OECD Pensions Outlook 2018

OECD

BETTER POLICIES FOR BETTER LIVES

Please cite this publication as:
OECD (2018), *OECD Pensions Outlook 2018*, OECD Pensions Outlook, OECD Publishing, Paris.
https://doi.org/10.1787/pens_outlook-2018-en

ISBN 978-92-64-30540-3 (print)
ISBN 978-92-64-30541-0 (pdf)

Annual: OECD Pensions Outlook
ISSN 2313-7630 (print)
ISSN 2313-7649 (online)

The statistical data for Israel are supplied by and under the responsibility of the relevant Israeli authorities. The use of such data by the OECD is without prejudice to the status of the Golan Heights, East Jerusalem and Israeli settlements in the West Bank under the terms of international law.

Corrigenda to OECD publications may be found on line at: *www.oecd.org/publishing/corrigenda*.

Foreword

The *OECD Pensions Outlook* provides an analysis of different pension policy issues in OECD countries covering both public and private pension systems. This fourth edition discusses policy options to help governments ensure that people will get the most out of the pension system.

This report is the joint work of staff of the Insurance, Private Pensions and Financial Markets Division of the OECD Directorate for Financial and Enterprise Affairs and the Social Policy Division of the OECD Directorate for Employment, Labour and Social Affairs. It has benefited from contributions from national government delegates, particularly delegates to the Insurance and Private Pensions Committee, the Working Party on Private Pensions and the Working Party on Social Policy. The views expressed here do not necessarily correspond to those of the national authorities concerned.

The editorial team for this report was led by Pablo Antolin. Chapter 1 was prepared by Pablo Antolin, Ole Beier and Emmy Labovitch; Chapter 2 by Stéphanie Payet; Chapter 3 by Pablo Antolin and Emmy Labovitch with contributions from Diana Hourani; Chapter 4 by Emmy Labovitch; Chapter 5 by Stephanie Payet; Chapter 6 by Jessica Mosher; and Chapter 7 by Christian Geppert, Maciej Lis and Tomoko Onoda under the supervision of Hervé Boulhol. Comments and inputs from Romain Despalins, Richard Hinz and Diana Hourani are gratefully acknowledged. The authors of Chapter 7 would like to thank Boele Bonthuis, Jessica Mosher, Stephanie Payet, Monika Queisser and Andrew Reilly for their useful comments. Editorial and communication support was provided by Pamela Duffin, Kate Lancaster and Edward Smiley.

The OECD gratefully acknowledges the financial support from the European Union. The opinions expressed and arguments employed herein in no way reflect the official views of the European Union or its member countries. The research on private pensions contained in this publication has also benefited from the financial support of Principal International Group, and the Chilean Ministry of Finance.

Monika Queisser and Stefano Scarpetta of the Directorate for Employment, Labour and Social Affairs, and Flore-Anne Messy, and Greg Medcraft of the Directorate for Financial and Enterprise Affairs provided useful advice and feedback.

Table of contents

Tables

Figures

Boxes

Editorial

People's trust in pension systems is low. Population ageing, low returns on retirement savings, low growth, less stable employment careers and insufficient pension coverage among some groups of workers have been eroding the belief that all types of pension systems, pay-as-you-go or funded, will deliver on their promises once workers reach retirement age. This is supported by evidence in the recent OECD *Risks that Matter* survey. People are also concerned about whether the institutions managing their retirement savings in funded pension arrangements have their best interests at heart.

This mistrust may surprise some, given the wide range of pension policy reforms across OECD countries in recent decades. These reforms have improved the sustainability of pension systems, in particular of pay-as-you-go defined benefit public pensions. Many countries, for example, have introduced automatic mechanisms to adjust pension benefits to economic and demographic developments while taking measures to strengthen safety nets to prevent old-age poverty.

Regulators and policy makers have taken steps to make regulatory and supervisory frameworks for funded pension arrangements more robust. This includes improving pension fund governance, investment policies and strategies, and investment risk management, with the goal of ensuring a more solid focus on the best interest of members. Progress has also been made in better aligning the charges and fees individuals pay with the actual cost of providing funded pensions. Measures to improve transparency are essential, but they work best when supported by pricing regulations and structural solutions.

Policy makers have also implemented measures to improve the design of funded pension arrangements to address the challenges of insufficient financial knowledge and behavioural biases and assist people make better choices for their retirement. These include providing targeted financial incentives, including matching contributions; automatic mechanisms; default options; simplification of information and choice; and financial education initiatives.

All of these reforms have made pension systems more robust today and better placed to deliver pensions. However, people's concerns are at least partially grounded in some remaining challenges. To ensure higher retirement income, people need to increase retirement savings, pension contributions, and/or the length of the contribution period in both pay as you go and funded pension arrangements. This is even more necessary as improvements in mortality and life expectancy lead to ever longer periods in retirement.

Policy makers have a range of options, including linking the statutory retirement age to improvements in life expectancy, keeping in mind that there are large socio-economic differences in life expectancy in many countries. The interaction between different pension arrangements, old-age safety nets and the tax system may sometimes address the potentially regressive effect of increasing the retirement age, when this age is fixed for everybody. More flexibility around the age at which people can access their pension savings may help reduce this regressive feature. Financial service providers need to develop innovative products and approaches to manage longevity risk. In addition, higher funded retirement savings could be achieved both by linking increases in contributions over time to increases in real wages and through better designed financial incentives. Governments are also examining how to integrate workers in non-standard forms of work, such as those active in the platform and gig economy and those working as independent contractors, into public pensions and encourage them to save for retirement.

Finally, pension reforms need to be better communicated so that the rationale and effects of such reforms become clearer. People need a better understanding of what they themselves can do to secure their retirement incomes, why contributions to all types of pension arrangements are important, which vehicles are available for retirement saving, and how they are protected. These key steps could help to restore trust and confidence in pension systems.

Stephano Scarpetta

Director, OECD Directorate for Employment, Labour and Social Affairs

Greg Medcraft

Director, OECD Directorate for Financial and Enterprise Affairs

Executive summary

Combining funded and pay-as-you-go pensions, automatic mechanisms, and a strong safety net for pensioners improves retirement outcomes

Policymakers designing pension systems should reflect on their objectives (poverty relief, redistribution, sustainability, and consumption-smoothing) and risks (demographic, social, labour, macroeconomic, and financial).

A robust safety net for pensioners, as well as a diversified and balanced pension system that incorporates a funded component is important, especially when promoting and reallocating national savings toward long-term investment is a policy goal. Additionally, well-designed pension systems need automatic mechanisms that align benefits with economic and demographic realities. Systems should be financially sustainable and provide some of the certainty conveyed by defined benefit arrangements.

Countries should introduce funded arrangements gradually when diversifying pension systems, especially when contributions will partially, or fully, replace an existing pay-as-you-go system. Policymakers should carefully assess the transition as it may put an additional, short-term, strain on public finances and increase risks for individuals.

Countries can improve the design of financial incentives to save for retirement

Tax and non-tax financial incentives can promote saving for retirement by providing an overall tax advantage to individuals through a reduction in total lifetime tax paid, although this has a fiscal cost. Incentive design should account for retirement saving needs and capacities for all income groups and, as a minimum requirement, provide for tax neutrality between consumption and savings.

Tax rules should be straightforward, stable and consistent across all retirement savings plans. Tax credits, fixed-rate tax deductions or matching contributions can be used to provide an equivalent tax advantage across income groups. Countries using tax credits may consider making them refundable and paying them into pension accounts. Non-tax incentives, in particular fixed nominal subsidies, help to boost low-income earners' savings. Countries with an "EET" tax regime should maintain the deferred taxation structure and all countries considering the introduction of financial incentives should examine their fiscal capacity and demographic trends.

Aligning charges levied with the cost of managing retirement savings requires better disclosure, pricing regulations and structural solutions

Providing pension services involves costs such as administration and investment activities which are paid for by members and employers. These costs can greatly affect the ultimate value of accumulated retirement savings. Some pension arrangements can be also more expensive, such as those providing more choice.

Market mechanisms have often been insufficient to align charges with the actual cost to providers due to market failures, such as asymmetric information or behavioural biases.

Measures to improve transparency are essential, but are not enough to align costs and charges. They work best when supported by pricing regulations and structural solutions. To maximise net returns, policy makers and regulators can also use measures such as benchmarking and tying investment expenses more closely to portfolio performance.

The governance and investment approaches of nationally significant investment institutions provide useful guidelines to strengthen regulatory frameworks

Several nationally significant investment institutions have common features and provide evidence of good governance and investment approaches. They have regulatory and legal frameworks at arm's length from government; clearly stated missions to guide investment policy; an oversight board that is accountable to the competent authorities and to members; and transparency about their governance arrangements and their investment and risk management to keep them accountable to different stakeholders.

These institutions express their performance objectives in terms of their mission and monitor performance against this long-term goal rather than against a market benchmark. Target date and lifecycle funds are the preferred strategy for institutions with individual accounts. Long-term return strategies may offer better returns, but at a higher risk that insufficient funds will be available to members at retirement.

Automatic features, default options, simple information and choice, financial incentives and financial education lead to better retirement outcomes

Low levels of financial knowledge and behavioural biases can lead people to make unsuitable decisions for retirement.

Mechanisms such as automatic enrolment and escalation of contributions can harness inertia to make pension systems more inclusive and help increase contribution levels. People unable, or unwilling, to choose a contribution rate, a pension provider, an investment strategy or a post-retirement product, may benefit from default options.

There are also other tools to help with decision making, including: web applications, limiting options and making comparisons easier, and financial incentives. Pension statements can convey key information simply, while financial education seminars and financial advice can help people understand the information.

Increased flexibility on retirement age and progressive public pensions and tax rules address financial disadvantages of populations groups with shorter life expectancy

Individuals in low socioeconomic groups have a lower life expectancy than high socioeconomic groups. They may be financially disadvantaged if they spend a shorter time in retirement relative to their working life, receiving a lower "return" on contributions made towards their funded pension source. Public pensions and tax rules can help to offset some of this disadvantage.

Policies to improve the sustainability of pension systems in light of increases in life expectancy will need to consider how those in different socioeconomic and gender groups may be impacted. Generally, working for longer will be required, but not all groups will necessarily be able to. Increased flexibility around retirement age is key to improving pension outcomes for all groups and ensuring that lower socioeconomic groups are not penalised in retirement for having shorter life expectancies.

Survivor pensions still play an important role, but should not limit incentives to work or redistribute from singles to couples

Survivor pensions are still needed to smooth living standards after a partner's death. However, recipients should not be eligible for a permanent survivor pension before retirement age. Instead, temporary benefits should be available to help adapt to the new situation.

The cost of survivor pensions should be internalised within each couple or, as a minimum, among all couples. In a budget-neutral reform, this means that the pension level of singles will be higher than someone living in a couple and benefiting from survivor pensions.

Partners from former unions should not be eligible as they have no current consumption to smooth. Splitting pension rights offers some advantages, although some countries favour the individual treatment of partners, including to promote gender equality.

Chapter 1. The role of supplementary pension provision in retirement

This chapter considers the growing role of supplementary pensions in supporting retirement outcomes across the OECD. It sets out the principal objectives that pension systems may aim to meet and the various risks that individuals face in saving for retirement. The chapter then examines how different design features of supplementary pensions can be deployed to achieve different objectives and offset individual and collective risks, in light of the features of the national pay-as-you-go (PAYG) public pension system. It outlines the trade-offs faced by policy makers as the role of supplementary pensions increases, and discusses the advantages and disadvantages of different features of PAYG and funded, defined benefit and defined contribution, and public and private pension provision.

Economic security in old age is an integral part of individual wellbeing. Pensions are intended to offer people this security once they can no longer earn their living themselves. The public sector or the private sector could entirely, and in principle, provide economic security. Pensions could be financed by the state from general revenues or earmarked levies on a pay-as-you-go (PAYG) basis, or they could be fully funded through individual contributions and accumulated assets. Pension payments could be defined according to a formula (defined benefit, DB) or they may depend on the amount of assets accumulated (defined contribution, DC) (Chapter 1, (OECD, 2016[1])).

In practice, national pension systems combine PAYG and funded, DB and DC, and public and private elements. Public pensions have typically been DB in nature and financed on a PAYG basis.[1] Increased longevity and the declining ratio of actively employed contributors to retired beneficiaries are threatening the financial sustainability of PAYG DB public systems. Reforms to ensure fiscal sustainability affect the adequacy of the pensions they can provide. Many countries have introduced supplementary pensions or are considering doing so in order to reduce the pressure on public finances and raise the overall level of benefits that a participating individual will receive. Typically, supplementary provision takes the form of funded, defined contribution pensions, managed by private institutions, pension funds.

The OECD encourages countries to diversify the sources of retirement income and to strengthen the degree of funding in the overall pension mix through a combination of PAYG and funded, public and private provision (Chapter 1, (OECD, 2016[1])). PAYG public and funded private pensions can be complementary. They offer different solutions for meeting the competing objectives of pension systems and have different capacities to cover the various types of risks that people face throughout their lives, both before and after retirement.

To exploit this complementarity and enhance the resilience of the pension system, policy makers need to understand how their national system addresses the objectives and risks inherent to pension provision, as well as the role that supplementary pensions are expected to play. They can then determine which features of pension design best support this role and whether these design features should be implemented via PAYG public or funded private pensions. For example, consumption smoothing could be achieved through raising contributions to either PAYG public or funded private arrangements, and the choice between the two may come down to practical issues of implementation. Redistribution, on the other hand, is easier to achieve through a mandatory public PAYG system.

The primary design features that policymakers should consider when optimising the combination of public and private provision are whether participation in a pension scheme is mandatory or voluntary; whether benefits are backed by accumulated assets or paid from current contributions, and whether the scheme is defined benefit or defined contribution. A number of different outcomes are possible. Policy objectives, risk tolerances, legacy systems and institutions, and fiscal and demographic constraints all vary across countries. Pension systems interact with other policy areas (e.g. with the tax regime or labour markets) resulting in changed incentives and economic distortions.

This chapter aims to provide a framework for assessing how to design funded pensions to complement PAYG public provision in meeting different objectives and sharing risks. It outlines the trade-offs faced by policy makers as they increase the role of supplementary pensions, and discusses the advantages and disadvantages of different features of PAYG and funded, DB and DC, and public and private pensions in providing retirement income.

The chapter first briefly describes the status of pension systems across the OECD, in terms of the role of PAYG public and funded private provision and the level of contributions to each part. It then outlines the various objectives and risks that pension systems need to address and the broad roles that PAYG and funded, DB and DC, public and private pensions can play individually in meeting multiple objectives and sharing risks. Section 1.3 considers the need for supplementary funded pensions in addition to PAYG public pensions to achieve sufficient levels of consumption smoothing. It also discusses how different elements of pension design can contribute to these objectives. Section 1.4 looks at interactions within pension systems, how these interactions affect both the complementarity between different pension designs, and the potential transition costs of changing the PAYG DB public system and introducing supplementary funded DC pensions. The chapter ends summarising the advantages and disadvantages of different combinations of PAYG and funded, public and private pension provision.

1.1. Public and private provision in national pension systems

The mix of PAYG and funded, public and private pensions and their relative importance in ensuring that individuals have adequate resources in retirement varies across economies. Figure 1.1 shows theoretical gross replacement rates from mandatory public, mandatory private and some voluntary private pension schemes based on the current rules of the pension systems in OECD countries.[2] The replacement rate measures the ratio of post-retirement to pre-retirement income. The outcomes shown in Figure 1.1 apply to an individual who enters the labour market in 2016, earns the average income and contributes for a full career.[3]

Figure 1.1. Gross pension replacement rates from mandatory public, private and voluntary private pension schemes

Percent of individual earnings, average earner

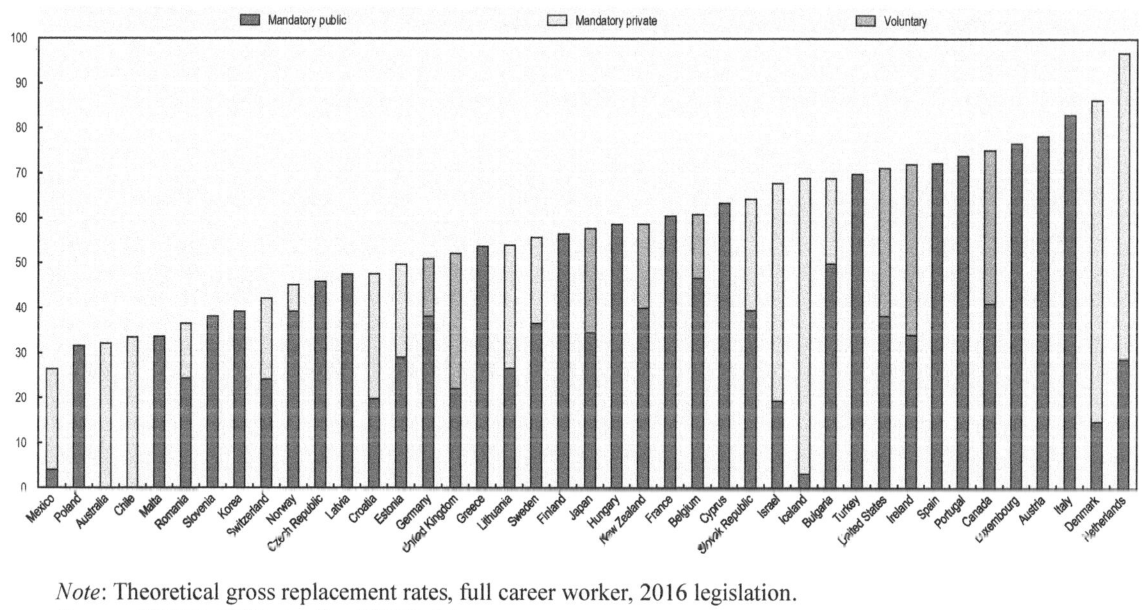

Note: Theoretical gross replacement rates, full career worker, 2016 legislation.
Source: (OECD, 2017$_{[2]}$), other OECD data.

StatLink http://dx.doi.org/10.1787/888933850051

Public pensions are expected to remain the most important source of pension income for current workers for most OECD countries. Several countries have a fully PAYG public system, and these provide gross replacement rates of between 32% (Poland) and 83% (Italy). Only Chile has a fully funded system for average earners (low-income workers receive public pension benefits in the form of a solidary pillar). Within the mixed systems, mandatory funded private pensions are the most important source of pension income in countries such as Denmark, Iceland, Israel and the Netherlands, while voluntary funded private schemes provide over half of the gross replacement rate in Ireland and the United Kingdom. In Switzerland, the public PAYG system aims to replace about a third of average earnings with mandatory funded DB benefits supplementing it for average and higher earners (workers earning below 40% of average earnings are not required to belong to a private scheme). In the United States, the replacement rate provided by Social Security is similar to the Swiss PAYG system for average earners at above 30%, with income from voluntary funded pensions, primarily DC, topping it up.

The most common form of public pensions in OECD countries is a PAYG, DB, earnings-related arrangement. The benefit formula determines the level of the replacement rate; its sustainability depends on the level of contributions and the willingness and ability of policymakers to divert budgetary resources to make up any shortfall between revenues and payments. The fiscal strains of high replacement rates have led to reforms of PAYG DB pension arrangements that have affected pension adequacy and have increased responsibility on funded, private pensions to fill the gap (OECD, 2015$_{[3]}$).

A high level of contributions to the public system can reduce the scope for supplementary pensions, especially if there is a close relationship between the level of contributions and the level of benefits. Figure 1.2 shows the contributions to different sectors of national pension systems, where this data is available. If contributions to or benefits from public pensions are low, then supplementary pensions are more likely to be needed to ensure pension adequacy for individuals. Putting a greater reliance on private, funded pensions can give policy makers more leeway to implement reforms necessary to improve the sustainability of the public system.

Figure 1.2. Mandatory pension contribution rates for an average worker in 2016

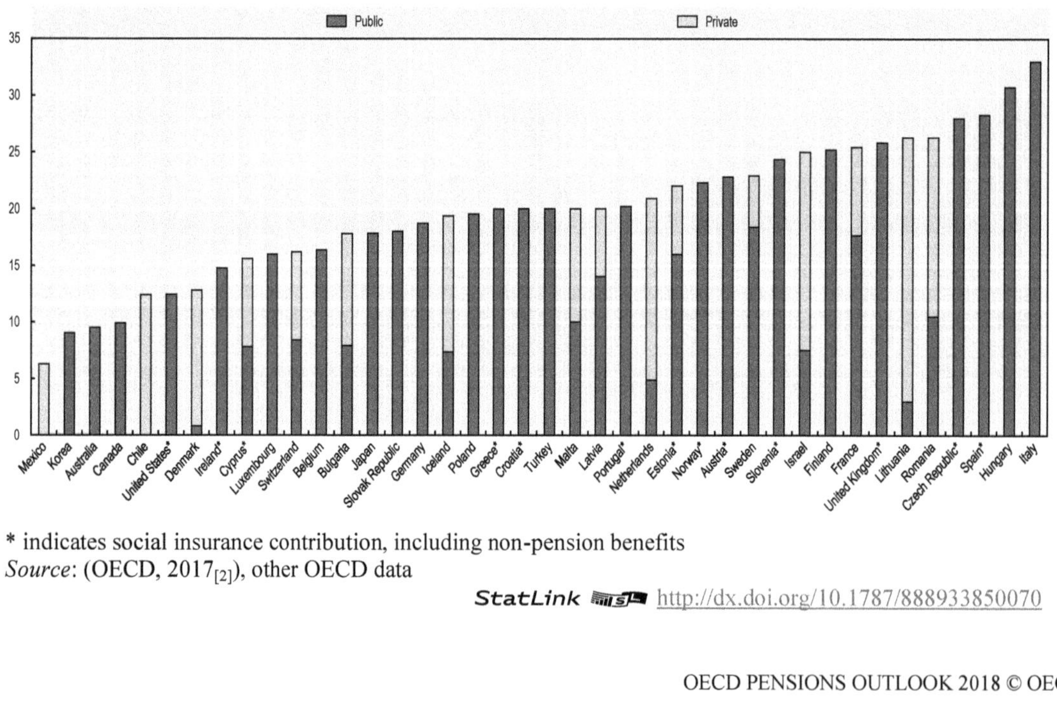

* indicates social insurance contribution, including non-pension benefits

Source: (OECD, 2017$_{[2]}$), other OECD data

StatLink http://dx.doi.org/10.1787/888933850070

It is not only the level of entitlements from public pensions that determines the potential role of supplementary pensions but also their nature. Both DB and notional defined contribution (NDC)[4] models of PAYG pensions offer a lifetime guaranteed benefit that is linked to the level of individual contributions: indirectly in the case of DB pensions and directly in the case of NDC. Funded public pensions, where they exist, typically provide only a small share of the overall public pension benefit and are mostly DC in nature.

Public pensions that provide an annuity-like benefit may create more scope for supplementary DC pensions that offer a less certain pay-out pattern. PAYG DB public pensions may have built-in progressive or redistributive features such as benefit caps or differential accrual conditions. Supplementary pensions can reinforce or partially offset these elements, for example through the tax treatment of private pensions. To play an effective role in ensuring adequate income in old age, the design of supplementary pensions should reflect the full range of objectives of the overall pension system and the capacity of existing provision to meet those objectives and mitigate related risks.

The volume of assets in funded and private pension arrangements has grown steadily in the majority of OECD in the last decade and a half. This has led to a more diversified and balanced pension landscape, in line with the OECD message to diversify the sources to finance retirement (Chapter 1, (OECD, 2016[1])). Figure 1.3 shows that assets earmarked for retirement account for more than the overall economy in eight countries. Total assets earmarked for retirement represent more than 50 per cent of the GDP of OECD countries on average.

Figure 1.3. Total assets in funded and private pension arrangements, in 2002 and 2017

As a percentage of GDP

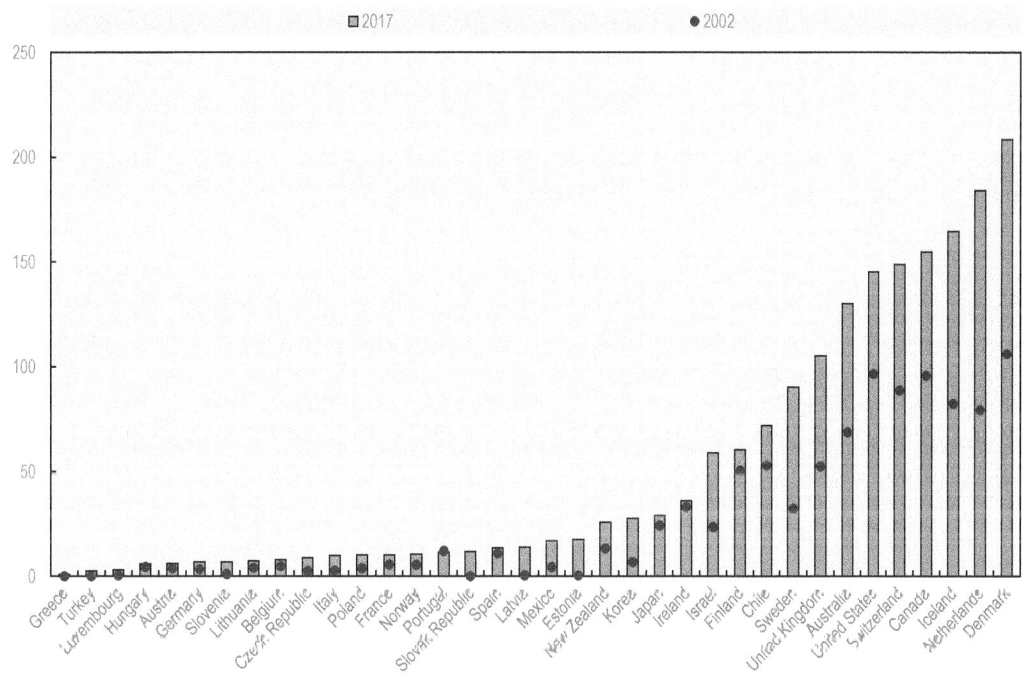

Source: OECD Global Pension Statistics and Pension Markets in Focus, 2018.

StatLink http://dx.doi.org/10.1787/888933850089

1.2. Pension system objectives and risks

Pensions systems have multiple and often competing objectives. They must provide financial security and "adequate" income for retirees and they must be financially sustainable. They need to offer mechanisms for people to save enough to finance future consumption. They should be flexible enough to weather long-term demographic and economic change. They may be used to deliver social and political goals such as poverty alleviation in old age and income redistribution across and within generations.

Pension systems must also provide insurance against multiple risks. Saving for retirement is saving for the future. The future is uncertain, and thus involves risks. Risks may be common to the system as a whole, such as macro-economic or financial market risks, or they may be related to the situation of the individual. Operational risks exist in both public and private pension systems. PAYG, funded, DB, DC, and public and private pensions play different roles in addressing the objectives and risks of pension systems.

Multiple objectives

The primary objective of pension systems is to make sure that people have resources at old age, that is, income security. This includes poverty relief, consumption smoothing and insurance against risks during working life and in old age. Protecting people from falling into poverty after their working life ends is the responsibility of the state across OECD countries. Encouraging people to put money aside during their working life in order to finance their consumption during retirement, as well as providing insurance against risks, is done through both PAYG public and funded private pension arrangements.

Realising these objectives entails secondary goals: financial and fiscal sustainability; adequate retirement income (what is adequate may vary across different countries and jurisdictions); redistribution (from those who would otherwise have a big pension income to those who will have lower pension payments); maximising coverage (how many people the system reaches, both as contributors and as beneficiaries); and preserving inter- and intra-generational equity (such that the benefits of one group are not maintained at the expense of another). Pension systems may have targets in terms of replacement rates and – increasingly – labour force participation (encouraging people to work and contribute beyond the age of retirement).

Poverty relief at a minimum level is provided through public pensions or other social benefits in all OECD member jurisdictions. This universal provision is part of the public safety net and cannot been successfully substituted by the private sector; the OECD recommends that it is financed from general taxation (Chapter 1 (OECD, 2016[1])). Universal basic benefits are also important contributors to the secondary objective of redistribution, although in some countries redistribution is limited by eligibility criteria. This brings up the issue of what universal means. Everyone could get universal basic pension benefits or everyone could be entitled to them once certain criteria is met. For example, individuals may have to contribute for at least a short period to be eligible for the basic benefit, which means that those who have never participated in the formal economy remain at high risk of old-age poverty. A number of countries, including Australia, Denmark and Chile, offer means-tested basic benefits.

The objective of consumption smoothing is central to achieving pension adequacy. It can be achieved through either public PAYG or private funded pensions. Public PAYG schemes are the primary instrument for achieving consumption smoothing in Spain, Italy and France. Private funded arrangements are used in Australia (DC), Chile (DC),

Switzerland and the Netherlands (both DB). Sweden uses a combination of public, PAYG notional defined contribution, public funded defined contribution and private occupational pensions which are increasingly moving from a DB to a DC structure. The common feature of all the arrangements that bear the primary responsibility for consumption smoothing is that they are mandatory.

Mandatory systems are also well placed to achieve the objective of high coverage. These can be public or private. The minimum basic public benefit will generate the highest levels of coverage, as individuals do not need a complete employment history to be eligible. Usually, such old-age benefits are pro-rated according to how well the individual meets the qualifying criteria for the minimum basic pension – such as a few years' contributions or residency – and are supplemented by other aspects of the safety net (e.g. housing allowance).

Mandatory, earnings-related pension arrangements can play an important role in achieving the coverage objective. However, private funded occupational plans will tend to focus on full-time employees and exclude groups such as the low paid, part-time workers and the self-employed. The United Kingdom's automatic enrolment programme is mandatory for employers and has enjoyed very low opt-out rates among employees. However, over 5 million people (21% of the total employed population) are ineligible for automatic enrolment because they do not meet the earnings or age criteria of the programme; women, ethnic minorities and disabled workers are disproportionately affected. A further 4.5 million self-employed workers are also excluded in the United Kingdom (PPI, 2017[4]); the Chilean and Australian mandatory enrolment arrangements similarly do not cover the self-employed although Australia offers incentives to encourage self-employed workers to contribute voluntarily to the superannuation system. Malaysia extended its public funded DC scheme to part-time workers in 2010, and coverage was thereby expanded to include a further 12 million people.

The redistribution objective is commonly achieved through the public PAYG, DB system. Within DB design, a number of components can be used to alter the balance between contributions and benefits, such as whether any floors and ceilings are applied to contributions, benefits, accrual rates and indexation. These can be adjusted to redistribute across generations or to target specific groups within a generation. Redistribution is also possible within private funded DB arrangements; however, if one group makes a bigger claim on the assets of the scheme than is justified by its contributions, the difference will ultimately have to be made up by reducing benefits to other groups or by injections of funding from the sponsor. Conde-Ruiz and Gonzalez (2016[5]) note that the minimum pension in Spain has grown faster than the minimum contribution limit since 1984, while the maximum pension has failed to keep up with increases in the maximum contribution, thus redistributing from higher to lower earners within each cohort. As discussed in OECD (2018[6]), redistribution also takes place through private, funded pensions via tax incentives for retirement saving, which may favour higher earners.

Funded, private pensions may be expected to support broader economic growth and accelerate the development of local capital markets by creating a pool of pension savings that must be invested. The role of funded, private pensions in economic development is likely to become more important still as countries place a higher priority on the objective of labour force participation. Funded pensions increase the incentives to work and save, and by encouraging older workers to stay in the labour market they can help to address concerns about the sustainability and adequacy of public, PAYG pensions in the face of demographic changes.

Table 1.1 summarises how different pension designs can help to fulfil the various objectives of pension systems.

Table 1.1. Pension system objectives and pension design features

	Public pension Non-contributory	Public pension Contributory PAYG	Public pension Contributory funded	Private funded pension Mandatory DB[1]	Private funded pension Mandatory DC	Private funded pension Voluntary
Poverty relief	Most efficient method	Some, through lifelong benefit	Some through lifelong benefit	Some through lifelong benefit	Not if exhausts resources	n/a
Consumption smoothing	No	Some, may be targeted to specific groups	Some, according to parameters	Inherent through lower wages	Most direct link savings/benefits	May divert other savings
Financially sustainable	n/a	Depends on parameters	Depends on link between benefits and contributions	Sponsor responsible	Individual responsible	Yes
Redistribution	Yes, via tax system	Yes, depends on parameters	Yes, depends on parameters	Possible within the plan but not a goal. Tax incentives can be redistributive	Not possible in individual DC. Tax incentives can be redistributive	Not possible in individual DC. Tax incentives can be redistributive
Inter-generational equity	Within tax system	In legacy systems, may mean lower guarantees for individuals	In legacy systems, may mean lower guarantees for individuals	Yes	Not possible in individual DC	Not possible in individual DC
Intra-generational equity	n/a	Possible	Possible	Possible	Not possible in individual DC	Not possible in individual DC
Benefit adequacy /replacement rate	Depends on policy /fiscal implications	Depends on target (note potential sustainability issues)	Depends on target	Depends on parameters	Only non-binding target can be set	n/a
Labour force participation	n/a	May weaken incentives if DB	Depends on link between benefits and contributions	May be less suited to future labour market	Strong incentive	Limited incentive
Coverage	Universal	Only if participated in formal economy	Only if participated in formal economy	Tend to exclude lower paid	Tend to exclude lower paid	Usually for higher earners

n/a: not applicable.
1. Applies also to voluntary DB where applicable (e.g. Canada, the United Kingdom).

Multiple risks

Saving for retirement, like any form of saving for the future, involves risks. Planning for retirement requires making assumptions about the value of several parameters going forward. These parameters include GDP and productivity growth, employment, unemployment, wage growth, career real wages, inflation, returns on investment, interest and discount rates, and life expectancy. The future is uncertain and assumptions rarely materialise exactly as expected, which brings risks that pension benefits and assets accumulated may be insufficient to achieve expected income targets, or that promises cannot be met. These risks need to be accounted for and monitored.

The growing role of DC funded pensions may leave individuals more exposed to those risks. In PAYG DB pension arrangements the State bears those risks. In DB funded systems the employer or plan sponsor bears them.

Pension systems and the individuals that they cover face multiple risks. These include risks to the individual's ability to contribute to both public and private pension arrangements (labour market and social risks); risks to the capacity of those contributions to fund an adequate retirement (macro-economic, financial market and operational risks) and the risk that an individual will outlive their assets (longevity risk).

As the role of private pensions in meeting the objectives of pension systems grows, so must their role in addressing the risks. Their capacity to do so will depend on their design. For example, DB schemes are likely to be more efficient than DC schemes at insuring individuals against income shocks both before and after retirement, because they are able to exploit risk pooling (albeit on a smaller scale than public DB schemes). However, funded pensions are in general more vulnerable to macro-economic and financial risks than PAYG pensions.

Labour market risks – such as loss of employment and unfavourable earnings patterns – can have a significant impact on the rate at which pension rights are accrued or the rate at which pension assets are accumulated, and thus on the level of pension income received.

These risks can be offset by either public or private pension arrangements. Non-contributory basic benefits provide a back-stop security against the failure or inability to pay into contributory schemes, or to pay enough to at least build up entitlements that are above the level of the basic benefit. Within public contributory schemes, employees are usually protected against some of the risk of disrupted career earnings: they may receive top-up contributions/accruals in certain circumstances (e.g. military service, parental leave), or a number of "bad years" may be excluded when their entitlements are calculated. The United States Social Security system takes account of the best 35 years of contributions when calculating retirement benefits. Most Central and Eastern European funded public systems include protection mechanisms for periods of economic inactivity (Kawiński, Stańko and Rutecka, 2012[7]).

A similar analysis applies to social risks, which include disability and lack of financial independence. The public non-contributory benefit provides a safety net for individuals who suffer an income shock either before or after retirement. All OECD countries offer additional disability benefits and usually some protection of the future retirement income of those whose working career is cut short by disability. These may be flat-rate or earnings-related.

These safeguards within public systems are a form of insurance, but because they are often funded outside the pension system they may not be recognised as such by individuals (they may be interpreted as entitlements). For example, in Sweden non-contributory individual credits to the PAYG system during spells of unemployment are allocated to the central budget line for unemployment costs.

Within private funded arrangements, the nature of the insurance may be made more explicit. It is compulsory to purchase insurance against social risks in Chilean individual accounts and (partly optional) life insurance is integrated within the Australian Superannuation system. Most DC schemes however do not provide cover against lost contribution periods, as it is expensive to insure such risks on an individual basis. Collective private schemes are better able to pool such risks and so provide insurance.

Macro-economic risks make it less likely that an individual will receive an adequate pension income. Low growth and productivity affect both public and private pension systems. They limit the fiscal capacity to fund non-contributory pensions and result in lower contributions to PAYG and funded schemes. It may well be difficult to raise contribution levels in both public and private schemes in a weak economic environment without reducing the pre-retirement consumption by too much compared to post-retirement consumption, especially for low earners. Low wage and productivity growth makes it harder to meet the promises embedded in DB arrangements, whether PAYG or funded.

Inflation reduces the future purchasing power of income put aside today for the purposes of consumption smoothing. Benefits in public PAYG schemes are usually indexed to price or wage inflation. The extent of indexation in funded DB schemes varies across the OECD: while automatic indexation is offered by few schemes in the United States, both benefits and accruals must be indexed to CPI in the United Kingdom, and pensions in payment are indexed to a minimum of CPI and a maximum of wage inflation in German *Pensionsfonds*. Indexation may threaten the sustainability of both PAYG and funded DB schemes – the Netherlands has introduced conditional indexation of occupational DB pensions to reduce risks to the funding levels of these schemes. Benefits in DC arrangements are less likely to be indexed but indexation can be introduced, as in Chile where life annuities must be linked to inflation.

Low interest rates pose a more immediate risk to funded pensions than to PAYG pensions. They can lead to lower pay-outs from funded DC schemes by reducing the returns on invested assets and lowering annuity values. They may also damage the sustainability of funded DB schemes as liability values increase.

Financial market risks similarly are more relevant for funded pensions than for non-contributory or PAYG arrangements. Retirement benefits in funded systems are financed by accumulated assets; financial market shocks can reduce the value of those assets. This will be particularly damaging for members of individual funded DC arrangements if the shock occurs towards the end of the accumulation period, when the individual has less time to rebuild their savings before beginning to draw down their assets. Investment strategies such as lifecycle or target date funds can help to reduce volatility in investment performance but potentially at the expense of lower overall returns (the *OECD Roadmap for the Good Design of DC Pension Plans* recommends the use of lifecycle funds as the default strategy in DC plans).

Operational risks also principally affect funded systems, since excessive operating costs or badly-designed investment strategies will have a direct impact on the assets in a funded scheme. Ultimately, a funded scheme can go bust. However, just as public arrangements will almost certainly be bailed out by the government, lifeboats and bailouts can be put in place for the private sector. Germany, Switzerland, the United Kingdom, the United States and Ontario (Canada) all have pension guarantee schemes in place for the private funded DB sector.

In principle, publicly-managed pensions should be at less risk of being high cost than privately-managed schemes, because they can exploit economies of scale and simplified administration (thanks to less personalisation) and do not incur marketing costs. For example, the Swedish public funded DC scheme, the Premium Pension (PPM), introduced a clearinghouse model to control investment costs and has a monopoly over the provision of annuities. Private funded arrangements can take measures to reduce their costs: the four sector-based occupational schemes in Sweden have introduced their own clearinghouse systems. Policies have been introduced in many OECD countries to contain costs and align charges and costs of privately-managed DC pensions.[5]

Furthermore, publicly-managed arrangements may not necessarily be more efficient than private providers across their operations. Palmer (2011[8]) reports that contributions to the PPM are not actually invested in the member's portfolio for up to 18 months, during which time they earn bond returns from the National Debt Office. Core Principle 5 of the *OECD Core Principles of Private Pension Regulation* specifies that investment decisions should be implemented in a timely manner.

Longevity risk is the risk that an individual will live longer than expected and so exhaust their resources. DB pensions, whether PAYG or funded, offer protection against longevity risk to individuals by providing a lifetime stream of benefits. However, this leads to issues of sustainability and inter-generational equity if a relatively smaller working population is required to support the pensions of a relatively larger retired population over a longer period. PAYG DB systems are the most vulnerable to demographic shifts that alter the ratio between the size of the cohort that is working and contributing and the size of the cohort that is receiving benefits paid for by those contributions.

Longevity risk within public arrangements can be reallocated more neutrally across generations by adjusting benefit levels and accruals. In Sweden and Germany, balancing mechanisms have been introduced whereby benefit levels are linked to demographic and economic developments, thus shifting a part of both macro-economic and longevity risk away from the state and onto individuals. Risk in an occupational DB scheme is ultimately borne by the sponsor although it can be spread amongst current workers, retirees, shareholders, and future employees through adjustments to benefit levels, accrual rates, indexation and contractual terms. However, the rising cost of longevity insurance is leading sponsors to withdraw DB provision in favour of DC.

In DC schemes, the risk of outliving one's assets is borne by the individual, who has the choice of saving more, retiring later or spending less in retirement. A functioning annuity market would allow DC arrangements to guarantee their members a lifelong income, with annuity providers bearing some proportion of the longevity risk. As discussed in OECD (2016[9]), this will vary according to the discount rate used in calculating the annuity and whether the guarantee is issued before or at retirement.

Longevity and longevity increases differ substantially within a given population (Chapter 6, (OECD, 2016[10])). If annuity rates do not reflect these differences, annuities may favour higher earners in conflict with redistribution objectives. On the other hand, if annuities accurately reflect gender differences in longevity, they will offer less generous benefits to women who are already the most at risk from old-age poverty (they are less likely to have a full contribution history and more likely to be reliant on survivors' pensions).

Overall, members of individual DC pension plans are exposed to more of the multiple risks that can affect pension systems than are members of DB or NDC plans. This is because individual DC arrangements establish a direct link between the value of accumulated assets and the level of retirement income. Collective funded and PAYG arrangements have greater scope for risk pooling and burden sharing but are also vulnerable in the event of lower contributions, lower returns on assets and higher claims. Table 1.2 summarises the exposure of different pension designs to different risks and highlights that the ultimate safeguard against the risk of old-age poverty is the universal basic public pension.

Table 1.2. Pension system risks and design features

	Public pension Non-contributory	Public pension Contributory PAYG	Public pension Contributory funded	Private funded pension Mandatory DB[1]	Private funded pension Mandatory DC	Private funded pension Voluntary
Labour market risks	Full cover at basic level	Protection can be built in, e.g. for missed contributions	Protection can be built in, e.g. for missed contributions	Risk pooling possible	Expensive to insure on individual basis	n/a
Social risks	Full cover at basic level	Protection can be built in, e.g. for disability	Protection can be built in, e.g. for disability	Risk pooling possible	Can be built in, e.g. Chile	n/a
Macro-economic risks	May affect fiscal capacity	Lower contributions, loss of purchasing power if not indexed	Lower contributions; cost of indexation	Contributions, indexation, sponsor health, annuity values	Contributions, annuity values. Indexation less likely	Lower contributions
Financial market risks	n/a	n/a	Investment returns	Investment returns	Investment returns	Investment returns
Operational risks	n/a	n/a	May fail to exploit scale	Governance risks	Governance risks	Governance risks
Longevity risk	Full cover at basic level	Full cover at given level	Full cover at given level	Full cover at given level but move to risk sharing	Can be built in but at higher cost	n/a

n/a: not applicable

1. Applies also to voluntary DB where applicable (e.g. Canada, the United Kingdom).

1.3. Pension arrangements for consumption smoothing

Consumption smoothing requires setting aside income today in order to spend it post retirement. The income that is set aside should not lose its value over time, so it should either accrue entitlements to future real purchasing power or be invested in assets that will increase in value. This can be achieved through either PAYG or funded, public or private pension provision.

Pressures on PAYG systems

Many countries initially introduced public PAYG systems for consumption smoothing. However, demographic changes mean that the number of retirees has grown faster than expected, while at the same time economic and market pressures have hit contributions into public systems and investment returns in funded systems, making it harder to finance benefits. PAYG pensions represent a significant fiscal burden in many countries. Across the EU, public expenditure on pensions represents over 10% of GDP (European Commission, 2018[11]).

In response to these fiscal pressures, countries have reformed their PAYG systems, introduced funded pensions (either public or private) or done a combination of both (OECD Pensions Outlook and OECD Pensions at a Glance, *passim*). Sweden reformed its public PAYG system, moving from a DB structure to a mixture of notional DC and funded DC. This signalled that individuals would have to take more responsibility for ensuring that they had an adequate retirement income while leaving poverty relief with the state, which maintained a minimum pension guarantee of around 25% of the average wage financed from the general budget. Most workers are also covered by an occupational scheme, usually DC, and these benefits are exempted from means testing for the guaranteed pension. The Swedish system provides a strong incentive to contribute to both public and private schemes for most groups of workers although the lowest paid will enjoy a high level of financial security from the minimum entitlements alone.

NDC may be a means for public PAYG pension arrangements to preserve some of the risk-sharing and insurance characteristics of DB while changing the accumulation structure to DC, creating more incentives for individual participation and improving fiscal sustainability. Individuals' contributions are credited to a notional account and the accumulated capital is converted into a lifetime annuity at retirement. Funding is on a PAYG basis. Contributions earn a notional interest rate linked to economic growth or wage growth. An additional risk-sharing mechanism of some NDC systems is a cohort-specific annuity conversion factor that adjusts for the effect of life expectancy gains. There is no intrinsic redistribution within cohorts in an NDC scheme but this can be created, for example by adding features such as offsetting contributions for missing periods, sick leave and survivors' insurance. As in a pure DC scheme, benefits adjust automatically to economic and demographic developments: each cohort should be self-funding.

Funded versus PAYG pensions

Some countries, by contrast, do not have a PAYG, earnings-related public pension and have introduced private funded DC pensions as the primary vehicle for consumption smoothing; this is the case in Australia and Chile. In the Netherlands the role of funded private pensions as a complement to universal basic public benefits was explicitly recognised by employers' and employees' organisations, which in 1969 adopted the principle that the combined replacement rate should be 70% of final salary for an individual with a 40-year contribution history. This understanding held during the 1980s: cuts in public benefits were compensated by increases in private occupational benefits. Such complementarity may be difficult to sustain going forward as private DB schemes, the main funded arrangement in the Netherlands, face sustainability issues and do not cover newer types of employment contract.

Funded pensions offer a number of advantages compared to PAYG pensions. They provide stronger incentives to participate in the labour market and to save for retirement. They create a pool of savings that can be put to productive use in the broader economy. Increasing national savings or reallocating savings to long-term investment supports the development of financial markets. However, adequate regulatory frameworks and regulation to promote competition and avoid captive markets are necessary for having a positive impact on developing financial markets. More domestic savings reduces dependency on foreign savings to finance necessary investment. Higher investment may lead to higher productive capacity, increasing GDP, wages and employment, higher tax revenues and lower deficits.

It is important that pension funds invest contributions in the best interest of members, through assets providing the best risk-adjusted, net of expenses, returns, and with diversification (*OECD Core Principles of Private Pension Regulation*). For example, pension funds may invest mainly in government bonds, which may give them the best return. This raises many questions. Those government bonds may be risky, and too much concentration in government bonds means investments are not diversified. Moreover, questions about differences with PAYG financed pension arrangements become pertinent. The issue comes down to whether governments use those funds to increase public investment or finance current expenditure, and to the legal system enforcing private contracts.

Invested assets can exploit opportunities in the financial markets to earn more than the rate of the wage bill growth, which is the implicit rate of return of PAYG schemes. This is more so in a context of population ageing and low productivity growth. Within DC schemes, each cohort is self-funding, reducing labour market distortion. Funded schemes may enable employers to offer targeted recruitment packages to attract employees.

However, funding reduces the opportunities for inter- and intra-generational risk sharing that is a source of economic efficiency within PAYG systems. Within a PAYG DB scheme, risks can be shared between workers and retirees by adjusting contribution and benefit levels. The gains in social solidarity that are available through inter- and intra-generational redistribution within PAYG schemes may also offset some of the fiscal costs. This type of redistribution could be partially restored via a non-contributory basic pension financed out of general tax revenues, or by adjusting the parameters of private funded DB schemes.

Some countries intend that funded pensions will ultimately replace public pensions as the main source of retirement income as the system matures, while public pensions continue to provide a minimum level of protection to individuals who fall outside the private system. Australia's pension system consists of the Age Pension, a means-tested universal benefit funded by current taxpayers; the Superannuation Guarantee, a mandatory DC scheme funded by employers; and voluntary superannuation, a tax-advantaged personal savings scheme. As individuals build up their DC assets, their entitlement to benefits from the Age Pension reduces. The Age Pension is a DB type arrangement so protects against longevity risk, labour market and social risks while the Superannuation Guarantee provide consumption smoothing and a higher replacement rate.

Furthermore, policy makers need to ensure that private schemes work in the best interests of members, by requiring high standards of governance and of investment and operational expertise, as outlined in the *OECD Core Principles of Private Pension Regulation*. In extreme circumstances, they may need to establish mechanisms to bail out private schemes.

Defined benefit or defined contribution

Funded pensions can be either defined benefit or defined contribution. DC arrangements establish a direct link between contributions and retirement income, so are the most effective method of smoothing consumption and provide the greatest incentive to contribute. Therefore, DC arrangements can be thought of as mechanisms that automatically adjust benefits to demographic, economic and financial realities. However, DC plans transfer the responsibility for financial security in retirement onto individuals without offering them insurance against the multiple risks that can affect funded pensions.

It is possible to introduce elements of insurance into DC pensions. Chile covers some labour market and social risks with compensatory pension contributions from the state for periods of missed earnings such as maternity leave. Many countries require DC providers to offer a default strategy that either follows a lifecycle approach or offers some protection against financial market risks. In Estonia, Latvia and the Slovak Republic, individuals who do not make an active choice will be allocated to a conservative strategy. By contrast in Sweden, where the public NDC system means that individuals are relatively well insured, the default strategy in the Premium Pension Fund is quite aggressive.

Individual DC pensions adjust automatically to demographic changes, although at the risk of inadequate pensions: if life expectancy increases, payments from a DC pot will run out. Individuals find it difficult to smooth their consumption post retirement – there is evidence from Australia that retirees underspend because they are afraid of exhausting their savings. Some longevity protection can be added to DC systems – the *OECD Roadmap for the Good Design of DC Pension Plans* recommends a combination of programmed withdrawals with a deferred life annuity as a default option for the pay-out phase – but payments must necessarily be lower if they have to last over a longer period. Norway imposes a pay-out phase for accrued pension capital of at least 10 years while Belgium allows lump-sum pay-outs. Mandatory annuitisation could call for an enhanced role for the public sector, as in Sweden, to maximise the benefits of risk pooling and avoid self-selection issues, and overcome behavioural barriers to choosing the right annuity.

DB schemes provide insurance against longevity risk in the pay-out phase and risk pooling in the contribution phase. However, Westerhout, Jan Bonenkamp and Broer (2014[12]) argue that collective systems may not be welfare-enhancing overall. This is because their design does not take members' ages into account. Contribution levels and benefits are age-independent and contribution and indexation policies are not matched with each other, leading to inefficient consumption smoothing. In addition, investment strategies target solvency ratios rather than total member wealth, whereas DC schemes may follow a lifecycle approach.

Although DB schemes are intended to cover individual longevity risk, they do not adjust automatically to demographic trends. Funded DB schemes in the Netherlands and Canada did not prove robust to the demographic shocks of increased longevity and an imbalance between the sizes of the working and retired cohorts. As the sustainability of pure DB systems has come under threat, different methods of risk sharing have been introduced that push more of the longevity, economic and market risk onto members but retain the risk pooling of DB. An example is the conversion of public sector schemes in New Brunswick (Box 1.1). The new designs may be referred to as "shared risk schemes" or "collective defined contribution". Automatic adjustments to demographic change can be built into the design of PAYG DB schemes, as in Sweden and Germany, although policy makers may retain the ability to override such mechanisms.

Individual DC plans are probably better suited to changing labour market patterns, such as multiple employers and increased self-employment, than DB schemes. Within DB plans a uniform contribution rate combined with a uniform accrual rate (i.e. how quickly rights are built up) will lead to redistribution from lower earners to higher earners and from new members to long-standing members, which could impede labour mobility. However, career breaks early on are especially costly for members of DC plans in terms of building up retirement assets (because the opportunity for compounding returns is lost). Pooled DC plans that are not tied to a specific employer, such as the Canadian Pooled Registered Pension Plans, could be a means of addressing changing labour market patterns while offering more risk pooling than individual DC arrangements.

Box 1.1. New Brunswick shared risk schemes

Shared risk schemes were introduced in New Brunswick in response to sustainability issues brought on by demographic and investment risks. Existing DB schemes were converted to the new model, which constrained some of the choices available to policy makers in terms of changing the parameters of the schemes.

The shared risk schemes were designed to achieve the objectives of sustainability and intergenerational equity. They expressly did not set a target replacement rate or benefit adequacy standard, prioritising the stability of payments rather than the level.

Benefits were made contingent on the solvency of the fund. "Base benefits" have to have at least a 97.5% probability of being paid and "ancillary benefits" (such as indexation) a 75% probability. The retirement age was increased and routes to early retirement closed off.

Employers participated in the risk sharing. They had to build a buffer fund so that the first cohort of contributors under the new design were not penalised, and their contributions were fixed for 5 years.

Employees continue to benefit from risk pooling in longevity insurance as the schemes internally annuitise on behalf of their members.

Mandatory versus voluntary pensions

If funded pensions are introduced, a decision will be needed as to whether to make them mandatory or voluntary, or a combination. Switzerland has a funded occupational system whereby contributions are mandatory up to a level of around 120% of average earnings and voluntary thereafter.

Funded pensions are intended to encourage individuals to take on more responsibility for their financial security in retirement, so mandating could be seen as contradictory since it removes individual choice. Voluntary provision is less likely to distort labour markets and may be the only possibility in countries without the institutional capacity to establish mandatory pensions. Funded, private pensions require both institutions that are capable of administering and investing large volumes of contributions and an appropriate supervisory regime. In addition, Holzman and Hinz (2005[13]) remind us that the least well off may have more immediate needs than saving for retirement and so forcing them to contribute to pensions would be welfare-reducing. By the same token, high income individuals might not need to be forced into consumption smoothing as they are well placed to take advantage of voluntary schemes.

In terms of performance, it is not clear whether mandatory or voluntary arrangements do better. Musalem and Pasquini (2012[14]) found that occupational schemes generally earn higher returns on their investments than pension systems with personal pension schemes. Countries with long-standing mandatory systems such as Australia, the Netherlands and Switzerland have seen assets grow to a significant proportion of GDP, implying that mandating has been successful at smoothing consumption. However, they have also seen a build-up of many small funds with relatively weak governance, to the detriment of members. This, together with the potential for large funds to reap economies of scale, implies that there may be a case for restricting competition within a mandatory system.

Behavioural studies provide strong support for mandatory or quasi-mandatory arrangements. There is considerable evidence that individuals find it difficult to plan ahead for their retirement and would likely not save enough during their working lives. Mandating can take different forms. In the United Kingdom, companies must offer pension schemes and employees are automatically enrolled with the option of opting out; in Australia, superannuation is compulsory from the perspective of employers. In New Zealand, soft compulsion in the form of automatic enrolment is combined with individual incentives such as matching contributions.

Tax incentives can be used to encourage contributions to both mandatory and voluntary systems and to share risks between the individual, the state and other tax payers. Tax breaks on contributions can encourage people to contribute more and may make the overall tax treatment of consumption more consistent across the pre- and post- retirement periods (depending on how benefits are taxed). Wealthier individuals who are in a position to save more into private pensions will enjoy a higher value of tax breaks, which may offset some of the redistribution effect of the public pension system. Furthermore, it is unlikely that lost taxes on contributions will be recouped through taxes on other parts of the pensions system, contributing to sustainability concerns.[6]

An important design feature of mandatory arrangements is the extent of their coverage. Australia excludes the self-employed from its mandatory system on the grounds that they need the flexibility to invest in their businesses and that these will provide a form of financial security for retirement. However, the line between "self-employed" and "gig economy" remains fluid for now.

There can be operational difficulties in implementing a mandatory private system. In Germany, there was concern that companies that did not previously offer voluntary schemes to their employees would free ride on existing collective agreements once occupational pensions became mandatory. Where a well-established voluntary system already exists, it may be easier to move to a mandatory system (as was the case in Switzerland).

1.4. Building a complementary system

Within the pension system, different design elements interact. Policymakers can improve the resilience of the overall pension system and target specific objectives by using different combinations of PAYG and funded, DB and DC, public and private pensions to introduce new design elements. A combination of public and private actors may be used to deliver different aspects of the pension system. The Polish system was split between the state-run administration body, ZUS, and private sector asset managers (PTE). However, making changes to the pension system may result in transition costs for both individuals and governments.

Pension system interactions

Mixed pension systems should be able to exploit complementarities. For example, a combination of a basic pension, some PAYG public and funded private pension arrangements may provide insurance against longevity risk, labour market and social risks (primarily through public arrangements) as well as consumption smoothing and higher retirement income (primarily through private funded arrangements). To the extent that outcomes from a defined benefit PAYG system are linked to wage growth and outcomes from funded DC arrangements are linked to capital markets, a mixed system provides diversification benefits to individuals that may reduce the overall level of risk to their retirement.

Different elements within a system may conflict, however. In New Zealand, the 2010 review by the Retirement Commission found that the universal Superannuation scheme and the voluntary KiwiSaver scheme were in effect competing for government subsidies (either direct funding or tax benefits). In Sweden, the mismatch between the ages at which benefits can be drawn from the minimum guaranteed pension system, the public NDC system and the funded system can be exploited to finance early retirement (Palmer, 2011[8]). The insurance against social risks provided by PAYG arrangements (e.g. public disability benefits) could be used to pay benefits until individuals are eligible for their retirement payments. The gap between the age at which public and private retirement benefits can be accessed may widen as countries introduce reforms to raise the statutory retirement age and so offset some of the effects of these reforms.

In the United States, the potential for different elements of the pension system to encourage individuals to retire early is addressed by incentives for people to stay in the labour market for longer. Social Security benefits are increased by 8% for each year that the claim is deferred beyond Normal Retirement Age and there are also disincentives for accessing plan balances before the age of 59.5.

Means testing of public pension benefits can create distortions, depending on which assets are captured in the assessment. For example, excluding housing from the calculation of assets may redistribute benefits from people who do not own property to those who do and discourage retirees from downsizing if selling their home would trigger extra effective taxes that would not otherwise be due. This in turn can make it harder for younger generations to buy property.

Means testing could also discourage people from working beyond retirement, if their earnings from employment mean their benefits are reduced. Income testing – excluding assets from the calculation of eligibility for benefits but including earnings on those assets – tends to provide disincentives for lower earners to save beyond the minimum requirement.

Pension systems also interact with other policy areas, especially the tax system, which can have a significant impact on how objectives and risks are addressed. For example, taxing retirement income at higher rates than lump sums could discourage retirees from converting retirement pots into drawdown products such as annuities, leaving them more exposed to longevity risk.

Implicit taxes may also be important. Gruber and Wise (1999[15]) found that in the EU, there were high implicit taxes on earnings for people who worked beyond the state retirement age, stemming from three sources. Firstly, DB benefits from the PAYG system were not increased to take account of the shorter time in retirement; secondly, payroll taxes were high; and thirdly, generous benefits were foregone by staying in work. The incentive to stay in the labour market was thus reduced. Reforms in the last decade and a half in many EU countries, have focused on reducing those implicit taxes.

Tax treatment affects redistribution. ICI (2015[16]) finds that within the United States retirement system, tax deferral for higher earners saving into private pensions generates similar levels of benefits as a proportion of total lifetime compensation as does Social Security for medium earners. Figure 1.4 shows total lifetime benefits for different groups, decomposed into tax effects and Social Security effects. The highest paid group (people earning USD 234 000) gets benefits with a net present value of 3.1% of lifetime earnings, compared to 3.4% for the third-lowest paid group (people earning USD 69 000), but the high earners get 3.0 percentage points of their overall gains from tax deferral while the lower earners get 2.0 percentage points from net Social Security benefits. The study concludes that higher earners get more benefit from tax deferral than do lower earners because they need to realise more of their consumption smoothing via voluntary pensions.

Figure 1.4. Present value of tax benefits of the United States retirement system

Percent of lifetime earnings

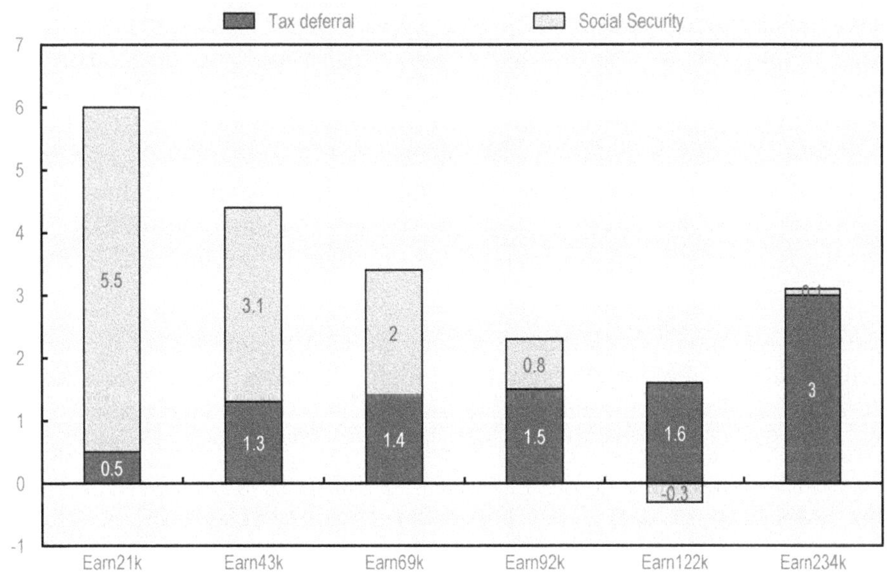

Source: (ICI, 2015[16])

All pension designs create labour market distortions. Ultimately all PAYG and funded pension contributions are paid for by employees through contributions or lower wages (employers will cut current or future pay to offset the cost of pension contributions). This will have an impact on labour supply and on unit labour costs. Some economists argue that labour market effects will vary according to the way contributions are collected: from the employer, the employee or through income taxes.

Introducing new design elements can strengthen pension systems and give more flexibility to policy makers, however it may create complexity that is difficult for governments to administer and for individuals to navigate. In Denmark, the income test for the minimum pension takes into account all household taxable income.[7] This means that benefits are highly targeted to those households in greatest need, but it creates a complicated incentive structure as benefits are affected by both spouses' financial situation and time to retirement. Complexity tends to make outcomes more regressive, conflicting with the objective of redistribution.

Transition costs

Introducing supplementary pensions can create transition costs for both the state and individuals. Supplementary funded pensions are intended to relieve the fiscal burden of public PAYG systems by creating additional consumption smoothing in new pension arrangements. However, this consumption smoothing can carry a big fiscal cost if it diverts contributions from the PAYG system to the funded system.

If contributions into the old PAYG system fall, then unless benefits to retired generations are reduced, the government will have to divert revenues, borrow more, or raise taxes to make up the shortfall. This means that the costs of transition are ultimately likely to fall indirectly on current workers, who have to pay into the new funded pensions and still bear the cost of paying for benefits due under the old PAYG system. An abrupt move to funded pensions can be especially costly for older workers, who have less time to build up their individual entitlements before they leave the workforce.

A number of countries, notably France, with a well-established PAYG public system are introducing more funded provision. Such a move can be made gradually in order to smooth the fiscal costs, as was the case in Sweden. Sweden introduced NDC accounts with a small element of funding and created a points system for transferring entitlements from the old PAYG system to the new system. Individuals born before 1953 are entitled to some benefits calculated under the old rules and some under the new system, with the weighting between the two varying by age.[8] Chile, by contrast, moved directly to a fully-funded, DC model without a long transition period and smoothed the fiscal cost by introducing a Recognition Bond to credit contributions to the previous system to new individual accounts.

The fiscal costs of moving to a funded system are exacerbated as the move makes the implicit liabilities of the PAYG system explicit. Poland's experience illustrates the potential difficulties of implementing pension reforms, even with a relatively long transition period. In 1999, Poland replaced the public, PAYG system with private, DC accounts. Younger generations were required to join the new system, workers aged between 30 and 50 years at the time of the reform were offered a choice between NDC and DC accounts, and older generations remained in the PAYG arrangement. The resulting budget deficit was expected to be offset by reduced expenditures from measures such as standardising the retirement age and other pension parameters and by the gains from privatisation. However accounting rules meant that the liabilities of the PAYG system could not be set against the assets being built up in the private funded arrangements.

Introducing funded pensions in order to promote consumption smoothing will be less effective when funded pensions are financed out of social insurance contributions which would otherwise go to the public PAYG system. Sweden's public funded DC scheme, the Premium Pension, represents only 2 percentage points of contributions, so this effect is relatively small. However, some CEE countries that combine PAYG public benefit with individual private DC accounts diverted a relatively large proportion of contributions from the public to the private system, exacerbating the transition costs.[9] This explains to a large extent the reversals from funded pension arrangements back to PAYG arrangements in many CEE countries.

Over the long term, transition costs may be at least partially offset by additional positive economic effects associated with introducing private pensions rather than relying solely on public provision. Rein and Turner (2001[17]) cite evidence that poverty rates have declined in Australia, the Netherlands and Switzerland since mandatory funded pensions were introduced. The initial transformation of Poland's public PAYG system into a multi-pillar DC approach helped to encourage Warsaw's development as a financial centre. As outlined in OECD (2011[18]), the introduction of funded DC pensions in Chile encouraged the growth of financial markets and provided a source of domestic financing.

1.5. Conclusions and policy implications

Public and private arrangements can be used to introduce different elements of pension design – funded or PAYG, DC or DB –into the overall system. While public pensions are well equipped to achieve the objective of poverty relief, other objectives – especially consumption smoothing – can be addressed in a variety of different ways. The United States largely combines a PAYG system with voluntary DC, the Netherlands has a public basic pension plus mandatory funded DB, Australia and Chile have a means-tested basic pension plus mandatory DC, and France and Spain rely primarily on PAYG.

Most countries are increasing the role of funded pensions in meeting the objective of consumption smoothing (Chapter 1, (OECD, 2016[1])). This raises the possibility that individuals will be exposed to more of the risks associated with building up savings over their working lives and ensuring that these are sufficient to last over their full lifetime in retirement. These risks are greatest for individuals saving into DC schemes.

Table 1.3 summarises the various objectives of pension systems, how different pension designs can help to achieve them, and the risks to which these designs are vulnerable. It can be seen that there are trade-offs involved in determining priorities and allocating responsibilities for pension provision, giving rise to a number of policy implications:

- Non-contributory public pensions are the most efficient vehicle for achieving the objective of poverty relief; they also contribute to goals of equity and redistribution with only a limited negative effect on labour market participation.
- The primary risk to individuals within PAYG arrangements is demographic risk; they are insured against all other types of risk. However, fiscal sustainability concerns may lead policy makers to adjust pre- and post-retirement benefit formulas.
- As private, funded DC arrangements play an increasing role in pension provision the insurance against all risks will be lost. Policy makers may require that insurance is built into the funded system (e.g. through the purchase of individual or group insurance) or continue to provide insurance via a PAYG arrangement.
- Compulsion generally leads to higher coverage. There are, nevertheless, useful mechanisms (Chapter 5 in this volume) to improve coverage in voluntary pension arrangements.
- Higher retirement income may require higher savings, contributions, and longer contribution periods, especially in a context of low returns, low growth and improvements in mortality and life expectancy.
- Introducing a funded pension arrangement is intended to make pension systems more sustainable and to improve consumption smoothing. However the transition may put additional strain on the PAYG system or public finances while increasing the proportion of risks borne by individuals, if contributions to the new arrangements are made at the expense of the existing scheme. Such moves should therefore be introduced gradually.
- However, a pension system that includes both PAYG and funded arrangements is better able to achieve its various objectives and more resilient to the multiple risks to old-age financial security.
- DC pension arrangements are more sustainable than DB pension arrangements because DC pensions adjust automatically to any changes in the parameters (e.g. contributions, returns, longevity).

Table 1.3. Summary of pension designs, objectives and risks

	Public pension Non-contributory	Public pension Contributory PAYG	Public pension Contributory funded	Private funded pension Mandatory DB[1]	Private funded pension Mandatory DC	Private funded pension Voluntary
Poverty relief	General taxation is the most equitable and efficient way of providing poverty relief in a redistributive system Provides backstop insurance against labour market, social and longevity risk Depends on ability of tax base to support it	May be used to determine eligibility for poverty relief and/or consumption smoothing Covers longevity risk	Covers longevity risk	Covers longevity risk	Safeguards required against resources being exhausted (longevity risk) – e.g. compulsory annuitisation	Not suitable for poverty relief
Consumption smoothing		May be primary vehicle for consumption smoothing for all individuals (e.g. France) or primarily for low earners (United Kingdom)	Contributes to consumption smoothing according to the parameters for contributions and benefits	Employer and employee contributions ultimately come out of salaries therefore contributes to consumption smoothing	Direct link between contributions and benefits Where private DC is partially funded at the expense of public contributory arrangements, the impact on consumption smoothing will be reduced	Contributes to consumption smoothing to the extent that savings into voluntary schemes do not just divert savings from other vehicles
Financial sustainability	Depending on benefit level and entitlement, may conflict with other priorities for public expenditure	Can be vulnerable to macro-economic and demographic risks. Sustainability depends on benefit levels, retirement age, indexation Transition to funded systems can worsen sustainability of PAYG systems	Can be vulnerable to macro-economic and demographic risks. NDC may improve sustainability by closely linking benefits to contributions Potential for operational risks Transition from PAYG to partial funding can make the PAYG system less sustainable	Vulnerable to demographic risks and low interest rates Potential for operational risks	Sustainability achieved by pushing more risk onto individuals – creates a requirement for a public system to provide some insurance Potential for operational risks	Fully sustainable
Redistribution	Part of progressive taxation. Means testing can increase redistribution effect	Can adjust parameters to increase redistribution e.g. link between contributions and benefits, floors and ceilings, accrual rates, indexation	Can adjust parameters to increase redistribution e.g. link between contributions and benefits, floors and ceilings, accrual rates, indexation	Not an objective of DB schemes Tax incentives may be less progressive than overall tax system	Not possible within individual DC schemes Tax incentives may be less progressive than overall tax system	Not possible within individual DC schemes Tax incentives may be less progressive than overall tax system

	Public pension Non-contributory	Public pension Contributory PAYG	Public pension Contributory funded	Private funded pension Mandatory DB[1]	Private funded pension Mandatory DC	Private funded pension Voluntary
Inter-generational equity	Within tax system	Demographic changes mean redistribution from current contributors to current retirees. This can be offset by adjusting benefit levels and accruals – this shifts part of macro-economic and longevity risk onto individuals	Demographic changes mean redistribution from current contributors to current retirees. This can be offset by adjusting benefit levels and accruals – this shifts part of macro-economic and longevity risk onto individuals	Longevity risk shared across generations. Risk sharing mechanisms can be introduced	Not possible within individual DC	Not possible within individual DC
Intra-generational equity		Can use compensatory mechanisms to offset missed contribution periods – therefore provides insurance against labour market and social risks. However this may be interpreted as a right so weakens incentive to contribute	Can use compensatory mechanisms to offset missed contribution periods – therefore provides insurance against labour market and social risks	Collective systems can provide insurance against labour market and social risks	Not possible within individual DC Insurance against labour market and social risks can be purchased but at a higher cost than in a collective arrangement	Not possible within individual DC
Benefit adequacy/replacement rate	Can be set as minimum or target replacement rate for average earner (note potential fiscal implications)	Can be used for minimum income guarantee or for target replacement rate Target may vary by income level	Target replacement rate may vary by income level.	Target replacement rate, though increasing move towards conditional indexation i.e. less protection against macro-economic risk	Vulnerable to macro-economic, financial market and operational risks. Investment strategy has significant impact on benefit levels.	Generally used to increase replacement rate for higher earners
Labour force participation	May weaken incentives	May reduce incentives to work past retirement age: close routes to early retirement and align age at which public and private benefits can be accessed	Incentive depends on link between contributions and benefits: close routes to early retirement and align age at which public and private benefits can be accessed	Uniform accrual rates penalise younger workers/those with less seniority – DB may be less adaptable to changing labour market conditions	Strong incentive	Limited incentive, unless no other savings vehicle available
Coverage	Universal	Excludes people who have never participated in formal economy	Can be extended to all workers within formal economy relatively easily	Tend to exclude the low-paid, part-time workers, self-employed	Tend to exclude the low-paid, part-time workers, self-employed	Generally used by higher earners. Incentives such as matching contributions can encourage more people to participate

1. Applies also to voluntary DB where applicable (e.g. Canada, United Kingdom).

Notes

[1] Most PAYG systems are DB; notional defined contribution (NDC) PAYG systems are in place in Italy, Latvia, Poland and Sweden.

[2] It only shows gross replacement rates for voluntary private pension arrangements with a significant coverage among the working population, generally 40% or more.

[3] For a fuller explanation of methodology, please see (OECD, 2017[2]).

[4] NDC arrangements are PAYG, i.e. current contributions pay for current benefits. However contributions are also credited to a notional account for each individual contributor, whose pension benefits at retirement are based on the capital accumulated in the account, as in a DC arrangement.

[5] These are discussed in Chapter 3.

[6] A full discussion of the impact and cost of tax incentives on contributions into private pensions is available in (OECD, 2018[6]) and in Chapter 2.

[7] Special regulations exempt work income up to a certain threshold.

[8] For example, someone born in 1939 receives 15/20 of their entitlements from the old system while 5/20 of their PAYG pension credits were transformed into NDC pension credits.

[9] Chapter 2 in (OECD, 2012[19]) provides a full discussion and analysis of these issues.

References

Conde-Ruiz, J. and C. Gonzalez (2016), "From Bismark to Beveridge: the other pension reform in Spain", *SERIES* 7, August 2016, pp. 461-490. [5]

European Commission (2018), *The 2018 Ageing Report: Economic and Budgetary Projections for the EU Member States (2016-2070)*, European Commission. [11]

Gruber, J. and D. Wise (1999), "Social Security programs and retirement around the world", *NBER Working Paper* 6534. [15]

Holzman, R. and R. Hinz (2005), "Old Age Income Support in the 21st Century", *World Bank* 32672. [13]

ICI (2015), "Who Benefits from the U.S. Retirement System", *ICI Research Perspective*, Vol. 21/7, November 2015. [16]

Kawiński, M., D. Stańko and J. Rutecka (2012), "Protection mechanisms in the old age pension systems of the CEE countries", *Journal of Pension Economics and Finance*, Vol. 11/4, pp. 581-609, https://doi.org/10.1017/S147474721200008X. [7]

Musalem, A. and R. Pasquini (2012), "Private Pension Systems: Cross Country Investment Performance", *World Bank Discussion Paper*, Vol. 1214/May. [14]

OECD (2018), *Financial Incentives and Retirement Savings*, OECD Publishing, Paris. [6]

OECD (2017), *Pensions at a Glance 2017: OECD and G20 Indicators*, OECD Publishing, Paris, http://dx.doi.org/10.1787/pension_glance-2017-en. [2]

OECD (2016), *Life Annuity Products and Their Guarantees*, OECD Publishing, Paris, http://dx.doi.org/10.1787/9789264265318-en. [9]

OECD (2016), *OECD Business and Finance Outlook*, OECD Publishing, Paris, http://dx.doi.org/10.1787/9789264257573-en. [10]

OECD (2016), *OECD Pensions Outlook 2016*, OECD Publishing, Paris, http://dx.doi.org/10.1787/pens_outlook-2016-en. [1]

OECD (2015), *Pensions at a Glance 2015: OECD and G20 indicators*, OECD Publishing, Paris, http://dx.doi.org/10.1787/pension_glance-2015-en. [3]

OECD (2012), *OECD Pensions Outlook 2012*, OECD Publishing, Paris, http://dx.doi.org/10.1787/9789264169401-en. [19]

OECD (2011), *Chile: Review of the private pensions system*, http://www.oecd.org/finance/private-pensions/49497472.pdf. [18]

Palmer, E. (2011), *Promoting Personal Responsibility with a Strong Public Commitment*, World Bank. [8]

PPI (2017), *The impact of automatic enrolment in the UK as at 2016.* [4]

Rein, M. and J. Turner (2001), "Public-Private Interactions: Mandatory Pensions in Australia, the Netherlands and Switzerland", *Review of Population and Social Policy*, Vol. 10. [17]

Westerhout, E., J. Jan Bonenkamp and P. Broer (2014), "Collective versus Individual Pension Schemes: a Welfare-Theoretical Perspective", *CPB Discussion Paper*, Vol. 287, https://www.cpb.nl/sites/default/files/publicaties/download/cpb-discussion-paper-287-collective-versus-individual-pension-schemes-welfare-theoretical-perspectiv.pdf. [12]

Chapter 2. Can countries improve the design of financial incentives to promote savings for retirement?

This chapter examines whether countries can improve the design of financial incentives to promote savings for retirement. After describing how countries currently design financial incentives, it assesses the overall tax advantage that these incentives provide to individuals, how these incentives affect the way individuals save for retirement, and the fiscal cost these incentives represent to governments. The chapter also compares different approaches to designing financial incentives, based on their inherent characteristics within a common framework, to assess the various implications for individuals and governments. It concludes with policy guidelines to help countries improve the design of their financial incentives to promote savings for retirement.

Governments have long used financial incentives to promote savings for retirement. Financial incentives encourage participation in retirement savings plans and boost overall retirement income by making private savings, typically a complement to public pension systems, more attractive and inclusive. Historically, tax incentives have been the dominant form of these incentives, providing favourable income tax treatment to savings for retirement relative to other types of savings. More recently, new types of financial incentives, not directly linked to the income tax system, have become more frequent. These non-tax incentives include matching contributions and fixed nominal subsidies paid into the pension account of eligible individuals.

These financial incentives represent a fiscal cost for governments. Therefore, it is important to evaluate whether they are effective tools for encouraging people to save for retirement, taking into account the different needs across the population.

The goal of this chapter is to discuss whether countries can improve the design of financial incentives to promote savings for retirement. It presents policy guidelines that can be used for that purpose. It provides a summary of four years of analysis conducted by the OECD under the project on Financial Incentives and Retirement Savings. It uses two measures to compare the outcomes of different designs of tax and non-tax incentives for individuals and governments.[1] The analysis focuses on funded and private pension arrangements in 42 OECD and selected non-OECD countries.

All of the countries analysed offer financial incentives to promote savings for retirement. These incentives are found to be effective tools to promote savings for retirement as they are shown to provide a meaningful tax advantage for contributions to a retirement plan relative to other savings vehicles. As a result of this tax advantage, people react by increasing their participation in, and contributions to, retirement plans. The evidence reviewed indicates that low-income earners are likely to be more sensitive to non-tax incentives than to tax incentives. Although the total fiscal cost of financial incentives varies greatly across countries, it is projected to remain in the low single digits of GDP for most. While different designs of financial incentives may be economically equivalent in certain circumstances, the way individuals perceive them may affect their behaviour and influence the amount saved in retirement plans. Countries can, therefore, improve the design of financial incentives by considering policy guidelines based on the analysis and experience to date.

The chapter is structured as follows. Section 2.1 briefly describes how different countries have designed their financial incentives. Section 2.2 assesses the overall tax advantage that these incentives provide when individuals save for retirement in comparison to a benchmark savings instrument. Section 2.3 examines evidence of the effectiveness of financial incentives at increasing retirement savings, while Section 2.4 assesses their fiscal cost. Section 2.5 compares the pros and cons of different approaches to designing financial incentives. Section 2.6 presents conclusions and provides policy guidelines to help countries improve the design of their financial incentives with a view to promoting savings for retirement.

2.1. How do countries design financial incentives to promote savings for retirement?

Countries use two primary types of financial incentive to encourage individuals to save for retirement, tax incentives and non-tax incentives. Traditional forms of savings are taxed the same way as other income and earnings: contributions are paid from after-tax earnings; the investment income generated is taxed; and withdrawals following retirement age are exempted from taxation. This is generally referred to as the "Taxed-Taxed-Exempt" or "TTE" tax regime. Tax incentives for retirement savings arise from deviating from this benchmark. Non-tax incentives include matching contributions and fixed nominal subsidies. These are payments made by the government or employers directly into the pension account of eligible individuals.[2]

To establish the tax treatment of retirement savings, it is necessary to know how contributions, returns on investment and withdrawals are taxed. A preferential tax treatment on those three flows can take the form of tax deductions, tax exemptions, tax credits or tax rate relief. Tax deductions and tax exemptions reduce an individual's taxable income. The value of the reduction in tax liability associated with the deduction or exemption depends on an individual's marginal tax rate. For example, contributions may be deducted from taxable income (fully or partially) before calculating the tax due, while returns on investment may be excluded from the tax base. By contrast, tax credits directly reduce tax liability. A tax credit may be calculated as a proportion of the contributions paid into a retirement savings plan or can be a fixed nominal amount. Tax credits are classified as "non-refundable" when the value of the credit cannot exceed the tax liability. Finally, tax rate reliefs reduce the tax rate applied on the income flow. For all these tax treatments, caps can be introduced to limit tax relief.

The most common tax treatment of retirement savings exempts contributions and returns on investment from taxation while taxing pension benefits and withdrawals as income. Figure 2.1 classifies countries according to the tax treatment of contributions, returns on investment and withdrawals for the main retirement savings plan. Half of OECD countries use a variant of the "Exempt-Exempt-Taxed" ("EET") tax regime. However, a wide range of other tax regimes can be found as well, from the "EEE" regime where contributions, returns on investment and pension income are all tax exempt, to regimes where two of three flows are taxed.[3]

Figure 2.1. Tax treatment of retirement savings, 2018

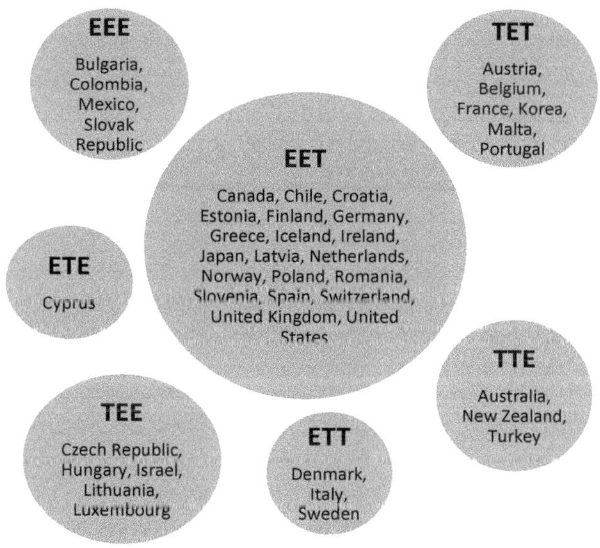

Notes: Main pension plan in each country. "E" stands for "exempt" and "T" for "taxed". Countries offering tax credits on contributions are considered as taxing contributions, as the tax credit may not cover the full amount of tax paid on those contributions. [4] [5]
Source: (OECD, 2018[1]).

Public pay-as-you-go (PAYG) pension arrangements are also generally subject to the "EET" tax regime. This is an argument in favour of providing the same tax treatment, "EET", to funded pension arrangements. In most OECD countries, employees' social security contributions are deductible from income, the (implicit or explicit) internal rate of return of the PAYG scheme is exempt from personal income tax, and pension benefits are taxed as income. Of the 18 OECD countries applying the "EET" tax regime to their main retirement savings plan, 13 also apply it to their mandatory PAYG pension arrangement (OECD, 2017[2]).

Figure 2.1 masks the heterogeneity that exists within countries. The tax treatment of contributions to retirement savings plans may vary according to the source of the contributions (the employee, the employer or the government), their mandatory or voluntary nature, the type of plan into which they are paid (personal or occupational), or the income of the plan member. In addition, limits to the amount of contributions eligible for tax relief may differ for various types of contributions. In countries where returns are taxed, tax rates may vary according to the holding period of the investments, the type of asset class, or the income of the plan member. Finally, the tax treatment of pension income may differ according to the source of the contributions, the form of the post-retirement product or the age of retirement.

The complexity of the tax treatment of retirement savings may prevent individuals to save for retirement. Consequently, some countries have introduced more direct, non-tax financial incentives to promote savings for retirement (Table 2.1). These include matching contributions and fixed nominal subsidies. These incentives are provided to eligible individuals who participate in, or make contributions to, retirement savings plans. Matching contributions correspond to a certain proportion of the individual's contributions (match rate), up to a maximum, while with fixed nominal subsidies all eligible individuals receive the same amount.

Table 2.1. Government non-tax financial incentives, 2018

	Matching contributions (match rate)	Fixed nominal subsidies
OECD countries	Australia (50%), Austria (4.25%), Chile (50% or 15%)[1], Czech Republic (scale), Hungary (20%), Mexico (325%)[2], New Zealand (50%), Turkey (25%), United States (50% to 100%)[3]	Chile, Germany, Lithuania, Mexico, Turkey
Selected non-OECD countries	Colombia (20%), Croatia (15%)	

1. Chile has two different matching programmes, one for young low earners (50% match rate) and one for voluntary contributors (15% match rate).
2. The matching programme for Mexico only applies to public sector workers.
3. The matching programme for the United States refers to the Thrift Savings Plan for federal employees. The first 3% of employee contribution is matched dollar-for-dollar, while the next 2% is matched at 50 cents on the dollar.

2.2. Does the design of financial incentives provide a tax advantage when people save for retirement?

This section assesses whether the design of financial incentives in OECD and selected non-OECD countries provides an advantage when people save for retirement. This assessment requires a common metric to compare the outcome of the different tax and non-tax incentives across countries. This section first introduces such a metric and then calculates it for all of the countries.

How to assess the way in which financial incentives provide an advantage to individuals

Comparing the present value of taxes paid when an individual saves in an incentivised retirement plan rather than a traditional savings vehicle makes it possible to assess how much tax is saved by the individual due to the financial incentives. Table 2.2 illustrates how much tax would be paid under two tax regimes that commonly apply to traditional savings vehicles ("TTE") and to retirement savings plans ("EET"). The calculations assume that an initial contribution of EUR 1 000 is invested for 10 years and earns a constant 5% return. The individual is subject to a 25% marginal income tax rate that remains constant over time. Under the "TTE" tax regime, the individual pays EUR 250 in tax when the contribution is made, so that, after tax, only EUR 750 are actually invested. At the end of each year, the individual also pays taxes on the investment income, amounting in total to EUR 84.7 in present value. Upon withdrawal, no tax is due and the after-tax value is equal to EUR 1 083.8. Under the "EET" tax regime, tax is only due upon withdrawal, so that the present value of tax paid amounts to EUR 250 and the after-tax withdrawal to EUR 1 221.7. The individual therefore pays EUR 84.7 less in taxes in present value terms when contributing to an "EET" plan rather than to a "TTE" plan. The difference in after-tax withdrawal is also equal to EUR 84.7 in present value. Provided the discount rate is equal to the rate of return, the benefit that accrues to the individual can be expressed as either a tax advantage or as a retirement income advantage.

Table 2.2. Overall tax advantage: illustration (in EUR)

	EET		TTE		Difference
	Nominal	PV	Nominal	PV	PV
Pre-tax contribution	1 000.0		1 000.0		
Tax paid on contribution	0.0	0.0	250.0	250.0	
Amount invested	1 000.0		750.0		
Tax paid on returns during investment period	0.0	0.0	111.3	84.7	
Account balance after 10 years	1 628.9		1 083.8		
Tax paid on withdrawal	407.2	250.0	0.0	0.0	
After-tax withdrawal	1 221.7		1 083.8		84.7
Total tax paid		250.0		334.7	84.7
Overall tax advantage					8.5%

Notes: "E" stands for exempt, "T" for taxed and "PV" for present value. The calculations assume that an initial contribution of EUR 1 000 is invested for 10 years and earns a constant 5% return. The individual is subject to a 25% marginal tax rate, constant over time. The discount rate is equal to the rate of return.

The analysis calculates the "overall tax advantage", by extending the simulation to the entire lifetime of the individual and considering the specific tax regimes of different countries. The overall tax advantage should not be confused with the incentive to save (Box 2.1). The overall tax advantage is defined as the difference in the present value of total tax paid on contributions, returns on investment and withdrawals when an individual saves in a benchmark savings vehicle compared to an incentivised retirement plan assuming a constant contribution rate during the entire career. It is expressed as a percentage of the present value of pre-tax contributions. The overall tax advantage represents the amount saved in taxes by the individual over working and retirement years when contributing the same amount (before tax) to an incentivised pension plan rather than to a benchmark savings vehicle. The impact of both tax and non-tax incentives is reflected in the overall tax advantage by evaluating non-tax incentives as refundable tax credits paid into the pension account.

Box 2.1. Difference between the overall tax advantage and the incentive to save

A positive overall tax advantage means that the individual would save in taxes paid when contributing to an incentivised retirement plan rather than to a benchmark savings vehicle. It does not mean that the individual has an incentive to save.

The incentive to save is measured by the after-tax rate of return. A tax system is neutral when the way present and future consumption is taxed makes the individual indifferent between consuming and saving. This is achieved when the after-tax rate of return is equal to the before-tax rate of return.

Taxing returns creates a disincentive to save because the present value of the income is greater if it is used for consumption today than if it is used for consumption tomorrow (Mirrlees et al., 2011[31]). A "TTE" tax regime therefore incentivises consumption rather than savings. In the example from Table 2.2, the after-tax rate of return with the "TTE" tax regime is equal to 3.75%, which is lower than the before-tax rate of return of 5%.

By contrast, an "EET" tax regime is neutral between saving and consuming (the after-tax rate of return is equal to 5%), provided that the individual faces a constant personal income tax rate over time. When the tax rate on withdrawals is lower than the tax rate at which contributions were deducted, the after-tax rate of return is greater than the before-tax rate of return, creating an incentive to save. When the opposite is true, for example due to a loss of entitlement to a means-tested public pension, the after-tax rate of return is lower than the before-tax rate of return, leading to an incentive to consume.

Upfront taxation of retirement savings, "TEE", also achieves tax neutrality between saving and consuming, as long as returns are not above the "normal return to saving". The normal return to saving is the return that just compensates for delaying consumption. It is also often called the risk-free return (Mirrlees et al., 2011[31]).

Overall tax advantage offered in different countries

Across OECD and selected non-OECD countries, a hypothetical average earner pays less in taxes over their lifetime by contributing the same pre-tax amount to a retirement savings plan rather than to a traditional savings account.[6] This amount varies from 8% of the present value of all contributions in Sweden, to around 50% in Israel, Lithuania, the Netherlands and Mexico (Figure 2.2).[7] Countries with the largest private pension markets, such as Australia, Canada, Denmark, Switzerland, the United Kingdom and the United States, provide overall tax advantages between 20% and 40% of the present value of contributions, with the United States at the higher end of the range and Australia, Denmark, and the United Kingdom at the lower end.[8]

Figure 2.2. Overall tax advantage provided to an average earner

Present value of taxes saved over a lifetime, as a percentage of the present value of contributions

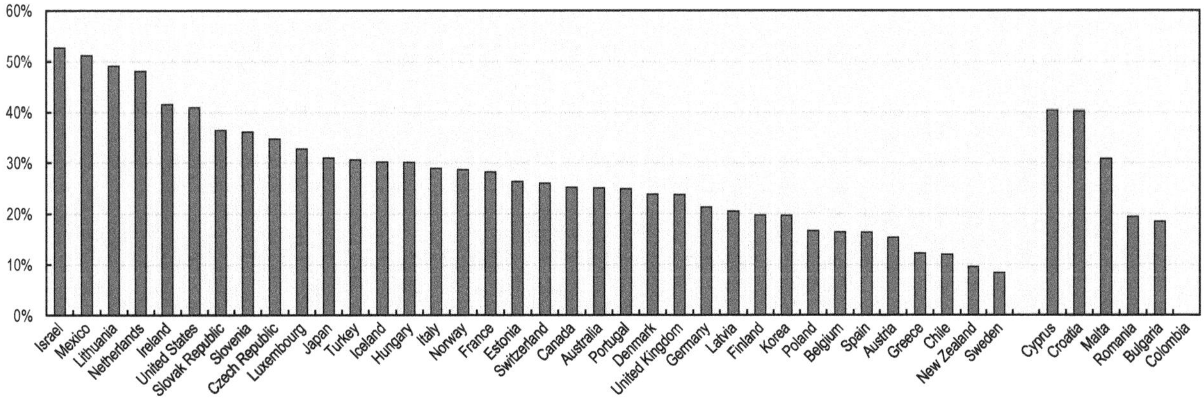

Note: Calculations based on the 2018 tax treatment of the main pension plan in each country.
Source: (OECD, 2018[11]).

StatLink http://dx.doi.org/10.1787/888933850108

The differences observed across countries are due not only to the characteristics of the tax regimes applied to retirement plans and savings vehicles and to the presence of non-tax incentives, but also to the characteristics of the personal income tax system in each country (i.e. the tax brackets and the tax rates). In Canada and Greece for example, the overall tax advantage of contributing to a private pension plan is different (25% and 12% of the present value of contributions respectively), even though the same tax regime applies to retirement savings (contributions and returns are tax exempt and withdrawals are taxed, “EET”). However, an average earner in Canada has a marginal tax rate of about 30%, while an average earner in Greece has a 22% marginal tax rate. A lower marginal income tax rate results in a lower value of the tax relief.

The overall tax advantage provided to individuals is sensitive to the assumptions used, especially the assumed contribution rate. In voluntary pension systems people contribute at different rates. Therefore, to compare the overall tax advantage across countries there is a need to assume a single rate of contribution for voluntary components of the pension system.[9] The analysis shown in Figure 2.2 assumes a 5% of earnings contribution for each country. Figure 2.3 shows the impact of increasing the assumed contribution rate from 5% to 10% for countries with voluntary private pension systems. Everything else equal, a higher contribution rate translates into higher assets accumulated at retirement and higher pension benefits. In systems where pension benefits are taxed, these higher benefits may be taxed at a higher rate because they may push total taxable pension income into a higher tax bracket or because the share of total taxable pension income in the last tax bracket is bigger. This would lead to a reduction in the overall tax advantage. In Ireland, the United States and Malta, the overall tax advantage falls by 10, 11 and 5 percentage point respectively when increasing the contribution rate to 10%. In the other countries with voluntary pension systems, the change in the overall tax advantage provided to the average earner from increasing the contribution rate is not significant. The relative value of the tax incentive across countries is therefore significantly affected by the assumed rate of contribution.

Figure 2.3. Overall tax advantage provided by voluntary pension systems according to the assumed contribution rate, average earner

Present value of taxes saved over a lifetime, as a percentage of the present value of contributions

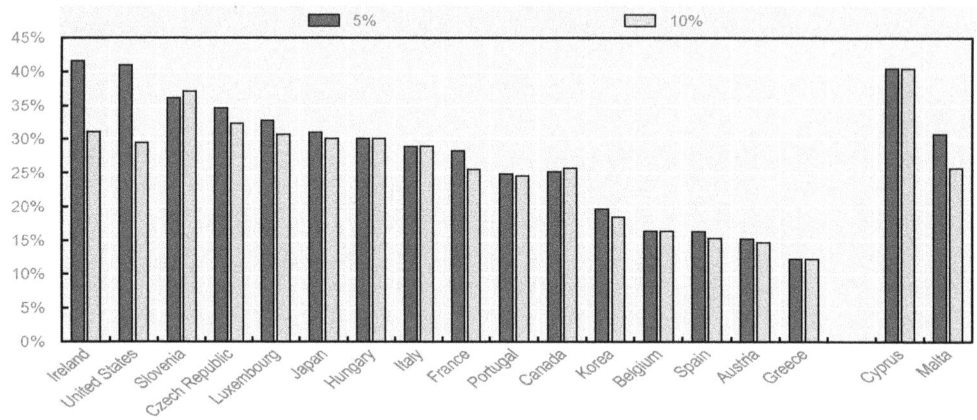

Note: Calculations for countries with voluntary private pension systems only, assuming a contribution rate of 5% or 10%.
Source: (OECD, 2018[1])

StatLink http://dx.doi.org/10.1787/888933850127

The value of the overall tax advantage varies with the income level of the individual. Figure 2.4 shows that, in some countries, high-income earners (earning four times average earnings) benefit from a higher overall tax advantage than average earners and low-income earners (earning 60% of average earnings). This is the case in Canada, Chile, Denmark, Italy, Japan, Poland, Switzerland and the United Kingdom (black triangles are on top). Low-income earners receive higher financial incentives in Estonia, Ireland, Latvia, Lithuania, New Zealand, Norway and Turkey for example (white diamonds are on top). These include countries offering fixed nominal subsidies (e.g. Lithuania, Turkey) or matching contributions with a low maximum entitlement (e.g. New Zealand). This type of incentive is found to be more valuable to low-income earners because the payment represents a larger share of their income. Other countries provide the largest tax advantage to average earners. These include France, Iceland, the Netherlands and Slovenia (blue bars are higher than the other symbols). Finally, countries with fixed personal income tax rates that tax all retirement savings equally regardless of income level offer the same overall tax advantage across the income scale, for instance, as in Bulgaria.

Figure 2.4. Overall tax advantage provided to individuals, by income level

Present value of taxes saved over a lifetime, as a percentage of the present value of contributions

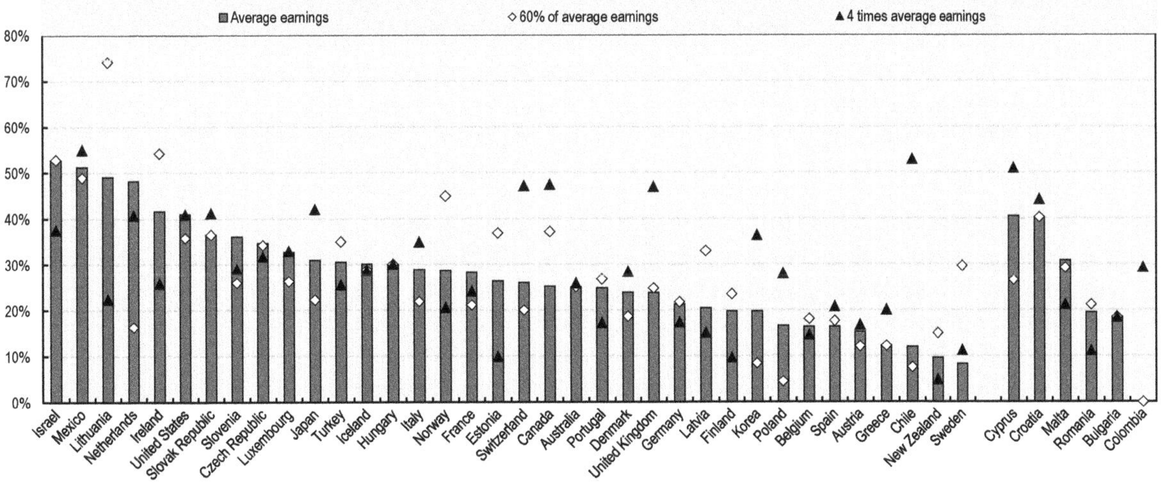

Note: Calculations based on the 2018 tax treatment of the main pension plan in each country.
Source: (OECD, 2018[1]).

StatLink http://dx.doi.org/10.1787/888933850146

2.3. Are financial incentives effective tools to promote savings for retirement?

Countries use tax incentives to promote savings for retirement, in particular by taxing retirement savings only upon withdrawal ("EET" tax regime). This translates into a tax advantage for individuals contributing an equivalent amount to an incentivised retirement plan rather than to a traditional savings vehicle by reducing total taxes paid over their lifetime. This section examines whether financial incentives are effective tools to promote savings for retirement by analysing whether individuals actually respond to financial incentives by increasing their participation in, and contributions to, retirement savings plans.

The best way to measure the effectiveness of financial incentives is with respect to the intended policy objective. Some countries may want to increase overall savings because they have low national savings relative to their investment needs. National savings are a source of funds for domestic investment which is a key driver of labour productivity growth and higher future living standards. Even a country that has large overall savings may want to reallocate savings into retirement savings plans. Increasing saving for retirement could increase long-term investment, enhance the depth and characteristics of the financial sector and facilitate long-term growth. Furthermore, research in behavioural economics indicates that people tend to save too little for retirement because of procrastination, inertia and short-sightedness.[10] Encouraging a reallocation of savings might not increase overall national savings but could earmark a greater share for retirement thereby increasing the long-term income security of the population. In addition, recent reforms to PAYG public pension systems have increased the need to enhance the role of private funded pensions in the provision of retirement income in some countries (OECD, 2017[4]). Increased private sources of retirement income can also help reduce reliance on the public safety net which helps to rein in public expenditures.

The effectiveness of financial incentives in part depends on the design and generosity of the public pension system. In countries where the public pension system already offers high replacement rates, the need for supplementary retirement savings may be relatively low although this may change as potential financial sustainability issues associated with generous public systems arise. If contributions to the public pension system are already large, individuals may not be willing to part with additional pension contributions. In both cases, financial incentives would need to be larger to overcome impediments to putting money aside for retirement.

In light of those broad objectives, the following section summarises the main findings from the literature evaluating the effectiveness of financial incentives in promoting savings for retirement. It discusses first the impact of financial incentives on participation in, and contributions to, retirement savings plans, and then whether financial incentives lead to an increase in national savings or to a reallocation of savings.

The impact of tax incentives on participation in, and contributions to, retirement savings plans

"EET" tax incentives encourage participation in, and contributions to, retirement savings plans in progressive personal income tax systems, where tax rates increase with taxable income, because individuals respond to the upfront tax relief on contributions. When contributions are deductible from taxable income, tax relief on contributions increases when taxable income jumps from one tax bracket to the next. Empirical studies in Canada (Milligan, 2002[5]), France (Carbonnier, Direr and Slimani Houti, 2014[6]), the United Kingdom (Crawford, Disney and Emmerson, 2012[7]) and the United States (Power and Rider, 2002[8]) show that individuals whose income is subject to a higher marginal tax rate are more likely to participate in, and to contribute more to, an "EET" retirement savings plan.[11] In all these studies, the authors include controls for the level of income, so that the tax effect is not distorted by the effect of income.

Among low-income earners, however, the combination of a progressive tax system and an "EET" tax incentive may not be effective in encouraging savings for retirement. For example, Carbonnier, Direr and Slimani Houti (2014[6]) compare contribution levels to "EET" tax-favoured pension plans for two groups of French individuals: those whose taxable income is higher than, but close to, a given tax threshold, and those whose taxable income is just below the same threshold. They conduct this comparison at different tax thresholds and for different age groups.[12] They find that low-income earners aged 45 to 55 do not increase their contribution level when their marginal tax rate increases. This suggests that the structure of the income tax system is not the main factor for low-income earners in deciding about their contribution level. In addition, in retirement income systems where low-income earners receive large income replacement rates through public pensions, this observed low responsiveness to tax incentives may be less of a concern.

Despite the limited sensitivity to variations in income tax rates, low-income earners have been found to respond to changes in some of the parameters of tax incentives by adjusting their participation in, and contribution level to, retirement savings plans. Although the impact may be small. For instance, Disney, Emmerson and Wakefield (2007[9]) show that low-income earners increased their participation in, and contributions to, personal pensions in the United Kingdom following a 2001 reform that increased the contribution limit for them. Private pension coverage increased by around three percentage points more among individuals who were affected by the reform than among those who were not affected. Evidence also suggests an increase in contributions among those affected by the reform of around GBP 0.8 per week for singles and GBP 4.3 per week for couples. Similarly, Harju (2013[10]) shows that an increase in tax incentives for low-income earners in 2005 in Finland slightly increased their participation in personal pension plans.[13] Among low-income earners, coverage increased between one and two percentage points because of the reform. The reform, however, did not prompt a significant increase in contribution levels.

The limited responsiveness of low-income earners to tax incentives may be due to insufficient income to afford contributions, insufficient tax liability to enjoy tax relief, or low understanding of tax-related issues. For example, in the United Kingdom in 2012, only 46% of survey respondents knew that money paid into private pensions qualifies for tax relief (Macleod et al., 2012[11]). In addition, Sandler (2002[12]) provides evidence that understanding of tax-related matters with respect to savings increases with the income level.

Tax incentives can also take the form of tax credits. The only available studies on tax credits refer to the Saver's Credit in the United States, which supplements "EET" tax incentives for low and middle-income earners.[14] According to the Internal Revenue Service, in 2015, only 5.4% of all tax filers received a tax credit for an average amount of USD 178, far below the maximum USD 1 000. This low participation number is partially explained by the fact that the statistics consider all tax filers while only low and middle-income earners are eligible for the credit. Brown and John (2017[13]) argue that the limited impact of the programme is due to a general lack of awareness of the credit and the complexity of the claim form, the fact that many low and middle-income earners do not have access to occupational pension plans, and the fact that low-income earners may not have sufficient tax liability to receive the tax credit. In addition, Ramnath (2013[14]) finds no statistically significant evidence that a higher tax credit rate increases individual contributions to private pensions.

Do tax incentives lead to an increase in national savings or to a reallocation of savings?

The literature is far from conclusive on whether tax incentives lead to an increase in national savings or instead to a reallocation of savings. Empirical studies provide a range of estimates that between 9% and 100% of savings in tax-favoured plans represent new savings. All studies examining this issue focus on retirement savings plans for which contributions are tax deductible (either "EET" as in the United States or "EtT" as in Denmark).[15]

A first group of studies find that tax incentives increase retirement savings through a moderate increase in national savings. Poterba, Venti and Wise (1996[15]) found that due to tax incentives, the assets accumulated in IRAs and 401(k) plans in the United States are mostly net additions to savings. Papers with similar findings include: Hubbard and Skinner (1996[16]), Benjamin (2003[17]), Ayuso, Jimeno and Villanueva (2007[18]), Guariglia and Markose (2000[19]), Rossi (2009[20]), and Gelber (2011[21]).

Another body of the literature argues that the increase in retirement savings following the introduction of tax incentives is mostly the result of a reallocation of savings rather than new savings. For example, Engen, Gale and Scholz (1996[22]) conclude that most of the reported increase in financial assets in IRAs can be attributed to stock market booms, higher real interest rates, and shifts in non-financial assets, debt, pensions and Social Security wealth. They conclude that tax incentives have a strong effect on the allocation of savings and wealth, but not on the level. Other papers with similar findings include:

Attanasio and DeLeire (2002[23]), Pence (2002[24]), Attanasio, Banks and Wakefield (2004[25]), Antón, Muñoz De Bustillo and Fernández-Macías (2014[26]), Chetty et al. (2014[27]) and Paiella and Tiseno (2014[28]).

The empirical measurement of whether tax incentives for retirement savings lead to an increase in national savings is inconclusive because of a number of constraints and methodological issues. For example, it is difficult to construct the counterfactual scenario, to control for all of the other factors that can influence saving decisions, and to choose the appropriate dependent variable (savings, wealth or consumption).

There is, however, more consistent evidence in the literature that low-to-middle income earners are more likely to respond to tax incentives by increasing their overall savings, while high-income individuals tend to reallocate their savings. For example, Engelhardt (2000[29]), Engen and Gale (2000[30]), Chernozhukov and Hansen (2004[31]) and Engelhardt and Kumar (2011[32]) argue that, since low-income earners have little wealth, when they contribute to a tax-favoured retirement savings plan their contributions represent new savings because they have few other assets to reallocate. By contrast, high-income earners are more likely to finance contributions to tax-favoured accounts by shifting assets from other taxable accounts or taking on more debt, rather than reducing their consumption, although they need to balance the advantage of tax incentives with the illiquidity of retirement products.

Therefore, the proportion of new savings in tax-favoured retirement plans will depend on the marginal propensity to save of different income groups, and on whether tax incentives are designed in a manner that will make them more accessible by, or attractive to, individuals at different income levels.

The impact of non-tax incentives on participation, contributions and savings

Adding employer matching contributions to tax-favoured ("EET") occupational pension plans has been shown to increase participation in retirement savings plans, but not necessarily total contributions (employer plus employee). Choi (2015[33]) and Madrian (2013[34]) review the rich literature in the United States related to employer matching contributions and conclude that the presence of a matching contribution and a higher match rate increase participation. They also find that the rate of increase in the match rate is directly related to the rate of increase in participation.[16] However, both authors note that the evidence on the link between the match rate and the overall level of contributions is inconclusive. Different levels of the match threshold, however, are found to be related to changes in participants' contribution rates. Choi et al. (2002[35]) show that increasing the match threshold (i.e. the rate of employee contribution up to which the employer offers the match), without changing the match rate, increases the proportion of employees contributing at higher rates.

Government matching contributions targeted at low-income earners may be more effective at increasing their contribution level than their participation rate. OECD (2012[36]) for example shows that, in Australia, despite the "super co-contribution" programme, low-income earners are less likely to make voluntary pension contributions than other income groups. However, those who do contribute voluntarily tend to have much higher contribution rates than other income groups, as they need to make a larger contribution effort to get the maximum entitlement (maximum 50% match rate up to AUD 500).

Finally, government fixed nominal subsidies are found to increase participation in retirement savings plans for low-income earners, but the impact on contribution levels and national savings is unclear. For example, Börsch-Supan, Coppola and Reil-Held (2012[37]) and OECD (2012[36]) show that Riester pensions in Germany, which offer fixed nominal subsidies (provided that individuals contribute at least 4% of income), achieve higher participation rates among low-income households than other types of private pension plans.[17] Pfarr and Schneider (2013[38]) also find a positive effect of the child subsidy on participation.[18] However, the design of the subsidies does not encourage individuals to contribute above the 4% threshold. OECD (2012[36]) shows that average contribution rates are similar across all income groups at around the 4% minimum required to obtain the full subsidy. This threshold may act as an anchor in people's mind and does not provide any incentive to go beyond it. Finally, the evidence regarding the impact of subsidies on national savings is mixed. Corneo, Keese and Schröder (2008[39]), Kolerus, Koske and Hüfner (2012[40]), and Pfarr and Schneider (2013[38]) argue that low-income households reallocate existing savings from taxable accounts to Riester plans. By contrast, Börsch-Supan, Coppola and Reil-Held (2012[37]) report that most households across all income groups declare that they increased their savings after being enrolled in a Riester plan.

2.4. What is the cost of providing financial incentives to promote savings for retirement?

Tax incentives translate into lower personal income taxes paid by individuals and thus create a fiscal cost for the government. Moreover, non-tax financial incentives come directly from the general budget. The total fiscal cost of those tax and non-tax incentives depends on the generosity of the incentives and the amount contributed into retirement savings plans in each year. This section first presents how countries report the cost related to financial incentives for retirement savings, introduces a measure that allows for cross-country comparisons, and then calculates the measure for a selection of countries, determined by their data availability.

Country reporting of the cost related to financial incentives to promote savings for retirement

Several OECD countries produce tax expenditure reports that provide an assessment of the estimated fiscal cost of providing financial incentives to promote savings for retirement. These national reports usually measure the amount by which tax revenues are reduced in a given year due to a favourable tax treatment compared to a counter factual scenario that assumes individuals continue saving the same amount in a non-tax favoured benchmark vehicle. Among countries offering non-tax incentives, some may also use these reports to provide information about the amount paid into retirement accounts through fixed nominal subsidies or matching contributions (e.g. Austria, Germany and New Zealand).

Some countries also report the distribution of tax expenditures across income groups. These tend to show that the tax expenditures are concentrated within high-income households. In voluntary pension systems, high-income earners are more likely to participate in private pension plans than other income groups, reflecting their higher propensity and capacity to save.[19] Moreover, their higher income results in a greater value of the tax relief per household even when the tax rate is the same for everyone. Finally, in progressive tax systems where tax rates increase in proportion to income, high-income earners typically face higher marginal tax rates, thereby benefiting more from every unit of the flows that attract tax relief. In United States for example, where tax qualified retirement savings are taxed only upon withdrawal ("EET" tax regime), households in the top 20% of the income distribution receive around 66% of the tax expenditure related to retirement savings (Congressional Budget Office, 2013[41]).[20]

Because they often use different methodologies, national tax expenditure reports do not allow for meaningful cross-country comparisons. For example, the items reported as tax expenditures for retirement savings vary by country. Some countries like Belgium, Ireland, France or Sweden only communicate tax revenues forgone in their tax expenditure reports. Other countries, like Canada, the United Kingdom and the United States also include the tax collected on pension withdrawals (reporting it as negative tax expenditure) providing a measure that nets the value of the different flows. There is therefore a need for a common measure of the cost of financial incentives across countries to facilitate comparisons.

How to compare the evolution of the fiscal cost across countries?

The "net tax expenditure" permits the comparison of the fiscal cost related to financial incentives for retirement savings over time and across countries. This measure sums up how much personal income tax is collected or forgone each year on contributions, returns on investment and withdrawals over the total population, as compared to a benchmark in which contributions and returns are taxed and withdrawals are tax exempt ("TTE").[21] As illustrated below, the maturity of the pension system and demographic trends influence the value of the net tax expenditure over time.

This measure of net tax expenditure stabilises only when the pension system is fully mature. For example, as illustrated in Figure 2.5, introducing "EET" tax incentives into a pension system creates a positive fiscal cost for the government that is larger during the early development of the system. The "EET" tax system, as compared to a "TTE" benchmark, produces a net tax expenditure stemming from the tax deferral and the tax exemption of returns on investment. During this maturing phase, aggregate assets and benefit levels increase over time until they reach a stable level. The lag in the growth of benefits behind that of assets and investment income creates a temporary increase in the net tax expenditure. Once the system has reached maturity (i.e. all retirees draw their pension based on a full career and constant contribution rules) the net tax expenditure stabilises at its steady-state level.

Demographic trends also affect the pattern of net tax expenditure. Figure 2.6 takes a mature "EET" system in year t and illustrates how the net tax expenditure varies when the sizes of the cohorts entering the labour market between t+5 and t+24 are 20% larger than that of previous and following cohorts. In t, the net tax expenditure is at its steady-state level. Larger cohorts entering the labour market translate into higher contributions and higher assets, bringing the net tax expenditure above the steady state for a while. When the larger cohorts retire, the net tax expenditure declines and reaches a minimum (below the steady state) the year in which all of the retired population is composed of individuals in the larger cohorts. The steady state is reached again when all the individuals in the larger cohorts have passed away.

Figure 2.5. Net tax expenditure for a maturing "EET" pension system, by components

As a percentage of GDP

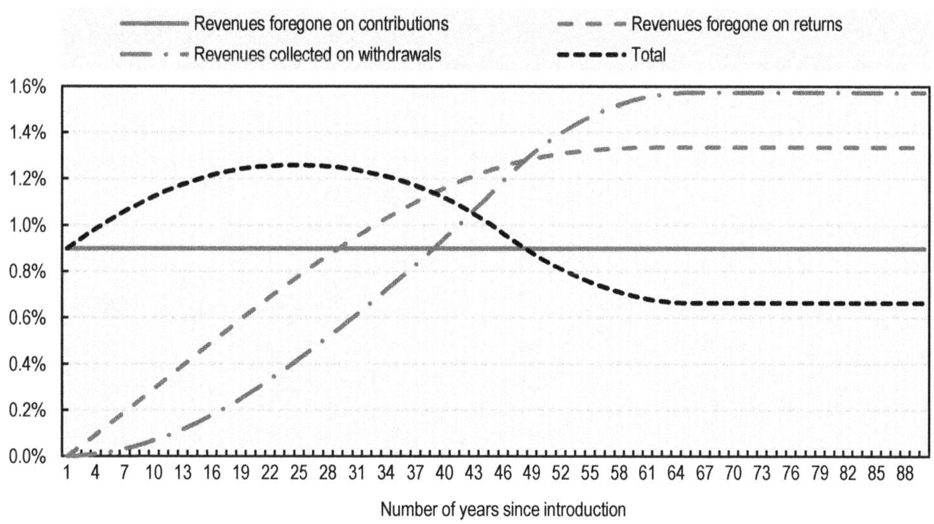

Notes: The calculations assume that individuals save from the age of 20 to 64 and draw pension benefits from age 65 to 84; contributions represent 3% of GDP; the number of people in each single-year age cohort is equal; the same average tax rate (30%) applies to all sources of income; a nominal rate of return of 5.06% (3% real return plus 2% inflation); and GDP growth at 3.28% (1.25% real growth plus 2% inflation).

StatLink http://dx.doi.org/10.1787/888933850165

Figure 2.6. Net tax expenditure for an "EET" pension system subject to a population bulge, by components

As a percentage of GDP

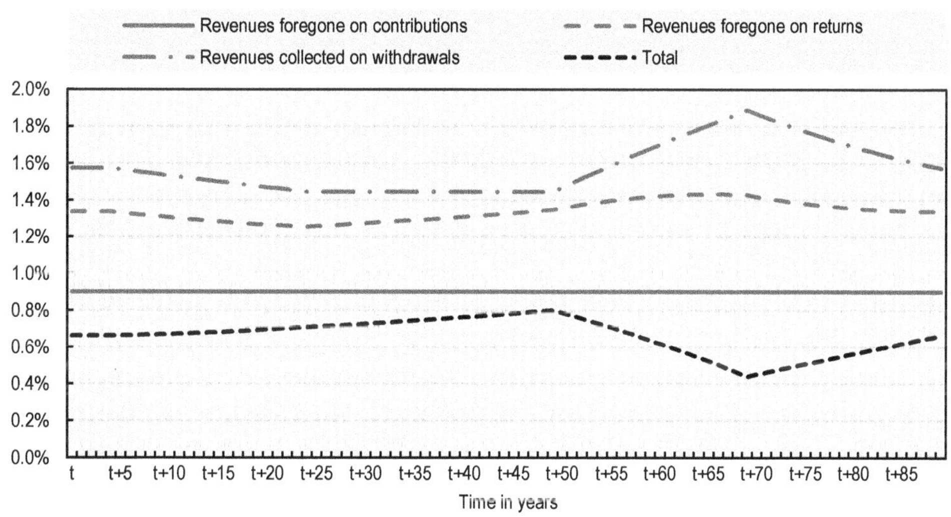

Notes: The calculations assume that individuals save from the age of 20 to 64 and draw pension benefits from age 65 to 84; contributions represent 3% of GDP; cohorts entering the labour market between t+5 and t+24 are 20% bigger than the other cohorts; the same average tax rate (30%) applies to all sources of income; a nominal rate of return of 5.06% (3% real return plus 2% inflation); and GDP growth at 3.28% (1.25% real growth plus 2% inflation).

StatLink http://dx.doi.org/10.1787/888933850184

Fiscal cost of financial incentives in selected OECD countries

The projected total fiscal cost of financial incentives to promote savings for retirement varies greatly across countries, but is generally expected to remain in the low single digits of GDP. Figure 2.7 shows the total fiscal cost of financial incentives, including both the net tax expenditure of tax incentives and the direct cost of non-tax incentives when they exist, for selected countries between 2015 and 2060.[22]

Figure 2.7. Projected fiscal cost related to financial incentives to promote savings for retirement in selected OECD countries, 2015-2060

As a percentage of GDP

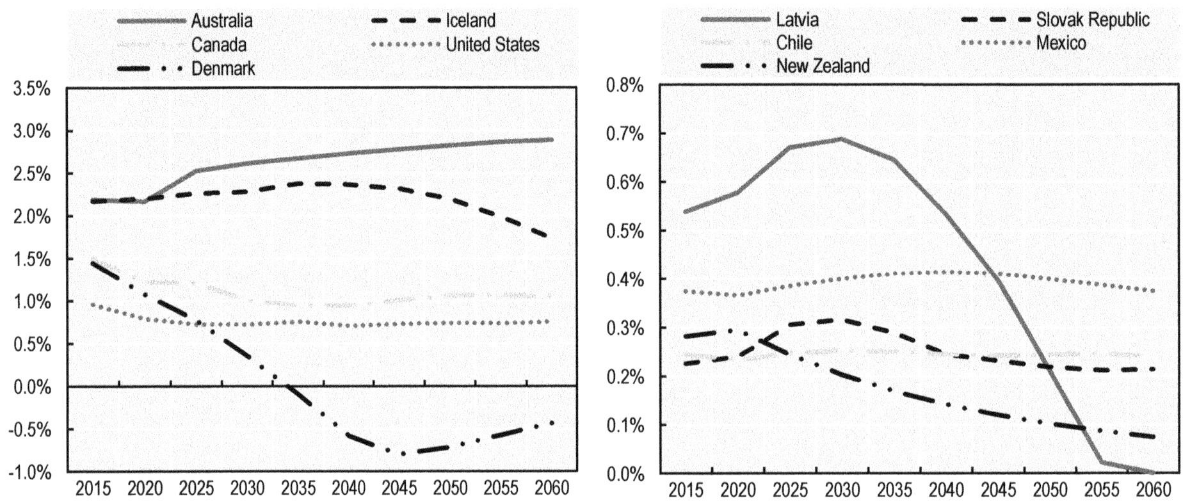

StatLink http://dx.doi.org/10.1787/888933850203

The fiscal cost varies from 2%-3% of GDP in Australia and Iceland to 0.1%-0.3% of GDP in Chile, Mexico, New Zealand and the Slovak Republic, and it even turns negative in Denmark, indicating an overall positive fiscal effect in the future.

Countries with mandatory private pension systems may expect a larger fiscal cost. For example, in Australia and Iceland, the mandatory private pension systems cover a large part of the population, contribution rates are above 10% and the tax incentives provide an overall tax advantage for an average earner of 25% of the contributions paid over a full career in Australia and 30% in Iceland (see Figure 2.2). In both countries, the fiscal cost is expected to vary between 2% and 3% of GDP over 2015-2060. Recent increases in contribution rates in these countries explain the upward trend in the fiscal cost.

Countries with mature voluntary private pension systems can expect a relatively stable fiscal cost. For example, the fiscal cost is anticipated to fluctuate between 0.7% and 1.5% of GDP in Canada and the United States, which have relatively mature voluntary pension systems and tax incentives that provide an overall tax advantage to the average earner, as measured earlier, of 25% in Canada and 41% in the United States. The ageing of baby-boom cohorts is the main factor driving the decline in the aggregate value of the net tax expenditure between 2015 and 2030-35 in these two countries. As baby-boomers start retiring and withdrawing their benefits, tax revenues collected on pensions will increase, thus reducing the annual value of the net tax expenditure. In both countries, the maturation of the private funded pension system is such that tax revenues collected on withdrawals are projected to exceed tax revenues forgone on contributions for the entire period of 2015-2060.

The maturing of the pension system will translate into large falls in the fiscal cost in Denmark and Latvia. In Denmark, the fiscal cost of the quasi-mandatory occupational pension plans will become negative (a positive fiscal impact) due to a large increase in tax revenues collected on withdrawals between 2015 and 2045. This is because coverage increased greatly in the 1990s through collective agreements, and contribution levels gradually increased to around 15% in the mid-2000s. This will translate into increased withdrawals as the system matures over time. The mandatory pension system in Latvia was introduced in 2001. During its initial phase, the net tax expenditure will increase and reach a peak at 0.7% of GDP in 2030, before declining and becoming negligible in 2060.

Including corporate income tax revenues and the potential tax impact of new savings would bring down the overall cost of financial incentives. When savings are invested in domestic equities or corporate bonds, they help companies improve their productive capacity, thereby raising the overall level of profits that are subject to corporate income tax and increasing future corporate income tax revenues. In addition, should financial incentives to promote retirement savings lead to new savings, this would affect tax revenues as well. Indeed, new savings are financed by a reduction in consumption and imply higher investment than otherwise, as new savings represent money that the individual would not have saved in the absence of the incentivised retirement plan. Therefore, new savings affect consumption tax receipts, as well as personal and corporate income tax revenues through higher investment income. As long as retirement savings are partly invested in the domestic economy and/or some of the saving would not have occurred in the absence of financial incentives, the fiscal cost of those incentives would be reduced compared to that shown in Figure 2.7. The exact reduction is, however, difficult to estimate as it depends on assumptions on how several parameters may evolve over time (see Chapter 5 (OECD, 2018[1])).

2.5. What are the comparative advantages and disadvantages of different approaches to designing financial incentives?

It is challenging to disentangle the effect of the design of different financial incentives from the effect of country-specific characteristics when analysing the implications for individuals and governments. Countries offering the same financial incentive can use different parameters such as the tax-deductibility limit, the tax credit rate, the proportion of contributions being tax deductible, the value of the subsidy, or the match rate. In addition, the characteristics of the personal income tax system in each country (i.e. the tax brackets and the tax rates) also affect comparability across countries.

This section, therefore, provides a theoretical assessment of different approaches to designing financial incentives to promote savings for retirement. The analysis compares different approaches to designing financial incentives based on their inherent characteristics and within a common framework to assess the implications for individuals and governments. The section starts with a description of the principal characteristics of the main current approach to designing financial incentives, taxing retirement savings upon withdrawal ("EET"), and then compares this approach to alternatives, such as taxing retirement savings upfront ("TEE") or using tax credits.

Principal characteristic of the current main approach to designing financial incentives

The overall tax advantage provided by the "EET" tax regime, as compared to a "TTE" benchmark, is essentially equivalent to exempting returns on investment from tax. When tax rates are the same at the time of contribution and withdrawal and the discount rate is equal to the rate of return, the reduction in taxes paid on contributions is exactly equal in present value to the increase in taxes paid on withdrawals, regardless of the income of the individual saver. In that case, the after-tax rate of return is equal to the before-tax rate of return and the tax regime provides neutrality between saving and consuming to all individuals (see Box 2.1). If the discount rate is lower than the rate of return, the overall tax advantage provided by the "EET" tax regime, the present value of the difference in the tax paid compared to the benchmark savings vehicle, is reduced because the tax on withdrawals will more than compensate for the initial tax relief on contributions.

The link between the overall tax advantage provided by an "EET" tax regime and the income level of the individual depends on the structure of the personal income tax system. In countries where all individuals have their entire income taxed at the same rate, the overall tax advantage provided by the "EET" tax regime (and any other tax regime) is the same across the income scale. When personal income tax rates increase with the level of taxable income (a progressive income tax system), the overall tax advantage increases with income because of the higher marginal tax rates. Indeed, individuals with higher marginal tax rates benefit more relative to a taxable alternative on every unit of investment income to which a zero rate of tax applies. However, the amount of investment income that would have been generated by an after-tax contribution into a benchmark "TTE" savings account is lower for individuals with higher marginal tax rates. The result is that the overall tax advantage increases with marginal tax rates, but the rate of increase slows as the marginal tax rate increases (Brady, 2012[42]). This is illustrated in the left panel of Figure 2.8.

The relative level of retirement income compared to income from work also affects the link between the overall tax advantage provided by the "EET" tax regime, and the level of income. Retirement income is usually lower than income from work, hence retirement income is likely to be taxed at a lower average rate than income from work. In that case, the tax paid on withdrawals may not compensate fully for the initial tax relief on contributions making the overall tax advantage larger than when the tax rate remains constant over the lifetime. This also means that the tax regime may favour savings over consumption, in particular for middle to upper-middle income earners (the after-tax rate of return is greater than the before-tax rate of return, see Box 2.1).[23] In addition, depending on the difference between the tax rates in the different tax brackets, and the size of the tax brackets, the reduction in taxes paid on withdrawals may increase the gap in the overall tax advantage across income groups. The right panel of Figure 2.8 shows that the overall tax advantage increases significantly for individuals earning between 80% and 2 times the average earnings when they face lower tax rates during retirement than while working. For high-income earners, there is a convergence towards tax neutrality (where neither savings nor consumption is favoured) because the higher the income level, the less likely is the individual to experience a fall in tax rate at retirement.

Figure 2.8. Overall tax advantage for an "EET" tax regime, by income level and components

Present value of taxes saved over a lifetime, as a percentage of the present value of contributions

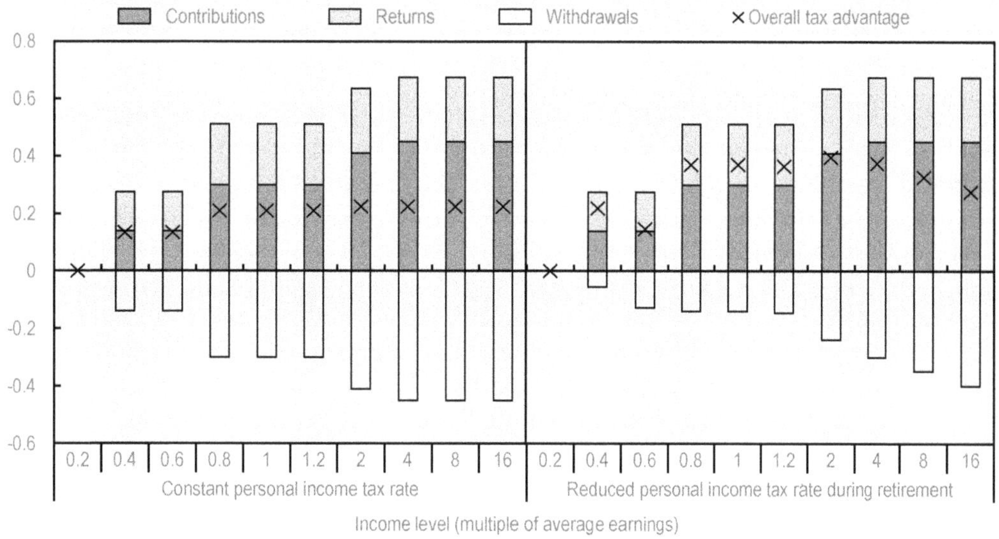

Notes: The calculations assumes an individual contributing 5% of wages from age 20 to 64 and withdrawing benefits from age 65 to 84 as a fixed-payment annuity. Personal income falls into five tax brackets with tax rates of 0%, 14%, 30%, 41% and 45% respectively. On the left panel, each individual remains in the same tax bracket over working and retirement years. On the right panel, the tax rate during retirement is defined according to the level of taxable pension income (including public pensions).

StatLink http://dx.doi.org/10.1787/888933850222

Finally, "EET" tax incentives always generate a long-term fiscal cost to governments. In mature pension systems, taxes collected on withdrawals are large and therefore fiscal costs are lower. As shown in Figure 2.5, once the system has reached maturity, i.e. all retirees draw their pension based on a full career and constant contribution rules, the net tax expenditure stabilises at its steady-state level. That level implies a long-term fiscal cost for the government. However, the size of withdrawals in a given year exceeds the size of contributions, as withdrawals are the result of several years of contributions accumulating with compound interest. Taxes collected on withdrawals each year therefore more than compensate for tax revenues forgone on contributions. For countries already using the "EET" tax regime that are entering into a demographic transition in which the population is ageing, the higher tax revenues will come at a time when pressure on public services may increase.

Taxing retirement savings upfront or upon withdrawal

Because they have the same present value under certain conditions, taxing retirement savings upfront (i.e. taxing only contributions, "TEE") is often seen as an equivalent approach to taxing retirement savings upon withdrawal ("EET"). Upfront taxation also achieves tax neutrality between savings and consumption as long as returns are not above the normal return on savings (Box 2.1). However, there are a number of different implications for the individual and the government between the two designs that are worth evaluating.

Upfront taxation ("TEE") and taxation upon withdrawal ("EET") provide the same overall tax advantage only when the income of the individual is subject to the same marginal tax rate throughout their working and retirement years. This is obviously the case in countries where the entire income is taxed at a single rate. However, in countries where tax rates increase with taxable income, not all individuals will be subject to the same tax rate over their entire life. In that case, the optimal tax treatment in terms of tax advantage depends on individuals' circumstances.

Individuals are better-off having their retirement savings taxed upfront or upon withdrawal depending on whether their income tax rate will be higher or lower during their working or retirement years. As discussed earlier, individuals usually face a lower tax rate during retirement than while working. When this is the case, taxation upon withdrawal will provide a higher overall tax advantage than upfront taxation. By contrast, individuals would be better-off paying taxes upfront when they expect tax rates during retirement to be greater than when they are working.[24] For example, when both public and private pension incomes are taxable, the individual may be subject to a higher tax rate during retirement than the one at which tax relief was granted on contributions.[25]

Low levels of financial knowledge may, however, affect individuals' behaviour and retirement plan choices when they are provided with the opportunity to choose between upfront taxation and taxation upon withdrawal. For example, Beshears et al. (2017[43]) show that employees in the United States who are offered a choice between a Roth 401(k) plan (upfront taxation, "TEE") and a traditional 401(k) plan (taxation upon withdrawal, "EET") do not contribute less to their occupational pension plan than employees who could only contribute to a traditional plan.[26] The authors find that the insensitivity of contributions to the introduction of the Roth option is partially driven by ignorance and/or neglect of the different tax rules.

In addition, behavioural biases may lead to a different perception of the two tax treatments. Contributions to plans with taxation upon withdrawal immediately reduce the amount of a participant's income tax due. Plans with upfront taxation do not provide tax relief today, they exempt future pension income from taxation. Because of present bias, individuals may want to secure the tax advantage earlier rather than later and therefore prefer taxation upon withdrawal.

By contrast, other behavioural factors could lead individuals to prefer upfront taxation. For example, Cuccia, Doxey and Stinson (2017[44]) show that uncertainty may lead to anxiety and influence plan choice. Plans with taxation upon withdrawal may be perceived as more uncertain than plans with upfront taxation because the amount of taxes that will be due on withdrawals is unknown, as tax rates may change due to tax reforms or to a change in the individual's economic status. Low levels of financial literacy and behavioural biases may therefore lead some individuals to choose the plan with the tax treatment that would not provide them with the largest overall tax advantage.

Taxation upon withdrawal may also discourage early withdrawals and lump sum payments. With taxation upon withdrawal, pension benefits are added to the individuals' earnings and taxed at their marginal rate. Early withdrawals when the individual is still working and earning work income may therefore push taxable income into a higher tax bracket. In the same way, lump sum benefits may represent large amounts that move an individual into a higher tax bracket than would apply to a lower annual level of pension benefits (annuities or programmed withdrawals) if the same tax treatment applies to all types of post-retirement product. By contrast, upfront taxation with no tax on withdrawals creates no financial disincentive for early withdrawals and lump sum payments.

Although upfront taxation may be appealing to the treasury because it does not defer tax collection, in the long run this tax regime may translate into a higher fiscal cost than taxation upon withdrawal. If we compare the yearly fiscal effects of the two tax regimes, we see that in the short term, upfront taxation leads to a lower fiscal cost than taxation upon withdrawal. This is because, when taxing only withdrawals, tax collection is deferred, while the cost related to tax revenues forgone on contributions is fully incurred as they are made. With upfront taxation, the net tax expenditure is simply equal to tax revenues forgone on returns. In the long term, once the two systems reach maturity, the fiscal impact is reversed: taxation upon withdrawal leads to a lower annual fiscal cost than upfront taxation. This is because, with taxation of withdrawals, the taxes collected more than compensate for tax revenues forgone on contributions, as the size of withdrawals in a given year exceeds the size of contributions in a mature pension system.[27]

Upfront taxation may be preferable when considering mobility across countries. If individuals initially contribute to a plan with taxation upon withdrawal and then move to another country later in their working life or after retirement, the original country faces a tax revenue loss if those individuals pay income tax in their new country of residence, unless there are perfectly offsetting movements in the opposite direction. With upfront taxation, mobility across countries does not impact tax revenues across countries. Retirement savings are taxed in the country where contributions are made and whether the individual later moves does not affect tax revenues.

Providing partial tax relief

Some countries deviate from the standard "EET" model to reduce the fiscal cost by lowering the overall tax advantage for individuals. This can be achieved by providing partial tax relief on returns (i.e. taxing returns at favourable rates compared to alternative savings vehicles like in Denmark and Sweden) or on contributions, while still taxing withdrawals.

Partial tax relief on contributions is widespread and can take a variety of forms. Most countries have ceilings on tax-deductible contributions, thereby limiting the amount of contributions attracting tax relief.[28] Some countries use partial tax deduction, whereby only a portion of the contributions is tax deductible (e.g. Portugal where 20% of an individual's contributions are tax deductible). Finally, in some countries, contributions are taxed at the same fixed rate for everyone, and that rate is usually lower than the marginal income tax rate, therefore providing a rate relief on contributions (e.g. Australia where contributions are taxed at 15% for most people).

There are other approaches, not yet implemented in any country that may be worth considering. For example, contributions could be tax deductible at the same fixed rate for everyone independent of the individual's marginal income tax rate. Alternatively, contributions could be tax deductible at a capped rate. In that case, contributions would be tax deductible at the individual's marginal income tax rate, as long as that marginal rate is below the capped rate. For individuals with a marginal tax rate above the capped rate, contributions would be deductible only up to the capped rate.

While providing partial tax relief can still promote contributions to retirement savings plans rather than to alternative savings vehicles, it may have a negative impact on the incentive to save. Taxing returns on investment or providing partial tax relief on contributions can still lead to a positive overall tax advantage for retirement savings in relation to other savings. For example, Figure 2.2 shows that Denmark and Sweden, that tax returns on investment at a preferential rate ("EtT" tax regime), provide a positive overall tax advantage to the average earner (representing 24% and 8% of the present value of contributions respectively). However, OECD (2018[45]) reports that average-rate taxpayers face a positive marginal effective tax rate on private pensions in these two countries (21.1% and 2.9% respectively). This means that individuals have a greater incentive to contribute to private pension plans than to other savings vehicles, but have a reduced incentive to save (because consumption tomorrow is taxed more heavily than consumption today).

Care is needed when providing partial tax relief as different approaches achieve different levels of overall tax advantage for different income groups. Figure 2.9 illustrates how the overall tax advantage varies with income for the different approaches to reducing the fiscal cost in tax systems where tax rates increase with taxable income.

Figure 2.9. Overall tax advantage provided by different approaches to reducing the fiscal cost, by income

Present value of taxes saved over a lifetime, as a percentage of the present value of contributions

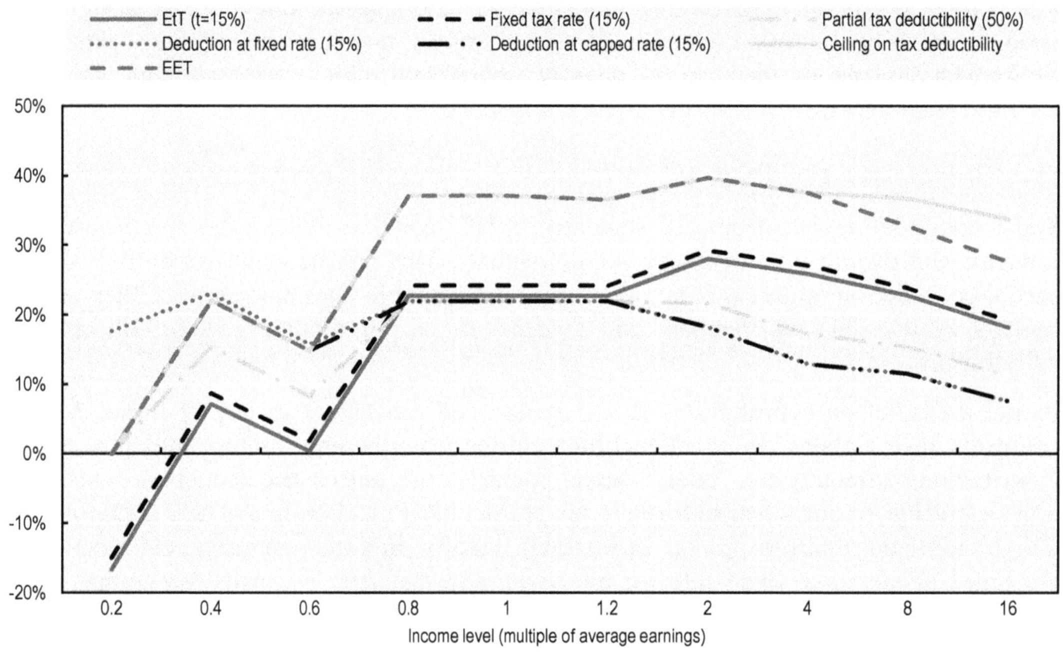

Notes: "E" stands for "exempt" and "T" for "taxed". The calculations assume an individual contributing 5% of wages from age 20 to 64 and withdrawing benefits from age 65 to 84 as a fixed-payment annuity.

StatLink http://dx.doi.org/10.1787/888933850241

- Moving from exempting to taxing returns on investment at a fixed rate reduces the overall tax advantage for all income groups but penalises low-income earners when the fixed tax rate exceeds their marginal tax rate, as they would pay tax on returns at a higher rate in the retirement plan than in the benchmark savings vehicle.
- Taxing contributions at a fixed rate penalises low-income earners when the fixed tax rate is larger than their marginal income tax rate.

- Reducing tax relief on contributions through partial tax deductibility hits middle-to-high income earners harder than low-income earners because low-income earners are the ones who benefit the least from the exemption of contributions.
- Capping the deduction rate only affects individuals with a marginal tax rate above the capped deduction rate.
- Tax deductions at fixed rate achieve a smoother overall tax advantage across income groups. While the "EET" tax regime provides a similar overall tax advantage to individuals earning between 80% and 4 times the average earnings, there are large differences with the other income groups. Tax deductions at a fixed rate reduce the overall tax advantage for individuals subject to a marginal tax rate greater than the fixed deduction rate, while they increase the overall tax advantage for individuals subject to a marginal tax rate lower than the fixed deduction rate. The differences across all income groups are therefore reduced compared to the "EET" tax regime.
- Introducing a ceiling on tax-deductible contributions likely affects the amount contributed into the plan, as individuals have no incentive to contribute above the ceiling. High-income earners are more likely to reach the ceiling and therefore they are more likely to reduce their contributions once a ceiling is introduced. This would lead high-income earners to accumulate fewer assets, have lower pension benefits, and therefore pay less tax. Lower pension benefits translate into a higher overall tax advantage for high-income earners once a ceiling is introduced because the proportion of their total pension income in the last tax bracket will be lower compared to a situation without the ceiling (cf. individuals earning 8 or 16 times the average earnings in Figure 2.9). Not indexing tax-deductibility ceilings, or only indexing them at the rate of inflation, increases the proportion of individuals reaching the ceiling over time and reduces their contributions to retirement plans.[29]

Using tax credits or tax deductions

Non-refundable tax credits and tax deductions are economically equivalent when the credit rate is equal to the individual's marginal tax rate. For example, for an individual facing a 30% marginal tax rate, it is equivalent to deduct contributions from taxable income or to get a tax credit of 30%.[30]

Tax credits achieve a smoother overall tax advantage across income groups than tax deductions at the marginal rate. Tax credits provide the same tax relief on after-tax contributions to all individuals with sufficient tax liability, independent of their income level and marginal income tax rate. They are equivalent to tax deductions at fixed rate, except for very low income-earners who benefit less from the tax credit if it is non-refundable.

Tax credits and tax deductions are, however, not very valuable for individuals with low or no income tax liability unless tax credits are refundable (i.e. when the tax credit is higher than income tax due, the treasury pays the difference to the individual). Individuals whose tax liability is lower than the value of a non-refundable tax credit will not receive the full credit. For individuals not paying income tax, deducting contributions paid into a pension plan at their marginal tax rate does not reduce their income tax due. Making tax credits refundable restores their attractiveness for low-income earners as long as claiming the credit is not too cumbersome. Additionally, tax credits may also be expressed as a fixed nominal amount and be used to target the tax advantage to low-income earners, as the nominal amount represents a higher share of their income.[31]

The structure of tax declaration and tax collection may influence individuals' perception of the two approaches and lead to different outcomes. For example, when pension contributions are deducted from pay before calculating and paying personal income tax, the tax relief is automatically provided and saved in the pension account. This may not be the case when tax deductions and tax credits need to be claimed through the income tax declaration. When contributions are first taxed at the individual's marginal rate, the tax refund may be provided later in the year or even the following year to the individual. If individuals anticipate that they will eventually get a tax refund, they can increase their after-tax contribution to save the whole tax relief in the pension account. However, if they do not anticipate it, the after-tax contribution may not be as high as with an automatic direct tax deduction.

Using tax incentives or non-tax incentives

Non-tax incentives are not linked to the individual's tax status making them attractive for all individuals. Matching contributions are calculated as a proportion of after-tax contributions. With fixed nominal subsidies, all eligible individuals receive the same amount in their pension account. As non-tax incentives are not linked to the individual's tax status, the value of the incentive is not limited by the tax liability.[32] Therefore all individuals can fully benefit from them as long as they fulfil the entitlement requirements (e.g. having an income below a certain level, contributing a certain proportion of income).

Moreover, non-tax incentives are paid directly into the pension account, which may not always be the case with tax incentives. Paying non-tax incentives directly into the pension plan increases the assets accumulated by retirement and future pension benefits. By contrast, individuals eligible for a tax credit or a tax deduction (when it needs to be claimed) may not save the value of the incentive in the pension account if they do not increase their after-tax contributions in anticipation of lower tax withholding or the receipt of a tax refund.

In addition, matching contributions may have a larger impact on retirement savings than economically equivalent tax credits.[33] A study by Saez (2009$_{[46]}$) shows that individuals receiving a 50% matching contribution participate more in retirement savings plans and contribute more than individuals receiving an equivalent incentive framed as a 33% tax credit.[34] This result suggests that taxpayers do not perceive the match and the tax credit to be economically identical. Some individuals may have perceived the 33% credit rate as equivalent to a 33% match rate, thereby reducing the incentive. Another factor could be that individuals had to wait for two weeks to receive the credit rebate. Due to loss aversion, contributing for example USD 450 and then receiving USD 150 back may feel more painful than contributing just USD 300 and obtaining a match of USD 150 to reach the same USD 450 total contribution.

Matching contributions alone, when not associated with other tax incentives, provide a higher overall tax advantage to low-income earners when tax rates increase with taxable income. This is despite the fact that the match rate is equal for everyone. When the matching contribution is associated with a "TTE" tax regime, the match rate applies to after-tax contributions, implying that individuals with higher marginal tax rates receive a lower tax advantage on their contributions. Moreover, returns on investment are taxable. Taxes paid on returns are higher compared to a traditional savings vehicle because matching contributions increase the level of total contributions and generate additional investment income. Therefore, the overall tax advantage provided by matching contributions declines with the individual's income level. This is an important difference with tax incentives, which tend to offer larger overall tax advantages to higher-income earners in tax systems where tax rates increase with taxable income.

Substituting deductible contributions for government matching contributions may increase participation in retirement savings plans. For example, in Turkey, participation in pension plans was initially encouraged through tax-deductible contributions. In order to make the system more inclusive and boost savings, tax relief on contributions was replaced by government matching contributions in January 2013.[35] Between 2012 and 2013, the number of new participants increased by 65%, suggesting that government matching contributions were more effective in increasing the attractiveness of saving for retirement for some people.

From the point of view of the government, the difference between tax and non-tax incentives stems from the salience of the cost of promoting savings for retirement. The budgetary cost of a financial incentive would ordinarily be the same whether incurred in the form of a direct spending (non-tax incentive) or an equal amount of tax expenditure (tax incentive). Tax expenditures however involve a cost that is less salient (or obvious) than the cost of direct government spending.

Adding non-tax incentives to tax incentives

Policy makers should keep in mind the starting point when designing financial incentives. Most OECD countries already have tax incentives in place. Policy makers could, however, add non-tax incentives on top of the existing tax incentives when the objective is to provide an equivalent overall tax advantage to all income groups.

For example, introducing matching contributions for a pension plan that is already subject to the "EET" tax regime increases the overall tax advantage provided to individuals and the fiscal cost to the treasury, but achieves a smoother overall tax advantage across income groups. The matching contribution increases the tax advantage on contributions for all earners in the same proportion (equivalent to the match rate). At the same time, it increases assets accumulated, pension benefits and the amount of tax due when the pay-out occurs. The increase in tax due on withdrawals hits higher-income earners harder, as they are the ones subject to the highest marginal tax rates. All in all, the introduction of a matching contribution increases the overall tax advantage for all individuals, but less so for high-income earners, achieving a smoother tax advantage across income groups.

Combining the "EET" tax regime with matching contributions would incur an additional fiscal cost. In the long run, this additional cost would be smaller than the direct spending on the matching contribution, as it is partially offset by an increase in taxes collected on the higher withdrawals. The additional cost could be contained by capping matching contributions, targeting matching contributions to specific groups, or capping the amount of contributions that can be deducted, although these approaches would modify the relationship between the overall tax advantage and the income level.

Using the financial resources allocated to financial incentives to pay higher public pension benefits

The question of how best to use government resources to enhance retirement income is an important issue to consider. Is it better to provide financial incentives to encourage people to save in supplementary funded pension schemes, or to increase benefits paid by a public pension scheme? The financial resources allocated to financial incentives could be used instead to increase pension benefits in a public scheme. To address this question, the analysis that follows uses hypothetical scenarios to illustrate some of the implications of removing financial incentives in favour of higher spending in public pension systems.

The baseline scenario represents a situation where financial incentives for retirement savings are in place. It assumes that an average earner subject to a constant 30% marginal tax rate contributes 10% of gross wages yearly to an "EET" retirement savings plan from age 20 to 64 and withdraws benefits afterwards in the form of a 20-year fixed nominal annuity. The overall cost to the government comes from the tax exemption of returns on investment. Assuming average earnings of EUR 35 000, inflation of 2%, productivity growth of 1.25%, real return of 3% and real discount of 3%, the total fiscal cost over the lifetime of the individual amounts to EUR 27 844 in present value terms and the after-tax yearly pension income the individual would receive from age 65 to 84 amounts to EUR 54 854.

Removing tax incentives and using the money to finance additional public pension benefits would reduce the overall level of benefits compared to the baseline. This new scenario assumes that the individual stops contributing to a supplementary pension plan because tax incentives have been removed. It keeps the fiscal cost constant by assuming that the equivalent amount of money (EUR 27 844 over the lifetime of the individual in present value) is used to finance additional public pension benefits for the individual. That money could finance a yearly after-tax additional public pension of EUR 19 706 from age 65 to 84, or only 36% of the annual pension income generated by a full career of contributions into a tax-incentivised retirement plan (EUR 54 854).

To cover the resulting gap in pension income while keeping the cost to the government constant, the individual would need to save some additional funds in a non-tax-favoured savings vehicle ("TTE"). Contributions to a "TTE" vehicle would not increase the fiscal cost for the government, as this tax regime is the assumed baseline for the taxation of savings. The individual would need to contribute 9% of gross wages pre-tax, or 6.3% after-tax, into a "TTE" vehicle to reach the same level of benefits as were produced by the tax-favoured savings and the lower level of public pension benefits in the baseline. This is less than the 10% contribution rate in the baseline.[36] However, it is not clear whether, without financial incentives, individuals would save that amount, in particular given that the "TTE" tax regime discourages savings (in favour of consumption) compared to the "EET" tax regime (Box 2.1).

The level of contributions in non-tax-favoured savings vehicles could be further reduced if the government were to create a fund to accumulate and invest the money allocated to the financial incentives over the lifetime of the individual. This would allow the government, as long as the accumulated resources are earmarked for this purpose only, to finance larger additional public pension benefits and reduce the amount of contributions that the individual would have to save in a non-tax-favoured plan to reach the same level of overall pension income as in the baseline scenario. The reduction in the contribution rate would depend on the returns earned by the investment of the government fund, which in turn would depend on whether this fund could invest in a large range of asset classes like any other pension fund or just in long-term government bonds.

This simple example shows that it could be difficult for a government to remove financial incentives and use the equivalent amount of money to increase public pension benefits. If this were done it might leave individuals with a lower retirement income if they do not make extra savings in a non-incentivised plan. In addition, it is contrary to the OECD principle of diversifying the sources to finance retirement income (Chapter 1 of (OECD, 2016[47])).

2.6. Policy guidelines for countries to improve the design of financial incentives

This chapter has examined whether countries can improve the design of financial incentives to promote savings for retirement. After describing how OECD and selected non-OECD countries currently design financial incentives, it has assessed the overall tax advantage that these incentives provide to individuals, how these incentives affect the way individuals save for retirement and the fiscal costs of these incentives to governments. The chapter has also compared different approaches to designing financial incentives in relation to their inherent characteristics within a common framework to assess the different implications for individuals and governments.

All countries provide financial incentives to promote savings for retirement. Those financial incentives can take the form of tax incentives, taxing retirement savings more favourably than other types of savings, or non-tax incentives, paying money directly in the pension account of eligible individuals (matching contributions and fixed nominal subsidies). The most common tax incentive exempts contributions and returns on investment from taxation, and taxes withdrawals ("EET").

In all countries, financial incentives provide an overall tax advantage to individuals when contributing to an incentivised retirement plan rather than to another type of savings vehicle by reducing the total tax paid over their lifetime. The differences in the overall tax advantage observed across countries are due to the tax treatments applied to retirement plans and savings vehicles, the specific features of these tax treatments (e.g. partial taxation, tax-deductibility limits, tax credits) and the presence of non-tax incentives, but also to the characteristics of the personal income tax system in each country (i.e. the tax brackets and the tax rates). In most countries, the value of the overall tax advantage varies with the income level of the individual.

Financial incentives, both tax and non-tax, can be effective tools to promote savings for retirement. Allowing individuals to deduct pension contributions from taxable income encourages participation in, and contributions to, retirement savings plans for middle-to-high income earners, because individuals respond to the upfront tax relief on contributions that reduces their current tax liability. Low-income earners are, however, less sensitive to tax incentives for retirement savings because they may lack sufficient resources to afford contributions, they may not have enough tax liability to enjoy fully tax reliefs, and they are more likely to have a low level of understanding of tax-related issues. Low-to-middle income earners, however, are more likely to respond to tax incentives by increasing their overall savings, while high-income individuals tend to reallocate existing savings or to offset retirement savings with increases in debt. Matching contributions and fixed nominal subsidies increase participation in retirement savings plans, especially among low-income earners, although the impact on contribution levels is less clear.

The total fiscal cost of financial incentives to promote savings for retirement varies greatly across countries, but remains in the low single digits of GDP. For example, in Canada and the United States, where the voluntary pension systems are relatively mature, the yearly cash-flow fiscal cost will fluctuate between 0.7% and 1.5% of GDP between 2015 and 2060. The time profile of the fiscal cost depends on the level of maturity of the pension system and the countries' demographic profile.

The way individuals perceive different designs of financial incentives may distort plan choices and savings levels even though those designs may be economically equivalent. Low levels of financial knowledge and behavioural biases may lead some individuals to fail to choose the tax treatment that will provide them with the largest overall tax advantage. In addition, the value of any tax relief on contributions may not always be saved in the pension account depending on the type of incentive (tax deduction or tax credit) and the way the tax system is structured (relief provided automatically or through a claim). Non-tax incentives that are deposited directly in the pension account represent a better assurance that the incentive helps to build larger pots of money to finance retirement. Finally, different designs can help to target financial incentives to different income groups.

Based on the analysis of country practices and the comparison of the inherent characteristics of different approaches to designing financial incentives to promote savings for retirement, the following policy guidelines could help to improve the design of financial incentives.

Financial incentives are useful tools to promote savings for retirement. Financial incentives usually result in lower participation levels than compulsion and automatic enrolment. However, they keep individual choice and responsibility for retirement planning, as individuals should ultimately be the best placed to evaluate their personal circumstances and determine the most appropriate level of retirement savings that takes into account all of their sources of income. Using the financial resources allocated to financial incentives to pay higher public pension benefits would require individuals to contribute to non-incentivised plans to reach the same level of benefits that would be achieved with just saving in an incentivised plan, although at a lower rate than into the tax-favoured vehicle. However, it is not clear whether, without financial incentives, individuals would save enough.

Tax rules should be straightforward, stable and common to all retirement savings plans in the country. Different tax rules applied according to who contributes (the employer or the individual), the type of retirement plan, or the income of the plan member may create confusion for people who may not have the ability to understand the differences and choose the best option for them. Frequent changes to tax rules may also reduce trust in the system and prevent individuals from adequately planning ahead.

The design of tax and non-tax incentives for retirement savings should at least make all income groups neutral between consuming and saving. This tax neutrality is achieved when the way present and future consumption is taxed makes the individual indifferent between consuming and saving. As PAYG public pension systems are under increasing strain due to population ageing and financial sustainability concerns, the tax treatment of retirement savings should at least not discourage savings and it may even be justified to incentivise savings more for certain groups of individuals, in breach of tax neutrality. A number of different designs can reach tax neutrality, including the "EET" and "TEE" tax regimes under certain conditions, most importantly constant tax rates over the lifetime. However, as people are likely to face lower marginal tax rates during retirement than while working, the "EET" tax regime is likely to breach tax neutrality and to incentivise saving, in particular for middle to upper-middle income earners. Interactions with the public pension system and the general tax system should also be carefully analysed. People will refrain from saving for retirement if doing so reduces their entitlements to public pensions or other forms of tax relief.

Countries with an "EET" tax regime already in place should maintain the structure of deferred taxation. The upfront cost incurred at the introduction of the pension system with deferred taxation is already behind in most countries and the rewards in the form of increased tax collections on pension income are coming in the future as these systems mature. Short-term and long-term impacts on the fiscal cost should be considered before modifying the "EET" tax regime.

Countries should consider the fiscal space and demographic trends before introducing a new retirement savings system with financial incentives. The maturity of the pension system and the demography influence the fiscal cost related to financial incentives. The fiscal cost also develops differently depending on the tax regime chosen, with, for example, a larger upfront cost in the case of the "EET" tax regime.

Identifying the retirement savings needs and capabilities of different population groups could help countries to improve the design of financial incentives. Individuals whose income is below or around the poverty line cannot afford to save in voluntary supplementary pension schemes and will rely on the safety net when reaching retirement. Specific incentives for those very-low-income earners are therefore not likely to be necessary. The need to save into complementary funded pension arrangements may differ across individuals, in particular when the public pension system delivers different replacement rates to different income groups. Financial incentives may need to be higher for those with higher savings needs.

Tax credits, fixed-rate tax deductions or matching contributions may be used when the aim is to provide an equivalent tax advantage across income groups. Financial incentives that equalise the tax relief provided on contributions for all individuals, independently of their income level and marginal income tax rate, achieve a smoother distribution of the overall tax advantage across the income distribution. They include tax credits and fixed-rate deductions (as opposed to deductions at the individual's marginal tax rate), as well as matching contributions. These approaches increase the attractiveness of saving for retirement for middle to low-income groups, while reducing it for high-income earners, compared to the widespread "EET" tax regime. The lower tax advantage for high-income earners may, however, reduce their incentive to save.

Non-tax incentives, in particular fixed nominal subsidies, may be used when low-income earners save too little compared to their savings needs. Non-tax incentives are better tools to encourage retirement savings among low-income earners who are typically less sensitive to tax incentives. In particular, fixed nominal subsidies are likely to be more attractive because they are easier to understand than tax incentives. These can be targeted at disadvantaged groups, such as young workers or women.

Countries using tax credits may consider making them refundable and converting them into non-tax incentives. Individuals with a low tax liability can still achieve the full benefit from tax credits when they are refundable, increasing the attractiveness of saving for retirement for low-income earners. The value of the credit is strengthened when it is paid directly into the pension account (converting the tax credit into a non-tax incentive), in order to help individuals to build larger pots to finance retirement.

Countries where pension benefits and withdrawals are tax exempt may consider restricting the choice of the post-retirement product when granting financial incentives. Taxing pension benefits discourages early withdrawals and lump sum payments when the amounts received are added to the individuals' earnings and taxed at their marginal rate. By contrast, when withdrawals are tax exempt, there is no financial disincentive for withdrawing early or choosing post-retirement products that fail to protect people from the risk of outliving their resources in retirement. Financial incentives may, therefore, lose their purpose if the policy objective when granting them was to encourage people to complement their public pension. To counter this, policy makers could restrict the choice of when and how to withdraw the money; take back part or all of the financial incentives when individuals take a lump sum or withdraw early; or promote selected post-retirement products that are more in line with the objective of people having a retirement income.

Countries need to regularly update tax-deductibility ceilings and the value of non-tax incentives to maintain the attractiveness of saving for retirement. Tax-deductibility ceilings for contributions tend to be updated yearly in line with price inflation only, so that, when wages grow faster than inflation, more individuals are likely to reach the ceiling over time and reduce their contributions to retirement plans. This will reduce, over time, the capacity of savings programmes to replace income. Similarly, keeping the same value of non-tax incentives (maximum matching contribution, subsidy) over time may reduce the attractiveness of saving for retirement and lower the positive impact on participation.

Notes

[1] For a more thorough discussion of the issues relating to financial incentives to promote savings for retirement, see (OECD, 2018[1]).

[2] Other types of financial incentive exist but are not considered in this analysis. These include non-tax incentives provided on social contributions (e.g. deduction of pension contributions for the calculation of social contributions, reduced social contribution rate on pension withdrawals) and tax incentives provided to employers (e.g. tax allowances when making contributions on behalf of certain employees).

[3] It is noteworthy that countries exempting all income flows ("EEE") have low personal income tax rates, below 20% for the average earner. Tax relief is therefore given at low rates.

[4] Note by Turkey: The information in this document with reference to "Cyprus" relates to the southern part of the Island. There is no single authority representing both Turkish and Greek Cypriot people in the Island. Turkey recognizes the Turkish Republic of Northern Cyprus (TRNC). Until a lasting and equitable solution is found within the context of United Nations, Turkey shall preserve its position concerning the "Cyprus" issue.

[5] Note by all the European Union Member States of the OECD and the European Union: The Republic of Cyprus is recognised by all members of the United Nations with the exception of Turkey. The information in this document relates to the area under the effective control of the Government of the Republic of Cyprus.

[6] The calculations assume that the average earner enters the labour market at age 20 in 2018 and contributes yearly until the country's official age of retirement at a rate equal to the minimum or mandatory contribution rate fixed by regulation in each country or 5% of wages in the case of voluntary plans. The total amount of assets accumulated at retirement is converted into an annuity certain with fixed nominal payments. Inflation is set at 2% annually, productivity growth at 1.25%, the real rate of return on investment at 3% and the real discount rate at 3%.

[7] In Colombia, the average earner does not pay personal income tax. There is therefore no tax advantage when contributing to a private pension plan rather than to a traditional savings account.

[8] Numbers are not directly comparable to those published in Chapter 2 of the *OECD Pensions Outlook 2016*. Beyond updating the tax rules from 2015 to 2018, several assumptions have been changed. In particular, the assumed contribution rate for voluntary pension schemes has been reduced from 10% to 5% because in some countries, a 10% voluntary contribution rate over a full career is likely to be rare and produces quite large pension benefits. Everything else equal, this

reduced contribution rate may increase the overall tax advantage provided by "EET" tax regimes because lower contributions translate into lower assets accumulated at retirement and lower pension benefits, which in turn may fall into a lower tax bracket. See (OECD, 2018[1]) for a full description of the methodology and changes in the assumptions.

[9] The calculations assume a common contribution rate across countries with voluntary funded pension systems to be able to compare. This means that the assumed contribution rate does not always represent the actual average contribution rate observed in some countries.

[10] See Chapter 5 in this volume for an analysis of the how behavioural biases can affect decision-making for retirement.

[11] Feng (2014[48]) conducts the same kind of analysis in Australia for voluntary pension arrangements (salary sacrifice) which are taxed favourably (with a fixed tax rate of 15% on contributions rather than the marginal tax rate), but fails to find a significant increase in participation for individuals whose income is subject to a higher marginal tax rate.

[12] The French personal income tax system has four tax thresholds. The authors test the impact of the three highest thresholds on contribution levels.

[13] The tax treatment of contributions to personal pension plans changed from being deductible from labour income (for which tax rates increase with income) to being deductible from capital income (for which a fixed tax rate applies).

[14] The Saver's Credit provides taxpayers who fall within certain income tax brackets with non-refundable tax credits equal to 50%, 20% or 10% of the amount contributed to private pension plans on up to USD 2 000.

[15] In Denmark, returns are taxed at a fixed rate of 15%. This represents a lower tax rate than the marginal tax rate for most people, hence the middle "t" in small letter in "EtT".

[16] Evidence in Australia also shows that the levels of the match rate and of the maximum entitlement influence participation. In July 2012, the government reduced by half both the match rate (to 50%) and the maximum entitlement (to AUD 500) for its "super co-contribution" programme, leading to a 40% decline in the number of individuals claiming the benefit.

[17] The basic subsidy amounts to EUR 175 and is reduced proportionately for contribution levels below 4%.

[18] The child subsidy amounts to EUR 300 for children born since 2008.

[19] This effect can be reduced by conditioning the access to a preferential tax treatment for high-income earners on reaching minimum participation and contribution levels among low and middle-income earners, as is done in the United States in occupational pension plans.

[20] It should also be noted that high-income earners pay a higher share of personal income taxes. In the United States, households in the highest income quintile paid 69% of federal taxes in 2013. The same year, they received 66% of the tax expenditures related to the tax treatment of private pensions (Congressional Budget Office, 2013[41]; 2016[50]).

[21] When the "EET" tax regime applies to retirement savings, the net tax expenditure in year t can be expressed as $NTE_t = \mu_C C_t + \mu_A(1-\mu_C)iA_{t-1} - \mu_B B_t$ where: C_t and B_t are contributions to and benefits paid out of retirement savings plans in year t; A_{t-1} is the aggregate level of assets in the plans at the end of the previous year; i is the nominal pre-tax rate of return on plan assets in the year; and μ_C, μ_A and μ_B are the average marginal personal income tax rates applicable to contributions, returns on investment and benefits respectively. See Chapter 5 of (OECD, 2018[1]) for more details.

22 As the amount of information necessary to make those projections is quite large, the analysis only covers 10 OECD countries for which appropriate data could be obtained.

23 OECD (2018[45]) shows that, when the taxpayer is assumed to earn less in retirement than when making contributions, the marginal effective tax rate (METR) on private pensions is negative in 22, 27 and 22 OECD countries for low-rate, average-rate and high-rate taxpayers, respectively. A negative METR increases the incentive to save.

24 Individuals may also face different marginal tax rates over their working life, making it harder to assess which tax treatment would be more advantageous for them.

25 Another example is when means-tested public pension benefits treat "EET" and "TEE" withdrawals differently, including the former for the means test but not the latter.

26 With upfront taxation, lower after-tax contributions are needed to achieve the same after-tax benefit in retirement as with taxation upon withdrawal (assuming that tax rates remain the same over the lifetime). The authors therefore expected that contributions would go down after the introduction of the Roth option in the occupational pension plan.

27 If the government invests the taxes collected on contributions with the upfront taxation regime instead of spending them, it could obtain the same gains when the system reaches maturity as with the tax regime that taxes retirement savings upon withdrawal.

28 Not indexing ceilings during several years or indexing them only in line with inflation is also a way to further reduce tax relief on contributions over time.

29 As wages increase in line with inflation and productivity, more people will reach the ceiling when this one is constant or just indexed to inflation.

30 With tax credits, contributions are included in taxable income. This implies that tax is paid on contributions and the tax credit is calculated based on the level of after-tax contributions.

31 This approach is common for mortgages but it is not implemented in any country yet for retirement savings.

32 This can also be achieved with refundable tax credits. Refundable tax credits could replicate the economic effects of non-tax incentives, as long as they are refunded directly into a pension account.

33 A credit rate of t is economically equivalent to a match rate on the contribution of t/(1-t). For example, a 25% refundable tax credit is economically equivalent to a matching contribution of one-third. This is because the tax credit rate is expressed as an inclusive rate (i.e. including the value of the credit), while the match rate is expressed as an exclusive rate (i.e. excluding the value of the matching contribution).

34 The study compares participation in and contributions to IRAs in the United States. An "EET" tax treatment applies to IRAs. The matching contribution and tax credit in the experiment supplement the already existing tax incentive.

35 The tax treatment of returns on investment and withdrawals has remained the same over time, with returns taxed upon withdrawals and withdrawals tax exempt.

36 The pre-tax and after-tax contribution rates are equal as contributions are tax deductible.

References

Antón, J., R. Muñoz De Bustillo and E. Fernández-Macías (2014), "Supplementary private pensions and saving: evidence from Spain", *Journal of Pension Economics and Finance*, http://dx.doi.org/10.1017/S1474747214000158. [26]

Attanasio, Banks and Wakefield (2004), "Effectiveness of tax incentives to boost (retirement) saving: Theoretical motivation and empirical evidence", *IFS Working Papers*, No. WP04/33, Institute for Fiscal Studies. [25]

Attanasio, O. and T. DeLeire (2002), "The effect of individual retirement accounts on household consumption and national saving", *The Economic Journal*, Vol. 112, pp. 504-538. [23]

Ayuso, J., J. Jimeno and E. Villanueva (2007), "The effects of the introduction of tax incentives on retirement savings", *Bank of Spain Working Papers*, No. 0724, Bank of Spain. [18]

Benjamin, D. (2003), "Does 401(k) eligibility increase saving? Evidence from propensity score subclassification", *Journal of Public Economics*, Vol. 87, pp. 1259-1290, http://dx.doi.org/10.1016/S0047-2727(01)00167-0. [17]

Beshears, J. et al. (2017), "Does Front-Loading Taxation Increase Savings? Evidence From Roth 401(K) Introductions", *Journal of Public Economics* 151, pp. 84-95. [43]

Börsch-Supan, A., M. Coppola and A. Reil-Held (2012), "Riester pensions in Germany: Design, dynamics, targetting success and crowding-in", *NBER Working Paper Series*, No. 18014, National Bureau of Economic Research, http://www.nber.org/papers/w18014. [37]

Brady, P. (2012), *The Tax Benefits and Revenue Costs of Tax Deferral (September)*, Investment Company Institute. [42]

Brown, J. and D. John (2017), "Improving the Saver's Credit for Low-and Moderate-Income Workers", *Issue in Brief*, National Institute on Retirement Security. [13]

Carbonnier, C., A. Direr and I. Slimani Houti (2014), "Do savers respond to tax incentives? The case of retirement savings", *Annals of Economics and Statistics*, Vol. 113-114, pp. 225-256. [6]

Chernozhukov, V. and C. Hansen (2004), "The effect of 401(k) particpation on the wealth distribution: An instrumental quantile regression analysis", *The Review of Economics and Statistics*, Vol. 86/3, pp. 735-751. [31]

Chetty, R. et al. (2014), "Active vs. Passive decisions and crowd-out in retirement savings accounts: Evidence from Denmark", *The Quarterly Journal of Economics*, Vol. 129/3, pp. 1141-1219, http://dx.doi.org/10.1093/qje/qju013. [27]

Choi, J. (2015), "Contributions to defined contribution pension plans", *Annual Review of Financial Economics*, Vol. 7/1, pp. 161-178. [33]

Choi, J. et al. (2002), "Defined contribution pensions: Plan rules, participation decisions, and the path of least resistance", *Tax policy and the economy*, Vol. 16, pp. 67-113. [35]

Congressional Budget Office (2016), "The distribution of household income and Federal taxes", *Congress of the United States, Congressional Budget Office*, Vol. Publication No. 51361. [50]

Congressional Budget Office (2013), "The distribution of major tax expenditures in the individual income tax system", *Congress of the United States, Congressional Budget Office*, Vol. Publication No. 4308. [41]

Corneo, G., M. Keese and C. Schröder (2008), "Can governments boost voluntary retirement savings via tax incentives and subsidies? A German case study for low-income households", *Economics Working Papers*, No. 2008-18, Christian-Albrechts-University of Kiel, Department of Economics. [39]

Crawford, R., R. Disney and C. Emmerson (2012), "Do up-front tax incentives affect private pension saving in the United Kingdom?", *IFS Working Papers*, No. WP12/05, Institute for Fiscal Studies. [7]

Cuccia, A., M. Doxey and S. Stinson (2017), "The relative effects of economic and non-economic factors on taxpayers' preferences between front-loaded and back-loaded retirement savings plans", *Working Papers*, No. 2017-7, Center for Retirement Research at Boston College. [44]

Disney, R., C. Emmerson and M. Wakefield (2007), "Tax reform and retirement saving incentives: Evidence from the introduction of Stakeholder Pensions in the UK", *IFS Working Papers*, No. W19/07, The Institute for Fiscal Policies. [9]

Engelhardt, G. (2000), "Have 401(k)s Raised Household Saving? Evidence from the Health and Retirement Study", *Syracuse Centre for Policy Research Working Paper*, Syracuse Centre for Policy Research. [29]

Engelhardt, G. and A. Kumar (2011), "Pensions and household wealth accumulation", *The Journal of Human Resources*, Vol. 46/1. [32]

Engen, E. and W. Gale (2000), "The effects of 401(k) plans on households wealth: Differences across earnings groups", *NBER Working Paper Series*, No. 8032, Nationl Bureau of Economic Research. [30]

Engen, E., W. Gale and J. Scholz (1996), "The Illusory Effects of Saving Incentives on Saving", *The Journal of Economic Perspectives*, Vol. 10/4, pp. 113-138. [22]

Feng, J. (2014), "The effect of superannuation tax incentives on salary sacrifice participation", *Economic Record*, Vol. 90, pp. 59-73, http://dx.doi.org/10.1111/1475-4932.12131. [48]

Gelber, A. (2011), "How do 401(k)s affect saving? Evidence from changes in 401(k) eligibility", *American Economic Journal: Economic Policy*, Vol. 3/4, pp. 103-122, http://dx.doi.org/10.1257/pol.3.4.103. [21]

Guariglia, A. and S. Markose (2000), "Voluntary Contributions to Personal Pension Plans: Evidence from the British Household Panel Survey", *Fiscal Studies*, Vol. 21/4, pp. 469-488, http://dx.doi.org/10.1111/j.1475-5890.2000.tb00032.x. [19]

Harju, J. (2013), “Voluntary pension savings and tax incentives: Evidence from Finland”, *FinanzArchiv: Public Finance Analysis*, Vol. 69/1, pp. 3-29. [10]

Hubbard, R. and J. Skinner (1996), “Assessing the effectiveness of saving incentives”, *Journal of Economic Perspectives*, Vol. 10/4, pp. 73-90. [16]

Kolerus, C., I. Koske and F. Hüfner (2012), “Selected Aspects of Household Savings in Germany: Evidence from Micro-Data”, *OECD Economics Department Working Papers*, No. 999, OECD Publishing, Paris, http://dx.doi.org/10.1787/5k8zpt6w2k7h-en. [40]

Macleod, P. et al. (2012), *Attitudes to Pensions: The 2012 survey*, Department for Work and Pensions. [11]

Madrian, B. (2013), “Matching contributions and savings outcomes: A behavioral economics perspective”, in *Matching Contributions for Pensions: A Review of International Evidence*, The World Bank, http://dx.doi.org/10.1596/978-0-8213-9492-2. [34]

Milligan, K. (2002), “Tax-preferred savings accounts and marginal tax rates: evidence on RRSP participation”, *Canadian Journal of Economics*, Vol. 35/3, http://dx.doi.org/10.1111/1540-5982.00139. [5]

Mirrlees, J. et al. (2011), *Tax by design*, Oxford University Press. [3]

OECD (2018), *Financial Incentives and Retirement Savings*, OECD Publishing, Paris. [1]

OECD (2018), *Taxation of Household Savings*, OECD Publishing, Paris, https://doi.org/10.1787/9789264289536-en. [45]

OECD (2017), *Pensions at a Glance 2017: OECD and G20 Indicators*, OECD Publishing, Paris, https://doi.org/10.1787/pension_glance-2017-en. [4]

OECD (2017), *Taxing Wages 2017*, OECD Publishing, Paris, http://dx.doi.org/10.1787/tax_wages-2017-en. [2]

OECD (2016), “Does the tax treatment of retirement savings provide an advantage when people save for retirement?”, in *OECD Pensions Outlook 2016*, OECD Publishing, Paris, http://dx.doi.org/10.1787/pens_outlook-2016-5-en. [49]

OECD (2016), *OECD Pensions Outlook 2016*, OECD Publishing, Paris, http://dx.doi.org/10.1787/pens_outlook-2016-en. [47]

OECD (2012), “Coverage of Private Pension Systems: Evidence and Policy Options”, in *OECD Pensions Outlook 2012*, OECD Publishing, Paris, http://dx.doi.org/10.1787/9789264169401-7-en. [36]

Paiella, M. and A. Tiseno (2014), “Evaluating the impact on saving of tax-favored retirement plans”, *Journal of Pension Economics and Finance*, Vol. 13/1, pp. 62-87, http://dx.doi.org/10.1017/S147474721300019X. [28]

Pence, K. (2002), "401(k)s and Household Saving: New Evidence from the Survey of Consumer Finances", *Finance and Economics Discussion Series*, No. 2002-6, Board of Governors of the Federal Reserve System. [24]

Pfarr, C. and U. Schneider (2013), "Choosing between subsidized or unsubsidized private pension schemes : evidence from German panel data", *Journal of Pension Economics and Finance*, Vol. 12/1, pp. 62-91, http://dx.doi.org/10.1017/S1474747212000170. [38]

Poterba, J., S. Venti and D. Wise (1996), "How retirement saving programs increase saving", *The Journal of Economic Perspectives*, Vol. 10/4, pp. 91-112. [15]

Power, L. and M. Rider (2002), "The effect of tax-based savings incentives on the self-employed", *Journal of Public Economics*, Vol. 85, pp. 33-52. [8]

Ramnath, S. (2013), "Taxpayers' responses to tax-based incentives for retirement savings: Evidence from the Saver's Credit notch", *Journal of Public Economics*, Vol. 101/1, http://dx.doi.org/10.1016/j.jpubeco.2013.02.010. [14]

Rossi, M. (2009), "Examining the interaction between saving and contributions to personal pension plans: Evidence from the BHPS", *Oxford Bulletin of Economics and Statistics*, Vol. 71/2, pp. 253-271, http://dx.doi.org/10.1111/j.1468-0084.2008.00525.x. [20]

Saez, E. (2009), "Details Matter: The Impact of Presentation and Information on the Take-up of Financial Incentives for Retirement Saving", *American Economic Journal: Economic Policy*, Vol. 1/1, pp. 204-228, http://dx.doi.org/10.1257/pol.1.1.204. [46]

Sandler, R. (2002), *Medium and long-term retail savings in the UK: A review.* [12]

Chapter 3. Pension costs in the accumulation phase: Policy options to improve outcomes in funded private pensions

This chapter examines policy measures implemented in different jurisdictions to help align the charges levied by pension providers on scheme members, sponsors and employers with the cost of the services provided, as well as ways to improve outcomes for members and sponsors. These policy measures have been introduced because market mechanisms alone have often been insufficient to achieve this goal. Aligning charges and costs is important as both visible charges – the fees paid to providers by different parties – and unreported charges – deductions from pension portfolios to pay suppliers such as asset managers – reduce the overall value of the pension pot. The most common policy response, improving transparency of charges and costs, works best when accompanied by additional measures such as pricing regulation or structural solutions. The chapter also considers how disclosure initiatives and pricing regulation can include benchmarking and performance related fee structures to improve outcomes for members and sponsors.

Funded pensions pay members' benefits out of assets generated during the accumulation phase. The higher the value of those assets, the more secure the benefit stream of a defined benefit (DB) pension and the higher the potential pay-out from a defined contribution (DC) pension.

The asset pool is made up of contributions from members, employers and sponsors, and the returns earned through investing those contributions. Pension providers carry out administration and investment activities in order to collect and grow pension assets. These activities are paid for out of contributions and investment gains. Therefore, all other things being equal, the higher the cost of providing the pension, the lower the amount of assets available to pay benefits and the worse the outcome for members and sponsors.

The cost of funded private pensions has come under increasing scrutiny with the growth in DC arrangements. In DB arrangements, the scheme sponsor is responsible for making up any shortfall in assets, so members do not directly bear the consequences of excessive costs. In DC funds, any fees that are levied on contributions to pay for administration services and any charges that are deducted from investment portfolios to cover investment expenses ultimately come out of members' retirement pots. Therefore, excessive fees and charges have a direct impact on individuals' future benefits. The impact on smaller pots – such as those of lower-income workers brought into the pension system through automatic enrolment – can be particularly high.

To maximise outcomes for members of DC schemes and to limit calls for extra funding on sponsors of DB schemes, it is therefore important that the administration and investment costs incurred by pension providers are as low as possible for a given level of service provided. In addition, providers should pass these costs on to members, employers and sponsors through appropriate charging structures.

In an efficient market, both the costs incurred by providers and the charges they apply to members, employers and sponsors, should be contained by competitive pressures. Pension providers would monitor and control their payments to external investment managers and other suppliers. Employers and employees would reward providers for keeping costs and charges low.

However, at times there appears to be a lack of such competitive pressures in both mature and more recently established pension markets across OECD and IOPS member jurisdictions (FCA, 2016[1]; Grattan Institute, 2014[2]; Ayres and Curtis, 2015[3]). The primary policy response has been to bolster market forces by creating greater transparency around costs and charges, but this has not been sufficient by itself to improve outcomes. Policy makers have therefore introduced additional measures to control costs and charges, including pricing regulation (e.g. charge caps in Costa Rica, Turkey and the United Kingdom) and structural solutions (e.g. auction mechanisms in Chile, India and New Zealand).

It is important that such measures do not encourage a "race to the bottom" among pension providers. Higher-cost services can represent good value for money: communication campaigns that encourage members of DC schemes to save more into their pension scheme will increase administration costs but can result in bigger individual pension pots; diversifying the investment strategy of DB schemes to include more expensive asset classes such as infrastructure can lead to better risk-adjusted returns.

Policy should therefore consider outcomes as well as costs and charges. Costs and charges are an important driver of outcomes, but administrative efficiency, and investment strategy and implementation, also influence how much both DB and DC pension portfolios grow. Administration cost and service levels, and investment cost and performance, can each be monitored against a relevant reference point, such as the pension provider's own policy statements, peer groups or a default fund. Such benchmarking exercises can highlight where there is scope for providers to improve outcomes, either by cutting costs or by modifying their administration or investment activities.

This chapter first provides an overview of costs and charges. It then analyses the reasons why market mechanisms have often been insufficient to align costs and charges in funded private pensions and analyses the effectiveness of different policies to strengthen or supplement market forces.[1] It finds that measures to improve transparency are essential but are not enough by themselves to align costs and charges. Rather, other solutions such as benchmarking, pricing initiatives, and structural solutions are also warranted. These policy options offer ways to better align costs and charges as well as ways to improve overall outcomes in DB and DC pensions.

3.1. Overview of costs and charges

Types of costs and charges

Pension providers carry out administration and investment activities in order to collect and invest contributions and provide other services (such as valuations and account statements) to members, employers and sponsors during the accumulation phase. Members and employers pay for the costs of these activities through visible charges – the fees levied by the provider – and unreported or not explicit charges – deductions from contributions or from the investment portfolio.

The potential impact of costs and charges on the value of retirement savings can be large. Table 3.1 shows the impact of total charges on the pension pot accumulated in a theoretical DC account under certain assumptions. Charges of 1.5% of assets would lead to a reduction of nearly 30% of the final pot at retirement, relative to a situation of no charges; halving charges to 0.75% of assets brings the reduction of the pot to less than 17%. The effect of compounding is likely to be significant in an asset-based charging structure: if an individual joins a DC scheme at age 25 and withdraws his entire pension pot at the age of 65, charges will be paid on the first contribution 40 times. Charges will also be paid each year on the prior years' investment returns.

Table 3.1. Comparison of charge levels and impact on retirement pot

Charges as % assets	Reduction of pension pot %
0.05	1.2
0.15	3.6
0.25	5.9
0.50	11.4
0.75	16.5
1.00	21.3
1.50	29.9

Note: Assumptions: contributions are 10% of wages; annual wage growth is 3.8% (2% inflation and 1.8% productivity growth); the contribution period is 40 years; portfolio investment returns are 7%. Lower returns would reduce the impact of charges on the pension pot, for example, the impact of a 1.5% charge drops by almost 3 percentage points if portfolio investment returns are 5% rather than 7%.
Source: (OECD, 2012[4]), Chapter 6.

To understand the total charges paid by members and sponsors, three pieces of information are needed: what are the total costs incurred by the pension provider; which of these costs are included in the fees; and which result in additional deductions.[2] However, costs may be difficult to observe and measure and fee structures differ across jurisdictions.

The costs incurred by pension providers can be direct or indirect. Most administration costs are direct – the provider will either incur operating expenses itself or receive an invoice from an external service provider. Some investment costs are direct, for example, compliance and regulatory costs, which are levied at the level of the pension fund. However, a number of the costs within the pension plan, especially investment costs, are typically indirect. An example of indirect costs is transaction costs, i.e. the costs of trading underlying securities in an investment portfolio such as commissions to brokers, clearing and settlement fees to custodians, and applicable taxes. These different costs are usually covered through a reduction in the returns to the portfolio as the transaction takes place, rather than through a separate billing procedure.

Getting a full picture of investment costs is further complicated by the fact that some indirect costs are "implicit", as illustrated in Figure 3.1. Transaction costs for equities are "explicit": brokers' commissions are contractually agreed, stamp duty rates are known and so on. Transaction costs for fixed income are "implicit": commissions and other costs are embedded in the bid-ask spread.

Figure 3.1. Explicit and implicit costs

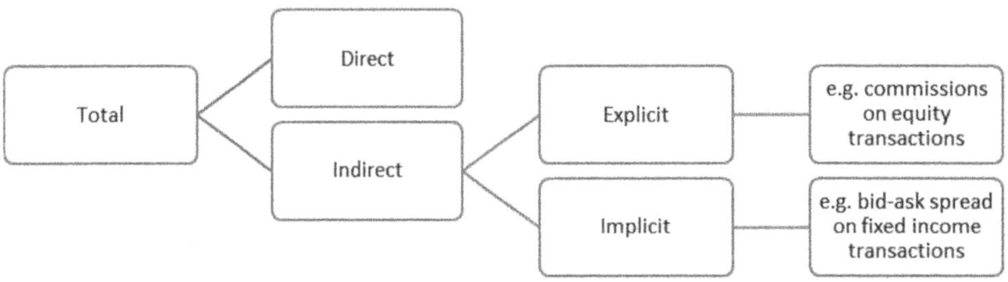

Different institutional arrangements will incur different types and levels of costs, depending on factors such as the number of intermediaries, the services offered and the investment strategy, so not all cost items are applicable or material to all providers. Table 3.2 gives an overview of the various different costs that private pension providers could incur. Whether these costs are recouped through fees or through unreported or not explicit charges, they constitute a reduction in the assets in the portfolio. Table 3.2 also illustrates how a focus on fees alone may obscure the full extent of fund charges.

Table 3.2. Overview of pension fund costs

	Description	Cost type	Fund type
Administration	Oversight/governance of fund	Direct	DB, DC
	Regulatory costs[1]	Direct	DB, DC
	Legal, accounting, actuarial	Direct	DB, DC
	Operations, IT	Direct	DB, DC
	General business expenses	Direct	DB, DC
	Communication	Direct	DB, DC
	Sales & marketing activities, commissions	Direct or indirect (explicit)	DC
	Investment platform	Direct or indirect (explicit)	DC
	Initial charge	Direct or indirect (explicit)	DC
	Additional features/benefits	Direct or indirect (explicit)	DB, DC
Investment	Oversight/governance of fund	Direct	DB, DC
	Regulatory costs	Direct	DB, DC
	Legal and accounting	Direct	DB, DC
	Consultants and advisors	Direct	DB, DC
	General business expenses	Direct	DB, DC
	Custodian, depositor	Indirect (explicit)	DB, DC
	Internal asset management	Direct	DB, DC
	External asset management	Indirect (explicit)	DB, DC
	Look-through costs	Indirect (implicit)	DB, DC
	Performance fees	Indirect (explicit)	DB, DC
	Additional costs of alternative assets	Indirect (implicit)	DB, DC
	Transaction costs	Indirect (implicit)	DB, DC
	Entry/exit costs of underlying funds	Indirect (implicit)	DC
	Platform fees	Indirect (implicit)	DC
	Switching between underlying funds	Indirect (explicit)	DC
	Non-cash costs e.g. opportunity cost, market impact[2]	Indirect (implicit)	DB, DC

1. Costs related to complying with regulation.
2. Costs related to how well a trade is executed, such as the speed of passing the order and whether the trade itself affects the market price.

There is a wide range of estimates of the magnitude of indirect costs, but evidence suggests that they can be substantial. Blake (2014[5]) finds that estimates of the implicit costs of investment funds range from 51% to 82% of explicit costs. Transaction costs and look-through costs are estimated to add 19 basis points (bp) to the investment costs of Australian Superannuation funds.[3] According to the Superintendence of Pensions, in the Chilean mandatory occupational DC system, estimated explicit indirect costs are 40% on top of direct costs, although this figure may not include all implicit costs.

The extent to which direct and indirect costs are included in fees varies by country. For example, in Ireland, voluntary occupational DC plans are required to include only administration costs and the costs of investing in primary funds in the fees levied on members. Portugal, by contrast, stipulates that fees cover more categories of direct cost and some indirect costs: administration costs, investment in primary funds, custodian fees and investment transaction costs (Han and Stanko, 2018[6]).

In assessing costs and charges, it is important to acknowledge that high costs are not necessarily bad and can offer good value for money. There is an argument that to be fully effective in improving outcomes, policy should not look at pension fund costs and fees in isolation but should consider the "value for money" offered by the pension provider. The logic is that pension providers that offer good value for money will grow assets through high quality administration and investment services at a competitive cost to members and sponsors. In these cases, higher costs may result in better outcomes for individuals through more sustained growth in pension assets. APRA (2016[7]) stated that "for any given pattern of contributions, members' retirement outcomes are primarily driven by investment performance". Higher costs could therefore result in more engaging communications with members or superior investment performance. Some jurisdictions specifically account for value - regulators in Australia and the United Kingdom require pension fund trustees to deliver good value for money, rather than low costs.

It is also important to balance any policy responses to high costs/charges against the risk that policy intervention may lead to higher regulatory costs. Rice Warner (2014[8]) found that the introduction of MySuper products in Australia led to additional compliance, product design and systems costs that were passed on through higher monthly fees; these partly offset the reduction in asset-based fees that resulted from their simpler investment design. Australia is re-evaluating RG97, which has proven burdensome for providers, and MiFIID 2 is also under scrutiny. Some commentators have raised concerns that retail savers will view new information on costs as amounting to a fee increase, rather than simply making explicit costs that were formerly implicit, and so be less willing to contribute to pensions.

How costs and charges differ in DB and DC funds

There may be additional costs incurred in running DC funds that do not affect DB plans, as Table 3.2 highlights. These are related to the elements of choice and liquidity within some DC arrangements. If either employers or employees are able to choose their DC fund, the provider is likely to spend money on sales and marketing activity. Where DC investment strategies have to accommodate inflows and outflows, there may be layers of cost such as platform or entry and exit costs that are charged to members' portfolios.

Sales and marketing activity that does not include education or information for members does little to improve outcomes, but the costs are borne by members[4]. These costs may be indirect, for example commissions paid to advisors that come out of contributions, or they may be direct as in Mexico and Poland, where they are counted as operating costs of the provider. Table 3.3 shows the cost of acquiring new business in Poland from 2008 to 2016 and the impact on operating costs of Pension Societies (PTE) when sales activity was banned from 2012. Notably, PTE did not return the savings from reduced sales activity to members; instead, they enjoyed an increase in operating margins.

Table 3.3. Costs of client acquisition and marketing of Polish PTE

	2008	2010	2012	2014	2016	Q2 2017
Acquisition costs (PLN million)	368.0	464.4	121.5	109.8	30.0	14.6
As proportion of operating costs	35.1%	37.6%	16.8%	14.7%	6.9%	5.8%
Operating margin	41.0%	32.3%	51.8%	61.2%	52.1%	49.1%
Number of client transfers	451 677	603 508	107 011	24 759	2 286	258

Note: A ban on acquisitions was introduced in 2011, effective 2012. Operating margins affected by other system reforms from 2016.
Source: OECD calculations based on quarterly bulletin of KNF.

Members may pay entry or exit fees to underlying vehicles when DC pension plans execute their investment strategy through investments in underlying vehicles such as mutual funds. This is because the plan has to adjust its holdings in the underlying vehicles when members make contributions or withdraw their assets. Entry and exit costs are implicit – they come out of the value of the member's portfolio – and can be hard to measure. DB plans may also invest via underlying funds, but they are typically able to buy share classes that do not carry entry/exit fees and they do not have to manage such frequent portfolio adjustments.[5] The UK Department for Work and Pensions found that among 14 providers handling 14.4 million pension pots, two were unable to say whether they applied entry costs, six applied entry costs but were unable to say what they amounted to, four did not apply entry costs, and two applied entry costs that amounted to a reduction of between 5 bp and 40 bp per contribution. Providers also said that they found it hard to get clear information on entry and exit costs from the managers of the underlying vehicles (DWP, 2017[9]).

When plan members can decide on the design of the investment strategy, then in addition to any entry or exit fees, the member may also pay fees to the provider for the ability to make changes to the selection of underlying funds and for using the provider's "platform". The platform provides a service (choice, customisation and easier implementation) but it may be hard to understand what members are paying for this service and what it is really worth.

As well as having additional layers of cost compared to DB funds, DC arrangements may have higher costs than DB funds for equivalent activities. Administration activity is likely to be more expensive within workplace DC plans than in DB plans. DC administrators handle large volumes of small inflows; they may also incur additional costs such as the need to provide middleware (connecting their IT systems to employers' payrolls) or to offer transfer services to members when they change employers.

DC providers may also have to invest more in communications designed to build member engagement, to help members make choices about their pension arrangements or to encourage them to contribute more. An alternative to such expenditure that would be more effective and lower cost would be to make auto-escalation compulsory, so that individuals' contributions increased automatically in line with their earnings.

3.2. How market mechanisms can fail

Market mechanisms should theoretically align the costs and charges of funded private pensions and keep them at competitive levels. However, studies in a number of jurisdictions point to a lack of competitive pressures in both DB and DC systems (FCA, 2016[1]; Grattan Institute, 2014[2]; Ayres and Curtis, 2015[3]). Johnson (2017[10]) estimated that the direct costs of the UK's Local Government Pension Scheme doubled as a percentage of assets over the period 2006-2016 and that indirect costs were as much again as direct costs. Calderón-Colín, Domínguez and Schwartz (2010[11]) concluded that "noise" in the Mexican pension fund market prevented workers from accurately interpreting market signals – instead of responding to price incentives, they were prompted to switch providers by intensive sales efforts. Australia's 2014 Financial System Inquiry found that "the superannuation system is not operationally efficient due to a lack of strong price-based competition".[6]

There are a number of reasons why private pension markets might fail to work. They include (1) lack of engagement by plan participants; (2) complex and opaque charging structures; (3) weak governance; (4) barriers to entry/switching; (5) failure to exploit potential economies of scale; and (6) ineffective fee structures.

Lack of engagement by plan participants

Plan participants cannot be relied upon to encourage competitive conditions among providers (Better Finance, 2017[12]). The problems that individuals have in engaging with and understanding financial products are well documented.[7] The problems are particularly acute with pension products, as neither the benefits themselves nor the reduction in benefits caused by excessive charges will be felt immediately. Consequently, members may not respond to high charges by switching plans or pressuring their provider to reduce fees and charges, or pressing their employer to do so on their behalf.

Employees, employers and sponsors may all be ill-equipped to select and monitor their pension fund. Figure 3.2 shows the quality of account transfers in Mexico over the period 2011-2015: over half of transfers were made into providers offering a lower net return than the current provider. OFT (2013[13]) described the buyer side of the UK DC workplace pensions market as "one of the weakest that the OFT has analysed in recent years." Their comment referred not only to plan members, but also to employers that were involved in selecting plan providers; they were concerned that smaller employers might lack the knowledge to select the most suitable provider for their employees and the resources to buy in expertise.

Figure 3.2. Quality of account transfers in Mexico (% of all transfers)

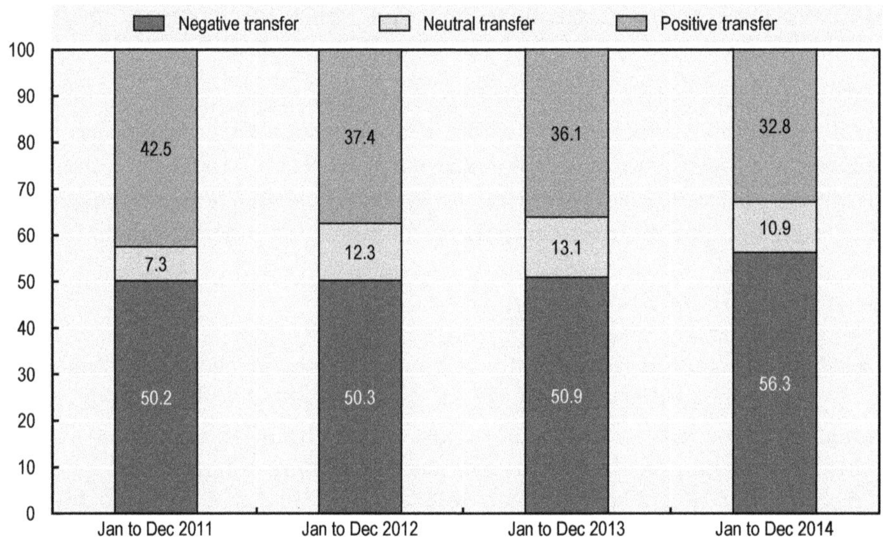

Note: A negative transfer is one to an AFORE offering a lower net return. A positive transfer is one to an AFORE offering a net return at least 5% higher than that offered by the previous AFORE. A neutral one is any other offer.
Source: OECD (2016[14])

Complex and opaque charges

The structure of charges is not standardised, making it difficult for employers and employees to compare what different providers charge in total for DC funds. Fees may cover different costs and be expressed in different ways. Deloitte (2014[15]) sampled 525 plans in the United States and found a variety of fee arrangements for similar services. For example, administration costs could be charged directly to the employer, to the participant, or at the level of the plan itself. These fees could be charged on a per-participant basis, per plan, or as a percentage of assets.

Complex charging structures may lead to wide variations in charges within a single jurisdiction. The Deloitte study found that the "all-in" fee (total charge) for the sample universe ranged from 0.28% to 1.38% of assets on a participant-weighted basis. Clearer communication of fees, such as expressing them in cash terms rather than as a percentage of assets, could help employers and members compare plans more easily, although this would not capture charges that are unreported, opaque or not explicit. Taking fees paid by employees directly out of their wages rather than deducting them from member contributions – as is done in Chile – could encourage awareness of fee levels as their impact on disposable income would be felt immediately.

In DB funds, there may be information asymmetries between sponsors and boards and their suppliers. RailPen, which manages pension assets of over GBP 20 billion, calculated that the total amount it was paying for external investment management were up to four times more than the GBP 70 million that they were paying annually in direct fees. In response, they started to bring more investment management in house.[8] Investment managers might charge different fees for segregated accounts to different clients and impose non-disclosure agreements so that pension providers cannot compare the fees they are paying to those being paid by their peers. This has led to a wide range in the fees paid by institutional investors for similar services (Table 3.4).

Table 3.4. Cost range in basis points for selected asset classes

	Externally-managed passive global fixed income	Internally-managed active real estate	Externally-managed active global equity
90th percentile	8.5	60.2	83.3
75th percentile	7.8	41.2	62.7
Median	7.1	27.3	49.2
25th percentile	4.0	15.8	38.8
10 percentile	1.6	7.1	24.0

Note: The CEM global universe covers around 360 DB funds, Sovereign Wealth Fund, buffer funds and DC platforms with almost USD 7 trillion of assets.

Source: CEM Benchmarking presentation to World Bank Global Pension and Savings Conference, April 2014.

An important part of these charging structures is investment expenses, which are likely to be a major cost item and potentially one that can be compressed in both DB and DC funds. Ramsey (2002[16])found that charges to recover the cost of investment management typically were the largest ongoing charges and had the most direct relationship to the performance of retirement funds in Australia. Net investment returns – that is, portfolio performance after deducting investment expenses or costs, are a significant driver of pension outcomes.

However, investment costs warrant special attention because they do not exist in isolation from the investment strategy. Low cost, low risk strategies generally generate lower returns than high risk strategies over time. It may be possible to reduce the transaction costs of an active emerging equity fund by negotiating with external managers and brokers; it is not possible to reduce them to the same level as the transaction costs of a passive bond fund. Most of the investment cost savings made by Dutch pension funds in the wake of their transparency initiative came from changing their investment strategies and implementation styles, although they also made savings by putting pressure on external managers and other intermediaries to offer them lower prices. In particular, pension funds reduced their allocations to high-cost alternative strategies and brought active management in-house.

Focusing only on cost may have unintended consequences. Morkoetter and Wetzer (2016[17])found that the introduction of TER reporting may have led Swiss pension funds to avoid higher-performing asset classes because they are focusing on absolute costs rather than costs in the context of returns. However, Ainsworth et al. (2016[18])found that while higher fees were associated with higher returns, they were also associated with higher risk, so that outcomes were not necessarily better.

Weak governance

Weak governance can result in a failure to identify and align costs and charges. Smaller schemes in particular may lack the resources for effective oversight of costs and be in a weak position to negotiate with their suppliers.

Conflicts of interest may weaken governance: external trustees of small plans might vote against scheme consolidation if it would put their jobs at risk, while the boards of providers that are part of a larger financial institution might be reluctant to reduce costs that are a source of revenue for their parent company.

Governance failings could also arise from agency problems, or from a dilution of fiduciary responsibilities as the intermediary chain gets longer. Employers who are responsible for selecting providers may not focus on the costs borne by employees, while employees may lack representation on fund boards.[9] Fund platforms might not use their bargaining power on behalf of members. Investment consultants could be tempted to increase their billings by proposing complex investment strategies or frequent changes to asset allocation. Advisors who benefit from built-in commissions (an implicit cost) are less likely to recommend switching providers. Investment managers who are not required to report indirect costs might not try to control them.

Barriers to entry/switching

Barriers to entry and to switching may exist at the level of the provider or at the level of the plan participant. Competition between plan providers should be strongest when a new plan is being set up or when participants (including employers, if they select the plan for their employees, or plan members if they have a free choice of provider) are thinking of switching plans.

Providers may face barriers to entry due to the high proportion of up-front costs in setting up a new plan - fixed costs such as IT are incurred before significant pools of assets are collected. This may make it especially difficult to attract new providers for automatic enrolment schemes targeting smaller employers and lower paid workers. New plan providers and external asset managers might be at a competitive disadvantage from lower brand recognition or a shorter track record. Vertically-integrated providers might limit access to their platforms by external asset managers or benefit from lower internal management costs thanks to the breadth of their internal trading platforms. On the other hand, if it is too easy for new providers to enter the market there is a risk that they will not achieve sufficient scale and be forced to increase charges or reduce the quality of the plan, or withdraw from the market completely.

When plan participants consider changing plan provider, they may be discouraged from doing so by regulatory barriers, such as taxes, or by commercial barriers such as explicit charges. They may also be unwilling to spend the time and effort researching a new plan, resulting in inertia and the failure to switch out of poorly performing plans. Employees who are enrolled into schemes that are selected by their employer may not have the option of switching provider.

Although the threat of switching can encourage competition among providers, participants should avoid excessive churning of pension portfolios, as this can create additional administration expenses for providers and unnecessary trading costs for members.

Failure to exploit potential economies of scale

As noted in OECD (2016[19]), there has been a significant decline in the number of private pension funds and plans since 2005 in several OECD member jurisdictions. A number of countries with mature pension systems, including the Netherlands and Australia, are actively encouraging further consolidation of funds. Pension plan size varies considerably across OECD and IOPS members and it is not clear that there is an "optimal" plan size, but the existence of high fixed costs in pension plan administration implies that larger plans will be more efficient. They could also benefit from better governance: the decrease in the number of pension funds in the Netherlands since 2005 from 800 to less than 400 has been accompanied by tougher qualification requirements for trustees.

Administration costs are largely driven by the size of the plan, as shown in Figure 3.3. Cost items such as IT, oversight, communications and collections have a substantial fixed element and there is evidence that scale economies can be captured relatively quickly. Di Gialleonardo and Marè (2015[20]) found that the administrative costs per participant of supplementary closed pension funds in Italy fell from EUR 31.43 for funds with 10 000 - 50 000 members to EUR 19.63 for funds with over 50 000 members. Furthermore, there were no diseconomies of scale for bigger funds. Bikker (2013[21]) reached similar conclusions for Dutch pension funds and found also that the size at which funds could continue to reap scale economies was increasing over time, suggesting that "average administrative costs per participant now decline without limit", in part because of more expensive technology and more complex regulation.

Figure 3.3. Administrative costs of pension management per participant relative to total participant numbers in the Netherlands

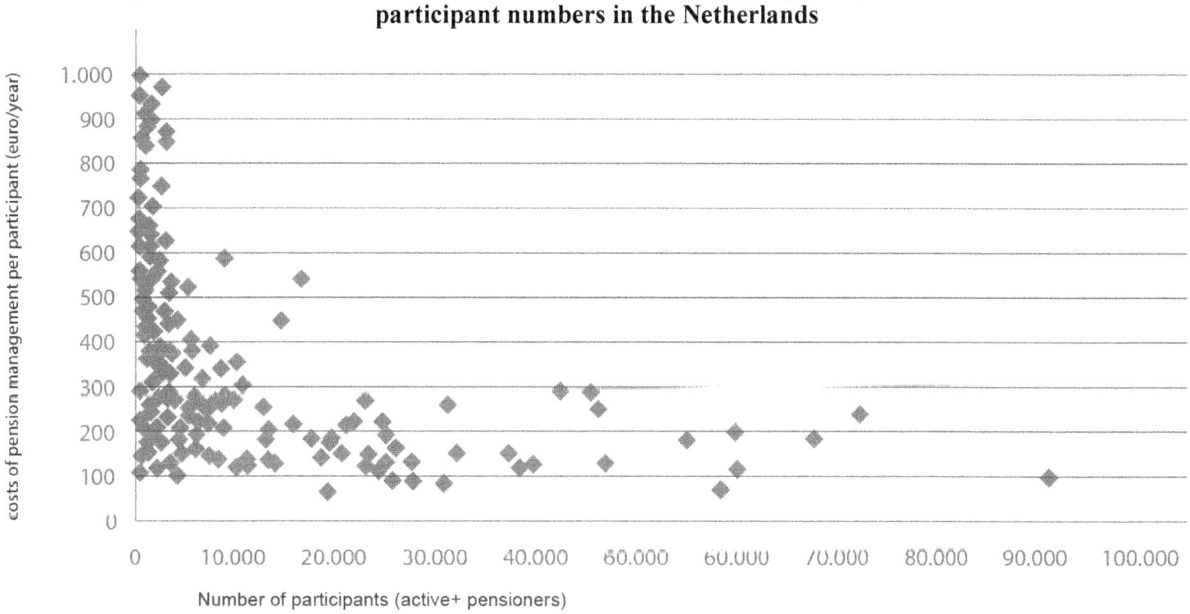

Note: Excludes pension funds with > 100 000 participants; all such funds had administrative costs below EUR 120 per year per participant.
Source: Pensioen Federatie (2016[22]).

Both studies found that the evidence for economies of scale in investment costs was less conclusive. Sources of economies of scale in investment costs include negotiating power with asset managers and other suppliers such as custodians, spreading semi-fixed costs such as research on external managers, and bringing investment management in house, especially for complex asset classes. Table 3.5 shows the fees charged by external managers to different types of US institutional investor in a range of asset classes – bigger investors pay less than smaller investors in every case.

Table 3.5. Fees by asset class and US investor type

%	Small endowment	State pension fund	Quality foundation
US TIPS	0.27	0.15	0.16
US high yield bonds	0.50	0.34	0.42
EM government bonds	0.60	0.45	0.49
US small cap equity	0.84	0.30	0.35
EM equity	0.95	0.28	0.42
Private equity	1.00	0.89	0.56
Real estate	0.76	0.50	0.41
REITS	0.75	0.43	0.51
Diversified hedge fund	1.63	1.33	0.89
Event-driven hedge fund	1.67	1.35	0.89
Macro hedge funds	1.70	1.41	0.95

Note: EM = emerging markets; REIT = real estate investment trust.
Source: Jennings and Payne (2016[23]).

Di Gialleonardo and Marè (2015[20]) suggest that the relatively low level of management fees for closed funds in the Italian market might leave fewer opportunities for further cost reduction and that larger funds implement more complex and so more costly investment strategies. Bikker (2013[21]) found that larger funds used more expensive asset classes and that scale economies were exhausted at an asset size of EUR 690 million. However, Broeders, van Oord and Rijsbergen. (2016[24]) found significant and sustained economies of scale for all pension funds with assets over EUR 20 million. Dyck and Pomorski (2011[25]) found that investment economies of scale worth between 43-50 bp per year for the largest DB funds, driven by insourcing asset management and increasing allocations to alternative asset classes.

However, there may be diseconomies of scale arising from concentration risk (investors may have limits on the proportion of an underlying asset that they can own, or of the share of an individual manager's business that they can represent), from market impact (market delays or adverse price movements from passing large trades) or from the temptation to go into riskier asset classes. Larger DB plans may find it difficult to implement LDI strategies because there are fewer counterparties for large derivatives trades. Reducing the number of plan providers too far could stifle innovation by both providers and external investment managers, although this is unlikely to be a problem in countries such as Australia, the United States or the United Kingdom where there are multiple providers (Axa, 2013[26]).

Ineffective fee structures

Fee structures should be designed to provide the right incentives to managers to achieve the best outcomes for members and plan sponsors. In traditional asset classes, investment manager fees are usually ad valorem, that is they are calculated as a percentage of assets under management. Managers of alternative assets, such as hedge funds or absolute return funds, may charge a combination of an asset-based fee and a performance-based fee. Neither fee structure will necessarily reward managers appropriately.

Ad valorem or asset-based fees provide few incentives for investment managers to become more efficient or to share efficiency gains with clients. They can reward poor performance and penalise good performance. In other words, this fee structure may not provide good value for money. For example, a portfolio manager who generates returns of only 8% when the market rises by 10% will earn more in absolute terms, while one who returns -10% when the market falls by 50% will earn less in absolute terms, even though he has provided a much better service to his clients by limiting their losses. As shall be discussed below, performance-based fees can help avoid this problem but need to be carefully designed so that managers do not keep a disproportionate share of the value they create, and they do not distort incentives.

3.3. Policy options

Policy makers have introduced different measures to bolster or replace weak market mechanisms. Some options are aimed at better aligning fees and charges, while others are geared towards providing better value for fees and charges. The range of measures includes disclosure-based initiatives, price regulations, and structural solutions.

3.3.1. Disclosure-based initiatives

Disclosure-based initiatives have been the principal focus of regulatory efforts to strengthen competitive pressures on providers. There are different types of disclosure initiatives. Efforts to increase transparency of charges and costs are intended to influence their level. Disclosure-based initiatives can also be used to improve outcomes for members and plan sponsors by getting better value. These initiatives include the use of benchmarks to compare the value that pension funds deliver to members, and the reporting of outcomes alongside different investment strategies.

Greater transparency to influence the level of costs and charges

Making costs and charges more transparent has been a key objective of policy in all jurisdictions, with measures to improve reporting, communication and benchmarking of investment costs and plan charges. Such measures target market failures arising from lack of engagement by plan participants, complex and opaque charging structures, and weak governance.

Cost transparency has been successful in encouraging providers to monitor and control their costs in both DB and DC occupational pension markets. In the Netherlands, pension funds are required to provide granular information on administration and investment costs and this has led to greater cost awareness among sponsors and fund boards, resulting in better outcomes (see Box 3.1). Funds must report on their costs to a level of detail similar to that in Table 3.2, and the Dutch National Bank benchmarks the costs and investment performance of plans against their peer group and calls “expensive” plans to account.

Box 3.1. The Netherlands Recommendation on Administrative Costs

The Dutch Authority for Financial Markets (AFM) published in 2011 a report on pension fund costs that highlighted:

- The influence of costs on retirement incomes
- That costs differed markedly among pension funds of similar size
- The potential for economies of scale
- Under- reporting of costs by pension funds

The report sparked a considerable backlash in the press and prompted the industry to address the issue of transparency. Over time, the Netherlands has introduced a series of legal and voluntary requirements for pension funds to publish more and more detail on their cost structure, service levels and performance. It is now mandatory for pension funds to report their administration costs, investment costs and transaction costs.

The evolution of plan providers' costs since the start of the reforms demonstrates the effectiveness of the Netherlands' cost disclosure framework. Table 3.6 shows cost data for five of the largest DB funds.

Table 3.6. Reported costs of asset management

Costs of asset management (bp)	2010	2011	2012	2013
ABP	39	64	73	76
PFZW	48	55	57	61
PMT	17	62	54	40
BPF Bouw	52	46	50	58
PME	70	53	37	29

Note: ABP restated its 2010 figure to 70 bp.
Source: Pensioen Federatie (2016[22]).

The reported costs suggest that pension providers had an incomplete picture of their costs before the authorities introduced reporting requirements. ABP and PMT understated their 2010 costs. The data also shows that pension funds were able to take action based on the new information – PME and PMT both reduced their costs over the period 2011-2013. It should be noted that the other funds took similar action, but made other changes that mean that overall costs did not decline.

The success of the framework reflects a number of factors:

- Regulatory pressure: although the development of reporting standards was led by the industry, there was a clear message from the Dutch Central Bank, DNB, that it would intervene if progress was too slow (public pressure also contributed).
- Industry leaders: the biggest funds adopted the voluntary Recommendations on Administrative Costs quickly; the Recommendations are burdensome for smaller funds but compliance is now close to 100%.

- A gradualist, pragmatic approach: reporting requirements have become stricter and more detailed over time. For example, look through costs have to be reported since 2017 only. The usefulness of data is set against the cost of collecting it.
- Benchmarking: the data is intended to enable participants to understand the relative performance of their plan on a number of criteria. Standard definitions and calculations are therefore used.
- Explaining cost drivers: pension plans' costs are heavily influenced by the choice of investment strategy, the scale of the fund, the complexity of the membership base, and service quality. Pension plans are benchmarked against plans with similar characteristics and annual reports contain detailed information about investment strategy and about service levels (for example, query handling).

Disclosure requirements are accelerating in many jurisdictions (Box 3.2). However, cost transparency can be cumbersome. The potential list of total direct and indirect investment costs is extremely long – the FCA Institutional Disclosure Working Group (IDWG) came up with over 300 discrete cost items – but many indirect costs are difficult to capture and may not be meaningful. Governing bodies, sponsors, regulators and members may be overwhelmed by too much data. In addition, some costs are relatively small, so may not be worth measuring; others are relatively large but cannot easily be compressed even once they are revealed. For example, stamp duty is a large part of trading costs, but cannot be avoided. An analysis of Local Government Pension Scheme costs in 2014 estimated that direct equity trading costs on a portfolio with turnover of 140% per annum were at least 75 bp. Of this, only around 10 bp was commission (which can potentially be squeezed through negotiation with brokers) while 65 bp was stamp duty and taxes. This figure was considerably higher than the direct investment management costs of 25.4 bp and administration costs of 12.6 bp (Sier, 2014[27]).

Regulators therefore need to decide which costs are relevant and whether and how they should be made transparent. Transparency does not have to create complexity. Meaningful cost reductions can be achieved even before detailed information about indirect costs is available. From 2011 to 2017, pension providers in the Netherlands were able to use standard, proxy spreads to measure transaction costs in fixed income portfolios and to use entry and exit charges as a proxy for look-through transaction costs. Despite the lack of detailed information about indirect costs, cost awareness increased and total costs fell.

A number of jurisdictions have introduced measures to improve transparency about DC costs and performance, in order to raise member engagement. The Danish government-backed site www.pensionsinfo.dk provides members with information on their individual accounts including direct and indirect administration and investment costs and past returns. The 2015 Communications Act in the Netherlands requires schemes to provide standardised information to members.

This type of information can enable members to make more straightforward comparisons between funds. In Mexico, individual pension statements include information on net-of-fees returns across AFORES (providers). Both Hong Kong (China) and Italy provide comparison websites and therefore impose a degree of standardisation on the way information about fund charges is collected and displayed.

Box 3.2. Accelerating disclosure requirements

Regulatory efforts to increase investment cost transparency are accelerating in several countries.

The Australian Securities and Investment Commission (ASIC) introduced enhanced fee disclosure requirements for most superannuation products and managed investment schemes in 2017 (ASIC, 2017[28]). Regulatory Guide 97 requires issuers of superannuation products to disclose indirect costs, defined as any amount that could potentially reduce the return of a product or the ultimate reference asset and that is not charged to the member as a fee. This includes the costs of interposed vehicles, such as fund-of-funds structures.

In the European Union, two new pieces of legislation came into effect at the start of 2018 that will increase transparency requirements on those providing investment services:

- MiFID II specifies that firms providing investment services shall provide ex ante and ex post disclosure on total costs and charges that are expected to be incurred by the client
- PRIIPS will require all entities advising on or selling Packages Retail and Insurance-based Investment Products to provide information on all direct and indirect costs to be borne by the retail investor.

In the United Kingdom, both the Financial Conduct Authority ("FCA", the regulator of contract-based schemes) and the Department for Work and Pensions ("DWP", the regulator of trust-based schemes) have imposed enhanced reporting requirements on providers but they have so far been reluctant to impose a standardised cost disclosure template on providers or asset managers. However, the regulators have tasked the industry to come with proposals to improve transparency.[10]

Since April 2015, all providers of contract-based pension schemes have been required to establish an Independent Governance Committee (IGC). IGCs are required to consider all the costs and charges of the scheme and produce an annual report demonstrating the value for money delivered by the scheme so that members can compare providers across the market.

FCA Policy Statement PS17/20 came into effect at the start of 2018 (FCA, 2017[29]). It requires firms managing money on behalf of DC workplace pension schemes to provide:

- Information about transaction costs calculated according to the *slippage cost* methodology (i.e. the difference between the price at which a transaction was executed and the price when the order to transact was transmitted to a third party, in line with MiFID standards)
- Information about administration charges
- Appropriate contextual information

Demands from the public or press for better disclosure of costs have spurred transparency initiatives in several countries, including Israel and the Netherlands. However, a clear signal from the regulator has been the decisive factor in ensuring that providers sign up to disclosure standards. The Netherlands reporting framework was developed by the pensions industry in response to demands from the regulator. The United Kingdom relies on a combination of regulation and industry co-operation, while binding transparency requirements have been introduced in Australia and the European Union. The United States approach is different: the law requires fiduciaries to act prudently and in the interests of participants, and implicitly relies on market forces, supervisory activity including disclosure and the right of legal redress by members to contain costs.

Disclosure will only be effective in bringing down costs and fees if providers, sponsors and members understand and act on the information. Most OECD and IOPS member countries have found that disclosure-based initiatives, giving members and sponsors the information they need to apply competitive pressure to pension providers, have had some effect but not enough to align charges with costs. Therefore, they have supplemented these initiatives with measures to regulate fees or influence the structure of the market or of the providers themselves.

Benchmarking to help improve outcomes for members

Improved transparency can help align costs and charges across funded pension systems but will not necessarily reveal whether there is further room to improve outcomes at the level of the individual provider. Would it be possible for a given pension provider to deliver more speedy and accurate administration services at the current cost, or is the provider offering expensive services that members did not value? Could investment costs be reduced to increase the net returns generated by the investment strategy?

Benchmarking providers could give regulators, members and employers and sponsors information about the relationship between costs and outcomes of their pension fund that would complement other policy efforts to bolster market mechanisms.

Finding a relevant point of comparison for pension funds is not straightforward. Cost and quality can vary widely, depending on the nature of the pension arrangement, the complexity of its administration and investment operations, its membership structure and the design and implementation of its investment strategy. Benchmarking can lead to herding behaviour in investment and less innovation in administration, resulting in weaker competition among providers, and might encourage short-termism in investment. However, peer groups, proxies and other reference points can be constructed.

It should be relatively straightforward to assess whether there is scope to improve outcomes being delivered by DB arrangements. DB providers have a clear target – to grow assets so that they meet future liabilities – and often have a strategic asset allocation to guide long-term investment strategy. Net portfolio returns give an indication of the quality and cost of the investment strategy and can be compared to market returns for equivalent asset classes, or to the investment gains made by other DB funds with similar portfolios. Administration costs can be identified and the quality of administration services can be judged using largely quantitative criteria. Absolute levels of cost and quality will vary across plans, but comparisons can be made across providers with similar activities.

Table 3.7 shows the information revealed in the financial statements of two large occupational DB plans in the Netherlands and two in the United Kingdom. Table 3.7 does not show that one fund offers better value than another, but it highlights areas where there may be scope for funds to reduce costs. Administration costs of the four funds range from 4 bp to 10 bp of assets under management and direct investment costs from 10 bp to 19 bp. The United Kingdom does not require funds to report total investment expenses.

Table 3.7. Cost comparisons in DB plans

	BT Pension Scheme (UK)	RBS Group Pension Fund (UK)	ABP (NLD)	PMT (NLD)
Assets under management (AuM)	GBP 46.1 bn	GBP 45.3 bn	EUR 381.8 bn	EUR 68.2 bn
Asset allocation:[1]				
Equity	25.6%	19.3%	31.7%	27.4%
Bills & bonds	39.5%	52.9%	35.6%	45.9%
Cash & deposits	5.6%	3.6%	-	6.1%
Alternatives	16.0%	19.6%	11.6%	9.2%
Property	11.3%	3.8%	11.5%	8.4%
Other	2.1%	0.9%	9.5%	3.0%
Administration expenses % of AuM	10 bp	4 bp	4 bp	10 bp
Investment expenses % of AuM:				
Direct only	19 bp	15 bp	10 bp	16.5 bp
Total	n.a.	n.a.	60.9 bp	47.8 bp
Direct transaction costs % of AuM	2 bp	2 bp	5 bp	8 bp
Equity transaction costs % of AuM[2]	0.6 bp	2.2 bp	1.4 bp	n.a.

1. Reconciled to the OECD Global Pension Statistics classification except for ABP where no breakdown is available for collective investment schemes.
2. For BT and RBS, mid-range of current and prior year AuM.
Source: Annual reports.

If DB providers understand their cost structures and they are able (or required) to benchmark the cost and performance of their administration and investment activities against relevant peers, they will be able to see where there is scope to improve outcomes. If there is an incentive to improve relative performance – or a sanction for being at the bottom of the range – then it is even more likely that pension providers will deliver good and improving value.

The supervisor enforces both transparency and benchmarking in the Netherlands. Pension plans are required to explain deviations from the cost structure of the peer group. The average investment costs for all pension funds were 58.5 bp in 2015; administration services for members (i.e. excluding the costs of governance and oversight of the plan) cost a further 7.5 bp; total costs across all funds ranged from 15 bp to 200 bp.[11]

In Switzerland, pension funds have been required to report their Total Expense Ratio (TER) in their annual reports since 2013;[12] in that year they were also obliged to collect TER data from underlying vehicles in which they were invested and publish a blacklist of those who did not comply. The Swiss supervisor, OAK, is expected to publish comparative data on more than 2 000 pension funds in the near future.

It is more difficult to assess and compare across DC funds. They have a wide range of administration service levels, investment strategies and liquidity constraints, especially in DC systems where there is an element of choice. Employers or employees may be able to choose their provider, they may select bespoke investment strategies or require different levels of administrative support. There may be intermediaries between the member and the provider. This means that a wide range of DC outcomes is possible, making it complicated to construct peer groups.

Unlike DB funds, which have a unique long-term investment objective (meeting liabilities), DC plans can have different goals. PPI (2016[30]) noted that while high charges erode returns, members may prefer a higher priced, lower volatility investment strategy to either a lower cost strategy or a higher risk strategy, depending on their risk tolerances and other sources of retirement income. Where members are allowed to choose between different strategies offered by their provider or to build their own asset allocation from a range of underlying investment options, they could have widely differing investment outcomes in terms of returns, risks and costs (Table 3.8). Absolute investment gains and performance relative to market benchmarks or peers could also vary markedly over different time horizons.

Table 3.8. Conoco Phillips Saving Plan Investment options, Performance and Expenses

Sample of funds available within 401k plans (United States).

Fund name	Expenses	Average annual total return		Beta	Benchmark
	% of assets	1 year	5 years		
Short-term reserves					
Stable Value Fund	0.32 %	2.28 %	2.16 %	n.a.	Bloomberg Barclays US 3-month Treasury Bellwether Index
Vanguard Prime Money Market Adm	0.1	0.98	0.33	n.a.	Money Market Funds Average
Bond funds					
PIMCO Total Return Institutional	0.51	2.8	2.31	0.98	Bloomberg Barclays US Agg Bond TR USD
Vanguard Inflation-Protected Securities Institutional	0.07	-0.18	-0.1	1.04	Bloomberg Barclays US TIPS Index
Balanced Funds (stocks and bonds)					
Target Retire Income Tr P	0.06	7.36	4.97	0.99	Target Retirement Income Composite Index
Vanguard Balanced Index Fund Inst	0.06	14.18	9.8	1	Balanced Composite Index
Domestic Stock Funds					
Vanguard Extended Mkt Index Inst	0.06	20.55	14.85	1	Spliced Extended Market Index
Vanguard PRIMECAP Fund Admiral	0.33	31.03	19.38	1.04	S&P 500 Index
Vanguard Small-Cap Growth Idx Inst	0.06	26.55	13.84	1	Spliced Small Cap Growth Index
Vanguard Windsor II Fund Adm	0.25	19.68	12.62	1	Russell 1000 Value Index
International Stock Funds					
Vanguard International Growth Adm	0.33	35.41	11.92	1.10	Spliced International Index
Vanguard Total Intl Stock Ix Inst Pl	0.07	23.80	7.82	0.95	Spliced Total International Stock Index

Notes: Returns are net of fees. Beta is volatility relative to the associated benchmark, calculated from trailing 36-month returns relative to the benchmark. "Spliced" refers to time-series that have been linked.
Source: Vanguard ConocoPhillips Savings Plan, 2017

Given the difficulty of creating DC peer groups of funds with similar administration and investment activities, a simpler method of assessing the relationship between provider costs and member outcomes could be to use default funds as a reference point for DC plans. Default funds are intended to provide an investment strategy that is suitable for the majority of DC members, which limits the design options. They are usually required to be low cost. Harrison, Blake and Dowd (2014[31])suggest that 50 bp is a reasonable TER for a default fund operating at scale. The OECD Roadmap for the Good Design of Defined Contribution Pension Plans recommends establishing appropriate default investment strategies, in particular lifecycle strategies.

Not all pension systems include a unique default fund. Countries may have a number of competing default funds offered by different providers, or no default option. Other, similar types of pension plan could serve as a benchmark, such as the lifecycle funds that are offered by the Thrift Savings Plan in the United States. Alternatively, a proxy portfolio that follows the principles of a default lifecycle option could be constructed as the basis for comparing the investment design and cost of actual DC arrangements. It would not, however, give information about administration activity.

DC plans could be assessed against the fees (to members and employers) and net returns of the default strategy or proxy. Members of other DC plans could reasonably ask their provider whether they were on track to achieve equivalent outcomes to the default for a similar cost, and if not, why not.[13]

Default funds with very similar investment designs can deliver different investment returns and charge a wide range of fees. Table 3.9 shows the investment strategy and fees for selected default funds or proxies in different jurisdictions. Return targets and investment performance differ between the funds, but the investment designs are similar: all include a form of de-risking as the member approaches retirement age. Fees vary from a minimum of 3.8 bp (United States) to a maximum of 95 bp (Hong Kong, China).

Table 3.9. Cost comparison across default funds

	NEST Retirement Date Funds (UK)	Thrift Savings Plan (US)	MySuper – Industry level (AUS)	AP 7 Safa (Sweden)	DIS – industry level (HK-China)
AuM	GBP 1.7 bn	USD 500 bn	AUD 474 bn	SEK 328 bn	HKD 15.4 bn
Investment strategy	Target date	Lifecycle/building blocks	Lifecycle and single strategy	Lifecycle	Lifecycle
Return target	CPI + 3% Volatility target for each stage	Market indices for each of bond and equity components	CPI over 10 years	Average return of private sector PPM funds	Market indices for each of bond and equity components
Returns (5-year annualised)	Range 1.9% - 11.4%	Range 4.5% -11.7%	6.6%	19.5%	n.a.
Fees *- asset-based*	3 bp	3.8 bp administration	49 bp	11bp in growth phase reducing to 6 bp at age 75	75 bp investment management
- other	180 bp per contribution	0-1.2 bp stock lending	AUD 87 annual administration fee per member*	-	20 bp recurrent operating expenses
- total as % of AuM	50 bp	3.8-5 bp	≈50 bp	6-11 bp	95 bp
Direct transaction costs as % AuM	Range 0-4.9 bp	n.a.	n.a.	n.a.	n.a.

Notes: excludes one-off fees e.g. entry/exit, switching fees. Payroll-related administration costs within TSP are borne by the employer and not included in the asset-based fees.
Source: Annual Reports, APRA, Orange Report 2016.

Benchmarking DC plans against a default could help to identify outliers in terms of outcomes, but it would remain complicated to draw conclusions about the potential to improve outcomes at individual funds in jurisdictions with a large number of providers and a wide variety of plan designs. Therefore, benchmarking should complement and not replace measures to align costs and charges at competitive levels.

Investment strategy reporting

Investment costs do not exist in isolation from the investment strategy. They should therefore be reported together. Indicators that take account of investment performance, manager skill and asset class are needed in addition to cost information to assess whether a fund's investment expenses are reasonable. This assessment of reasonableness can be made both in absolute and in comparison to the costs incurred by other portfolios.

These indicators would also make it possible to tie rewards more directly to outcomes. Investment managers and strategies can be analysed in terms of the returns generated per unit of risk taken, fees per unit of return and the amount of return that is retained in fees.

This analysis is robust across different asset classes and investment styles. For example, passive management will score highly in terms of cost versus risk because passive portfolios track the reference benchmark closely and have low management fees and transaction costs. However, passive management scores poorly in terms of cost versus alpha because passive funds are not designed to outperform the market. This type of analysis makes it easier to improve the value for money of investment activities by tying rewards for investment managers to outcomes.

3.3.2. Pricing initiatives

Governments have introduced pricing initiatives aimed at managing fees and charges or providing good value to members. Pricing regulation aims to specifically limit what providers can charge. Some jurisdictions have also introduced performance-based fees to ensure that investment managers are rewarded for delivering high returns per unit of risk taken. They are intended to incentivise investment managers to become more efficient or to share efficiency gains with clients.

Pricing regulation

Pricing regulation can contribute to disclosure efforts by simplifying fee structures, making it easier for participants to understand what services they are paying for and exactly how much they are paying. Alternatively, pricing regulation can force providers to take action on costs, by imposing limits on what they can charge.

DC arrangements are subject to this type of price regulation in several countries. Australia, Estonia and Hong Kong (China) have introduced low-cost plans. Chile, Sweden, Turkey and the United Kingdom have imposed charge caps. Mexico simplified fee structures in 2008 by stopping the use of fees on contributions, so that AFORES can only levy a fee calculated on assets under management, which was also capped. Costa Rica replaced its mixed fee structure with a single, asset-based fee in 2011. In Denmark and Poland, fees are levied on both contributions and assets under management, whereas in Spain only asset-based fees are permitted.

Different fee structures may be appropriate at different points in the development of the pensions system or the growth of a pension fund. Assets grow over time, so asset-based fees reward established providers who have had time to collect and grow contributions. Contribution-based fees enable new DC schemes to raise revenues more quickly, but may not cover costs as plans mature if members leave or defer. Pricing regulation may therefore need to evolve as pension systems mature.

However, unless both asset-based and contribution-based fees cover a significant part of total costs, including indirect and implicit costs, this may not be sufficient to deliver better pension outcomes. Therefore, more direct controls over pricing, such as charge caps, may be introduced. The United Kingdom introduced a charge cap of 0.75% of assets under management on workplace default funds from April 2015. The cap applies to all direct and indirect administration and investment costs, but does not include transaction costs. As well as putting an upper limit on default fees, the cap also helped to raise awareness of high charges in other DC arrangements. The charge cap appears to have been effective in reducing fees for DC funds: all qualifying schemes (those that are eligible to be used as defaults) are now priced below 75 bp and the prices of other schemes have also fallen.

Charge caps set a clear and simple standard for member charges but can have unintended consequences. If the cap is set too high, charges tend to rise to the level of the cap, as was seen earlier in the UK market when stakeholder pensions were introduced with a maximum charge of 1%, which quickly became the market price for all similar retirement savings products. In a similar manner, the German government's estimated total charge for Riester products of 10% has become the de facto standard charge (Better Finance, 2016[32]). If the cap is set too low, plan providers might try to cut costs by offering lower-quality plan designs or by reducing the number of transactions they undertake, even when the trades would be in the best interests of members.

If the cap does not include all direct and indirect costs, then providers might have an incentive to exaggerate uncapped costs in order to compensate for any lost profits in areas that do fall within the scope of the cap. Turkey reduced its charge cap quite significantly in 2013 and introduced a new charging structure consisting of a capped ad valorem fee that varies by asset class (ranging between 1.09% and 2.28%), a fee on contributions and a small fixed on-boarding fee. The cap takes into account all fees that pension providers can earn from participants and total fees are capped from the sixth year of a contract.

Establishing the correct level of the cap is especially complicated in markets where providers have different cost structures. Setting the cap in line with the cost structure of large, vertically integrated providers might squeeze out smaller providers. A low cap can also discourage new entrants. However, a relatively high cap could enable lower-cost providers to generate excessive profits if they chose to price at the level of the cap, unless there was pressure from participants or other stakeholders to reduce charges.

In order to capture economies of scale on behalf of members, charge caps should not be static. Costa Rica initially capped fees at 1.1% and this will reduce to 0.35% by 2020. In Estonia, fees must be reduced by 10% for each EUR 100 million increase in assets.

Charge caps focus on fees rather than design, putting the onus on providers to come up with a pension design that is profitable for them within the cap. An alternative form of pricing regulation is to introduce standardised pension designs with regulated fees. MySuper products in Australia have simplified product specifications and a limited range of fees, although this has not led to a high degree of standardisation in terms of product attributes, costs and outcomes. The Default Investment Strategy introduced by Mandatory Provident Fund (MPF) schemes in Hong Kong (China) in 2017 has a fixed asset allocation and maximum fees. MPF schemes were already required to offer a low-fee fund with no restrictions on design but with maximum management fees of 1% of assets.

Another form of price control is to change the basis for charges. Member-borne commissions have been banned in UK DC schemes; similar measures have been introduced in Australia and the Netherlands. Mexico changed the incentive structure of sales agents to limit negative-yielding switches.

Introducing performance fees to achieve better investment outcomes

Asset-based fees can fail to provide incentives to investment managers to become more efficient or to share efficiency gains with clients. Performance-based fees are one solution. Unlike price caps which specifically limit charges, performance-based fees aim to better align the interests of investment managers and pension fund members and sponsors. Hamdani et al. (2017[33]) use evidence from a regulatory experiment in Israel to demonstrate that funds with performance fees exhibit higher risk-adjusted returns than funds with asset-based fees operating in different competitive environments.

Performance-based fees can complement other pricing regulation such as price caps. This may be useful since ad valorem fees can limit the effectiveness of price caps. The average net profit margins of Mexican Pension Fund Providers (AFORES) rose from 33.5% in 2013 to 37.4% in 2017, despite pressure from the regulator, CONSAR, that pushed average fees down from 1.29% to 1.03% of assets under management over the same period (Table 3.10). Assets under management grew rapidly, implying that the AFORES were reaping economies of scale, and the cost of acquiring new contributions fell (Table 3.10). CONSAR will therefore start considering cost indicators, such as net profit, return on equity and return on assets, when assessing fee proposals from the AFORES. It also intends to introduce performance-based assessments, by taking into account historical investment performance, and investment performance relative to a benchmark portfolio.

Table 3.10. Fees and margins in Mexican AFORES

(million Peso)	2013	2014	2015	2016	2017	CAGR
Assets under management	2 546 915	2 877 673	3 027 296	3 244 518	4 358 958	14.4%
Revenues (inflows)	18 102	18 744	20 123	20 876	22 345	5.4%
Affiliation and transfer costs	5 252	5 723	5 195	5 008	5 115	-0.7%
Total operating costs	7 612	8 247	7 963	8 165	8 756	3.6%
Net earnings	6 057	6 693	6 810	8 094	8 366	8.4%
Net margin (earnings/revenues)	33.5%	35.7%	33.8%	38.8%	37.4%	
Average fee (as % of assets under management)	1.29%	1.20%	1.11%	1.06%	1.03%	

Source: CONSAR.

Performance-based fees must be structured in such a way as to give the right incentives to pension funds and their investment managers. Rewards should be paid for delivering high returns per unit of risk taken, and a fair share of returns should stay in the portfolio rather than being paid out in fees. The basic parameters of a performance fee design (there are many more complex structures in operation) are:

- The fee base (e.g. is the fee calculated on investment gains or on assets under management (AUM)) and the fee rate
- The performance reference point, i.e. the minimum return the fund must earn before a performance fee is due
- The measurement period, i.e. the length of time over which performance is calculated
- The high watermark (HWM), if any, which is the last highest value that the fund has reached

The performance reference point can be fixed (a "hurdle rate") or variable (e.g. a market index). It is important that the reference point reflects the investment strategy of the fund. An equity manager should not be paid a performance fee for outperforming a cash benchmark, since the bulk of any outperformance is likely to be due to the investment characteristics of equities relative to cash rather than to manager skill. Pension fund management companies operating in Latvia's mandatory funded scheme are benchmarked against a composite debt and equity index. In Poland, the reference point is competitors' performance. Performance fees are calculated as 0.06% of assets under management multiplied by the "percentage premium ratio", or the relative performance of the fund versus its peers. The ratio is 1 for the best performing fund – which receives a performance fee of 0.06% of AUM – and 0 for the worst performer – which receives no performance fee. Other funds receive an amount below 0.06% of AUM that reflects their relative position.

High watermarks (HWM) are intended to ensure that managers are not paid a performance fee for good performance in one period unless they have caught up any underperformance in previous periods. The fund value must always be above the previous HWM for a performance fee to be earned. The Czech Republic and the Slovak Republic both use HWM in the calculation of performance fees; the Czech Republic sets the HWM as the historic maximum value of the fund while the Slovak Republic looks back over a shorter period.

High watermarks can be effective in preventing a "double fee". Such double charging is a feature of ad valorem fees, where the fee basis is the full AUM. An individual, who joins a DC scheme at the age of 25 and retires at the age of 65, will pay annual fees on his first year's contributions 40 times. Fees will also be paid each year on the prior years' investment gains. Box 3.3 illustrates the application of a performance fee with a fee base of investment gains, a fee rate of 20%, a hurdle rate of 5%, a measurement period of one year and a HWM. Box 3.3 also shows that a high watermark can be effective in preventing a "double fee" (i.e. the fund manager is not rewarded for the Year 1 performance in both Year 1 and in Year 4). Conversely, if an asset class suffers a sharp fall, a manager might take several periods to get back to the HWM even if he outperforms the market consistently. This outperformance would not be rewarded. This can be resolved through the use of "relative high watermarks", relative to different asset classes.

However, this may not be enough to create alignment of interests. The upside potential of a strongly performing manager is potentially unlimited, while the downside risk is limited – especially since most performance fees are payable on top of an asset-based fee. Fee caps can help to create more symmetrical payouts; so can reserve systems, whereby a portion of any performance fees earned are "banked" in a reserve pool, and used to top up the portfolio if the manager subsequently underperforms. This cushions investors against a run of poor returns and leaves the possibility for the manager to earn back lost reserves and fees once performance improves.

There are practical difficulties in implementing performance fees. Parameters need to be negotiated and calculating fee accrual can be complex; performance fees may be higher than asset-based fees for strong managers and so increase investment expenses. They may also pose stability risks, as performance fees are more volatile than asset-based fees. Given the importance of investment manager fees and performance to outcomes, they are nonetheless a potentially powerful means of improving the value for money of the investment activities of pension funds.[14]

Box 3.3. Simple performance fee

The chart shows the path of a pension fund portfolio, with a starting value of 80 rising to 100 at the end of Year 1, falling to 82 at the end of Year 2, climbing back to 90 at the end of Year 3 and finishing Year 4 with a value of 110.

The fund manager receives a performance fee of 20% for performance above a hurdle rate of 5%, subject to a high watermark, HWM. The fee is calculated on the absolute increase in the value of the portfolio.

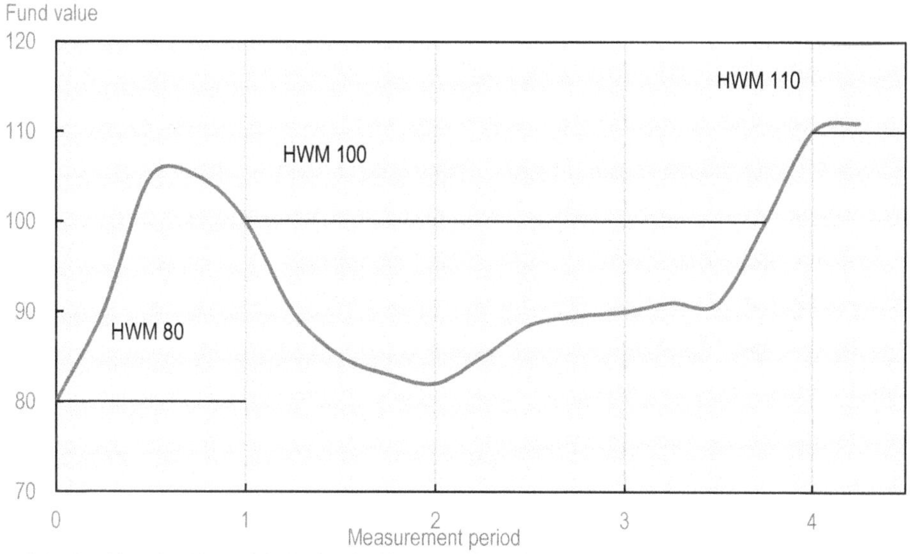

At the end of Year 1, the fund manager has earned a performance fee of 4. This is equal to 5% of AUM and 20% of investment gains. Absolute performance is 20 (100-80), equating to an investment return of 25% (20/80) and the hurdle rate is 5%. The performance fee is therefore calculated as [20 × (25% - 5%)]. The high watermark rises from 80 to 100.

The fund ends Year 2 with a negative performance and fails to meet the hurdle rate, so no performance fee is due. At the end of Year 3, the fund value has risen from 82 to 90, a return of 9.75% that is almost double the hurdle rate. However, the value of the fund remains below the HWM so no performance fee is due.

At the end of Year 4, the fund value has risen by 20, or 22%. The fund manager earns a performance fee of [20 × (22% - 5%) = 3.4]. This is equivalent to 3% of AUM and 17% of investment returns. The new HWM is 110.

Structural solutions

Structural solutions entail efforts to overcome market weaknesses by intervening in the structure of the market. These can include measures to strengthen market mechanisms or alternatively to circumvent them and their weaknesses by imposing new organisational structures.

Mexico and Chile provide examples of policies designed to strengthen market mechanisms. In Mexico, the number of providers (AFOREs) increased from 11 to 21 between 2003 and 2008 as the Regulator encouraged new entrants in order to stimulate price competition. However, because of weak member engagement and inappropriate incentive structures, this led instead to increased expenditure on commercial activity that did not benefit plan participants.

Chile followed a different approach, introducing an auction process in 2008.[15] Providers bid for the right to enrol new members of the mandatory DC system who remain captive for two years. Bids cover administration costs and internal investment costs and must be lower than the minimum fee currently available in the market. This appears to have been effective in reducing fees levied by Chilean providers (AFPs): the first auction in 2010 was won by a new entrant to the market with a bid of 1.14% of salary; by 2016 the lowest fee in the market had fallen to 0.41%. However, according to the Superintendence of Pensions, average fees, weighted by the number of contributors, have shown a smaller decline from 1.50% in January 2010 to 1.20% in June 2017. Furthermore, there were no bidders for the latest auction, most probably because providers could not improve upon the previous winning bid as required by the design of the auction process.

A fee-based auction system presents potential risks. Providers might make unsustainably low bids, in the hope that they would make enough gains from economies of scale to remain profitable if the won the auction. Eventually, they may raise their fees to compensate for this unsustainable position, eroding the benefits of the auction system, or they may reduce the quality of their investment and administration services. The Australian Productivity Commission (2017[34]) describes the potential risks.

A multi-criteria tender could partially address such risks. To select default providers, New Zealand uses a range of selection criteria in addition to fees (e.g. fund features, past investment performance). However, this approach is more expensive to implement and may introduce more subjective judgements into the tender process.

In some pension systems, regulators look to improved governance to create the conditions for market mechanisms to function. Australia and the Netherlands have imposed tougher qualification requirements on members of governing bodies, and the UK regulator is asking for more detailed reporting from the Independent Governance Committees of DC schemes. These reforms are in each case part of a much larger package of measures to improve outcomes for DC plan participants. In the United States, under the federal statute known as ERISA, plan administrators, sponsors and other parties have fiduciary responsibilities in terms of managing costs and imposing fees. Private lawsuits and compliance enforcement reinforce this regulatory approach.

Policymakers may consider measures to influence the operational set-up of pension providers or the organisational set-up of the market in which they operate in order to align costs and charges at competitive levels. Policymakers in several jurisdictions are encouraging schemes to consolidate to reap economies of scale. Fund mergers can be mandatory, as in Sweden, or a voluntary response to other regulatory pressures such as increased scrutiny of costs, as in the Netherlands and Switzerland. Canada's Pooled Registered Pension Plan system is designed to pool individual accounts in order to benefit from scale economies and participating providers must ensure that charges are no more than they would be for a plan with 500 members. The Australian Prudential Regulation Authority (APRA) found considerable scope for rationalisation and efficiency within the superannuation system, with over 40 000 investment options available across the industry (APRA, 2016[7]). Although APRA does not stipulate a minimum size for a provider, it suggests that better-resourced superannuation funds might be more sustainable as the system matures and cash flows turn negative. APRA applies a scale test to MySuper products to check that returns are not adversely affected by the size of a (smaller) fund.

Alternatively, rather than attempting to influence the cost structure of existing pension providers, policymakers may change the structure of the market by establishing new, centralised institutions. These can help to control total charges to members in a number of ways. They can provide additional competition to plan providers – the UK's NEST competes with other providers for auto-enrolment business. They can offer low-cost solutions directly to underserved populations – NEST has an obligation to take on smaller accounts. They can ensure that scale economies are available to all participants – Sweden's PPM clearinghouse offers very low platform fees to plan providers and has negotiated total investment costs including transaction costs for members of only 30 bp.

Table 3.11. National Pension System in India

Intermediary	Activity	Price-setting	Fees charged by client type		
			Private sector	Government	"Lite"
Central Record-keeping Agency	Account opening	Auction (2 suppliers)	INR 40 / INR 39.36	INR 40 / INR 39.36	INR 15 / INR 15
	Annual account maintenance		INR 95 / INR 57.63	INR 95 / INR 57.63	INR 25 / INR 14.4
	Charge per transaction		INR 3.75 / INR 3.36	INR 3.75 / INR 3.36	Free
Points of Presence	Initial subscriber registration and contribution upload	Regulator	INR 200	n/a	n/a
	Any subsequent transactions		0.25% of contribution, min INR 20, max INR 25 000. Non-financial INR 20	n/a	n/a
	Administration charge per 6 months or Rs 1 000 contribution		INR 50 per annum	n/a	n/a
	Contribution through eNPS		0.10% of contribution, min INR 10, max. INR 10 000	n/a	n/a
Trustee Bank	Flows between intermediaries		NIL (potentially gets benefit of sweeping cash)		
Custodian	Asset servicing	Auction	0.0032% per annum		
Pension funds	Investment management	Auction	0.01% AUM	0.0102% AUM	0.0102% AUM
NPS Trust	Fiduciary	Expenses only	0.01% from Trustee Bank		
Retirement advisers	Advice, onboarding	Regulator	INR 120 for onboarding, INR 20 for subsequent services, max. INR 100 per annum		

Source: PFRDA

However, it could be argued that centralised institutions have an unfair marketing advantage and can price in scale economies before they are realised thanks to government support. Furthermore, centralised institutions may add to complexity when employers or members have choices to make. NEST's annual management charge of 0.3% is low relative to the UK market, but it also charges employers a fee on contributions of 1.8% that makes comparisons with other providers more difficult (Now Pensions has a monthly charge of GBP 40 and People's Pension charges a one-off set up fee of GBP 500 or GBP 300 if the employer comes via an intermediary).

Countries could consider a combination of several potential solutions to reduce fees. For example, India's National Pension System (NPS) combines centralised institutions, an auction system and fee caps. Rather than having integrated providers, NPS has unbundled the various administration and investment activities and found a low-cost intermediary for each activity, as shown in Table 3.11. There are two providers of central record-keeping and clients can choose between them based on quality and cost criteria. The NPS is technology driven, both to enhance interactions with members and to contain costs.

3.4. Conclusions and policy implications

The cost of running pension funds – providing administration and investment activities – and the way those costs are passed on to members, employers and sponsors have a significant impact on outcomes. The value of pension assets is directly affected by fees that are levied on contributions before they are invested and by other charges that are deducted from the investment portfolio throughout the accumulation phase.

Market mechanisms cannot alone be relied upon to keep costs and charges at competitive levels. Initiatives to improve transparency are the principal policy tool that jurisdictions have implemented for strengthening competitive pressures in private funded pension systems. These policies have been supplemented by regulations to control pricing and/or structural measures to influence the set-up of the pension market or the products offered by pension providers.

There are a number of lessons that can be learned from the experience of different jurisdictions in addressing weak market mechanisms in both DB and DC pension provision.

- No single policy response is effective in isolation. Measures aimed at stimulating market mechanisms work best when they are reinforced by pricing regulation and structural solutions.
- Transparency is a pre-requisite for aligning costs and charges, but is not sufficient in itself to improve outcomes. Sponsors and trustee bodies must be prepared to act on the information to reduce the costs of DB plans, and employers and members must be able to benefit from greater disclosure to put pressure on DC providers.
- The role of the Regulator is critical. Plan providers may take action on costs and charges when faced with regulatory and compliance enforcement action (or the threat of such action). Plan participants are generally ill-equipped to tackle excessive costs and charges without support from regulators and policy makers.

Reducing costs leads to immediate gains, which can become significant over time through the effect of compounding. Targeting costs and charges may not, however, improve outcomes.

- It is difficult to get a true picture of total costs, so such policies may miss important indirect or implicit charges.
- Cost-cutting may lead to overly conservative investment strategies or lower quality administration services.
- Policy makers have therefore tried to address the "value for money" offered by pension providers as well as their costs.

The relationship between costs and outcomes determines whether a pension fund is offering good value for money.

- Benchmarking DB funds against relevant peer groups, and DC funds against a low-cost lifecycle strategy, can reveal whether administration and investment costs are competitive and investment performance is commensurate with investment expenses.

- For benchmarking to be effective, providers that underperform need to be held to account by the regulator, sponsor, or members.
- Direct investment costs are likely to be one of the biggest expenses for pension funds so it is important that they do not overpay for investment performance relative to other funds. Rewards for portfolio managers should reflect their contribution to outcomes, which is a function of performance, risk and costs. Performance-based fees can improve incentives for investment managers and avoid the double-charging inherent in asset-based fees.

Regulatory efforts to increase investment cost and charges disclosure are accelerating and reporting requirements are increasingly stringent. However, policy makers might find that putting in place a limited disclosure regime and making it more stringent over time is more effective than asking providers to introduce full cost disclosure in one go.

- Aiming for a very high level of investment cost transparency can create delays and generate new expenses.
- Compliance rates for less rigorous disclosure regimes are likely to be higher and the amount of data will be manageable for regulators as well as providers.
- Direct costs – especially direct investment costs – have a significant impact on outcomes and are relatively easy to identify.

Policy makers have been successful in reducing the costs and fees of pension funds in several jurisdictions through a combination of different measures to strengthen market mechanisms, restrict fee options and introduce structural changes in the overall system or at the level of the provider. These efforts could be complemented by data on the relationship between costs and outcomes offered by different funds, including performance metrics and cost comparisons, which would indicate whether individual funds have the potential to reduce costs further in order to generate better outcomes for their members and sponsors.

Notes

[1] The focus on the chapter is on charges and costs in the accumulation phase. It does not address the pay-out phase, which deserves a full analysis in itself.

[2] The provider's costs include its profit margin, where applicable.

[3] Chant West survey 2017

[4] While this may be true in many circumstances, if sales increase the size of funds and scale efficiencies, there may be, in this case, benefits to members.

[5] DC plans may also be able to access these share classes. Most DC plans in the United States, including those that are participant-directed, use lower-cost institutional plans.

[6] Financial System Inquiry (Murray) final report, Australia.

[7] See for example OECD/INFE International Survey of Adult Financial Literacy

[8] Source: Financial Times, 24 August 2014

[9] Member representation may be particularly difficult to implement in DC funds because of the individual rather than collective nature of fund membership.

[10] The Institutional Disclosure Working Group set up by the Financial Conduct Authority has prepared voluntary templates for pension trustees to gather cost data from their suppliers.

[11] Source: CEM Benchmarking

[12] The TER includes explicit investment costs that are deducted directly from members' assets and some administration costs.

[13] Short-term investment returns could differ e.g. if a bespoke strategy included more volatile asset classes than the default.

[14] There may be regulatory challenges in certain common law, trust-based environments where performance fees may be construed to give a fiduciary the capacity to control his own level of compensation. However such cases are not common across OECD or IOPS jurisdictions.

[15] Chile also introduced other reforms in 2008 to help drive competition, such as the elimination of fixed fees and including comparative fee information on members' account statements.

References

Ainsworth, A. et al. (2016), "Superannuation Fund Performance and Fund Fees", *Working Paper*, Vol. No. 115. [18]

APRA (2016), "Productivity Commission Issue Paper: Superannuation efficiency and competitiveness", *Submission from the Australian Prudential Regulation Authority*. [7]

ASIC (2017), "Disclosing fees and costs in PDSs and periodic statements", *Regulatory Guide 97*. [28]

Axa (2013), *Is Big Better?*, Axa Investment Managers. [26]

Ayres, I. and Q. Curtis (2015), "Beyond Diversification: The Pervasive Problem of Excessive Fees and "Dominated Funds" in 401(k) Plans", *The Yale Law Journal*, Vol. 124, p. 1476. [3]

Better Finance (2017), *Pension Savings - the real return*. [12]

Better Finance (2016), *Pension Savings - the real return*. [32]

Bikker, J. (2013), "Is there an optimal pension fund size? A scale-economy analysis of administrative and investment costs", *DNB Working Paper*, Vol. No. 376. [21]

Blake, D. (2014), "On the Disclosure of the Costs of Investment Management", *Pensions Institute discussion paper PI-1407*. [5]

Broeders, D., A. van Oord and D. Rijsbergen (2016), "Scale economies in pension fund investments: A dissection of investment costs across asset classes", *of International Money and Finance*, Vol. 67, pp. 147-171. [24]

Calderón-Colín, R., E. Domínguez and M. Schwartz (2010), "Consumer confusion: the choice of pension fund manager in Mexico", *Journal of Pension Economics & Finance* , Vol. 9/1, pp. 43-74. [11]

Deloitte (2014), *Inside the Structure of Defined Contribution:401(k) Plan Fees, 2013: A Study Assessing the Mechanics of the "All-In" Fee*, Deloitte/ICI. [15]

Di Gialleonardo, L. and M. Marè (2015), "The Efficiecy of Italian Pension Funds: Costs, Membership, Assets", *Siep Working Paper* , Vol. No. 687. [20]

DWP (2017), *Pension Charges Survey 2016: Charges in defined contributuion schemes.* [9]

Dyck, A. and L. Pomorski (2011), *Is Bigger Better? Size and Performance in Pension Plan Management.* [25]

FCA (2017), "Transaction cost disclosure in workplace pensions", *Policy Statement PS17/20.* [29]

FCA (2016), *Asset Management Market Study - interim report.* [1]

Grattan Institute (2014), *Super Sting: how to stop Australians paying too much for Superannuation.* [2]

Hamdani, A. et al. (2017), "Incentive Fees and Competition in Pension Funds: Evidence from a Regulatory Experiment", *NBER Working Paper*, Vol. No. 22634. [33]

Han, T. and D. Stanko (2018), "2018 Update on IOPS Work on Fees and Charges", *IOPS Working Papers on Effective Pension Supervision*, Vol. Forthcoming. [6]

Harrisson, D., D. Blake and K. Dowd (2014), *VfM: assessing value for money in defined contribution default funds*, Cass Business School/Pensions Institute. [31]

Jennings, W. and B. Payne (2016), "Fees Eat Diversification's Lunch", *Financial Analysts Journal*, Vol. 72/2. [23]

Johnson, M. (2017), *The LGPS: a Lost Decade*, Centre for Policy Studies. [10]

Morkoetter, S. and T. Wetzer (2016), *Investment Decisions of Swiss Pension Funds*, University of St. Gallen/SFAMA. [17]

OECD (2016), *OECD Reviews of Pension Systems: Mexico*, OECD Reviews of Pension Systems, OECD Publishing, Paris, http://dx.doi.org/10.1787/9789264245938-en. [14]

OECD (2016), *Pension Markets in Focus*, http://www.oecd.org/daf/pensions/pensionmarkets. [19]

OECD (2012), "A Policy Roadmap for Defined Contribution Pensions", in *OECD Pensions Outlook 2012*, OECD Publishing, Paris, http://dx.doi.org/10.1787/9789264169401-9-en. [4]

OFT (2013), *Defined contribution workplace study.* [13]

Pensioen Federatie (2016), *Recommendations on Administrative Costs - Revised version*, Federation of Dutch Pension Funds. [22]

PPI (2016), *Value for money in DC workplace pensions*, Pensions Policy Institute. [30]

Productivity Commission (2017), *Superannuation: Alternative Default Models - Draft Report*. [34]

Ramsey, I. (2002), *Disclosure of Fees and Charges in Managed Investments*. [16]

Rice Warner (2014), "MySuper Fees", *Financial System Inquiry 2014*. [8]

Sier, C. (2014), *Pension Fund Cost and Complexity - Quick Wins*, Pension PlayPen. [27]

Chapter 4. Strengthening the application of OECD Core Principles of Private Pension Regulation: Lessons from Investment Institutions

This chapter considers how the governance frameworks and investment policies of several nationally significant investment institutions contribute to realising the missions of these institutions. It maps the set-up and practices of the different institutions against the recommendations of the OECD Core Principles of Private Pension Regulation, especially Core Principle 3: Governance and Core Principle 4: Investment and Risk Management. The chapter builds on this analysis to determine how the application of the recommendations might be strengthened to help improve outcomes for members of private pension schemes. The institutions examined include pension funds, reserve funds and sovereign wealth funds.

The *OECD Core Principles of Private Pension Regulation* ("Core Principles") provide governments, regulators and supervisors with a common benchmark and high-level guidance on the design and operation of funded and private pension systems. They aim to strengthen the regulatory framework around funded pensions in order to promote the sound and reliable operation of funded and private pension plans.

Strong governance and appropriate investment strategies are essential if funded and private pensions are to generate good outcomes for plan members and generate trust and engagement by the public. Core Principle 3: Governance and Core Principle 4: Investment and Risk Management set out the characteristics and behaviours that regulators should encourage in the governance frameworks and investment policies respectively of pension providers.

Nationally significant investment institutions, such as reserve funds, pension funds and sovereign wealth funds, provide practical examples of how governance and investment standards can be framed, implemented and monitored. These institutions play different roles in their domestic pension systems, leading to different organisational structures and investment strategies. However, their governance and investment arrangements have many common features, and these correspond to the recommendations of the *OECD Core Principles of Private Pension Regulation*.

This chapter examines the governance frameworks and investment policies of several nationally significant investment institutions, in particular public and centralised institutions, and maps them against Core Principles 3 and 4. There is a close match between the set-up of these institutions and the recommendations of the Core Principles, demonstrating the relevance of the recommendations. The analysis also highlights key policy issues linked to the practical application of governance and investment standards, and how these investment institutions have addressed these. Based on this analysis, it proposes measures to strengthen the application of Core Principles 3 and 4 to private pension institutions.

The chapter sets out an examination of ten different investment institutions, including six pension funds, two reserve funds and two sovereign wealth funds. Five of the pension funds operate individual member accounts: the Mandatory Provident Fund (MPF) in Hong Kong (China), the Central Provident Fund (CPF) in Singapore, AP7 in Sweden, the National Employment Savings Trust (NEST) in the UK and the Thrift Savings Plan (TSP) in the USA.[1] The sixth pension fund under consideration in this report, Denmark's ATP, manages individual accounts within a common insurance scheme. The two reserve funds analysed are the Canadian Pension Plan Investment Board (CPPIB) and the funds AP1-4 in Sweden.

The chapter also examines Norway's two sovereign wealth funds, the Government Pension Fund Global (GPFG) and the Government Pension Fund Norway (GPFN), which despite their titles are not directly linked to the domestic pension system nor earmarked for specific liabilities. It further includes some information about the Australian Future Fund (AFF) and New Zealand Superannuation Fund (NZS) – both sovereign wealth funds – where these offer relevant illustrations of the topics related to investment institutions, governance and investment policies.

4.1. Overview of institutions analysed for this report

The institutions analysed for this report are shown in Table 4.1. They have been included because they provide examples of different approaches to governance and investment.

Table 4.1. Institutions analysed for this report

	Country	Type	Reason for inclusion
Canada Pension Plan Investment Board (CPPIB)	Canada	Reserve Fund	Governance framework Investment approach
ATP	Denmark	Pension Fund with Individual Accounts	Governance framework Investment approach
Mandatory Provident Fund (MPF)	Hong Kong (China)	System of Pension Funds with Individual Accounts	Investment approach
Government Pension Fund Norway (GPFN)	Norway	Sovereign Wealth Fund	Governance framework Investment approach
Government Pension Fund Global (GPFG)	Norway	Sovereign Wealth Fund	Governance framework Investment approach
Central Provident Fund (CPF)	Singapore	Pension Fund with Individual Accounts	Governance framework
AP1-4	Sweden	Reserve Fund	Governance framework Investment approach
AP7	Sweden	Pension Fund with Individual Accounts	Governance framework Investment approach
National Employment Savings Trust (NEST)	United Kingdom	Pension Fund with Individual Accounts	Governance framework Investment approach
Thrift Savings Plan (TSP)	United States	Pension Fund with Individual Accounts	Governance framework Investment approach

The six pension institutions are ATP, MPF, CPF, AP7, NEST and TSP. All of these institutions receive both employee and employer contributions except AP7 (employee only).

- ATP is a mandatory defined contribution (DC) occupational pension scheme established in 1964 under which members accrue guaranteed rights. ATP is set up as an insurance scheme and manages approximately USD 115 billion of assets.[2] In addition, ATP's 2 820 staff administer a variety of other social security benefits.[3]
- The MPF was introduced in 2000. It is a fully-funded occupational DC system consisting of 32 private pension schemes operated by 14 MPF trustees that are licensed and overseen by the Mandatory Provident Fund Authority (MPFA). Total savings across all providers are approximately USD 78 billion. A regulatory requirement of the MPF is that schemes must offer a default option that complies with specific design guidelines.
- The CPF is a mandatory retirement savings scheme set up in 1955. Members receive a guaranteed rate of return that is based on the return on Singapore government bonds. The state issues special bonds to provide this guarantee. Total assets are approximately USD 237 billion.
- AP7 provides the default option within Sweden's premium pension system, which is a mandatory funded pension scheme within the public system. Premium pensions were established in 2000 and employees contribute 2.5% of their pensionable income to them, bringing total assets to approximately USD 40 billion. AP7 has 27 employees.
- NEST was set up as part of the UK's workplace pension reforms in 2008 that included the introduction of auto-enrolment. It is a multi-employer DC pension scheme that has a public service obligation to be open to any employer that wants to use it and has a low-cost approach. Total assets are approximately USD 2.4 billion and staff numbers are around 240.

- TSP is a voluntary DC plan for federal employees and members of the uniformed services. It was set up in 1986 and offers similar services to 401k plans for private sector employees. The assets of the TSP amounted to approximately USD 575 billion as at Q4 2017 and are administered by a government agency, the Federal Retirement Thrift Investment Board (FRTIB). From January 2018, members of the uniformed military will be auto-enrolled into the TSP, taking participants to an estimated 5.6-6.0 million people.

The two Reserve Funds are designed to back up their domestic pension systems:

- CPPIB is an investment management organisation that was established in 1997 to invest the assets of the Canada Pension Plan. It manages an investment portfolio of approximately USD 250 billion and provides cash management services to the Canada Pension Plan. It has 1 392 staff.
- The funds AP1-4 constitute about 15% of the assets of the Swedish pension system and act as a buffer to cover future disbursements. The aim of having multiple funds is to diversify the investment risk of the buffer capital. The funds co-operate to provide transparency and cost efficiency but nevertheless are in competition with each other in terms of performance. Net inflows have been negative since 2009 and the Swedish Pension Agency expects to withdraw capital from AP1-4 over the next 25-30 years. Assets are approximately USD 152 billion; each of the funds AP1-4 has around 60 staff members.

The two sovereign wealth funds are owned by the Norwegian state.

- The domestic fund, GPFN, was established in 1967 with funds allocated from the national insurance scheme. No further inflows or outflows have occurred since then and returns are retained by the fund. Assets under management were approximately USD 29 billion at the end of 2017. GPFN is managed by the Folketrygdfondet, a special legislation company with 50 employees that is wholly owned by the State of Norway through the Ministry of Finance.
- The global fund, GPFG, was set up in 1990 to accumulate the country's surplus petroleum revenues. Assets are approximately USD 1 000 billion and are managed by Norges Bank, the Norwegian Central Bank, through its asset management unit, NBIM, which has close to 600 employees.

Some additional information about the Australian Future Fund (129 employees) and the New Zealand Superannuation Fund (over 100 employees) has been included. These institutions have not been presented in detail as their governance structures and investment practices are very similar to those of their peers listed in Table 4.1.

4.2. Governance frameworks

This section analyses the governance frameworks of the reference group of public investment institutions. It considers the different governance models of the selected institutions based on a mapping of the key features of their governance frameworks against the Implementing Guidelines (IG) of Core Principle 3 of the *OECD Core Principles of Private Pension Regulation*, which are described in Table 4.2.

Table 4.2. Mapping governance frameworks: key features

	Implementing Guideline Core Principle 3	Key features
3.1	Identification of responsibilities	Separation of operational and oversight responsibilities
3.2 – 3.4	Governing body	Creation, role and responsibilities of governing bodies
3.5	Accountability	To members, supervisor, competent authorities
3.6	Suitability	Membership of governing body
3.7	Delegation and expert advice	Sub-committees of the Board; internal and external expertise
3.8 – 3.10	Auditor, actuary, custodian	Independence
3.11 – 3.12	Risk-based internal controls	Organisational and administrative controls; codes of conduct; internal reporting systems
3.13	Disclosure	Timely communication of relevant information to all stakeholders

Identification of responsibilities

Core Principle 3 recommends that governance frameworks clearly separate oversight and operational activities (IG 3.1), and that a governing body is established with responsibility for oversight (IG 3.2). All the institutions analysed in this document follow this recommendation and have a Board of Directors, Trustee or other governing body (hereafter "the Board") entrusted with oversight. The Board is usually responsible for hiring the Chief Executive and setting out written descriptions of his or her duties, but leaves the day-to-day running of the institution to the executive team.

Governing body

One of the chief responsibilities of the governing body of a pension fund is to set out the fund's mission (IG 3.3). This is not the case for the Boards of the investment institutions examined: their missions are established by the state in accordance with their role in their domestic pension system and the Board's role is to interpret the mission or objective of the institution and transform it into a set of operating and investment strategies. The mission of these investment institutions may be specified in legislation or otherwise publicly stated, as shown in Table 4.3.

Governing bodies must observe prudential and fiduciary standards in carrying out their responsibilities, as outlined in IG 3.4. The way they meet these standards differs because their responsibilities can differ. In private pensions, their duties are towards members and beneficiaries, while in public institutions the Board must take into account the requirements of the state. The purpose of a Sovereign Wealth Fund is to shift public spending power from one point in time to another. There are no individual rights involved and there is no link to a specific purpose. Their Boards can fulfil their duties in this case by ensuring high professional standards and efficiency in the management of the fund's assets. By contrast, Reserve Funds are earmarked for specific uses and their mandates often reflect the needs of government, for example they may stipulate a liquidity requirement. Pension funds with individual accounts have a duty towards each member.[4] Boards must therefore additionally concern themselves with ensuring that such funds are protected from political interference in violation of the mission.

There may be instances when the state decides to change the mission of a public investment institution, as occurred in France and Ireland. The Fonds de Réserve pour les Retraites was established by the French government in 2001 as a reserve fund for the pension system. In 2010 its role became more like that of a sovereign wealth fund. Ireland's National Pension Reserve Fund was transformed into the Ireland Strategic Investment Fund in 2014 with a mandate to support local economic activity and employment.

Table 4.3. Stated mission

	Country	Type of Institution	Mission
CPPIB	Canada	Reserve Fund	Assist the Canada Pension Plan in meeting its obligations to contributors and beneficiaries. Manage assets in the best interests of the contributors and beneficiaries. Maximize long-term investment returns without undue risk of loss, having regard to factors that may affect the funding of the CPP and its ability to meet its financial obligations on any given day Provide cash management services to the Canada Pension Plan
ATP	Denmark	Pension fund with individual accounts	To pay supplementary pensions, to preserve the real value of the assets
MPF	Hong Kong (China)	Pension fund with individual accounts	To regulate and supervise privately-managed schemes within the Mandatory Provident Fund and occupational retirement schemes, to educate the working population about saving for retirement and to lead improvements in MPF schemes
GPFN and GPFG	Norway	Sovereign Wealth Fund	To support long-term considerations in the government's spending of petroleum revenues, as well as savings to finance pension expenditures under the National Insurance Scheme
CPF	Singapore	Pension fund with individual accounts	To enable Singaporeans to have a secure retirement
AP1-4	Sweden	Reserve Fund	To manage the fund capital in such a way that the utility for the national pension system is maximised. To manage the fund capital in the best interests of the income pension system by generating high returns at low risk
AP7	Sweden	Pension fund with individual accounts	To provide the default investment option in the Premium Pension system
NEST	UK	Pension fund with individual accounts	To ensure that every employer has access to a workplace pension scheme that meets the requirements of the UK pension reforms
TSP	USA	Pension fund with individual accounts	The FRTIB administers the Thrift Savings Plan. Its mission is to do so solely in the interest of participants and beneficiaries

In both cases, the new mission implied a meaningful change in the contributions and payments of the fund and in the investment horizon. Both institutions have been successful in implementing their new mission, but with some discontinuity in terms of the Board. These examples may be of relevance to private pension funds that are considering structural changes, for example introducing risk-sharing features into defined benefit schemes. Regulators should be confident that the funds' governing bodies can demonstrate that they are able to articulate the new mission and introduce new operating and investment strategies without disruption.

Accountability

The Boards of these investment institutions are accountable for the delivery of their mission. The accountability frameworks of these institutions are based on the "arm's length" principle. In an arm's length relationship, the two parties to an agreement are considered to be independent and on an equal footing, so that neither has control over the other for the purposes of that agreement. This means, for example, that the state may have the final say over Board recruitment but once the Board is established the government cannot influence Board members to invest in a particular project.

The arm's length relationship means that the Board is accountable to government, in line with IG 3.5, but has the independence to set out its strategy within the framework established by law, consistent with IG 3.4. The Board may report to Government or Parliament but it usually does not take instructions or directions from them, although the degree of independence can vary. For example, the New Zealand Minister of Finance may give directions to the Guardians of the Superannuation Fund, as long as these directions are "consistent with the duty to invest the Fund on a prudent, commercial basis".[5] Ministerial directions must be tabled in Parliament. Similarly, the Board of the US Thrift must seek Congressional approval for any changes to the investment instruments permitted in the TSP.

For such an arrangement to work, the mission of the institution must be clearly defined. This enables the Board to put in place appropriate policies and the competent authorities to spot inconsistencies even from an arm's length. Regulators may wish to consider whether the private pension funds under their supervision similarly have clearly stated objectives and coherent operating policies.

Suitability

As specified by IG 3.6 for private pension institutions, Board members (and senior managers) are expected to meet fit and proper criteria. These are spelled out in differing levels of detail according to the jurisdiction, but in general the criteria cover personal and financial integrity, conflicts of interest and business conduct. All institutions require that Board members have relevant experience, insight and professional background.

- ATP requires that Board members and managers have sufficient experience to undertake his/her responsibilities. Candidates cannot 1) have been guilty of specific offences; 2) be subject to liquidation, petition of bankruptcy or similar; 3) be involved in business activities that have led to losses for ATP; or 4) have demonstrated unsuitable behaviour.
- The AP funds apply a general standard requiring the Government to appoint board members based on their ability to advance the management of the fund.

If Board members no longer meet the relevant criteria, they are typically required to report the situation to the Chairman of the Board, the Regulator or other competent authority. The expectation is that the member will resign if required, therefore only a few of the institutions have a formal procedure for removing Board members. This procedure is carefully defined to avoid it being abused.

- The Canadian Governor in Council can remove Board members of CCPIB "for cause" (i.e. for misconduct or breach of duty).
- If the Danish regulator considers that an individual board member at ATP no longer meets the required standards, it should inform the Minister of Employment who will decide whether or not the individual can continue to serve.
- The Swedish Government has the authority to terminate Board members of the AP funds if it assesses that they no longer meet the required standards.

IG 3.6 also stipulates that "the governing body should collectively have the necessary skills and knowledge to oversee all functions". ATP, CPPIB, NEST, CPF, NZS and FRTIB require that the Board as a whole possesses a specific mix of skills and experience.

- The CPPIB applies a general behavioural standard and sets criteria related to the different competences of the Board overall.
- The Secretary of State for Work and Pensions selects Trustee Members for NEST on the basis of merit, fairness and openness and considering that the Board of Trustees overall should have experience of investment, portfolio management, member representation, finance, auditing, governance, and business management.

It is customary for Boards to conduct annual self-assessments and verifications of Board member suitability. This type of information could be valuable to regulators of private pensions, as it would help to identify areas where members of governing bodies needed extra technical advice or training as well as potential sources of governance failings.

Delegation and expert advice

The majority of Boards have established committees with mandates to work on specific aspects of the operations of the institution, as described in IG 3.7. These committees are intended to strengthen the Board's control and strategic foresight and to enable them to work more closely with management on specific issues. In some cases, the committees are mandated by law. Forming committees is an important way to ensure depth and continuity in the Board's work on particular aspects. A risk related to the use of committees - and particularly so if the number of committees becomes high - is that the Board and its individual members become distanced from their collective and personal responsibility.

- The Board of CPPIB is legally required to form an Investment Committee and an Audit Committee.
- The Board of ATP has formed a Management Committee, an Audit Committee and an ORSA (Own Risk and Solvency Assessment) committee. It has delegated the typical responsibilities of a Remuneration Committee to its Management Committee.
- The Board of MPFA has established a large number of committees: Administration, Audit, Finance, Guidelines and Remuneration Committees, Tender Board, Working Group on MPF Reform Issues, and Working Group on Review of Adjustment Mechanism for Minimum and Maximum Levels of Relevant Income.
- The Boards of GPFN and GPFG have formed Risk Management Committees, Audit Committees and Remuneration Committees. The Board of GPFG has also formed an Ownership Committee.

Consistent with IG 3.7, where external experts or investment managers are hired, the Board has ultimate responsibility for the terms of their contracts.

Actuary, auditor, custodian

As part of their internal control and verification system all institutions examined are subject to external audit and many of them have created special functions to facilitate this process – e.g. Internal Auditor, Appointed Actuary, Chief Risk Officer and Risk Unit. In most cases such special functions are set up and appointed by the Board and they report directly to it. This is in keeping with IG 3.8 – 3.10.

Risk-based internal controls

Just as the Boards of the examined investment institutions operate at arm's length from government, their management operates at arm's length from the Board. Executive management is responsible for the day-to-day management of the institution and the execution of the investment strategy.[6] The Board is not involved in these tasks but it puts in place sufficient guidelines and control procedures to be able to monitor the activities of the management team, in line with IG 3.11 and 3.12. In the majority of cases, the chief risk officer is a member of the executive committee and in some cases the internal control teams report directly to the Board of Directors or to the relevant sub-committee of the Board.

Several schemes have internal and external whistle-blower schemes in place, a more rigorous control mechanism than those suggested by the Core Principles. It is usually a requirement for the Board to establish and enforce a code of ethics, a code of conduct or a framework of policies or guidelines for management and staff.

Disclosure

IG 3.13 states that the governing body should make accurate and timely disclosures to all relevant parties. The type and extent of the disclosure made by these investment institutions depends on how they are supervised, but in general these institutions are subject to stringent reporting requirements to both members and supervisors, and their detailed financial information is publicly available.

Funded public pension schemes with individual accounts tend to be supervised in the same way as their private equivalents. For example, ATP is supervised by the Danish financial services regulator on an equivalent basis to a commercial insurance company; AP7 is supervised by the Swedish financial services regulator similarly to a private fund management company; and the Pensions Regulator supervises NEST in the same way as other trust-based occupational schemes. This creates a level playing field between the public and private sectors and reinforces the arm's-length relationship between the institution and the government.

Reserve funds and Sovereign Wealth Funds are subject to other supervisory arrangements, typically involving direct supervision by a Government ministry. For example, all AP funds report to the Swedish Government that in turn reports to Parliament. CPPIB is accountable to, but not supervised by, Parliament: it submits its annual report to the Minister of Finance and to the appropriate provincial ministers. The Minister of Finance puts the report before Parliament. The Minister must undertake a special examination at least once every six years.

All the institutions examined submit audited annual accounts to government (some also submit quarterly reports). Most provide additional qualitative reporting on the operations, performance and strategic outlook for the business. Most of the institutions publish detailed data on the investment portfolio, risk measures and management and responsible investment practices. Supervisors of private pension systems should be able to request the same amount and type of information from the private sector, with the caveat that they must therefore also have the capacity to analyse and act on this information.

In most cases these reports are issued shortly after the end of the reporting period. In the case of the FRTIB, the financial report is issued within the statutory time frame, more than a year, after the end of the reporting period although fund information is published more regularly.

In addition to government, these reports are directed at a professional audience such as financial analysts, peers, policy makers and the financial press. This audience can provide a useful service in terms of performance evaluation, policy evaluation and peer pressure, compensating for the lack of direct competitive pressures on a number of the institutions. Providing transparency about the state of the public institution can help to build its credibility. In the case of private pension funds, it may not be appropriate to release detailed information to the public, especially where it is financially sensitive or may confuse members of the scheme.

Those institutions that operate schemes with individual accounts issue regular policy/account statements to their clients. Statements include information on contributions, accrued rights/savings, current risk choices if relevant, returns on investments, individual costs, benefit forecast and other benefits. They also direct members to sources of further information. In the case of ATP and AP7 the statement also includes a link to web-based national integrated pension rights and pension overview services where the individual can get a complete overview of his or her expected financial situation in old age across all public and private pension schemes and savings arrangements. Regulators may use such statements as a basis for comparison for private pension funds' communications with members.

Appointment of Board members

The Board plays the key role in ensuring effective governance of investment institutions. It is therefore essential that the institutions are able to attract and recruit suitable candidates to their Boards. Regulators may wish to consider whether the recruitment criteria and remuneration policies of the different investment institutions examined here could usefully be applied to private pension institutions, especially in jurisdictions where there is a shortage of qualified candidates.

Appointments procedure

In the case of the public institutions discussed in this report, the government has an important role in Board appointments, but Board members are not political appointees. Other stakeholders are usually involved in the appointment process and there is no instance of Board members being removed following a change of government.[7]

In Norway, Singapore, Sweden and the United States, the appointments procedure is consultative but driven primarily by the government:

- Board members of Folketrygdfondet and Norges Bank, (the managers of GPFN and GPFG) are appointed by the Ministry of Finance and the King in Council respectively.
- In Singapore, the Minister of Finance appoints the Board of the CPF in consultation with the President.
- Board members of the AP funds in Sweden are appointed by the government; for some of the positions other stakeholders are consulted. For AP1-4, social partners can propose two board members each.
- In the USA, the President appoints the Board members of the FRTIB (which manages the assets of the Thrift Savings Plan) and the appointments are confirmed by the Senate. Three Board members are appointed by the President and two are appointed by the President in consultation with the minority leader in the House of Representatives and the majority leader in the Senate.

In Canada and Denmark the appointments procedure is driven primarily by other stakeholders who propose candidates to the government. Such a process helps to create confidence and ownership in the institution among stakeholders. Stakeholders must respect all professional and other criteria when proposing candidates.

- In Canada, appointments are made by the Governor in Council on the recommendation of the Finance Minister. The Minister can form an advisory committee with one representative from each of the participating provinces and must consult the appropriate provincial Ministers of the participating provinces before making any recommendations on Board appointment.

- Board members of ATP are formally appointed by Denmark's Minister of Employment but candidates are proposed by the two parties to the labour market. Each party nominates 15 members to a Board of Representatives and 6 members from each side are selected for the Board of Directors (specific organisations have the right to propose members).

Trustees of NEST in the UK are currently appointed by the Secretary of State for Work and Pensions but it is intended in future that Trustee members are appointed by NEST itself based on input from the Members Panel (an advisory body designed to provide NEST with members' views and considerations). This corresponds to the proposal in IG 3.5 that the accountability of the governing body is improved when plan members and beneficiaries can nominate members.

Recruitment criteria for Board members at the institutions under review also pay close attention to potential conflicts of interest. This issue is addressed in several of the Core Principles, notably in IG 3.1, which highlights the importance of setting out clear contractual responsibilities when a pension fund is managed by a financial institution. This reduces the risks of a conflict in cases where a financial institution appoints the members of the governing body of pension funds that it administers, and there is a clash between the commercial interests of the financial institution and the fiduciary responsibilities of the pension funds. The examined investment institutions additionally apply specific conflict of interest rules to Board members and emphasise transparency to reduce conflicts.

- Directors of the MPFA (who are unpaid) are required to make a general declaration of their interests, and to report any pecuniary interest in a matter placed before the management board. These reports are available for public inspection.
- The Board of the New Zealand Future Fund has set up a Conflicts Committee to address possible conflicts of interest for Board members.

Board size and structure

The number of Board members appointed varies across the institutions analysed, depending on the mandate of the institution and the range of competences needed for the Board to deliver that mandate. The size of the Board of the institutions examined ranges from 5 (FRTIB, which manages the assets of the TSP) to 15 (NEST, CPF). The FRTIB is responsible for investment strategies that are externally managed, and its mandate is quite constrained (the legislation gives the Board very little leeway in setting investment policy). While a small Board may have gaps in expertise (which could be filled by using external advisers), a large Board may face logistical problems in trying to organise regular meetings.

Some countries apply additional political or social criteria when determining the composition of the Board:

- ATP targets equal gender representation on the Board.
- GPFN and GPFG have a quota of 40% female Board members.
- The AP funds require members of the Board to be Swedish citizens.
- A maximum of three of the Board members of CPPIB can reside outside Canada; the Board must have regard to the desirability of having directors representative of various regions of Canada.

Duration of terms, timing of appointments and re-appointment

The different institutions apply similar policies to ensure continuity and avoid having to replace several Board members at the same time. This is not a matter addressed by the Core Principles.

- CPPIB, ATP and the AP funds all set three-year terms for Board members and allow multiple re-appointments.
- Folketrygfondet (GPFN) sets four-year terms and allows re-appointment for up to 12 years.
- FRTIB members are appointed for four years terms.
- Some institutions have legal limits on the number of Board members they can replace at one time; others set practical limits.

Remuneration of the Board and management

Most of the institutions under review publish details of the remuneration of Board members and top executive management in their annual report.[8] The remuneration of Board members among the different institutions ranges from pay scales in line with market standards to zero or very low payments. None of the institutions examined allows performance-related pay for the Board. In all cases, non-executive Board members are permitted to hold positions in other organisations. In most cases, Board members hold non-executive positions elsewhere but in some instances (e.g. the CPF) they have executive functions.

Market-matching remuneration may help to attract good candidates. Table 4.4 has examples of market-matching remunerations. A number of the institutions that pay their Board members at market rates specify that this is to enable them to recruit suitable people, as well as being an appropriate reward for the responsibilities and time commitment involved in the role. They also specify that the institution should not drive market rates higher. For example, the remuneration of Board members at CPPIB is set out in the bye-laws and takes account of the remuneration of persons with similar responsibilities and activities. A similar approach is followed in ATP through a remuneration policy set out by the Board.

Table 4.4. Board remuneration examples

	Chair	Board Member
Australia Future Fund	USD 160 000	USD 80 000
New Zealand Superannuation Fund	USD 50 000	USD 35 000
NEST (UK)	USD 125 000	USD 30 000
CPPIB (Canada)	USD 156 000	USD 40 000 + per diem USD 1 400 + travel time
AP2 (Sweden)	USD 12 000	USD 6 000 + around USD 4 000 for Committee work

Note: Exchange rate at 13/10/2017.
Source: Annual reports.

However in several jurisdictions salary limits are placed on public functions, so offering high market-rate remuneration to Board members could be controversial. Their respective governments set the remuneration for Board members of the AP funds and the GPFN. The remuneration of the Board of the Australian Future Fund is determined by the public sector remuneration tribunal, but is at the top end of the public sector scale so corresponds to market-matching rates.

The Board usually has the authority to establish the remuneration of senior management.

- In GPFN the Board sets the remuneration of the Executive Director and informs the Ministry of Finance.
- In the AP funds the Board sets the remuneration of the Executive Director and other senior managers; Government guidelines exist for the remuneration of senior managers of the AP funds.
- The Board of Directors sets the remuneration of the senior management team in ATP and in CPPIB taking account of market comparisons.

Executive management all receive market-based pay. Many of the institutions under review are market leaders in terms of their asset base and their role within the investment community, and this is reflected in their compensation structures.

- NZS considers that it is competing in a global market for executive talent.
- ATP offers market-level compensation based on national and international standards and taking into account the size and scope of the institution.
- AP4 aims to pay salaries that are competitive but not market-leading.
- The levels of executive compensation at CPPIB are consistent with those at other comparable Canadian financial institutions. The government of Canada actively monitors executive compensation in relation to the size of assets under management.

Table 4.5 shows some examples of executive pay. There is a wide range of both fixed and variable compensation. Some institutions offer performance-based remuneration as part of their senior managers' remuneration. Others believe that such incentives may lead to suboptimal and short-term business conduct and they exclude their senior managers from any performance-based remuneration.

- GPFN does not allow performance-related pay for its Chief Executive but it does apply performance-based incentives to other senior managers.
- CPPIB has an extensive and quite complex incentive programme for senior managers. Its managers are among the highest paid in the pensions industry globally, reflecting their expertise in managing a very large, actively-managed portfolio.
- ATP, AP4 and AP7 do not allow performance-based pay for senior managers.
- All staff – including non-investment staff – at the Australian Future Fund have some element of their variable pay linked to the performance of the investment portfolio. This helps to keep them focused on the mission of the AFF.

Table 4.5. Executive remuneration examples (in USD)

	Fixed	Variable	AUM
AP4			
Chief Executive Officer	400 000		42 billion
Australia Future Fund			
Chief Executive Officer	483 000	Up to 120%	105 billion
Chief Investment Officer	447 275	Up to 120%	
CPPIB			
President & CEO[1]	518 000	2 702 700	252 billion
Chief Investment Strategist[2]	370 000	1 030 440	
MPFA			
Managing Director	730 000		n/a
NEST			
Chief Executive	290 000		2.4 billion
New Zealand Superannuation Fund			
Chief Executive Officer	511 000	378 000	26 billion

Note: Exchange rate as at 14/02/2018.
1. Target full year compensation, excludes LTIP and other non-direct payments of USD 3.5 million.
2. Excludes deferred of USD 1 million.
Source: Annual reports. Summary of key policy issues: governance frameworks

Summary of key policy issues: governance frameworks

The nationally significant investment institutions analysed fulfil different roles in their domestic pension systems, and this is reflected in differences in their governance frameworks. Nevertheless, they have a number of features in common that are relevant to the regulation of private pensions:

- The governance frameworks of these investment institutions closely reflect the recommendations of Core Principle 3, especially in the establishment of an oversight Board that is accountable to the competent authorities as well as to members.
- The missions of the institutions are clearly stated. Their Boards are held accountable for delivering the mission and are subject to extensive disclosure requirements. This enables the supervisory authorities and stakeholders to monitor performance and compliance with the mission.
- The institutions operate within a regulatory and legal framework but at arm's length from government. This places considerable responsibility on the Board. Board recruitment is therefore a key determinant of the success of the institution.
- There is no consensus on the appropriate level of remuneration for Board members of the investment institutions under review, but fit and proper criteria are rigorously applied in all cases and attention is paid to the overall range of skills of the Board. Conflict-of-interest policies are transparent.
- The Boards have oversight of operational and other internal risks and several institutions have implemented whistle-blower schemes.

4.3. Investment and risk management

The investment strategies of the nine investment institutions fall into two main types, target date/lifecycle funds and long-term return strategies. The ways in which these strategies have been formulated and are executed have been examined in light of the implementing guidelines of Core Principle 4 of the *OECD Core Principles of Private Pension Regulation* which addresses investment and risk management. The implementing guidelines are described in Table 4.6.

Table 4.6. Mapping investment policies: key features

	Implementing Guideline Core Principle 4	Key features
4.1	Retirement income objective and prudential principles	Alignment with retirement income objective; risk management techniques
4.2 – 4.4	Prudent person standard	Prudent person standard, fiduciary duty, requirement to establish investment process with adequate safeguards
4.5 – 4.12	Investment policy	Written policy; clear risk and return objectives appropriate for the characteristics of the fund. Asset allocation strategy with tolerances. Investment options for members. Review procedures.
4.13 – 4.21	Portfolio limits and other quantitative requirements	Definition; respect for diversification and liability matching
4.22 – 4.27	Valuation of pension assets	Transparent basis
4.28 – 4.29	Performance assessment	Monitoring procedure

Table 4.7 provides an overview of the processes followed by each of the institutions in establishing and implementing its investment strategy. As discussed below, these processes largely cover the points raised in the Implementing Guidelines of Core Principle 4, especially IG 4.1 – 4.12 which cover the alignment of a fund's investment policy with its objectives. The implementation of these policies, including more detailed information on portfolio design, asset allocation and risk control (IG 4.13 – 4.21) and performance assessment (IG 4.28 – 4.29), is discussed in the "Investment Strategy" section.

Retirement income objective and prudential principles

IG 4.1 stipulates that the regulation of pension fund investment should be aligned with the retirement income objective and the eventual liabilities of the fund. The equivalent for a nationally significant investment institution is that the Board of Directors be held accountable for establishing an investment policy in line with the mission of the institution. This means setting the return expectation, the risk tolerance and any asset allocation limits. This is the case for most of the institutions under review.[9]

Prudent person standard

The Core Principles emphasise the obligations of pension fund governing bodies towards members and beneficiaries, especially their fiduciary duty and the expectation that they will act prudently (IG 4.2 – 4.3). As shown in Table 4.7, the investment policies of the reserve funds and the pension funds with individual accounts include the concepts of member best interest and prudential requirements.[10]

Table 4.7. Investment policy overview

	Canada CPPIB	Denmark ATP	Norway GPFN	Norway GPFG	Sweden AP 1-4	Sweden AP7	United Kingdom NEST	United States TSP
Classification	Reserve Fund	Pension fund with individual accounts	Sovereign wealth fund	Sovereign wealth fund	Reserve fund	Pension fund with individual accounts	Pension fund with individual accounts	Pension fund with individual accounts
Key investment objectives implied by mission	Maximise long-term returns without undue risk Funding of Canada pension plan	Liability matching Preserve real value Liquidity Best interests of members	Risk/return profile Responsible investment	Risk/return profile Responsible investment	Conservative risk/return profile	Risk/return profile Best interests of members Lifecycle option	Best interests of members Universal access to workplace scheme	Best interests of members
Investment constraints in law and regulation	Prudential requirements	Formerly, some quantitative limits were set to ensure adequate diversification. These were removed in 2017.	Ministry of Finance stipulates a strategic benchmark of 50-70% equities and 30-70% fixed income, with a regional split of 85% in Norway and 15% across the rest of the Nordic region	Ministry of Finance sets investment constraints. Equity weighting in strategic benchmark to be raised from 62.5% to 70%. High yield instruments max 5%; non-listed real estate maximum 7%. Tracking error limit 1.25%.	Minimum 30% allocation to interest-bearing assets. Maximum currency exposure 40%. Maximum 5% unlisted equity. At least 10% of assets must be managed externally.	Covered by UCITS legislation.		The Board must provide 5 different index funds with characteristics defined by law and lifecycle funds based on these index funds.
Ownership limits	Max. 10% of assets can be invested in a single issuer (except Canadian government entities) Max. 30% of voting rights of a company	Controlling interest not permitted	Maximum ownership 15% for Norwegian company, 5% in other Nordic countries	Maximum ownership 10% in listed companies (excluding real estate)	Per fund/ maximum 2% of market capitalisation of Swedish stock exchange and 10% of an individual issuer.	Maximum 5% of voting shares. AP7 may only exercise voting rights in a Swedish company in exceptional cases.	NEST invests in pooled funds	
Investment policy definition process	Board must establish written policy – including asset allocation and risk limits - for the Investment Portfolio and the Cash for Benefits portfolio based on the	Board must establish a written framework for investments and risk limits, on the advice of management. It also establishes the degree of autonomy for management to	Board sets out investment policy based on Ministry of Finance requirements and with advice from management. Investment policy covers asset allocation, risk limits	Board sets out investment policy based on Ministry of Finance requirements and with advice from NBIM (management unit). Investment policy covers asset	The Board must publish an annual business plan including investment guidelines and risk management, with advice from management.		The Trustee has determined that the best interests of members are served by default Target Date Funds. The Trustee prepares a Statement of Investment Principles	Asset allocations for the lifecycle funds were prepared by an external consultant. The TSP must review the assumptions at least annually to see if changes in allocation are

	framework provided in law and drawing on the advice of management	act in the event that the portfolio develops differently from expectations	and tolerances	allocation, risk limits and tolerances			with written advice from the Chief Investment Officer.	warranted
Aligning Board and management with long-term investment policy	Management operates under the direction of the Board through its Investment Committee and reports regularly to the Board. The Board must evaluate investment strategy at least annually.	Management operates under the direction of the Board. Regular reporting to the Board including a daily set of key figures.	Management operates under the direction of the Board and reports regularly to the Board	Management operates under the direction of the Board and reports regularly to the Board	Asset allocation set by management on the basis of the Board's guidelines. Management reports regularly to Board on investment performance and risk.		Asset allocation set by management. The Investment Committee meets quarterly to review investment operations and decisions, with advice from the Chief Investment Officer.	Management operates under the direction of the Board of Directors and reports regularly to the board.
Targets set	The Cash for Benefits portfolio should outperform a domestic money market benchmark. The Investment Strategy should deliver higher returns than the reference portfolio with equivalent risk.	Nominal net return target of 7% on free reserves	Measures itself against reference portfolio	Outperform the strategic benchmark	Each fund has set itself a long term return target (AP1, AP3: 4% real; AP2, AP4: 4.5% real)	Perform at least in line with private sector options	Investment target: net returns in excess of inflation over the long term. Other objectives: maximise pension income and any lump sum at retirement by taking appropriate risk; seek to deliver similar outcomes for cohorts with similar contribution histories; dampen volatility over the savings phase.	While the chosen indices may indirectly provide a target benchmark, the Board does not systematically make available an evaluation of performance.
Valuation of pension assets/liabilities	Assets valued at market value. The Government Actuary performs a liability valuation that informs but does not determine the investment strategy.	Mark-to-market. Requirements similar to Solvency II	Market value Estimates used for non-traded assets	Market value Estimates used for non-traded assets	Market value Estimates used for non-traded assets	Market value Estimates used for non-traded assets	Market value	Market value

Investment policy

All of the institutions have a written investment policy, in keeping with IG 4.4 – 4.5, that outlines the type of investment and risk exposures the institution will take on in order to achieve its mission and objectives. It is translated into an investment strategy by the Board, usually with the advice of management, which determines the final shape of the portfolio.

- The mission of the CPPIB is "to invest its assets with a view to achieving a maximum rate of return, without undue risk of loss, having regard to the factors that may affect the funding of the Canada Pension Plan and its ability to meet its financial obligations on any given business day."[1] It should also "provide cash management services to the Canada Pension Plan so that they can pay benefits." The Board of Directors has translated this into a strategy of maintaining two separate portfolios, one to manage liquidity and one to seek high returns.
- The mission of AP7 is to provide the default investment option for the Premium Pension System based on a lifecycle approach. The Board has translated this into an investment strategy of building the default fund with two underlying building block portfolios, for which it lays down the investment constraints.
- The mission of ATP includes maintaining the real value of members' benefits and providing insurance-like guarantees. The Board has translated this into a liability-driven strategy combining a hedging portfolio and a return-seeking portfolio.

The degree of freedom that the Board has in establishing the investment policy reflects the nature of the institution. This mirrors the requirements of IG 4.6 for private pensions, that the investment objectives be consistent with the retirement income objective and specific attributes of the fund. Pension funds are expected to provide their members with retirement income and their investment policies are designed accordingly. ATP is designed as an insurance company and its investment policy is essentially driven by its liabilities. Sovereign Wealth Funds and Reserve Funds do not face the same expectations from members, but their investment policy might be influenced by liquidity requirements. Sovereign Wealth Funds and Reserve Funds may face cash calls at relatively short notice, whereas public pension funds with individual accounts can usually plan their liquidity needs long into the future.

Similarly, the degree of risk that the institution can bear depends on its mission (IG 4.9). In general, pension institutions with individual accounts have a direct responsibility towards each member to build their retirement assets and make them available on retirement. They therefore have a lower risk tolerance as they seek to avoid capital losses and illiquidity risk.

Risk management is the chief mechanism for aligning both Board and management with the long-term investment policy. Within the limits of its mandate, the Board of Directors sets out a risk budget specifying overall risk as well as risk composition and it receives regular reports from management on whether or not it is being respected. The degree of tolerance around the risk budget (and other investment constraints) is an important determinant of the management's ability to react to extreme events such as a market crash or significant events in particular markets or sub-markets without having to wait for approval from the Board. This could have a significant outcome on the performance of the portfolio.

IG 4.7 states that the written investment policy should include guidelines on asset allocation, overall performance objectives and monitoring, and the degree of tolerance around these guidelines. In the case of the examined investment institutions, some of these guidelines are set by the state rather than by the Board. In Sweden, the asset allocation of AP1-4 is set in legislation and the mandate of AP7 specifically includes providing lifecycle funds. By contrast, the Board of CPPIB (Canada) faces no asset allocation constraints. In the UK, it is the Board of NEST, rather than the government, that has determined that offering lifecycle funds is the best way to fulfil the mandate of the institution.

The investment institutions may have either absolute or relative performance targets. There is considerable variation in the absolute return targets: NZS's mandate is to achieve annualised performance of 2.7% above cash over any 20-year moving average period; AFF aims to achieve annual returns of 4.5% - 5.5% above the Consumer Price Index, with an "acceptable" level of risk and while minimising the impact on Australian financial markets;[2] AP4 targets real returns of 4.5% per annum. CPPIB and the Norwegian sovereign wealth funds have relative return targets, as they aim to outperform a reference portfolio with equivalent risk.

The reserve funds and sovereign wealth funds under review all integrate environmental, social and governance (ESG) factors in their investment policies. Their emphasis is on risk reduction, especially climate change-related risks. Some institutions, notably CPPIB and the Australian Future Fund, also highlight the potential return opportunities from ESG investment. The Swedish reserve funds AP1-4 have established a Council on Ethics to support their ESG activities.

Among the institutions with individual accounts, Denmark's ATP and the UK's NEST point to ESG factors as drivers of long-term risk-adjusted performance. AP7 is an "active owner", engaging with its portfolio holdings on ESG issues. ESG integration is not addressed in the Core Principles, although Core Principle 4 draws attention to the long-term nature of pension fund investment and refers regulators to the *G20/OECD High-Level Principles of Long-Term Investment Financing by Institutional Investors* in this regard.

Portfolio limits and other quantitative requirements

The quantitative restrictions placed on the investment institutions are consistent with their risk-return objectives and with prudential requirements (IG 4.13 – 4.21). With the exception of the Norwegian domestic fund, their asset allocations are relatively unconstrained. This may reflect the high level of investment expertise of these institutions and their relatively large asset base, which means that they are able to take advantage of investment opportunities across a wide range of asset classes. Notably, the CPPIB invests over 20% of its portfolio in real assets, whereas direct investment in real estate is prohibited in six OECD countries and a number of jurisdictions restrict investment in other less liquid asset classes.[3]

Valuation of pension assets

The institutions all use market value to measure their assets and have established transparent procedures for valuing assets where no market price is available (IG 4.22-4.27).

4.4. Investment strategy

The institutions considered in this report primarily use one of two types of long term investment strategy: target date/lifecycle funds (which have a multi-year investment horizon and become more conservative over time), or long-term return strategies (which have a multi-generational investment strategy and no pre-determined evolution in their risk profile. ATP (Denmark) is unusual in having an insurance-based approach; this includes a long-term return-seeking portfolio, and it is therefore considered as part of the second group.

Target date and lifecycle funds

Among the pension funds with individual accounts, four out of five offer a target date or lifecycle strategy as the default option for members who do not wish to select an investment strategy for themselves (Table 4.8). In these institutions such approaches are used to obviate the need for members to make complicated decisions about their pension investments while providing a relatively high degree of certainty about future benefits. They can equally be used by schemes in which members do not have a choice about how their funds are invested. The exception is the CPF in Singapore, which offers a guaranteed rate of return on savings. Both the Core Principles (in IG 4.10) and the *OECD Roadmap for the Good Design of Defined Contribution Pension Plans* recommend that pension plans provide a default option, and the Roadmap recommends that the default be a lifecycle strategy.

Table 4.8. Target date funds (TDF) and lifecycle strategies overview

	Hong Kong (China) MPFA	Singapore CPF	Sweden AP7	United Kingdom NEST	United States Thrift Savings Plan
TDF/lifecycle offered	✓	×	✓	✓	✓
TDF/lifecycle is default	✓		✓	✓	✓
TDF/lifecycle description	Initial allocation to riskier assets of 60%; reduced linearly from age 50 to an allocation of 20% at age 64		Initial allocation to equity of 100%. Annual rebalancing from age 56 to allocation of 33% equity, 67% fixed income at age 75	Up to 50 single-year retirement date funds; multi-phase glide path and dynamic risk management	5 lifestyle funds for different cohorts. Quarterly rebalancing to target asset allocation; rate of change increases as the target date approaches
Active/passive underlying investments	Schemes can use passive or active funds but costs are capped		Mix of externally and internally managed active equity funds; fixed income is internally managed	Externally-managed passive funds are used to build the TDF	Externally-managed passive funds are used to build the TDF
Other funds or strategies offered	The MPF scheme has 462 approved constituent funds	Guaranteed interest savings scheme	A wide range of investment options is offered by the private sector	Ethical (lifecycle approach); Sharia; Higher Risk; Lower Growth	Five single asset class funds are available

Note: ATP is excluded from this table as it operates individual accounts within a common scheme; members are invested in a collective insurance scheme with a long-term return component (see Table 4.9).

Target date funds (TDF) are multi-asset funds that reduce their weighting in riskier asset classes as a specific event – in this case the retirement date – approaches. Members are allocated to the TDF that corresponds to their retirement date, for example the NEST Retirement Fund 2021. The de-risking path is known as a "glide path". In addition to providing the benefits of a classic multi-asset strategy of diversification and rebalancing, TDF adjust automatically as the risk profile of the member evolves. In theory, members will become more risk-averse as they age, although the example of NEST shows that this may not always be the case in practice (Box 4.1).

In addition, by allocating most or all of the portfolio to low risk assets ahead of the retirement date, TDF aim to protect members from market volatility at the moment when they may want to cash in their assets to buy an annuity or, if they stay invested, have less time to recover their losses through future market growth.

Box 4.1. Target date glide paths

The asset allocation of a target date fund typically becomes more conservative over time. Members are expected to become more risk averse as their time horizon shortens, as they have less time to make additional contributions or to recover from losses. Thus, TDF usually have a high exposure to risky assets such as equities in early periods in order to build up the asset pool and switch into safer but lower-yielding assets such as bonds over time.

Figure 4.1. Typical glide path

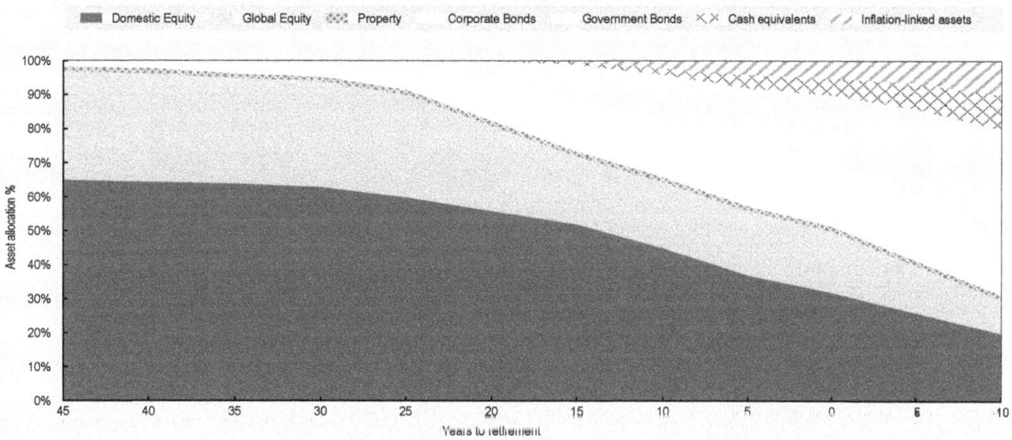

NEST, the UK auto-enrolment provider, has implemented a different glide path. Its TDF have three phases: the foundation phase (40+ years to retirement); the growth phase (from around 40 to around 10 years to retirement) and the consolidation phase (less than 10 years to retirement). NEST's research found that young savers were very concerned by the risk of extreme loss; the foundation phase therefore aims at capital preservation rather than high growth, with a target long-term volatility of 7%. This is to encourage younger members to get into the habit of saving and avoid a sharp one-off fall in their retirement pot that might make them stop contributing. The growth phase concentrates on growing the retirement pot by at least 3% per annum in real terms and has a target volatility of 10-12%. In the consolidation phase, portfolio gains are locked in via low-risk assets.

Figure 4.2. NEST glide path

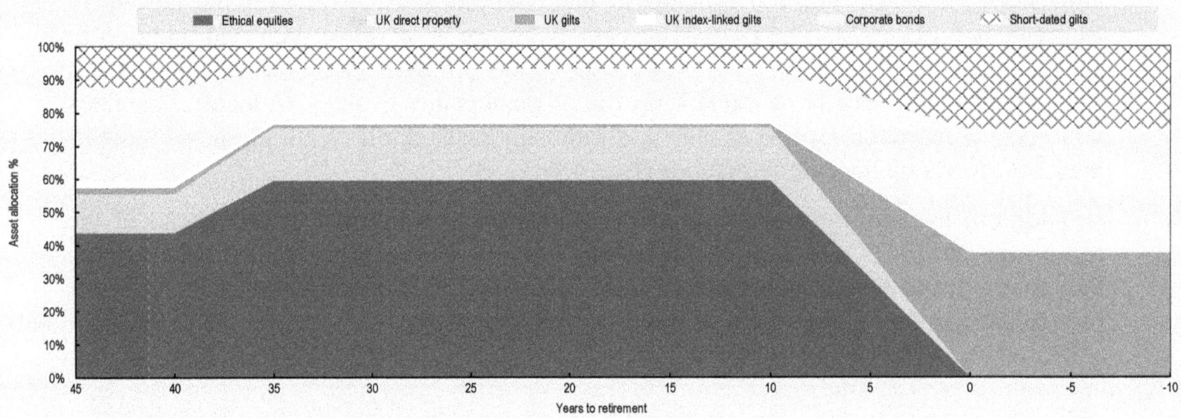

Note: Based on NEST Ethical Fund lifecycle.
Source: NEST Investment implementation document, end Sept. - end Dec. 2016.

Lifecycle funds follow an equivalent approach of reallocating assets away from riskier asset classes as the member gets older. Instead of being allocated to a specific fund, the member's own portfolio is adjusted over time. There are administrative differences between the two approaches – TDF are pooled vehicles whereas lifecycle funds are individual accounts – but the investment objective is almost identical. The key consideration is that there is effective asset allocation and risk budgeting in every period.

Figure 4.3. Risk allocation - MPFA Default Investment Strategy (DIS)

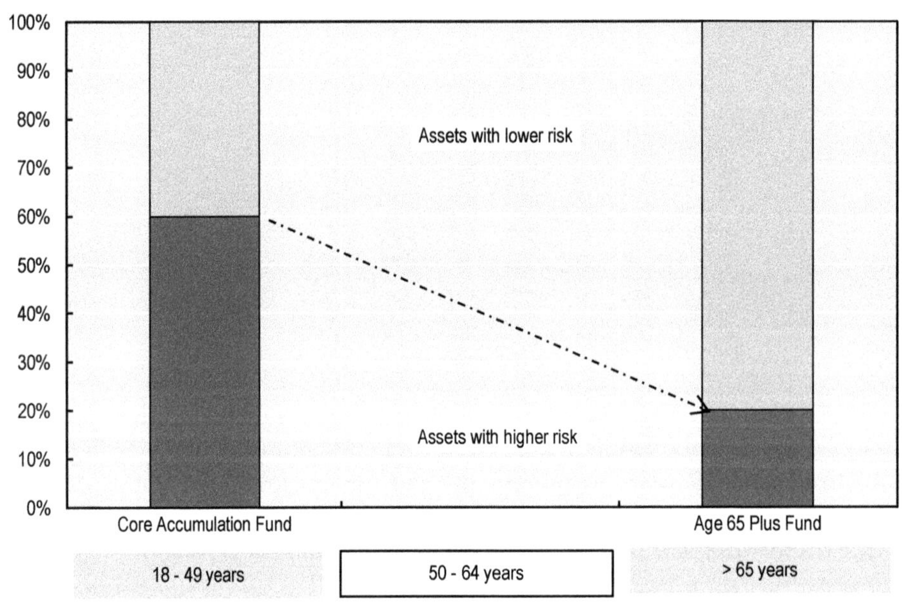

Source: MPFA Newsletter March 2017.

TDF and lifecycle funds can be more or less targeted to different cohorts. The asset allocation of the Default Investment Strategy (DIS) in Hong Kong, China is adjusted annually for members aged between 50 and 64 years; the default fund of AP7 in Sweden is adjusted annually for members aged between 56 and 75 years. NEST (UK) offers up to 50 Retirement Date Funds as its default strategy: members choose the fund that corresponds to the year they will retire, for example a member who will want to take their money out in 2040 will select the NEST 2040 Retirement Fund. The Thrift Savings Plan (USA) groups members into larger cohorts, offering TDF for 2020 (retirement date 2015-2024), 2030 (retirement date 2025-2034), 2040 (retirement date 2035-2044) and 2050 (retirement date 2045-2054).

Schemes differ in terms of the methodology used to establish the glide path, the number of different asset classes used as building blocks to construct the overall asset allocation, and the extent to which risk is managed along the glide path in response to prevailing market conditions. For members of the DIS in Hong Kong (China), the asset allocation of their portfolio is static between the ages of 18 and 49, is adjusted linearly each year between the ages of 50 and 64 and is static thereafter (Figure 4.3).

By contrast, NEST in the UK actively manages asset allocation along the glide path within pre-set risk budgets, taking account of economic and market conditions (Figure 4.4).

Figure 4.4. Risk allocation – NEST funds

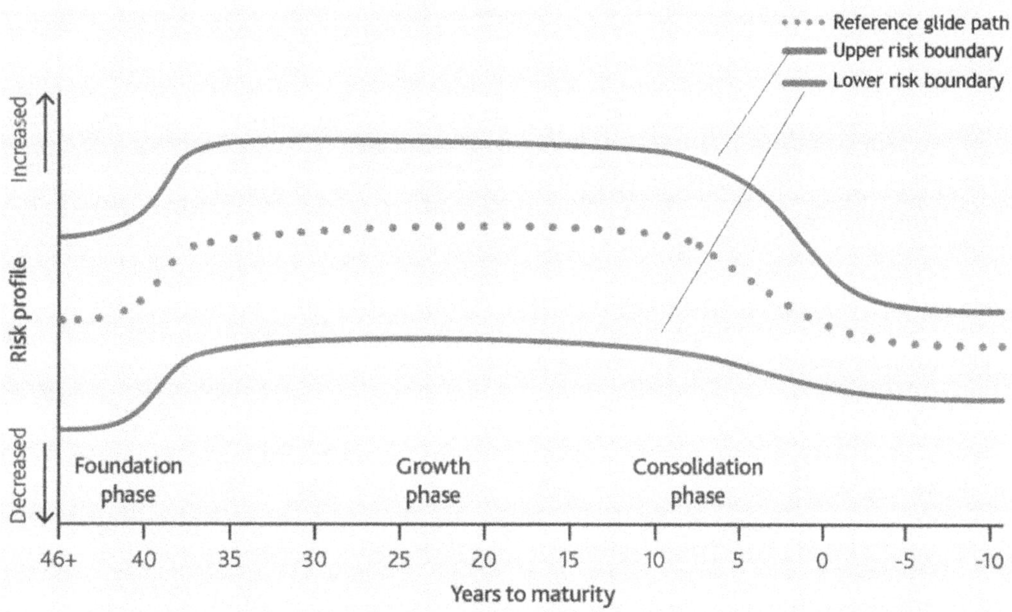

Source: NEST, "Looking after members' money" 2017.

Schemes also differ in terms of the underlying building blocks used to create their asset allocation. The Thrift Savings Plan uses 5 underlying funds covering US and global equities, US bonds and US government bonds. NEST uses 14 underlying funds covering nine asset classes - its default funds have exposure to emerging market bonds and to property, which are not included in the asset allocation of the Thrift Savings Plan. Both NEST and TSP use passively managed funds as building blocks, to reduce costs. AP7 has two building blocks - fixed income and equity - but its equity building block itself contains a number of actively managed underlying funds. AP7's equity portfolio has very broad exposure to non-domestic equity markets and employs leverage to boost returns, making it higher risk than the equity investments of NEST and the Thrift Savings Plan.

Long-term return strategies

Reserve funds and sovereign wealth funds follow long-term return investment strategies. Their focus is on asset growth at an acceptable level of risk, without the constraint placed on TDF to reduce portfolio risk as the target date approaches. The investment institution may have a higher or lower tolerance for risk depending on its mission or mandate, the source of the funds and the size of its asset base.

Of the institutions under consideration, the CPPIB has the most aggressive and diversified long-term return investment strategy. It has a large in-house investment team and considerable exposure to direct investments and illiquid asset classes. It has generated annualised net nominal returns of 6.7% over the past ten years in local currency. The GPFG, which has a different risk tolerance and follows a less diversified strategy in terms of asset classes, has returned almost 6% per year in local currency over the same period. Table 4.9 provides an overview of long-term return strategies employed by different institutions.

Table 4.9. Long-term return strategies overview

	Canada CPPIB	Denmark ATP	Norway GPFN	Norway GPFG	Sweden AP 1-4
Classification	Reserve fund	Pension fund with individual accounts	Sovereign wealth fund	Sovereign wealth fund	Reserve fund
Investment objective	Maximise returns without undue risk of loss. Aim is to generate sufficient returns that there is no need to raise contributions	Investment portfolio: generate sufficient returns to preserve the long-term purchasing power of benefits	Maximise long-term returns after costs with a moderate level of risk, while investing responsibly	Maximise long-term returns after costs with a moderate level of risk, while investing responsibly	To help create stability in the pensions system. Maximise returns for a low level of risk.
Source of funds	Employer and employee contributions	Employer and employee contributions	Surplus social security contributions	Government funds from oil production	Historic surplus social security contributions
Investment strategy	Highly diversified across asset classes and geography. Significant direct investment and investment in long-term real asset projects	Highly diversified, significant exposure to illiquid assets	Dominated by domestic assets	Recent enlargement of investment universe to include Real Estate. Exploit the fund's long-term approach and its size to capture investment opportunities.	Diversified in terms of asset class and geography
Investment risk tolerance/control	Overall risk target established through a reference portfolio (85% global equity, 15% Canadian government bonds). Size of the fund means able to withstand short-term losses.	Pension liabilities are hedged. For the growth portfolio, risk diversification follows a factor risk approach.[4] Additional insurance against very negative events. Risk budget adjusted for size of reserves.	Overall risk target established through a reference portfolio (60% Nordic equity, 40% Nordic fixed income; 85% weighting to Norway)	Overall risk target established through a reference portfolio (62.5% equity, 37.5% fixed income).	Low risk tolerance built into mandate. At least 30% of the portfolio must be invested in high-grade fixed income. Currency exposure maximum 40%.
Active/passive approach	Active	Active	Active	Active	Active
In-house/external management	In-house	Both in-house and external	In-house	In-house	Between 17% and 31% internally managed in AP1-4

While long-term return strategies may generate higher absolute returns than TDF investments, they are likely to be more volatile. It may also be necessary to tie up assets in illiquid investments in order to generate performance. They are also more expensive to implement and may demand a higher degree of investment expertise of the Board as well as management.

One institution in the survey – Denmark's ATP – applies an insurance approach to provide life-long guaranteed benefits at age 65. New contributions are converted into deferred annuity rights based on a guaranteed interest rate. ATP is subject to a regulatory framework similar to the European Solvency II requirements and is subject to absolute solvency requirements at all times on a marked-to-market basis. ATP is very sensitive to interest rate risk and the majority of its assets are allocated to the "hedging portfolio" that hedges interest rate risk on the pension liabilities (i.e. the individual annuity rights); a small portion of the assets are allocated to the "investment portfolio" that aims to generate sufficient returns to preserve the long-term purchasing power of benefits. ATP is the only institution in the reference group to have liabilities.

Summary of key policy issues: investment and risk management

The investment institutions included in this report have different missions and therefore have different investment policies. The ways in which they implement these policies are however quite similar: they primarily use one of two types of long term investment strategies, target date/lifecycle funds or long-term return strategies. Regulators may therefore wish to consider how relevant these strategies are for private pension institutions.

- Target date funds (TDF) / lifecycle funds is the preferred strategy for institutions with individual accounts. They have two chief advantages: they preserve members' assets ahead of their retirement date, and relieve members of the requirement to manage their own retirement funds.
- These advantages come at the cost of lower performance potential than a long-term return strategy, reducing the target size of the retirement pot. They may be less relevant where the member is not involved in the investment decision-making process.
- Long-term return strategies should offer better return potential than TDF/lifecycle, but their higher expected volatility makes them less suitable for individual accounts. They carry a higher risk than TDF/lifecycle funds that sufficient sums will not be available to members at the moment of retirement.
- The institutions express their performance objectives in terms of their mission and monitor performance against this long term goal rather than against a market benchmark. The relevant supervisory body is able to assess whether the performance objective is appropriate and whether the Board is on track to achieve it.
- All the nationally significant investment institutions examined except the US Thrift Savings Plan integrate ESG analysis in their investment policies.[3] ESG integration is not directly addressed in the Core Principles.

4.5. Conclusions

The nationally significant institutions analysed in this report have different objectives and employ different organisational and operational structures to achieve them. However, there are many common features in the approaches taken, indicating that the recommendations of the Core Principles are relevant and applicable to the full range of pension systems and institutions.

The missions of the different institutions are clearly stated, and guide the investment policy. The institutions provide a high level of transparency about their governance arrangements and their investment and risk management. This reinforces their accountability to their different stakeholders. Regulators may wish to apply similar disclosure standards to private pension institutions.

The role of the Board in ensuring that the institution achieves its mission is critical. Board members are therefore expected to have high levels of expertise in all areas related to the running of the institution. The recruitment and remuneration policies of the different institutions may provide some guidance as to how to avoid lack of experience or conflicts of interest in the Boards of private pension funds.

In terms of investment policy, the mission of each institution has implications for the type of risk-return profile it should target, and this broad profile may be included in legislation. However it is not usual for legislation to set out how that profile should be achieved - only Norway sets out investment constraints in law.

All but one of the nine investment institutions examined in this chapter integrate ESG analysis in their investment policies. Regulators may consider clarifying their approach to ESG integration.

Most institutions offering pension funds with individual accounts have opted for target date funds or lifecycle strategies. These offer a smoothed return profile to members and are especially appropriate as default investment strategies. Where the institutions are able to bear higher risk, they have implemented more aggressive, long-term return-seeking strategies and often built up significant asset management expertise in-house. Regulators might want to examine the capacity of funds in their jurisdiction to implement similar strategies.

Notes

[1] The MPF System consists of several privately-managed schemes, rather than a single, national investor. However, the MPF is included because its Default Investment Strategy is relevant for the examination of the investment policies of the pension funds that operate individual accounts.

[2] All AUM data as at 21 July 2017 unless otherwise stated.

[3] Employee numbers were not found for MPF, CPF, TSP.

[4] In the case of the MPF, it is the trustees of the constituent funds rather than the Board of the MPFA who have fiduciary responsibilities towards members.

[5] New Zealand Superannuation Fund website

[6] The arm's length nature of Board relationships both upwards and downwards within the investment institutions examined in this report is one of the main lessons distilled from the analysis of their governance structure.

[7] Hong Kong is excluded from this section as the MPF consists of private sector funds, each with its own Board structure

[8] Board remuneration is not part of the OECD Core Principles or its implementing guidelines. However, it is an important aspect in the setting of nationally significant investment institutions and it could be considered for inclusion in a future revision of the OECD Core Principles.

[9] In the case of GPFG, the Norges Bank is responsible for the operational implementation of the mandate laid down by the Ministry of Finance. The Ministry decides the strategic asset allocation and tracking error while Norges Bank's executive board sets supplementary risk limits.

[10] In the case of the MPF, fiduciary responsibilities lie with the trustees of the constituent funds. The Board of the MPFA oversees licensed providers and does not have its own investment policy.

[1] Source: Section 5 of CPPIB Act.

[2] The "Investment Principles" of the Korean National Pension Fund (a reserve fund) similarly include a "Principle of Public Benefit" which takes into account the potential impact of the fund on the national economy, given its size. The fund has assets of over USD 500 billion and invests almost 70% of this on the domestic market.

[3] Source: *OECD Annual Survey of Investment Regulation of Pension Funds 2017*

[4] Factor risk investing decomposes each asset class into its underlying risk factors. For example, corporate bonds contain both interest rate factor risk and equity factor risk, while government bonds contain only interest rate factor risk. This means that a portfolio made up of equity plus corporate bonds is less diversified than a portfolio made up of equity plus government bonds.

[5] The MPFA (Hong Kong, China) does not establish an investment policy.

Chapter 5. Improving retirement incomes considering behavioural biases and limited financial knowledge

This chapter identifies policies to improve retirement incomes through a better design of funded pension arrangements in the context of behavioural biases and low levels of financial knowledge. It discusses five key decisions that people need to make when planning and saving for retirement: participation, contribution, plan provider, investment strategy, and post-retirement withdrawal option. The chapter concludes with a set of policy guidelines that could help policy makers improve the design of funded pension arrangements.

Individuals must increasingly take responsibility for their retirement. In many OECD countries, funded private pension arrangements play a growing role in retirement-income provision, relative to pay-as-you-go public pensions. Moreover, within funded pensions, personal and defined contribution plans, where individuals need to make a range of decisions, are growing in importance (OECD, 2016[1]). This changing retirement-income provision landscape implies that individuals must acquire more financial skills and take more responsibility for their retirement planning, as risks related to retirement saving (i.e. investment and longevity) are transferred to individuals.

More individual choice could be welfare enhancing if individuals can make informed decisions in line with their specific needs. Conventional economic theory assumes that individuals are rational agents who process all available information consciously to maximize their expected utility. In the field of pensions, this implies that people rationally plan their consumption over their whole life, by saving a portion of their earnings during working years to achieve a desired level of income during retirement.

Unfortunately, behavioural economics shows that psychological factors affect people when making decisions for retirement and induce behaviours that are inconsistent with the rational model of utility optimisation. Generally low levels of financial knowledge compound the problem. Empirical research shows that many people fail to meet the retirement savings goals suggested by conventional economic models.[1]

Improving levels of financial literacy should help to tackle the issue. The OECD International Network on Financial Education (INFE) defines financial literacy as "a combination of awareness, knowledge, skill, attitude and behaviour necessary to make sound financial decisions and ultimately achieve individual financial wellbeing". It has developed Recommendations, High-Level Principles and Frameworks to promote financial education, both for adults and young people, as a tool to improve financial inclusion and individuals' well-being over their entire lifetime.[2] Adequate levels of financial literacy among the general population will, however, take time to materialise. In the meantime, other approaches like improving the design of retirement plans are needed to raise retirement incomes.

This chapter identifies policies to improve retirement incomes through a better design of funded pension arrangements in the context of behavioural biases and low levels of financial knowledge. The focus in this chapter is narrower than financial literacy, as it only addresses the impact of behavioural biases and low levels of financial knowledge on decision-making for retirement. As behavioural biases and low levels of financial knowledge can affect different decisions that people need to make for their retirement in different ways, the chapter discusses separately different retirement-planning decisions.[3] The analysis concludes with a set of policy guidelines that could help policy makers improve the design of funded pension arrangements.

Policies that improve the design of funded pension arrangements while adjusting for observed patterns of behaviours can be divided into five categories.

- *Automatic features* are increasingly used to make funded pension systems more inclusive and help participants reach an adequate contribution level (e.g. automatic enrolment and automatic escalation of contributions). They harness the power of inertia to keep people saving for retirement.
- *Default options* help people who are unable or unwilling to choose a contribution rate, a pension provider, an investment strategy or a post-retirement product.

- *Simplification of information and choice* can help people make better choices. Developing web applications, reducing the set of options, better disclosure of information or facilitating the comparison of options can achieve this.
- *Financial incentives* are widely used to promote private pension arrangements as they exploit individuals' tendency to respond to immediate gratification.
- Finally, *financial education* plays an important role in supporting individuals to make appropriate decisions. Conveying key information in a simple way through pension statements, financial education seminars and financial advice can improve decision making.

Section 5.1 describes the challenges in decision-making for retirement and the varying needs for financial skills according to the type of pension arrangement. Section 5.2 explains why these challenges become problematic in the context of behavioural biases and low levels of financial knowledge. Sections 5.3 to 5.7 each focus on one key decision that people need to make when planning and saving for retirement (participation, contribution, provider selection, investment strategy selection, post-retirement option selection). Each section highlights how behavioural biases and low levels of financial knowledge specifically affect that decision and presents policies that may be used to address these issues and eventually improve retirement incomes. Section 5.8 concludes by providing policy guidelines to assist policy makers to improve the design of their funded pension system considering behavioural biases and limited financial knowledge.

5.1. Challenges in decision-making for retirement vary according to the type of pension arrangement

This section presents the challenges faced by individuals when planning for retirement. As developed in OECD (2016[2]), those challenges vary according to the type of pension arrangement and are likely to be greater for people covered by: i) funded private pension arrangements rather than pay-as-you-go (PAYG) public pension arrangements; ii) personal plans rather than occupational plans; and iii) defined contribution (DC) schemes rather than defined benefit (DB) schemes.

General challenges common to all pension arrangements

There are some challenges that are common to PAYG public and funded private pension arrangements. In particular, people need a basic understanding of the main rules of the pension system. This includes being aware of the level of mandatory contributions, eligibility rules to receive benefits, how benefits are calculated, as well as how contributions, investment returns and benefits are taxed. In addition, when public pensions are means-tested, individuals need to be aware of the extent to which private pension benefits may affect their entitlement for and the level of their public pension.

People also need to be able to evaluate how different risks may affect their individual retirement situation. Several factors that influence the level of retirement benefits are inherently uncertain and risky. These include labour market risks (spells of unemployment and trajectory of wages during the career), financial risks (investment returns, inflation and interest rates), demographic risk (longevity) and political risk (uncertainty about future pension rules). For example, individuals in DC schemes need to accumulate more assets if life expectancy increases in order to maintain the same level of spending in retirement.

To grasp the potential impact of financial risks on retirement income, individuals need basic numeracy and financial knowledge. For example, people need to understand the concept of compound interest in PAYG notional DC schemes as well as in funded DC schemes to appreciate how pension wealth accumulates over time in such arrangements. Knowledge of inflation is also important, in particular to understand mechanisms of revalorisation of pensions in payment.

Individuals also need skills to assess the need for pension reforms. They need to understand how wages and changes in the economy may impact PAYG pension arrangements. In particular, individuals need to comprehend that a pension promise in a DB arrangement may end up being too generous if the parameters of the pension system (e.g. age of retirement, accrual rate) are not adjusted to reflect new conditions (e.g. life expectancy improvements, decreasing working population).

Individuals' own decisions may also impact their future retirement income, in particular with respect to the age of retirement. Most OECD countries have a statutory retirement age upon which people are entitled to get their pension, but allow people to retire earlier and/or postpone retirement within certain limits. Depending on the retirement age, pension benefits may be adjusted downwards or upwards, with the adjustment not necessarily actuarially neutral in order to incentivise or, conversely, discourage certain behaviours (OECD, 2017[3]).[4] Decisions about the retirement age therefore require individuals to have a basic understanding of how benefits are calculated.

This basic knowledge and understanding of the pension system is necessary to be able to form appropriate expectations about the level of future retirement benefits. It is important that people assess their retirement income needs, so that they can formulate a desired level of retirement income and react in case there is a gap between the expected and desired levels.

Specific challenges related to funded pensions

In addition to the challenges mentioned above, there are specific challenges related to funded pensions, which are often privately managed. What people need to know and be able to do varies according to the type of scheme, and in particular whether pension plans are mandatory or voluntary, occupational or personal, DB or DC.

Mandatory versus voluntary plans

In mandatory funded pension arrangements, individuals have a more limited set of decisions to make. They do not have to decide whether to participate in the plan and the contribution rate is set by law or regulation. Individuals or their employer can decide to make additional contributions. Individuals may also be able to choose the pension provider, the investment allocation and in which form benefits are received.

Voluntary funded pension arrangements usually offer greater choice and therefore require greater financial knowledge to make appropriate decisions during the accumulation and retirement phases. People may need to make a number of key decisions for their retirement at different stages of their lives, including whether to participate in the plan, how much to contribute, which pension provider to choose, how to invest their contributions and which post-retirement product to choose. Moreover, the number of available plans and investment portfolios can be quite large, adding to the complexity of making a choice.

Occupational versus personal plans

Personal pension plans usually require greater financial skills than occupational pension plans as they offer more choice. In occupational plans, plan sponsors take care of a number of plan design features, such as the choice of the provider, the amount contributed (possibly as a default), the investment strategy (possibly as a default) and the post-retirement product (possibly as a default). They can also negotiate lower fees for the administration of the accounts and the management of the assets. All those decisions typically fall under the responsibility of individuals in personal pension plans.

DB versus DC plans

DC pension arrangements provide a clear, straightforward link between pension contributions and pension benefits, but put most risks onto individuals. In these plans, assets accumulated at the end of one's working life (contributions plus investment income earned on those contributions) are used to generate a stream of income, thereby directly determining the amount of retirement income. However, individuals have to bear investment, inflation and longevity risks. As they bear the risks, individuals have more discretion about a number of plan design features in DC plans. In DB plans, the employer bears most of those risks.

DC plans require more financial skills than DB plans with respect to the benefit calculation. In DB plans, benefits are usually calculated according to a formula based on past earnings, making it relatively straightforward for individuals to estimate their future level of retirement income. By contrast, benefits received from a DC plan depend on the amount contributed, the performance of the underlying investment and the remaining life expectancy at retirement. This means that they are more uncertain and difficult to predict.

DB plans usually automatically protect individuals from longevity risk, while longevity protection relies on individual choice in DC plans. DB plans are usually paid out in the form of immediate life annuities, with employers bearing longevity risk and limited choice for individuals. DC plans often offer choice for the post-retirement product between lump sums, programmed withdrawals, annuities, or any combination of the above. Decisions about the post-retirement product require an understanding of the characteristics of the different products available and of longevity risk to be able to assess the implications for the individual's future standard of living during the whole retirement period. When choosing an annuity, people also need to figure out whether they want fixed-term or life annuities, single or joint, immediate or deferred, variable payments or fixed in nominal terms, and with or without guarantees. Moreover, individuals should also appreciate how interest rates at the time of retirement may impact their annuity payment.

Finally, individuals need greater awareness of fees charged by pension providers to administer pension accounts and manage assets in DC than in DB plans. In DB plans, plan members have a promise on the level of pension they will receive and employers usually cover the costs of running the pension plan, meaning costs and fees do not directly affect retirement benefits. By contrast, in DC plans, fees have a direct adverse impact on retirement income. People need to realise that even a difference in fees charged of a few basis points can translate into large differences in assets accumulated at the end of the career.

5.2. Decision-making for retirement is complicated by behavioural biases and low levels of financial knowledge

Given the growing importance of funded pension arrangements, and especially DC plans, in retirement-income provision across most OECD countries, individuals are required more and more to take responsibility for their retirement planning. However, most individuals may not be able or prepared to assume this role. A combination of lack of general financial knowledge and awareness of risk, poor pension-specific knowledge, as well as behavioural biases undermines people's ability to make appropriate decisions for their retirement.

Low levels of financial literacy are prevalent in many countries. Financial literacy is a broad concept that the OECD International Network on Financial Education (INFE) defines as "a combination of awareness, knowledge, skill, attitude and behaviour necessary to make sound financial decisions and ultimately achieve individual financial wellbeing". Cross-comparable data from 30 countries and economies show that overall levels of financial literacy are relatively low, with an average score of 13.2 out of a maximum of 21 (OECD, 2016[4]). On average, only 56% of adults achieve the minimum target score on financial knowledge, with significant differences by gender, as 61% of men achieve the minimum target score, compared to 51% of women. The study identifies budgeting, planning ahead, choosing products and using independent advice as weaknesses in financial behaviour. The analysis reveals low levels of understanding of basic principles relating to retirement savings, such as compound interest and risk diversification.

People's knowledge, understanding and engagement with pensions also tend to be low. In the United Kingdom for example, the 2017 Financial Conduct Authority's Financial Lives Survey reveals that 32% of DC plan members do not know the size of their pension savings. This share is reduced to 26% for people aged 55 and over and not retired. Less than 20% of people aged 35 to 44 have thought seriously about how they will manage financially in retirement. This increases to 35% of 45-54 year olds and 55% of 55 and over and not retired. Finally, most people (81%) with a DC pension state they have not given much thought to how much they should contribute to maintain a reasonable standard of living when they retire. In Germany, households with low education, low income and less financial knowledge did not adjust their retirement behaviour or enrol themselves in complementary pension arrangements following 20 years of reforms that gradually reduced the generosity of public pension benefits (Börsch-Supan et al., 2015[5]).

Behavioural biases can cause people to misjudge important facts or to be inconsistent over time. Behavioural biases "refer to the systematic, and most often unconscious, deviations from a strict economic model of rationality that many people exhibit in the face of (economic) decisions" (Lefevre and Chapman, 2017[6]). They can be categorised according to the drivers of the decision that is affected: preferences, beliefs and decision-making processes (Table 5.1).

Table 5.1. Classification of behavioural biases related to retail financial services

Category	Bias	Description
Preferences	Present bias or hyperbolic discounting	People respond to urges for immediate gratification resulting in overvaluing the present over the future. As such, choices may be regretted in the future. Present bias can lead to self-control problems such as procrastination.
	Reference dependence and loss aversion	When evaluating a product or future prospects, people do not think of the choice or product in isolation. Instead they assess it with respect to changes relative to a reference point, thinking in terms of gains and losses from that reference point. Preferences may therefore change when the reference point changes. In addition, psychologically, losses are felt roughly twice as much as gains of the same magnitude. Loss aversion may lead to the endowment effect (valuing a good more just because the individual owns it), a preference for the status quo and distortions in attitudes to risk.
	Regret and other emotions	People avoid choice or are willing to pay for products just to avoid making a decision that they may come to regret. They may also shy away from ambiguity, uncertainty or stress even if making a choice is likely to result in a positive outcome for them. Their choices can also be distorted by temporary strong emotions (e.g. fear).
Beliefs	Overconfidence	People can show overconfidence about the likelihood of good events occurring or their own ability and success at different tasks, including the accuracy of their judgements.
	Over-extrapolation	People often make predictions on the basis of only a few observations, when these observations are not representative. As a result, people also underestimate uncertainty.
	Projection bias	People expect their current tastes and preferences to continue in the future and underestimate the possibility of change.
Decision making	Mental accounting and narrow bracketing	Mental accounting describes how people treat money or assets differently according to the specific purpose that they have assigned to them, instead of treating all money as the same. Narrow bracketing describes how people often consider the decisions they take in isolation, without integrating these decisions with other decisions that affect their overall wealth and level of risk they take on.
	Framing, salience and limited attention	People may react differently to essentially the same choice situation because the problem is framed differently. Frames usually work by triggering a particular bias (e.g. loss aversion, reference dependence, regret, a rule of thumb), as certain information is made more salient and limited attention is paid to other factors.
	Decision-making rules of thumb	Consumers simplify complex decision problems by adopting specific rules of thumb (heuristics). When choosing from a wide range of options, people may choose the most familiar, avoid the most ambiguous or uncertain, choose what draws attention most (e.g. the first option on a list), or avoid choice, including sticking to the status quo. When estimating unknown quantities, people may anchor estimates to some relevant or irrelevant figure and adjust from there.
	Persuasion and social influence	Emotions and norms in social interactions are important: consumers may allow themselves to be persuaded to buy a product just because the sales person is 'likeable' and therefore trustworthy. Emphasising good personality traits or overemphasising bad personality traits may substitute for a reasoned judgement. Consumers may also be influenced by usage patterns without adequately considering whether those apply to their own circumstances.

Source: (Financial Conduct Authority, 2013[7]).

Several behavioural biases particularly affect people when making decisions for retirement. First, *present bias* can be strong as saving for retirement is for the long term and may compete with short-term needs. Therefore, the combination of delayed benefits until retirement and small short-term costs (e.g. transaction costs, paperwork) can be a real barrier to action, potentially impeding participation in retirement savings plans. Second, financial products, and in particular retirement products, are complex. Individuals usually view making financial decisions as difficult, unpleasant and time-consuming. They often lack the motivation to invest time and effort in making informed decisions and cannot evaluate many products given their complexity. They are therefore more likely to rely on *simple rules of thumb* and be sensitive to *framing* and *persuasion*. Third, effective retirement decisions require sophisticated risk assessments (e.g. longevity and investment risks). Most people lack the skills, practice or intuition to assess risk and uncertainty when making important decisions. *Overconfidence* and *over-extrapolation* may therefore lead individuals to underestimate uncertainty and risk. Fourth, many financial decisions are emotional. *Emotions*, whether positive (like optimism or excitement) or negative (like stress, anxiety, fear and regret), can drive decisions rather than a logical cost/benefit analysis. Finally, it can be difficult to improve one's ability to deal with retirement products over time. Decisions related to retirement planning are made infrequently. The consequences of these decisions are often only revealed long after the decision has been made, with little opportunity to learn and correct past decisions. Because of *loss aversion* and fear of *regretting* one's decisions later on, people may therefore fail to act.

The key decisions that people need to make for their retirement at different stages of their lives are whether to participate in a pension plan, how much to contribute, how to choose the pension provider, how to invest, and how to choose the post-retirement product. Financial literacy, and in particular behavioural biases and low levels of financial knowledge, may affect those decisions in different ways. The following sections therefore cover each of those decisions separately. The analysis focuses on the design of funded pension arrangements, as they pose more challenges in decision-making for retirement than PAYG pensions. OECD and non-OECD jurisdictions have implemented different policies to address the implications of behavioural biases and low levels of financial knowledge that have improved the design of funded pension arrangements. These policies either simplify the decision-making process or aim to harness the power of behavioural biases to nudge people into acting in their own long-term interest.

5.3. Participation decision

How behavioural biases and low levels of financial knowledge affect the participation decision

Present bias or hyperbolic discounting is one of the main behavioural biases affecting participation in voluntary funded pension arrangements. Because of present bias, individuals fail to commit to save for retirement. Procrastination, myopia and inertia lead many individuals to postpone or avoid making the commitment to save for retirement even when they know that this is ultimately in their best interest. In addition, retirement planning competes with other short-term needs, especially at younger ages (e.g. buying a house, paying tuition fees, raising a family).

Saving for retirement involves making complex financial decisions. One potential consequence of this complexity is that individuals delay facing these decisions. For example, Iyengar, Jiang and Huberman (2004[8]) find that participation rates in 401(k) pension plans in the United States decline as the number of fund options increases. Other things equal, every ten options added is associated with a 1.5% to 2% drop in participation rates.

Additionally, many people seem to have a misperception of their retirement preparedness. As a result, they may fail to take action in case their future retirement income falls short of their expectations. For example, Munnell, Hou and Sanzenbacher (2017[9]) show that 43% of households in the United States have a misperception of their retirement readiness, with 24% of households reporting that they are inadequately prepared while the index calculated by the authors says they are not at risk and 19% of households being less worried than they should be about their retirement preparedness. Those people who do not realise that they are at risk of being financially unprepared for retirement are unlikely to remedy the situation. Moreover, Balasuriya, Gough and Vasileva (2014[10]) find that overconfidence is one of the most important factors explaining non-participation in pension plans.

Effective approaches to promote participation

Policies aiming to increase participation in voluntary funded pension arrangements, while addressing the issues posed by behavioural biases and low levels of financial knowledge, fall into four broad categories: changing the default enrolment mechanism (active decision, automatic enrolment or compulsion), simplifying choice, providing incentives, and providing financial education.

Changing the default enrolment mechanism

In voluntary pension systems, individuals must take a decision on whether or not to enrol in a pension plan. For most plans, individuals do not participate in a pension plan until they actively decide to opt in. Removing or changing that opt-in default mechanism may result in increased participation rates.

Requiring an active decision on whether or not to enrol in a plan may increase participation compared to opt-in enrolment. This mechanism requires employees to decide whether or not to participate in their employer occupational plan within a certain timeframe. Requiring employees to explicitly state an enrolment preference encourages them to think about an important decision and not procrastinate. However, under such an active decision mechanism, individuals have to deal with a potentially time-consuming and complex issue at a time which may be inconvenient. Carroll et al. (2009[11]) compare two kinds of 401(k) enrolment in the United States: opt-in enrolment (i.e. the default is not to participate) and active decisions (i.e. there is no default but rather a compulsory choice between participating or not). The authors find that compelling new hires to make active decisions about 401(k) participation within 30 days raises participation after three months of tenure by 28 percentage points relative to a standard opt-in enrolment. Keller et al. (2011[12]) suggest that using loss aversion together with the active decision mechanism, highlighting losses incurred by not joining (e.g. not getting the employer matching contribution), would increase participation even further. Benartzi et al. (2017[13]) show that this type of nudge is more cost effective than financial education, matching contribution and tax incentives.[5]

Automatic enrolment has gained popularity in the last decade. It involves signing people up automatically to a pension plan while giving them the chance to opt out with specified timeframes and conditions. The policy uses individual behavioural traits, such as inertia and procrastination, to keep people in a pension plan, as the default is to participate. At the same time, the opt-out option maintains individual choice and responsibility for the decision to participate in a pension plan. The popularity of this policy to increase participation in voluntary funded pension arrangements is growing. It was initially developed in U.S. private occupational pension plans as a way for employers to comply with non-discrimination rules, which condition the access to a preferential tax treatment for high-income earners on reaching minimum participation and contribution levels among low and middle-income earners. It is currently implemented in eight OECD countries: Canada, Chile (for self-employed workers), Germany, Italy, New Zealand, Turkey, the United Kingdom and the United States. Chile (for employees), Ireland, Lithuania and Poland may follow soon.[6] Table 5.2 describes the automatic enrolment schemes already in place.

Table 5.2. Description of automatic enrolment schemes

	Year of implementation	Mandatory for employers	Target population	Opting-out window	Contribution rates	Government financial incentives
Canada (1)	2014-2017	No, except in Quebec	Employees with at least 2 years of tenure	60 days	Employee: no minimum; Employer: voluntary	"EET" tax treatment
Chile	2012-2017		Self-employed workers	Submission of the income tax declaration	10% of covered earnings	"EET" tax treatment
Germany	2018	No	Private sector employees	Depend on agreement	Depends on agreement	"EET" tax treatment
Italy	2007	Yes	Private sector employees	6 months	Employee: voluntary; Employer: 6.91%	"ETT" tax treatment
New Zealand	2007	Yes	New employees aged 18 to 64	Between 2 and 8 weeks	Employee: 3% minimum; Employer: 3% minimum	50% matching contribution up to NZD 521.43; grants for homeownership
Turkey	2017	Yes	Employees younger than 45	2 months; re-enrolment every 2 years	Employee: 3% minimum; Employer: voluntary	one-time TRY 1 000 contribution; 25% matching contribution; subsidy equal to 5% of assets at retirement if 10-year annuity
United Kingdom	2012	Yes	Employees aged at least 22 and earning over GBP 10 000	1 month; re-enrolment every 3 years	From 2019, minimum 8%, including employer (3% minimum)	"EET" tax treatment
United States (2,3)	1998 (occupational plans)	No	New employees, potentially extended to all employees ("auto-sweep")	90 days	Depends on plan rules	"EET" or "TEE" tax treatment
	2017 (state auto-IRAs)	Yes in certain States	Private sector employees with no occupational plan coverage	Depends on state	Employee: depends on state; Employer: no contribution	"TEE" tax treatment

Note: "E" stands for exempt and "T" for taxed.

1. The Pooled Registered Pension Plan framework was introduced in 2012 at the federal level. So far, six provinces (British Columbia, Quebec, Manitoba, Nova Scotia, Ontario and Saskatchewan) have issued implementing regulations.

2. Employers in the United States have been able to use automatic enrolment basically from the start of occupational DC plans. In 1998, the Treasury and the Internal Revenue Service issued a ruling clarifying that automatic enrolment in 401(k) plans is permissible for newly hired employees.

3. As of 15 May 2018, five states have enacted auto-IRA programmes for private sector workers (California, Connecticut, Illinois, Maryland and Oregon). Only Oregon had implemented its programme at the time of writing this chapter.

There is clear evidence that automatic enrolment increases participation in occupational pension plans at the company level. In the United States, automatic enrolment is estimated to increase 401(k) participation by 35 to 67 percentage points relative to voluntary opt-in arrangements (Madrian and Shea, $2001_{[14]}$; Choi et al., $2001_{[15]}$; $2004_{[16]}$). In the United Kingdom, for eligible private sector employees, automatic enrolment led to an increase of 37 percentage points in the probability of participating in an occupational pension plan (Cribb and Emmerson, 2016[17]).

The success of automatic enrolment in raising overall participation at the country level cannot be taken for granted, however, and depends on several factors: the scale of implementation of the policy, the size of the target population, the presence of incentives, and the opt-out prevalence.

Overall participation rates are likely to be higher when offering a pension plan with automatic enrolment is mandatory for employers. The role of employers is essential in automatic enrolment schemes. In Italy, Canada (in the province of Quebec only), New Zealand, Turkey and the United Kingdom, employers are mandated to automatically enrol their employees into a pension plan (occupational or personal). By contrast, in Canada (in the provinces of British Columbia, Ontario, Manitoba, Nova Scotia and Saskatchewan), Germany and the United States, employers can voluntarily offer an occupational pension plan and implement automatic enrolment. This difference may have large implications for participation, as the success of the policy in the case of voluntary involvement from employers will depend on the proportion of employers offering an occupational pension plan and, among them, the proportion implementing automatic enrolment. For example, in the United States, participation in occupational pension plans has remained constant over the last decades despite the increased use of automatic enrolment by employers.[7] This is because the proportion of private sector workers being offered an occupational pension plan has stayed roughly at 50% since 1979 (Munnell, Belbase and Sanzenbacher, 2016[18]).

The target population of automatic enrolment schemes usually excludes the self-employed. The only exception is Chile, where the automatic enrolment policy between 2012 and 2017 was specifically directed at certain categories of self-employed workers.[8] In the other countries, only employees can be automatically enrolled. This restriction excludes an increasing share of the workforce.[9] In Canada, New Zealand and the United Kingdom, self-employed workers can voluntarily join the schemes directly with a plan provider. This may not be sufficient however to reach high participation rates among these workers.

Other criteria may restrict the size of the target population of automatic enrolment schemes, such as age, earnings and tenure in the company. A minimum entry age exists in New Zealand (18) and the United Kingdom (22). There are discussions in the United Kingdom to reduce the age limit to 18 years old, acknowledging the fact that people should start contributing as early as possible in order to accumulate significant pension assets. An earnings limit of GBP 10 000 is in place in the United Kingdom.[10] The rational is to exclude people for whom pension contributions may not be affordable. Unfortunately, this may lead to the exclusion of employees with multiple jobs who do not meet the criteria for automatic enrolment in any individual job although they could afford contributing to a pension plan. Finally, the impact of the policy on overall participation rates is likely to be lower when only newly hired employees are automatically enrolled. This applies in New Zealand and the United States, although in the United States, more and more plans with automatic enrolment extend the policy to all employees (Vanguard, 2017[19]).

Countries can offer financial incentives to encourage automatically enrolled workers to stay enrolled and minimise opt-out rates, but also to nudge people outside the target population of the automatic enrolment scheme to voluntarily opt in. Financial incentives include employer contributions (Italy, New Zealand, the United Kingdom and the United

States), tax incentives in the form of a favourable tax treatment compared to other savings vehicles (Canada, Chile, Germany, Italy, the United Kingdom and the United States), and non-tax financial incentives in the form of government matching contributions and fixed nominal subsidies paid in the pension account (New Zealand and Turkey).

Early withdrawals and contribution holidays can also be viewed as incentives to encourage people to stay in the scheme. Early partial withdrawals may be allowed to face financial hardship or serious illness, or to buy a home. It may however divert too much money that was initially intended to finance retirement and negatively affect future retirement income adequacy. Canada, Italy, New Zealand and the United States allow for early withdrawals under certain conditions.[11] Similarly, allowing contributions holidays can reassure savers that they can temporarily stop contributing in case other expenses come along. However, it can also raise adequacy concerns, unless individuals increase their contributions to fill the gap afterwards. This option is available in New Zealand.

Overall, financial incentives may represent an important motivation to join or remain in a pension plan once automatically enrolled. According to a 2010 survey of KiwiSaver members in New Zealand, some of the most commonly reported reasons for joining the plan were the government payments (67% of respondents), the employer contributions (56%), the mechanisms facilitating the purchase of a home (24%), and the contribution holidays (12%) (Inland Revenue, 2015[20]).[12]

Opt-out rates vary greatly across countries. These rates, jointly with participation rates, can provide a measure to assess the success of automatic enrolment. Self-employed workers in Chile opt out in large numbers, with on average 75% deciding not to contribute to individual retirement accounts each year. Preliminary information for Turkey suggests opt-out rates of around 60%. Large opt-out rates can also be inferred for Italy as, by the end of 2016, members automatically enrolled only represented around 6% of new membership of private sector workers since 2007 (COVIP, 2017[21]). At the other extreme are New Zealand and the United Kingdom. As of June 2017, 17% of all employees automatically enrolled in KiwiSaver plans had opted out and remained out of the scheme. In the United Kingdom, around 10% of people currently opt out of their workplace pension.[13] The length of the opting-out window may have an impact on opt-out rates, but there is no empirical evidence demonstrating whether shorter windows reduce opt-out rates or not.

People who opt out tend to be in younger or older age groups and have lower earnings and less stable employment (Inland Revenue, 2015[20]; Department for Work and Pensions, 2013[22]; 2014[23]). The main reason for opting out is being financially constrained. Older workers may also feel that retirement is too close to consider saving for retirement or that they already have sufficient savings. Preference for other forms of savings may also prompt people to opt out.

Opt-out rates may be larger when other incentives compete and interact negatively with the introduction of automatic enrolment. In Italy for example, automatic enrolment into a private pension fund is competing with the previously existing TFR system (*Trattamento di Fine Rapporto*). Private sector workers have to choose whether the future flows of severance pay contributions (set at 6.91% of salary) remain in the firm or are transferred to a pension plan. As both employers and employees highly value the TFR system, it creates an incentive to opt out of the pension arrangement (Rinaldi, 2011[24]). In Turkey, automatic enrolment supplements existing pension provision. Employees already contributing to a personal pension plan, that already enjoys the government matching contribution, may not want to cumulate both schemes.

Re-enrolling workers who have opted out may help bring opt-out rates down. In Turkey and the United Kingdom, employers are required to re-enrol their eligible workers who chose to opt out or cease membership at regular intervals (every two and three years, respectively). This gives employees the opportunity to think again about their finances and pension savings options in case their situation has changed since they decided to opt out. Early results in the United Kingdom show that around 60% of employees working for medium employers and 45% of employees working for large employers, who originally stopped saving and have been automatically re-enrolled, are now saving into an occupational pension plan (Department for Work and Pensions, 2017[25]). This re-enrolment system however also implies an additional burden on employers who have to keep track of each employee's membership status, re-assess the eligibility of employees who opted out or ceased membership, and automatically re-enrol them.

Finally, compulsory enrolment is ultimately the most effective policy in reaching high and uniformly distributed coverage rates (OECD, 2012[26]). Under compulsion, all eligible individuals have to participate in a pension plan, without the option to opt out. Compulsion addresses the issues posed by procrastination, myopia and inertia, ensuring that individuals save for retirement and start saving early in their career.

However, compulsion has its limitations. It may be difficult to implement, because mandatory contributions could be perceived as another tax. Moreover, people may perceive the level of compulsory contribution as the one endorsed by policy makers and therefore as adequate, potentially leading to lower contribution rates than what would have been saved voluntarily. In addition, when there is already a mandatory public pension arrangement, participation in a complementary funded pension arrangement may not be beneficial for all individuals. If low-income workers can expect high replacement rates from the public pension system, forcing them to contribute may not be justified as it may lead them to become more indebted or divert funds from other necessary expenses, such as children's education or housing. Finally, compulsory enrolment is of limited effectiveness when the informal sector is large and people shun paying mandatory pension contributions.

Simplifying choice

Simplifying the enrolment process, in particular by using default mechanisms, can increase participation in funded pension arrangements. In 2010, the single most popular reason for joining KiwiSaver was that it was an easy way to save, as reported by 77% of KiwiSaver members (Inland Revenue, 2015[20]). The features that make it easy to join KiwiSaver are the default mechanisms (automatic enrolment, default contribution rate and default provider), as well as the fact that it is administered by the employer, with deductions made at source.

Using default options for the contribution rate and the investment strategy can reduce choice overload and simplify the decision about whether to participate in a pension plan. In the United States, some employers have voluntarily tested an alternative form of enrolment to traditional opt-in programmes (i.e. the default is not to participate) and automatic enrolment (i.e. the default is to participate) called Quick Enrollment™. This programme gives workers the option of enrolling in the 401(k) plan provided by their employer by opting into a pre-set default contribution rate and asset allocation. The goal of this policy is to reduce complexity. Instead of evaluating all possible contribution rate and asset allocation options, employees just face a binary choice between participating based on the default options provided by the programme and not participating. Studies show that Quick Enrollment results in substantial 401(k) participation increases, although typically smaller than automatic enrolment (Choi, Laibson and Madrian, 2009[27]; Beshears et al., 2013[28]). They also find that the participation increases produced by Quick Enrollment are durable and that employees who join the pension plan in this way often remain at the default contribution rate and asset allocation for years.

Providing incentives

Financial incentives for retirement savings reduce the cost of saving and therefore encourage people to save in pension arrangements rather than to consume or save in other types of vehicle. Even when people know that saving for retirement is in their own best interest, present bias represents a real barrier to action. People need extra motivation to put money aside for retirement. Financial incentives harness individuals' tendency to respond to immediate gratification to encourage them to save for retirement. Loss aversion can also be a driver of taking advantage of financial incentives, in particular employer and government contributions, if people do not want to "leave money on the table" by not joining a pension plan or contributing below a certain level.

Financial incentives, tax and non-tax, are effective in promoting retirement savings (see Chapter 2). Tax incentives arise from deviating from the typical tax treatment of savings (i.e. contribute from after-tax earnings, pay tax on the investment income and withdraw money tax free). Allowing individuals to deduct pension contributions from taxable income encourages participation in retirement savings plans for middle-to-high income earners, because individuals respond to the upfront tax relief on contributions that reduces their current tax liability. Low-income earners, however, are less sensitive to tax incentives, because of insufficient income to afford contributions, insufficient tax liability to fully enjoy tax reliefs and lack of understanding of tax-related issues. Nevertheless, if low-to-middle income earners do respond to tax incentives, they are more likely to increase their overall savings, while high-income individuals tend to reallocate their savings. Non-tax incentives are payments made by the government or the employer directly in the pension account of eligible individuals. They include matching contributions and fixed nominal subsidies. These incentives increase participation in retirement savings plans, especially among low-income earners.

Tax incentives are, however, difficult to understand, potentially leading individuals to misjudge them and fail to pick the most appropriate tax regime when choice is provided. For example, some occupational plans in the United States provide choice between taxation upon withdrawal ("EET" tax regime, e.g. traditional 401(k)) and upfront taxation ("TEE" tax regime, e.g. Roth 401(k)). Beshears et al. (2017[29]) show that less than half of DC plan participants surveyed online respond correctly to questions related to the tax rules of Roth and traditional 401(k) plans.

In addition, behavioural biases may lead to a different perception of the "EET" and "TEE" tax treatments. Contributions to plans with taxation upon withdrawal ("EET") immediately reduce the participant's income tax due. Plans with upfront taxation ("TEE") do not provide tax relief today. Because of present bias, individuals may want to secure the tax advantage earlier rather than later and therefore prefer taxation upon withdrawal. Other behavioural factors could lead individuals to prefer upfront taxation. For example, Cuccia, Doxey and Stinson (2017[30]) show that uncertainty may lead to anxiety and influence plan choice. Plans with taxation upon withdrawal may be perceived as more uncertain than plans with upfront taxation because the amount of taxes that will be due on withdrawals is unknown, as tax rates may change, as well as the individual's economic status. Behavioural biases and low levels of financial knowledge may therefore lead some individuals to fail to choose the plan with the tax treatment that would provide them with the largest overall tax advantage.

Attractive product features can also be provided to encourage participation. Allowing participants to access their funds before retirement or to temporarily stop making contributions have already been discussed above in the context of automatic enrolment. Providing investment return guarantees is another possibility.

Investment return guarantees alleviate the impact of market risk on retirement income by setting a floor on the value of accumulated assets at retirement, either in nominal or real terms. They provide some predictability in the savings phase with respect to future pension benefits. They may increase the attractiveness of saving for retirement in DC pension plans as they overcome people's fear of losing the nominal value of their contributions. However, their need should be assessed in the context of the overall pension system, as other mechanisms, such as public pensions' automatic stabilisers and old-age safety nets, may already provide a floor or minimum income at retirement.

Investment return guarantees have to be paid for, and this cost reduces the expected value of benefits from DC plans relative to a situation where there are no guarantees (OECD, 2012[31]). The cost of the capital guarantee, that makes sure that people will get back at least their contributions (in nominal terms), is affordable over sufficiently long holding periods. Guarantees above the capital guarantee may be too costly, however. In addition, in the current environment of low interest rates, investment return guarantees require higher technical provisions, meaning that the investment opportunities of the pension providers are limited to investment products with lower risk and thereby lower expected returns. Lower risk eases the pressure on solvency, but eventually, lower expected returns can make it difficult for pension providers to generate returns that are sufficient to provide a good retirement income. Some countries are therefore moving away from investment return guarantees, such as the Czech Republic, Denmark and Germany.

Providing financial education

Policy makers increasingly recognise the role of financial education in supporting individuals to plan for their retirement. OECD (2016[2]) summarises the different financial education tools used in different jurisdictions to address various financial education needs in relation to retirement planning. These can be split into three broad categories:

- Information and awareness: this includes general information on retirement options through websites, awareness campaigns covering retirement issues, comparison tools presenting plan features in a standardised way, personalised pension statements, access to personal information online, as well as calculators and simulators;
- Instruction: this takes the form of seminars and workshops about retirement planning, helping participants acquire financial knowledge and skills relevant for retirement, explaining the risks that individuals may be exposed to and suggesting how to manage them, and helping individuals estimate their retirement income needs;
- Advice: this ranges from factual information to fully personalised advice.

Evidence on the effectiveness of financial education for retirement is currently limited but suggests that instruction at the workplace can be effective in increasing enrolment in occupational pension plans (Atkinson et al., 2015[32]). For instance, Duflo and Saez

(2003[33]) studied a university that encouraged a random sample of its employees to attend to an annual event providing information on benefits, including an occupational pension plan. They found that 5 to 11 months after the event, plan participation was higher in treated departments (i.e. those where a random sample of employees received an invitation letter promising a reward for attending the event) than in control departments. Collins and Urban (2016[34]) show that online financial education courses offered to employees increase self-reported IRA participation by six percentage points. Anderson and Collins (2017[35]) find that a multi-media education effort towards women, providing information through emails, webinars and live events, reduces the gender gap in participation in retirement savings plans.

Providing more information on the employer's pension plan and how to join it can also increase participation. Clark, Maki and Morrill (2014[36]) find that young employees (18 to 24 years old) who received a flyer containing information about their employer's 401(k) plan and the value of contributions compounding over a career, were more likely to begin contributing to the plan compared to workers of a similar age that did not receive the flyer. Lusardi, Keller and Keller (2009[37]) study the impact of helping employees form and implement a savings plan through the provision of a planning aid that (a) encourages individuals to set aside a specific time for enrolling in their savings plan, (b) outlines the steps involved in enrolling in the plan (e.g., choosing a contribution rate and an asset allocation), (c) gives an approximation of the time each step will take, and (d) provides tips on what to do if individuals get stuck. This planning aid increased enrolment in the occupational pension plan by 12 to 21 percentage points for newly hired employees.

However, not all types of information lead to increased participation in retirement savings plans. For example, Beshears et al. (2015[38]) show that information about peers' saving behaviour may discourage participation by generating "oppositional reaction". The authors conducted a field experiment to assess the impact on retirement savings choices of disseminating information about what a target population's peer usually do. The expectation was that individuals may realise that participating in their employer's 401(k) plan is more common than they had previously believed among their co-workers, and thereby that social influence would motivate them to enrol in the plan. In fact, the results show that the presence of peer information decreased the likelihood of subsequently enrolling in the plan, especially among employees with relatively lower income. This result suggests that information about peers' savings choices may discourage low-income employees by making their relative economic status more salient, reducing their motivation to increase their retirement savings.

5.4. How much to contribute

How behavioural biases and low levels of financial knowledge affect the level of contribution

People have to figure out how much money they will need in retirement in order to determine how much they should put aside to cover those needs. Determining the appropriate contribution rate is mostly relevant for DC pension arrangements, as in DB plans members usually have no choice regarding the contribution level and their benefits are pre-determined according to a formula. In mandatory systems, the contribution rate is determined by regulation but people need to assess whether they need to complement it with voluntary contributions. In voluntary systems, people can usually choose how much they want to contribute, although some minimum may be prescribed by regulation. In any case, people need the numeracy and financial skills to assess whether their contributions will translate into an income that will cover their needs in retirement. That assessment should be done given the level of retirement income that may be expected from the public pension system, which requires a good level of understanding of the rules used to compute public pension benefits. Unfortunately, behavioural biases affect this assessment.

The main behavioural biases affecting how much people contribute in DC pension arrangements are self-control, use of simple heuristics, projection bias and loss aversion.

Saving for retirement requires self-control. When surveyed about their low savings rates, many households report that they would like to save more but lack the willpower. For example, Choi et al. (2001[15]) report that 67.7% of their sample of 401(k) participants think that their contribution rate is "too low." However, procrastination makes them postpone action to increase their contribution rate. Among self-reported under-savers, 35% expressed an intention to increase their contribution rate in the next few months, but only 14% of this subgroup actually increased their contribution rate in the four months following the survey. People tend not to follow through on their good intentions. For the same reason, people automatically enrolled tend to stick to the default contribution rate for long periods, even when this default is not the optimal rate for them (Choi et al., 2004[16]).

There are no satisfactory heuristics that could help people approximate a good contribution rate. The most common heuristics in place appear to be to save the maximum allowed by law to get tax incentives or to save the minimum necessary to receive the full matching contribution offered by the employer or the state. Neither of these amounts, however, was most likely computed to be the most appropriate contribution rate for everyone.

Projection bias may also interfere with the contribution level chosen by individuals. People may indeed underestimate how much income they will need during retirement if they base their assessment on their current needs and preferences or if they underestimate their life expectancy. They may underestimate the fact that their preferences and circumstances may change when they get older and therefore fail to save enough for retirement.

Finally, loss aversion affects savings. Many studies show that people have the tendency to weigh losses significantly more heavily than gains (Kahneman and Tversky, 1979[39]). Losses hurt roughly twice as much as gains yield pleasure. Once people get used to a particular level of disposable income, they tend to view reductions in that level as a loss. Thus people may be reluctant to increase their contributions to their private pension plan because they do not want to experience a cut in take-home pay.

Effective approaches to promote appropriate contribution levels

The appropriate contribution rate to pay into a funded pension arrangement depends on the target retirement income, the risks involved in saving for retirement, and the risk aversion of the individual. Retirement income in DC pensions is uncertain and depends on the level of contributions, the contribution period and other unpredictable parameters such as life expectancy, investment returns, discount rates, and spells of unemployment. The larger the contribution rate, the higher the probability of reaching a given target retirement income for a given contribution period. For example, according to OECD calculations, a contribution rate of just below 13% over 40 years is needed to reach a target replacement rate of 30% with a 95% probability (OECD, 2016[40]). With a contribution rate of 7.75% the likelihood to reach that 30% target falls to 75%. Individuals therefore need to be aware that a given contribution rate may not be sufficient to reach their target retirement income in all circumstances.

Policies helping individuals to contribute at the appropriate level given their individual circumstances, while addressing the issues posed by behavioural biases and low levels of financial knowledge, include setting default contribution rates at higher levels than current practice, automatically increasing contribution rates over time, providing matching contributions, simplifying the contribution process and providing information about expected pension benefits.

Setting default contribution rates at high levels

Default contribution rates are a typical feature of automatic enrolment schemes to simplify the decision about whether to participate in a pension plan. To minimise opt-out rates, they are usually set well below 13%. The total minimum contribution rate is 6% in New Zealand (3% from employees and 3% from employers), 3% in Turkey (only from employees) and will reach 8% in the United Kingdom as of April 2019 (5% from employees and 3% from employers). In 2016, 52% of automatic enrolment plans managed by Vanguard in the United States had a default contribution rate of 3% or less (Vanguard, 2017[19]). Goldin, Homonoff and Tucker-Ray (2017[41]) show that more U.S. military service members chose to participate in the Thrift Savings Plan when the default contribution rate was low (1-2%) rather than medium (3-5%) or high (6-8%). Therefore, the current design of automatic enrolment schemes may not be conducive to contribution rates that allow people reaching their target retirement income.

Moreover, individuals tend to stick with default contribution rates even when they are too low to reach a target replacement rate. Default options in general reduce individuals' engagement regarding retirement planning. Because of inertia and procrastination, individuals may fail to consider other options in the presence of a default and remain in sub-optimal arrangements. Research suggests that some individuals who remained with the default contribution rate would have chosen a higher savings rate in the absence of automatic enrolment (Madrian and Shea, 2001[14]; Choi et al., 2004[16]).

Higher defaults may increase contribution rates without harming participation. Relative to a 6% default contribution rate, Beshears et al. (2017[42]) show that setting up higher defaults (from 7% to 11%), while leaving the possibility to the individual to select another contribution rate, increases average selected contribution rates 60 days after a website visit by 20 to 50 basis points of pay, without a decline in participation rates, except for the highest default (11%). The average selected contribution rates for the 7% and 11% defaults were not statistically different from one another, showing that employees did not seem to unthinkingly accept high defaults.

Default contribution rates are not a panacea, however, when they apply to a large number of people with heterogeneous needs and preferences. Default options are designed for an average or reference individual and therefore may not be optimal when they apply to individuals with highly heterogeneous situations. For example, a single contribution rate may not be appropriate for prime age workers and older workers. The former may be financially constrained because they face other important expenses (e.g. mortgages, education), while the latter may be worried about their retirement and willing to save more. In this context, it may be appropriate to have contribution rates increasing as people age (Blake, Wright and Zhang, 2014[43]). However, one needs to be careful about potential time inconsistency issues as contribution rates may need to reach extremely high levels at the end of one's career in order to attain the same target retirement income (OECD, 2012[44]).

Automatically increasing contribution rates

Automatically increasing contribution rates is an alternative way to the standard single rate for setting up default contribution rates. People can commit to future increases, preferably linked to wage increases, or can agree on immediate contribution increases.

Higher contribution rates can be achieved by allowing people to commit to future increases in the contribution rate. For example, Thaler and Benartzi (2004[45]) introduced Save More Tomorrow™ ("SMarT") in private occupational pension plans in the United States. The objective is to build on people's awareness of their own tendency to procrastinate and help those who would like to save more but lack the willpower to act on this desire. Employees have the option of committing themselves in advance to increasing their contribution rate in the future, with increases happening each time the individual gets a pay raise. This feature mitigates the perceived loss aversion of a cut in take-home pay and avoids the affordability issue of increased contributions for low-income earners. The contribution rate continues to increase on each scheduled salary increase until the contribution rate reaches a pre-set maximum. In this way, inertia and status quo bias work towards keeping people in the plan. The employee can opt out of the automatic escalation at any time. Results show that SMarT participants almost quadrupled their contribution rates over the course of 40 months, from 3.5% to 13.6% on average.[14]

Making it easy to increase contribution rates can also achieve positive outcomes. For example, Easy Escalation™ allows employees already participating in a pension plan to increase their contribution rate to a pre-selected level. The principle is that employees already participating in the company pension plan and whose contribution rate is below 6% receive a form in which they just need to tick a box to increase their total contribution rate to the 6% threshold. Beshears et al. (2013[28]) find that about 15% of low contributors who received an Easy Escalation form raised their contribution rate to the pre-selected threshold, compared to only about 1% of those who did not receive the form.

Providing matching contributions

Employer matching contributions encourage participation in occupational pension plans and can also be seen as a way to promote employee contributions. As the employer contribution is defined as a ratio of the employee's own contribution, the more the employee contributes, the higher the employer's contribution will be, up to a limit.

A higher match rate does not necessarily lead to a higher employee contribution. Choi (2015[46]) and Madrian (2013[47]) show that the empirical evidence in the United States on the impact of employer match rate on total contributions is mixed. Some studies find a positive relationship between the match rate and contributions, others find no relationship and yet other studies find a negative relationship. By contrast, when the Australian government reduced the match rate and the maximum entitlement by half in its super co-contribution programme in 2012, the number of beneficiaries and the co-contributions payments dropped by 40% and 60% respectively the following year.

However, increasing the rate of employee contribution up to the rate at which the employer offers the match - the match threshold - may have a positive impact on employee contributions. Choi et al. (2001[15]) study a company with a 50% match rate that increased its match threshold from 5% to 7% of income for union workers and from 6% to 8% of income for management employees. They observe an immediate change in the distribution of employee contribution rates, with the proportion of participants contributing between 7% and 8% increasing.

Simplifying the contribution process

Simplifying the contribution process may increase voluntary savings, in particular in personal pension systems. Individuals may find it difficult to save for retirement without the involvement of employers. Mexico introduced a new strategy to promote voluntary savings in the pension system to encourage all types of worker, formal and informal, to save for retirement. The strategy includes more and better information for people through communication campaigns and websites, a network of more than 7 000 convenience stores all around the country where people can deposit voluntary savings, the use of debit cards to save a proportion of spending through an application, and the launch of an application where people can have access to many services, including opening a pension account and saving online. The results are promising so far, with the balance of voluntary savings growing on average by 33% annually since 2014.

Sending reminders can also improve savings. Reminders provide associations between future expenditures and today's choices. They can thus help to mitigate present bias. For example, Karlan et al. (2016[48]) compare the savings patterns of individuals in three different banks in Bolivia, Peru, and the Philippines. Those who received a monthly reminder via text message or letter saved 6% more than those who did not. Reminders also made individuals 3 percentage points more likely to reach their savings goal by the end of the commitment period.

Providing information about expected benefits

Salient information about retirement and expected benefits can also increase contributions to private pension arrangements. For example, since 2004, the German pension authority has sent out annual letters which provide detailed and clear information about the pension system in general as well as the individual's expected pension payments. The letters also highlight the importance of additional voluntary retirement savings. Using tax return data from administrative records, Dolls et al. (2016[49]) find that receiving the letter increases contributions to a Riester pension plan.

Personalised information, as opposed to general information, could encourage people to increase contributions. Fuentes et al. (2017[50]) show the results of randomly giving low- to middle-income workers in Chile either personalised or generalised information regarding their pension savings. Individuals in the treatment group received a personalised estimate of their expected pension under different scenarios. Individuals in the control group received comparable general information and recommendations on how to improve their future pensions, but without any reference to their individual situation. Compared to the control group, the level of voluntary savings of individuals who received personalised information was 14% higher on average during the 6 months following the intervention. The positive effect of personalised information was not permanent however, with no difference in the level of voluntary savings between the two groups after nine months.

Finally, calculators and simulators can facilitate the estimation of the contribution rate needed to cover people's needs in retirement and reduce the difficulties related to lack of numeracy. By providing forward-looking information under different scenarios, they make the long-term benefit of saving more salient and improve awareness of the link between contributions and retirement income (OECD, 2016[2]). In addition, they usually allow users to assess how their retirement income would change if they change their expectation regarding the retirement age or the contribution rate for example, or if external parameters (e.g. rate of return, inflation) change. Moreover, by combining information about the different sources of retirement income (e.g. public and private), simulators and calculators help people realise whether their overall target replacement rate can realistically be achieved given their current saving behaviour. Such calculators are available for instance in Chile, Latvia, Mexico, the Netherlands, the United Kingdom and the United States.

5.5. Choice of the pension provider

How behavioural biases and low levels of financial knowledge affect the choice of the pension provider

Participants in private pension plans are expected to choose the pension provider that best fits their needs. This choice should be driven, among others, by comparing the services offered, the long-term performance, and the fees charged. Comparing pension providers, however, takes time and effort. In addition, behavioural biases and low levels of financial knowledge affect how people choose, which could lead to lower competition between pension providers and ultimately increase costs and fees and reduce future retirement incomes.

People may lack the skills to compare pension providers and choose the best one for them, in particular when many providers are available (choice overload) and pricing practices are complex. For example, when pension providers use different fee structures, it becomes difficult for individuals to compare pension plans. This is the case in Latvia, Poland, the Slovak Republic and Slovenia for example, where some private pension funds can use a mix of asset-based and contribution-based fees.

Behavioural biases may create or strengthen market power in what would otherwise be a competitive market (Financial Conduct Authority, 2013[7]). Because of procrastination and inertia, pension plan members tend to stick with their existing provider, do not shop around, do not compare providers based on their most critical characteristics, and do not switch to better providers. For example, in Mexico, weak member engagement and understanding reduced the effectiveness of two traditional competition policies: increasing the number of providers and allowing people to switch between providers. These policies have actually led to higher costs and less competition. In the United Kingdom, in 2012, 60% of individuals purchased an annuity with their existing provider, even though an estimated 80% of these individuals could have gotten a better deal elsewhere (Financial Conduct Authority, 2014[51]).

Finally, framing, persuasion and simplistic rules of thumb may guide individuals' choice of the pension provider rather than thorough analyses of the providers' most critical characteristics. Individuals may not choose the appropriate provider if they focus on the information highlighted by pension providers and underweight or ignore the non-salient, but potentially important, pieces of information. In addition, individuals may choose a specific provider because they know the brand name of the management company, because the sales person was nice to them, or because that provider was first in the list of options.

Effective approaches to facilitate provider choice

Competition between pension providers may not be effective because of behavioural biases and low levels of financial knowledge. Approaches facilitating provider choice while strengthening competition include defaulting people into providers chosen through a tender mechanism and enhancing information disclosure and standardisation. These policies need to be complemented by measures improving efficiency in the pension industry, so that individuals can expect good value for money independently of the choice of the provider.

Selecting default providers through tender mechanisms

Chile and New Zealand have introduced tender mechanisms to strengthen competition and reduce fees paid by members. There are a number of differences between the two systems. First, the number of providers selected at the end of each tender is different. Only one is selected in Chile, while several are in New Zealand (six in 2007, nine in 2014). Second, the provider winning the tender receives all new members of the pension system in Chile. In contrast, winning providers in New Zealand become default providers and only receive individuals not choosing their provider and working with an employer who has not designated a scheme.[15] Third, the period covered by the tender is longer in New Zealand, seven years, as opposed to two years in Chile. Fourth, there are more criteria to decide the tender for KiwiSaver default providers. The basic criteria for selecting default providers are investment capability, corporate strength, administrative capability, track record, stability, and fee levels. The 2014 tender also included a new criterion which requires providers to offer investor education to default members. In Chile, the tender only focuses on the fee charged to plan members.

Tender mechanisms are effective at driving average fees down but heterogeneity may persist across providers. In Chile, fees are charged on the salary. The weighted average fee charged to plan members has declined since the tender mechanism has been in place, from 1.49% of salary in 2009 to 1.19% in 2017.[16] For a typical NZD 7 000 balance in KiwiSaver default funds, the average total annual fee declined from NZD 69 for the period 2007-2014 to NZD 56 for the period 2014-2021. However, fee differences across pension providers are significant, especially in Chile. In January 2018, fees charged to plan members varied from 0.41% of salary to 1.48%. Since the tender mechanism has been in place, most pension providers have kept their fees at high levels or just moderately reduced them. Therefore, providers not winning the tender do not seem to feel pressure to reduce their fees. This may be due to the fact that inertia keeps plan members with their provider and prevents them from switching to cheaper providers.

Tender mechanisms need to include a range of criteria to be truly effective, not just fee levels. In Chile, the last two tenders were won by Planvital, the provider that was initially the most expensive; it reduced its fees from 2.36% to 0.47% of salary to win the 2014 tender. There are concerns that this provider may have offered a fee that is insufficient to cover its operating costs, increasing the solvency risk of the firm and compromising the quality of the services offered to members, including fund returns. This predatory pricing may also explain why the number of providers participating in the tender declined from four in 2010 to only one in 2016 and none in 2018.[17] In August 2018, Planvital increased its fees to 1.16% of salary, confirming that the previous fee level was not viable. In New Zealand, the government uses a range of criteria to evaluate the offers on top of fee levels, including the provider's organisational and investment capabilities. The number of default providers increased from six to nine between the two tenders, suggesting no predatory behaviour.

Enhancing disclosure

Enhanced disclosure primarily aims to encourage plan participants to react to differences in cost and fee levels. The Danish government-backed site www.pensionsinfo.dk provides individuals with comprehensive information about their own pension accounts including direct and indirect administration and investment costs and past returns. The 2015 Communications Act in the Netherlands requires schemes to provide standardised information to their members. Individual pension statements in Mexico include information on fees paid by the worker and compare net-of-fees returns across pension funds. In the United States, participant disclosure regulation 404(a) requires plan sponsors to ensure that participants and beneficiaries receive sufficient information on fees, expenses and performance to make informed investment decisions.

Simplified disclosures can help plan members switch to better providers. Thorp et al. (2017[52]) investigated whether simpler information on fees and investment returns helps plan members in Australia switch to a better pension provider. For both fees and returns, simplified information increased the proportion of people switching. Participants to the experiment reacted to changes in fees expressed in nominal terms and quickly switched to the lower-fee provider. Expressing fees as percentages slowed down the transition to a lower-fee provider. Return information is more difficult to process and participants delay switching to better performing providers. People may indeed wait for several years of outperformance (or underperformance) before switching as they do not consider investment performance as an exact measure of manager skill.

Changing the charge structure can facilitate comparisons between pension providers. Some countries replaced their mixed fee structures (usually with fees on both assets and contributions) with a single, asset-based fee. This is the case for example in Mexico (2008) and Costa Rica (2011). Avoiding mixed fee structures can contribute to disclosure efforts by making it easier for participants to compare offers. As a complement to a single charge structure, some countries have introduced more direct controls over pricing, such as caps on fees.

The main limitation of disclosure-based initiatives is that they do not always succeed in prompting members' action regarding their retirement savings. This is particularly the case for people with low financial knowledge. Indeed, as people do not always have a good understanding of the effect of compounding, they may not realise that small differences in fees (a few basis points) may translate into large differences in assets at the end of the accumulation period. In addition, while greater transparency and more straightforward comparisons should make it easier for plan participants to switch providers, switches may not always occur in the intended direction. For example, in Mexico, between 2001 and 2014, the majority of the workers who switched did so to a pension fund providing a lower net return (OECD, 2016[40]).

5.6. How to invest pension contributions

How behavioural biases and low levels of financial knowledge affect the choice of the investment strategy

In DC pension arrangements, participants usually bear the consequences of their investment decisions. When making investment decisions, people are confronted with a complex sequence of choices. To start with, they have to decide whether to remain invested in the default option. If not, they then have to decide in how many funds to invest, in which funds to invest and finally what percentage to invest in each fund. If participants behave as predicted by economic theory, such responsibility would be welfare-enhancing as members would invest and hold a portfolio of financial assets with a risk-return combination consistent with their investment horizon, degree of risk aversion and the portfolio of other assets they hold. This assumes that members have the knowledge to exercise choice and that their choice is not distorted by behavioural biases.

However, individuals lack good financial knowledge and are prone to various behavioural biases that can have an impact on investment choice. The main issues include choice and information overload, time-inconsistent preferences, heuristic decision-making, framing effects, overconfidence, over-extrapolation, and loss aversion (Tapia and Yermo, 2007[53]; OECD, 2017[54]).

Contrary to popular belief, more choice is not always better. Individuals can be prone to choice overload and therefore fail to act. For example, Iyengar, Jiang and Huberman (2004[8]) find that participation rates in 401(k) pension plans decline as the number of fund options increases.

Risk aversion and preferences vary over time, complicating optimal investment plan design. In addition, inertia and procrastination affect individuals' decisions, leading to sub-optimal choices. For example, Benartzi and Thaler (2002[55]) show that plan participants rarely rebalance their investment portfolios after joining plans and have relatively weak preferences for the portfolio they elect.

Faced with complex decisions, people rely on simple rules of thumb or heuristics that serve to reduce the complexity of the options to be assessed. Benartzi and Thaler (2001[56]) show evidence that participants make decisions that seem to be based on naive notions of diversification, such as the "1/n heuristic". The rule simply allocates assets evenly among the n options offered in the retirement savings plan. The authors show that reliance on the l/n heuristic can be costly, as individuals enrolled in plans with predominantly stock funds will find themselves owning mostly stocks, while those in plans that have mostly fixed income funds will own mostly bonds, independently of their degree of risk aversion.

Many participants are influenced by the way in which saving and investment issues are presented or "framed". For instance, Bateman et al. (2016[57]) show that individuals appear to focus on asset allocation information at the expense of risk and return information when comparing different investment options. When asset allocation information is not shown to participants, they revert to a risk-return trade-off. Moreover, if a number of different investment options are presented, issues such as numbering and the order in which they appear will affect choice, as people may not bother going through the whole list.

A large experimental literature finds that individuals are usually overconfident (Tapia and Yermo, 2007[53]). Overconfidence is the tendency for people to overestimate their knowledge, abilities and the precision of their information. Over-extrapolation occurs when people make projections on the basis of only a few observations, implicitly believing that these observations suggest real patterns or trends (e.g. assuming an investment will have the same performance in the future as in the past). These biases mean that investment decisions may become based on conjectures rather than fundamental value.

Finally, people often strongly prefer avoiding losses to acquiring gains. This may result in under-diversified portfolios with an over-reliance on fixed income.

Effective approaches to facilitate the choice of the investment strategy

In order to account for the implications of behavioural biases and low levels of financial knowledge on investment decisions, effective approaches to facilitate the choice of the investment strategy include simplifying choice by reducing the number of available investment options, establishing appropriate default investment strategies, and providing financial advice and financial education.

Reducing the set of available investment options

In DC pension arrangements, policy makers need to find the appropriate balance between a wide range of individual choices on the one hand, allowing people to take into consideration their individual risk profiles and preferences, and the simplicity of a restricted menu of choices on the other hand.

Some countries give priority to individual choice and allow a large number of investment options, complemented with default strategies for those unwilling or unable to choose. For example, in Sweden, individuals can choose up to five funds from the 830 registered with the Swedish Pensions Agency at the end of 2015. If an individual decides not to choose his/her own funds, the contributions go to the publicly-managed fund AP7. Most Swedes like having fund choice within the premium pension system, in particular younger ones (Swedish Investment Fund Association, 2013[58]). Despite this, only 1% of those who joined the pension system in 2016 declined the default fund and chose their own portfolios (Cronqvist, Thaler and Yu, 2018[59]).

By contrast, many countries in Latin America and Central and Eastern Europe allow participants to choose only from a restricted number of investment options. For example, participants can choose from five pension funds in Chile and Mexico, four funds in Estonia and three funds in Latvia.

Reducing and simplifying investment options can improve members' outcomes. Keim and Mitchell (2017[60]) examine how employees in a large U.S. firm changed their fund allocations when the employer streamlined its pension fund menu and deleted nearly half of the offered funds. The authors examine plan participants' investment choices prior to and after the streamlining event and evaluate what happened to participant fund allocations, risk exposure, and costs as a result of the change. Participants holding the deleted funds could either i) reallocate their money to funds kept in the list in advance of the deadline, or ii) be defaulted into the age-appropriate target date fund. Post-streamlining, participants who held the deleted funds adjusted their portfolio, ending up with fewer funds, significantly lower within-fund turnover rates, and lower expense ratios.

Establishing appropriate default investment strategies

Default investment strategies address the problem that some people lack the knowledge and/or the commitment to design and manage their own portfolio.

The default investment strategy may be designed according to a balanced investment strategy that keeps the same asset allocation throughout the investment period or following a life-cycle strategy.

In some countries, such as Estonia, Latvia and New Zealand, by default all contributions are invested in the most conservative strategy (no equity exposure) until the participant designates an alternative pension fund. The reasoning for such regulations may be that those unable to make choice may also be the most risk averse. It also gives members time to think about the strategy that best fits their needs. Thus, pension funds invest contributions in a fixed income portfolio under the expectation that at some point in the future, participant will make their own appropriate investment choice.

The drawback with a conservative strategy as a default is that it could be inconsistent with two financial principles. Indeed, conservative investment strategies account neither for the existence of an equity risk premium, nor for the principle that younger individuals are able to assume greater risk than older individuals because the former have more time to recover from periods of low returns and have more human capital. Moreover, people are prone to inertia and procrastination. If members are passive decision makers, the default option selected by policy makers or employers becomes the de facto member's choice. Some people may therefore remain with a conservative investment strategy for the entire accumulation period.[18]

The main trend in recent years is to establish a life-cycle investment strategy as the default. This allows younger individuals to take more risk and to reduce risk as people age. As members get older, their pension assets are invested in a more conservative investment strategy, reducing the risk of large losses in their account as the retirement age approaches.

There are three main models to design life-cycle strategies. Some countries follow a model based on multi-funds, with members assigned to one of the funds according to their age (e.g. Chile and Mexico). Members' assets are transferred from one fund to the next when they reach certain age thresholds. In some other countries (e.g. Hong Kong, China and Sweden), the default life-cycle investment strategy uses a mix of funds, the proportions of which evolve as members reach a certain age. Finally, target date funds are popular in the United States (Vanguard, 2017[19]). Portfolio allocations are based on an expected retirement date, with allocations growing more conservative as the participant approaches the fund's target date. The glide path is usually smoother than with the multi-funds model.

Although life-cycle investment strategies may alleviate the impact of investment risk, they do not necessarily provide the best investment outcome for the individual in all circumstances. Such strategies provide protection for those close to retirement in the case that a negative shock in financial markets happens just before retirement, as the amount of assets allocated to risky investments falls as people get closer to retirement. OECD work shows that life-cycle strategies tend to outperform fixed-portfolio strategies when a shock to equity markets occurs just before retirement (Antolin and Payet, 2011[61]). However, life-cycle strategies are not a panacea. The positive impact of life-cycle strategies dwindles as shocks to equity markets occur further from retirement age. Indeed, people with a fixed portfolio could have an opportunity to recover should returns to equities become positive in the remaining years before retirement, while with a life-cycle strategy, the automatic reduction in equity exposure reduces the chances of recovery. The Productivity Commission in Australia questions the inclusion of life-cycle investment strategies in MySuper produts, given the lower returns they achieve in the years approaching retirement (Productivity Commission, 2018[62]).

Providing financial advice and financial education

Financial advice should help members tailor their investment strategy to their needs but may be ineffective when it is unsolicited. For example, Hung and Yoong (2013[63]) show that individuals who actively solicit financial advice perform better, making fewer "portfolio mistakes" (i.e. having overly conservative portfolios, overly aggressive portfolios and/or under-diversified portfolios) than those not receiving advice. When individuals can choose whether or not to receive financial advice, those with low financial knowledge are more likely to take it. However, individuals who receive unsolicited advice disregard it almost completely and make as many portfolio mistakes as those not receiving advice.

Financial education for individuals making investment decisions can support and encourage long-term savings and investment and help individuals to feel more confident when investing their pension contributions. OECD (2017[54]) offers a policy framework to develop and implement national initiatives on investor education. It aims to remove the potential obstacles that may prevent individuals from participating in financial markets (e.g. lack of trust in the financial system, perceived participation costs) and to induce behavioural change (e.g. avoiding inappropriate risk-taking, excessive risk aversion). Investor education can also prepare individuals to understand financial advice and to better interact with financial advisors. IOSCO and OECD (2018[64]) also presents how behavioural insights can be used to develop financial education interventions.

5.7. Choice of the post-retirement product

How behavioural biases and low levels of financial knowledge affect the choice of the post-retirement product

One of the key goals of pensions is to provide a lifelong stream of income after retirement. DB plans usually pay pension benefits in the form of immediate life annuities. By contrast, in DC pension arrangements, people may have to choose between different post-retirement products. The biggest risk people face during retirement is to run out of money while they are still alive. Unlike lump sums and programmed withdrawals, life annuities guarantee a payment for the entire lifetime of the retiree and therefore protect them from longevity risk. Behavioural biases and low levels of financial knowledge, however, affect how people perceive annuities. They also affect the decision to get a lump sum and the way in which people may draw down their savings when choosing programmed withdrawals.

The effect of financial knowledge on annuity demand is unclear (Brown, 2009[65]). For example, Agnew et al. (2008[66]) find that, conditional on education, individuals with high levels of financial knowledge are significantly less likely to choose annuities. This may be due to the fact that more financially knowledgeable individuals are over-confident in their investment skills, perhaps leading them to believe that they can "do better" than an annuity by investing on their own. Brown, Casey and Mitchell (2008[67]) find that more highly educated individuals are less likely to annuitise. However, conditional on education, they find that more financially knowledgeable individuals are more likely to choose an annuity. In both studies, financial knowledge is measured based on the capacity to correctly answer three basic questions on interest compounding, inflation and risk diversification. However, the decision to annuitise may be linked to other types of financial knowledge, such as understanding the implications of longevity on retirement outcomes.

Loss aversion may lead people to dislike annuities. People feel that they lose money if they die early. Moreover, they may not like to give away a large amount of money (the annuity premium) for a stream of small amounts (the annuity payments). Finally, there is also the issue of insolvency risk. People wonder whether the institutions taking their money now for promised pension payments in 20-30 years will still be around over that time.

Framing also influences the way people perceive annuities. Brown et al. (2013[68]) argue that life annuities are more attractive when presented in a "consumption frame" rather than in an "investment frame". The two alternative frames, which are just two representations of the same financial choice, may lead to different perceptions of gains and losses. The consumption frame presents financial products by highlighting consequences for consumption in retirement. The investment frame focuses instead on the risk and return features of the financial products. In an experiment, the authors randomly assigned people over the age of 50 to choose between different financial products using the consumption or the investment frame. The financial products include life annuities, savings accounts, bonds and fixed-term annuities. The results show that life annuities are preferred when financial products are presented in a consumption frame. By contrast, when these same products are presented in an investment frame, savings accounts and other financial products are strongly preferred to annuities.

Financial literacy may also affect withdrawal behaviour. For example, in Turkey, about one-third of participants close their individual pension account before achieving full retirement entitlements and withdraw all of their assets, despite financial penalties.19 Yildiz, Karan and Bayrak Salantur (2017[69]) find a negative relationship between financial literacy and withdrawal probability. In the United Kingdom, individuals may not understand the consequences in terms of taxes paid of withdrawing funds from their pension account. Since 2015, individuals aged 55 and over can access their DC pension savings as they wish. The reform allowed the Treasury to collect far more taxes than anticipated.[20]

As programmed withdrawals do not provide full coverage for longevity risk, the withdrawal rate determines the amount of longevity risk left with the individual. On the one hand, withdrawing too much too early causes individuals to face an increased risk of outliving their pension assets. On the other hand, withdrawing too little may lead people to reduce the standard of living that they can enjoy in retirement. In Australia for example, people are required to withdraw a minimum amount every year under programmed withdrawals, from 4% of assets under age 65 to 5% between 65 and 74 years old and up to 14% at age 95 and older. According to the Australian Government (2016[70]), a majority of individuals drawdown account-based pensions at or close to the minimum rates. There is the concern that individuals are self-insuring against longevity risk at a high cost when measured in terms of foregone income.

Traditional rules of thumb to draw down pension assets in programmed withdrawals may not provide optimal outcomes. People adopt rules of thumb for drawing down their assets that are relatively simple to follow. Some retirees leave the principal in their retirement accounts untouched and spend only the investment income. This strategy may be desirable for those who want to leave a bequest but it reduces retirement consumption. A second drawdown strategy is to divide all financial assets by the remaining life expectancy each year, as predicted by life tables. However, people living beyond their cohort's life expectancy will outlive their resources. A third strategy is the so-called "4-percent rule" advocated by some financial planners, under which the retiree each year withdraws 4% of the initial amount of assets accumulated at retirement. However, this strategy lacks flexibility, as the withdrawn amounts do not adjust to the performance of the portfolio. Sun and Webb (2012[71]) build an optimal drawdown pattern that maximizes the expected utility of consumption during retirement and compare it to the three strategies described above. They find that the three strategies underperform this optimal drawdown pattern, with the life expectancy strategy being the closest and the 4-percent rule being the farthest from the optimal.

Effective approaches to facilitate the choice of the post-retirement product

The design of the pay-out phase needs to be determined in coherence with the overall structure of the pension system. The need to annuitize DC pension pots depends on how much is already received as an annuity from occupational DB plans and public PAYG pensions. Moreover, allowing lump sum withdrawals can help people cover expenses or reimburse debt and thereby improve their financial situation in retirement. The design of the accumulation and pay-out phases also needs to be internally coherent. For example, flexibility in the pay-out phase may not make sense when participation is mandatory or financially incentivised.

Policy options to help individuals transforming the assets accumulated in their pension account into retirement income include promoting the demand for annuities and facilitating product comparisons.

Promoting the demand for annuities

When mandating annuities is not an option, the role of annuities in the pension system may still be strengthened to help people cope with longevity risk by establishing them as defaults, providing financial incentives and fostering product design innovation.

Annuity take-up could be increased by establishing this post-retirement product as the default. For example, Gazzale, Mackenzie and Walker (2012[72]) show that offering an immediate life annuity as the default option, with a lump sum as the alternative, increases the demand for annuities. While only 28% of participants in their experiment chose an annuity when the default was the lump sum, 51% did so when the default was the annuity. Defaulting plan members into an annuity would increase longevity protection.

Financial incentives can be used to encourage individuals to purchase annuities. For example, both the Czech Republic and Estonia incentivise people to annuitize their pension income through a more favourable tax treatment for annuities as compared to programmed withdrawals (OECD, 2018[73]). In Turkey, the government promotes annuities by paying a subsidy equal to 5% of the account balance at retirement to participants in the automatic enrolment scheme purchasing an annuity paid over at least 10 years. In Denmark, a tax reform in 1999 reduced the deduction that high-income workers could take for contributions to "capital" pension accounts, which are accounts that provide lump-sum payments at retirement. That reform, however, left unchanged the treatment of contributions to accounts that provide annuity payments. Chetty et al. (2014[74]) show that individuals in the top income tax bracket reduced significantly their contributions to capital pensions following the reform, redirecting nearly all that saving to annuity pension plans and other savings accounts.

Product design innovations can help overcome the low demand for traditional annuity products. OECD (2016[75]) provides an overview of the different types of annuity product, describing the guarantees that they offer. It shows that there is a trend toward more flexibility and risk-sharing in the design of annuity products, which could help to mitigate loss aversion by providing the individual with increased access to the underlying capital and improving the perceived value of the product. For example, variable annuities provide flexibility by allowing the individual to surrender the policy instead of converting the accumulated capital into an annuity at the guaranteed rate. Risk-sharing features can be found in participating life annuities. These types of annuity products generally offer a minimum guaranteed level of income to the annuitant, but give additional bonus payments depending on an actual return or profit measure.

A product that strikes a balance between flexibility and protection from longevity risk could be established as a default post-retirement product. For example, OECD (2012[44]) advocates the use of a combination between programmed withdrawals and a deferred life annuity bought at the time of retirement that starts paying at old ages (e.g. 80-85). This type of combination may be appealing to individuals because only a limited portion of the total assets accumulated is needed to finance the deferred life annuity.[21] According to Gazzale, Mackenzie and Walker (2012[72]), when participants in an experiment were offered a deferred annuity as an alternative to the default lump sum, 60% selected the annuity (compared to 51% for the immediate annuity). The Australian government is developing a new retirement income framework that aims to promote products that strike a balance between longevity protection, cost and flexibility. This framework would aim to facilitate the development and take-up of products that better manage longevity risk through risk pooling while also potentially allowing for some liquidity.

Facilitating product comparisons

To overcome inertia, people should be encouraged to shop around before choosing their post-retirement product. In the United Kingdom for example, around 60% of annuity sales are being made to firms' existing members (Financial Conduct Authority, 2017[76]). In order to improve competition, the Financial Conduct Authority introduced new rules requiring providers to give members information to encourage shopping around in the annuity market. As of 1 March 2018, firms are required to provide information about the amount used to purchase the proposed annuity, whether the annuity is single or joint life, whether payment is in advance or in arrears of the start date, whether the income paid by the annuity is guaranteed for any period and whether the income will increase in line with inflation or some other specified rate. The document also gives the provider's own quote and explains how to shop around, encouraging use of the Money Advice service.

The burden of shopping around can be further reduced by introducing a platform where people can directly compare offers from all providers for different post-retirement products. In Chile, the Online Pension Consultation and Bidding System (*Sistema de Consultas y Ofertas de Montos de Pensión*, or SCOMP) allows members with sufficient accumulated balance in their individual DC account to see the bids from all insurance companies (for annuities) and pension funds (for programmed withdrawals) in one place. Search costs are significantly reduced as future pensioners simultaneously receive and compare a wide range of post-retirement options from all providers in the market. In addition, all offers are standardised, facilitating the comparison by individuals. This system therefore lowers the risk that, because of inertia, future pensioners remain with their current pension administrator even though better offers may be available from other providers.

A platform comparing post-retirement options and bids can increase competition and lead to better outcomes for individuals. Morales and Larraín (2017[77]) find that the SCOMP improved competition among providers. Between 2001 and 2008, annuity payments rose by 15%. Both individuals and providers have access to all bids simultaneously, providing transparency and reliability in the post-retirement option selection process, generating competition among bidders, and allowing individuals to make a decision based on comparable information. However, there is a concern that insurance companies are not giving their best offers through the SCOMP, because members can request external bids (i.e. insurance companies make an offer outside the system), thereby reducing transparency and potentially competition.

5.8. Conclusion and policy guidance

Given the growing importance of funded pension arrangements, and in particular DC pensions, for people's future retirement income in many countries, policy makers increasingly recognise the need to help people with their retirement planning. Planning for retirement is likely to require more financial knowledge and skills for people covered by funded private pension arrangements rather than PAYG public pension arrangements; personal plans rather than occupational plans; and DC schemes rather than DB schemes.

This chapter has reviewed the evidence that indicates that behavioural biases and low levels of financial knowledge can undermine people's ability to take action and make appropriate decisions for their retirement at all stages of their lives. It has then assessed policies implemented in different countries to improve the design of funded pension arrangements through motivating or facilitating the appropriate behaviour by individuals. These approaches complement general financial education policies, in particular those targeting the youth that will improve overall levels of financial literacy over time.

In this context, policies that improve retirement incomes while considering behavioural biases and limited financial knowledge can be divided into five categories: automatic features, default options, simplification of information and choice, financial incentives, and financial education.

Automatic features are increasingly used to increase participation in and contributions to funded pension arrangements. For example, automatic enrolment and automatic escalation of contributions harness the power of inertia to keep people saving for retirement. These policies maintain individual choice by allowing people to opt-out. They are sometimes referred to as "soft-compulsion" policies.

Default options help people who are unable or unwilling to choose a contribution rate, a pension provider, an investment strategy or a post-retirement product. The default option usually implies lower risks for individuals. However, default options may not be optimal for everyone failing to make a choice given different needs and preferences.

People can make better choices if the decision-making process is simplified. This can be achieved through the development of web applications (e.g. voluntary contributions), the provision of a reduced set of options (e.g. investment strategies), better disclosure of comparable information (e.g. cost information) or the facilitated comparison of options (e.g. bids by providers for post-retirement options).

Financial incentives harness individuals' tendency to respond to immediate gratification to make them save for retirement. They can take the form of tax incentives (more favourable tax treatment compared to other savings vehicles) and non-tax incentives (matching contributions and fixed nominal subsidies). Attractive product features (e.g. early access to funds in certain circumstances) can also be provided to encourage participation.

Finally, financial education plays an important role in supporting individuals to make appropriate decisions, as set out in the OECD Recommendation on Good Practices for Financial Education Relating to Private Pensions (OECD, 2008[78]). As people tend to focus on salient information, making sure that important information related to retirement saving is emphasised can improve decision making. This information can be conveyed through pension statements, financial education seminars and financial advice.

Based on the analysis of different approaches used in various countries to improve retirement incomes in the context of behavioural biases and low levels of financial knowledge, the following policy guidelines could help policy makers improve the design of funded pension arrangements.

Countries aiming for high participation in funded pension arrangements could introduce a national mandate for private pensions. Compulsion is the simplest, least costly and most effective way to reach high and uniformly distributed participation rates. Automatic enrolment is a second-best option. Under this mechanism, all employees not already covered by an occupational pension plan could be enrolled by their employer in a new scheme with the possibility to opt out. That scheme should not compete with already existing provision to avoid creating incentives for employees to opt out.

Self-employed and informal workers could be encouraged to voluntarily join the same scheme by offering easy access and financial incentives. Self-employed and informal workers could be nudged into the same scheme into which formal employees are enrolled, with the same incentives (apart from any employer contribution).

Using default options for the contribution rate, the pension provider, the investment strategy and the post-retirement product can simplify decision-making. Default options provide a reference point against which individuals can judge other options. They are essential for those who are unwilling or unable to make complex decisions with respect to retirement planning. Default options should however be carefully designed to avoid locking in passive individuals into sub-optimal arrangements.

- **Setting default contribution rates at a low initial level and implementing automatic escalation helps people to contribute enough to cover their needs in retirement**. Low default contribution rates can make it easier for people to accept compulsory enrolment, while in the context of automatic enrolment they can help reduce opt-out rates. However, low default contribution rates may prevent people from reaching an overall retirement income (including public pensions) that they will deem adequate. Automatically increasing contributions and linking these increases to pay rises can help people to reach their optimal contribution rate.
- **Countries could use tender mechanisms accounting for costs, quality of service and other variables to default new entrants that fail to choose a pension provider**. To avoid predatory behaviour, the tender should include a range of criteria reflecting the quality of service, not just fee levels. Only plan members not selecting their own provider would be defaulted into the winning entities. This should be combined with enhanced fee disclosure and members' education, as well as price regulation (i.e. fee structure and caps), to make sure that all individuals get good value for money with any provider.
- **A life-cycle investment strategy could be established as a default, while a limited set of available investment options should be provided for those able and willing to choose their own investment strategy**. For those unable or unwilling to track their investment and adjust it over time, a life-cycle investment strategy could be established as a default, allowing younger individuals to take more risk and to reduce risk as people age. This investment strategy is most appropriate as a default when policy makers are concerned about the risk of large losses in the years approaching retirement. Streamlined investment options on top of the default can facilitate individual choice when choice overload is considered as a serious issue.

- **Countries have to consider protection from longevity risk, flexibility and choice when designing the post-retirement phase**. A combination of programmed withdrawals, offering flexibility during the first years in retirement, with a deferred life annuity starting payments at the age of e.g. 85, offering protection against the tail risk of longevity, could be considered as an appropriate default post-retirement product. Facilitating shopping around different post-retirement products and providers, for example by using platforms to compare all options and bids, could enhance transparency, competition, and product innovation, as well as improve retirement income.

Countries should continue efforts to educate and inform people to increase engagement with respect to pensions. Workshops and seminars at the workplace, financial advice and personalised communication can prompt people's action and help them make decisions for their retirement at all stages of their lives. More standards, principles and guidelines on how to develop and implement financial education policies can be found at www.financial-education.org.

Notes

[1] See for example (Munnell, Hou and Sanzenbacher, 2017[9]) for the United States.

[2] See for example the OECD Recommendation on Principles and Good Practices for Financial Education and Awareness (OECD, 2005[80]), the OECD Recommendations on Good Practices for Financial Education Relating to Private Pensions (OECD, 2008[78]), the OECD/INFE High-level Principles on National Strategies for Financial Education (OECD/INFE, 2012[81]), the OECD/INFE Policy Framework for Investor Education (OECD, 2017[54]), the OECD/INFE Core Competencies Framework on Financial Literacy for Youth (OECD, 2015[82]), and the G20/OECD INFE Core Competencies Framework on Financial Literacy for Adults (OECD, 2016[83]).

[3] This chapter does not consider decisions made by employers and how employers can help their employees meet their retirement income goal.

[4] According to Queisser and Whitehouse (2006[79]), a pension system is actuarially neutral when the present value of pension benefits is not affected by the decision to retire at a given age or a year earlier/later.

[5] The authors compare the increase in pension contributions to the implementation cost of different policies. According to their calculations, the active decision mechanism generated USD 100 of additional savings per dollar spent. It was under USD 15 for all the other policies they looked at.

[6] A pension reform proposal sent to the Chilean Congress in August 2017 includes the possibility for employers to automatically enrol their employees into collective voluntary pension savings plans on a voluntary basis. Ireland has announced in September 2017 that automatic enrolment will be introduced within the next three years. Lithuania plans to introduce automatic enrolment for workers under 40 years old as of 2019. Poland envisages starting enrolling automatically employees into Employee Capital Plans (PPKs) from 2019.

[7] The proportion of all wage and salary workers aged 21 to 64 participating in an occupational pension plan has remained at around 46% between 1987 and 2013 (Copeland, 2013[87]). The percentage of Vanguard DC plans with automatic enrolment increased from 15% in 2007 to 45% in 2016 (Vanguard, 2017[19]).

[8] In Chile, participation in individual retirement accounts is mandatory for employees and voluntary for the self-employed. The target population for automatic enrolment consists of self-employed workers who are paid for services delivered to a third party and who issue an invoice against which a tax retention is collected.

[9] For example, in the United Kingdom, the share of self-employed workers in total employment has risen from 11.9% in 2000 to 14.9% in 2016 (Office for National Statistics, 2016[84]).

[10] This threshold is reviewed every year by the government. It used to be linked to the personal tax allowance but has been frozen at the GBP 10 000 level since 2014/15. This means that the threshold has increased in real terms, allowing more people to enter the target population.

[11] An alternative solution currently explored is to link a short-term savings, or "sidecar", account to a traditional retirement account to better meet consumers' short- and long-term financial needs (Mitchell and Lynne, 2017[85]; NEST Insight, 2017[86]).

[12] Government payments include the kick-start NZL 1 000 contribution that all individuals who joined before 21 May 2015 received.

[13] It remains to be seen how this rate will evolve when the contribution rate increases to 8% as of April 2019 (from 2% up to April 2018).

[14] Automatic increases in contributions could be made portable when individuals change jobs and enter a new pension plan. This would allow them to continue with the previous increase path and avoid they start all over again from a low contribution rate in the new plan. This may be difficult to implement, however. In addition, wage levels and salary increases may differ from one job to the next, making the contribution increase path of the previous job not appropriate anymore.

[15] In June 2017, only 21% of all KiwiSaver members were in a default scheme.

[16] Fees are weighted by the number of participants in each pension provider in August of each year.

[17] The absence of offers in the last tender can also be explained by the fact that bids have to be lower than the one previously in force.

[18] This fear may not be valid in every country however. For example, most participants in the Latvian mandatory funded pension scheme make an active investment choice getting out of the default conservative plan.

[19] Early withdrawal is penalised by a higher tax on returns and the foregone benefit of the 25% government matching contribution.

[20] The measure was initially estimated to raise around GBP 0.3 billion in 2015-16 and GBP 0.6 billion in 2016-17, but it has actually raised far more than anticipated: GBP 1.5 billion in 2015-16, while the latest estimate for 2016-17 is GBP 1.1 billion. The Treasury now expects the measure to bring in GBP 1.6 billion in 2017-18.

[21] According to OECD (2012[44]), only 15% to 20% of assets accumulated at retirement could be used to finance the deferred life annuity following standard premium calculations. The true premium may be higher however, as annuity providers may find it difficult to insure the tail risk of longevity.

References

Agnew, J. et al. (2008), "Who Chooses Annuities? An Experimental Investigation of the Role of Gender, Framing, and Defaults", *American Economic Review*, Vol. 98/2, pp. 418-422, http://dx.doi.org/10.1257/aer.98.2.418. [66]

Anderson, D. and J. Collins (2017), "Can knowledge empower women to save more for retirement?", *CRR WP* , No. 2017-12, Center for Retirement Research at Boston College, http://crr.bc.edu. [35]

Antolin, P. and S. Payet (2011), "Assessing the Labour, Financial and Demographic Risks to Retirement Income from Defined-Contribution Pensions", *OECD Journal: Financial Market Trends*, Vol. 2010/2, http://dx.doi.org/10.1787/fmt-2010-5kggc0z23fr5. [61]

Atkinson, A. et al. (2015), "Financial Education for Long-term Savings and Investments: Review of Research and Literature", *OECD Working Papers on Finance, Insurance and Private Pensions*, No. 39, OECD Publishing, Paris, http://dx.doi.org/10.1787/5jrtgzfl6g9w-en. [32]

Balasuriya, J., O. Gough and K. Vasileva (2014), "Do optimists plan for retirement? A behavioural explanation for non-participation in pension schemes", *Economics Letters*, Vol. 125/3, http://dx.doi.org/10.1016/j.econlet.2014.10.012. [10]

Bateman, H. et al. (2016), "As easy as pie: How retirement savers use prescribed investment disclosures", *Journal of Economic Behavior and Organization*, Vol. 121, http://dx.doi.org/10.1016/j.jebo.2015.10.020. [57]

Benartzi, S. et al. (2017), "Should governments invest more in nudging?", *Psychological Science*, Vol. 28/8, pp. 1041-1055, http://dx.doi.org/10.1177/0956797617702501. [13]

Benartzi, S. and R. Thaler (2002), "How Much Is Investor Autonomy Worth?", *The Journal of Finance*, Vol. 57/4, pp. 1593-1616, http://www.jstor.org/stable/3094518. [55]

Benartzi, S. and R. Thaler (2001), "Naive diversification strategies in defined contribution saving plans", *The American Economic Review*, Vol. 91/1, pp. 79-98, http://dx.doi.org/10.1257/aer.91.1.79. [56]

Beshears, J. et al. (2017), "How do consumers respond when default options push the envelope?", *SSRN Electronic Journal*, No. 3050562, Social Science Research Network, https://papers.ssrn.com/sol3/papers.cfm?abstract_id=3050562&download=yes. [42]

Beshears, J. et al. (2017), "Does Front-Loading Taxation Increase Savings? Evidence From Roth 401(K) Introductions", *Journal of Public Economics* 151, pp. 84-95, http://www.nber.org/papers/w20738. [29]

Beshears, J. et al. (2015), "The Effect of Providing Peer Information on Retirement Savings Decisions", *The Journal of Finance*, Vol. 70/3, http://dx.doi.org/10.1111/jofi.12258. [38]

Beshears, J. et al. (2013), "Simplification and saving", *Journal of Economic Behavior and Organization*, Vol. 95/130 145, http://dx.doi.org/10.1016/j.jebo.2012.03.007. [28]

Blake, D., D. Wright and Y. Zhang (2014), "Age-dependent investing: Optimal funding and investment strategies in defined contribution pension plans when members are rational life cycle financial planners", *Journal of Economic Dynamics and Control*, Vol. 38, pp. 105-124, http://dx.doi.org/10.1016/j.jedc.2013.11.001. [43]

Börsch-Supan, A. et al. (2015), "Savings in times of demographic change: Lessons from the german experience", *Journal of Economic Surveys*, Vol. 29/4, http://dx.doi.org/10.1111/joes.12116. [5]

Brown, J. (2009), "Financial Education and Annuities", *OECD Journal: General Papers*, Vol. 2008/3, http://dx.doi.org/10.1787/1995283x. [65]

Brown, J., M. Casey and O. Mitchell (2008), "Who Values the Social Security Annuity? New Evidence on the Annuity Puzzle", *NBER Working Paper*, Vol. W13800, https://papers.ssrn.com/sol3/papers.cfm?abstract_id=1092850. [67]

Brown, J. et al. (2013), "Framing Lifetime Income", *The Journal of Retirement*, Vol. 1/1, pp. 27-37, http://dx.doi.org/10.3905/jor.2013.1.1.027. [68]

Carroll, G. et al. (2009), "Optimal defaults and active decisions", *Quarterly Journal of Economics*, Vol. 124/4, pp. 1639-1674, https://www.ncbi.nlm.nih.gov/pmc/articles/PMC2798815/pdf/nihms-86882.pdf. [11]

Chetty, R. et al. (2014), "Active vs. Passive decisions and crowd-out in retirement savings accounts: Evidence from Denmark", *The Quarterly Journal of Economics*, Vol. 129/3, pp. 1141-1219, http://dx.doi.org/10.1093/qje/qju013. [74]

Choi, J. (2015), "Contributions to defined contribution pension plans", *Annual Review of Financial Economics*, Vol. 7/1, pp. 161-178. [46]

Choi, J., D. Laibson and B. Madrian (2009), "Reducing the complexity costs of 401(k) participation through Quick Enrollment™", in David A. Wise (ed.), *Developments in the Economics of Aging*, University of Chicago Press, Chicago, http://www.nber.org/chapters/c11310. [27]

Choi, J. et al. (2004), "For better or worse: Default effects and 401(k) savings behavior", in *Perspectives on the Economics of Aging*, National Bureau of Economic Research. [16]

Choi, J. et al. (2001), "Defined contribution pensions: Plan rules, participation decisions, and the path of least resistance", *Working Paper Series*, No. 8655, National Bureau of Economic Research. [15]

Clark, R., J. Maki and M. Morrill (2014), "Can Simple Informational Nudges Increase Employee Participation in a 401(k) Plan?", *Southern Economic Journal*, Vol. 80/February 2013, http://dx.doi.org/10.4284/0038-4038-2012.199. [36]

Collins, J. and C. Urban (2016), "The role of information on retirement planning: Evidence from a field study", *Economic Inquiry*, Vol. 54/4, pp. 1860-1872, http://dx.doi.org/10.1111/ecin.12349. [34]

Copeland, C. (2013), "Employment-Based Retirement Plan Participation: Geographic Differences and Trends, 2013", *EBRI Issue Brief* 405, http://www.ebri.org (accessed on 22 March 2018). [87]

COVIP (2017), *Annual report 2016*. [21]

Cribb, J. and C. Emmerson (2016), "What happens when employers are obliged to nudge? Automatic enrolment and pension saving in the UK", *IFS Working Papers*, No. WP16/19, Institute for Fiscal Studies. [17]

Cronqvist, H., R. Thaler and F. Yu (2018), *When Nudges Are Forever: Inertia in the Swedish Premium Pension Plan*, https://ssrn.com/abstract=3099886. [59]

Cuccia, A., M. Doxey and S. Stinson (2017), "The relative effects of economic and non-economic factors on taxpayers' preferences between front-loaded and back-loaded retirement savings plans", *Working Papers*, No. 2017-7, Center for Retirement Research at Boston College, http://crr.bc.edu. [30]

Department for Work and Pensions (2017), *Automatic Enrolment Review 2017: Maintaining the Momentum.* [25]

Department for Work and Pensions (2014), "Automatic enrolment: Experiences of workers who have opted out. A qualitative research study", *Research report* 862. [23]

Department for Work and Pensions (2013), "Automatic enrolment: Qualitative research with large employers", *Research report* 851. [22]

Dolls, M. et al. (2016), "Do savings increase in response to salient information about retirement and expected pensions?", *NBER Working Papers* 22684. [49]

Duflo, E. and E. Saez (2003), "The Role of Information and Social Interactions in Retirement Plan Decisions: Evidence from a Randomized Experiment", *The Quarterly Journal of Economics*, Vol. 118/3, pp. 815-842, http://www.jstor.org/stable/25053924. [33]

Financial Conduct Authority (2017), *Data Bulletin*, Financial Conduct Authority. [76]

Financial Conduct Authority (2014), *Thematic review of annuities*, Financial Conduct Authority. [51]

Financial Conduct Authority (2013), "Applying behavioural economics at the Financial Conduct Authority", *Occasional Paper* 1. [7]

Fuentes, O. et al. (2017), "Personalized Information as a Tool to Improve Pension Savings: Results from a Randomized Control Trial in Chile", *Documento de Trabajo IE-PUC* 483. [50]

Gazzale, R., S. Mackenzie and L. Walker (2012), *Do Default and Longevity Annuities Improve Annuity Take-Up Rates? Results from an Experiment*, AARP Public Policy Institute. [72]

Goldin, J., T. Homonoff and W. Tucker-Ray (2017), *Retirement contribution rate nudges and plan participation: Evidence from a field experiment*, http://dx.doi.org/10.1257/aer.p20171059. [41]

Hung, A. and J. Yoong (2013), "Asking for help: Survey and experimental evidence on financial advice and behavior change", in Olivia Mitchell and kent Smetters (ed.), *The market for retirement financial advice*, Oxford University Press. [63]

Inland Revenue (2015), *KiwiSaver evaluation: Final summary report.* [20]

IOSCO and OECD (2018), *The application of behavioural insights to financial literacy and investor education programmes and initiatives.* [64]

Iyengar, S., W. Jiang and G. Huberman (2004), "How Much Choice is Too Much?: Contributions to 401(k) Retirement Plans", in Olivia Mitchell and Stephen Utkus (ed.), *Pension Design and Structure: New Lessons from Behavioural Finance*, Oxford University Press, http://prc.wharton.upenn.edu/prc/prc.html. [8]

Kahneman, D. and A. Tversky (1979), "Prospect Theory: An Analysis of Decision under Risk", *Econometrica*, Vol. 47/2, pp. 263-291. [39]

Karlan, D. et al. (2016), "Getting to the Top of Mind: How Reminders Increase Saving", *Management Science*, Vol. 62/12, http://dx.doi.org/10.1287/mnsc.2015.2296. [48]

Keim, D. and O. Mitchell (2017), "Simplifying Choices in Defined Contribution Retirement Plan Design", *Journal of Pension Economics and Finance*, Vol. 1/22, http://dx.doi.org/10.1017/S1474747217000336. [60]

Keller, P. et al. (2011), "Enhanced active choice: A new method to motivate behavior change", *Journal of Consumer Psychology*, Vol. 21, pp. 376-383, https://ac.els-cdn.com/S1057740811000775/1-s2.0-S1057740811000775-main.pdf?_tid=55e833ad-5d21-4f31-9396-3a282476c4d7&acdnat=1523522654_3da3de8f31fc75eda65e1608f2fbc82f. [12]

Lefevre, A. and M. Chapman (2017), "Behavioural economics and financial consumer protection", *OECD Working Papers on Finance, Insurance and Private Pensions*, No. 42, OECD. [6]

Lusardi, A., P. Keller and A. Keller (2009), "New Ways to Make People Save: A Social Marketing Approach", *Working Paper*, No. 14715, National Bureau of Economic Research, http://www.nber.org/papers/w14715. [37]

Madrian, B. (2013), "Matching Contributions and Savings Outcomes: A Behavioral Economics Perspective", in *Matching Contributions for Pensions: A Review of International Evidence*, the World Bank, http://dx.doi.org/10.1596/978-0-8213-9492-2. [47]

Madrian, B. and D. Shea (2001), "The power of suggestion: Inertia in 401(k) participation and savings behavior", *The Quarterly Journal of Economics*, Vol. 116/4. [14]

Mitchell, D. and G. Lynne (2017), "Driving Retirement Innovation: Can Sidecar Accounts Meet Consumers' Short-and Long-Term Financial Needs?", *Issue Brief*, No. June 2017, Aspen Institute Financial Security Program. [85]

Morales, M. and G. Larraín (2017), "The Chilean Electronic Market for Annuities (SCOMP): Reducing Information Asymmetries and Improving Competition", *The Geneva Papers on Risk and Insurance - Issues and Practice*, Vol. 42/3, pp. 389-405. [77]

Munnell, A., A. Belbase and G. Sanzenbacher (2016), "State initiatives to cover uncovered private sector workers", *Issue in Brief* 16-4. [18]

Munnell, A., W. Hou and G. Sanzenbacher (2017), "Do households have a good sense of their retirement preparedness?", *Issue in Brief* 17-4. [9]

NEST Insight (2017), *Liquidity-and-sidecar-savings*, NEST Insight. [86]

OECD (2018), *Financial incentives and retirement savings*, OECD Publishing, Paris. [73]

OECD (2017), "Flexible retirement in OECD countries", in *Pensions at a Glance 2017: OECD and G20 Indicators*, OECD Publishing, Paris, http://dx.doi.org/10.1787/pension_glance-2017-5-en. [3]

OECD (2017), *OECD/INFE Policy Framework for Investor Education*, http://www.oecd.org/finance/financial-education/OECD-INFE-policy-framework-investor-edu.pdf. [54]

OECD (2016), *G20/OECD/INFE Core competencies framework on financial literacy for adults*, http://www.oecd.org/daf/fin/financial-education/Core-Competencies-Framework-Adults.pdf. [83]

OECD (2016), *Life Annuity Products and Their Guarantees*, OECD Publishing, Paris, https://doi.org/10.1787/9789264265318-en. [75]

OECD (2016), *OECD Reviews of Pension Systems: Mexico*, OECD Publishing, Paris, http://dx.doi.org/10.1787/9789264245938-en. [40]

OECD (2016), *OECD/INFE International Survey of Adult Financial Literacy Competencies*. [4]

OECD (2016), "The changing pensions landscape: The growing importance of pension arrangements in which assets back pension benefits", in *OECD Pensions Outlook 2016*, OECD Publishing, Paris, http://dx.doi.org/10.1787/pens_outlook-2016-4-en. [1]

OECD (2016), "The role of financial education in supporting decision-making for retirement", in *OECD Pensions Outlook 2016*, OECD Publishing, Paris, http://dx.doi.org/10.1787/pens_outlook-2016-8-en. [2]

OECD (2015), *OECD/INFE Core competencies framework on financial literacy for youth*. [82]

OECD (2012), "A Policy Roadmap for Defined Contribution Pensions", in *OECD Pensions Outlook 2012*, OECD Publishing, Paris, http://dx.doi.org/10.1787/9789264169401-9-en. [44]

OECD (2012), "Coverage of Private Pension Systems: Evidence and Policy Options", in *OECD Pensions Outlook 2012*, OECD Publishing, Paris, http://dx.doi.org/10.1787/9789264169401-7-en. [26]

OECD (2012), "The Role of Guarantees in Retirement Savings Plans", in *OECD Pensions Outlook 2012*, OECD Publishing, Paris, http://dx.doi.org/10.1787/9789264169401-8-en. [31]

OECD (2008), *Recommendation on Good Practices for Financial Education Relating to Private Pensions*, http://www.oecd.org/pensions/private-pensions/40537843.pdf. [78]

OECD (2005), *Recommendation on Principles and Good Practices for Financial Education and Awareness*, http://www.oecd.org/daf/fin/financial-education/35108560.pdf. [80]

OECD/INFE (2012), *High-Level Principles on National Strategies for Financial Education*, https://www.oecd.org/finance/financial-education/OECD-INFE-Principles-National-Strategies-Financial-Education.pdf. [81]

Office for National Statistics (2016), *Trends in self-employment in the UK: 2001 to 2015.* [84]

Productivity Commission (2018), *Superannuation: Assessing Efficiency and Competitiveness - Draft Report.* [62]

Queisser, M. and E. Whitehouse (2006), "Neutral or Fair?: Actuarial Concepts and Pension-System Design", *OECD Social, Employment and Migration Working Papers*, No. 40, OECD Publishing, Paris, http://dx.doi.org/10.1787/351382456457. [79]

Rinaldi, A. (2011), "Auto-enrolment in private, supplementary pensions in Italy", in *Improving Financial Education Efficiency: OECD-Bank of Italy Symposium on Financial Literacy*, OECD Publishing, Paris. [24]

Sun, W. and A. Webb (2012), "Can retirees base wealth withdrawals on the IRS' required minimum distributions?", *Issue in Brief* 12-19, http://crr.bc.edu/wp-content/uploads/2012/10/IB_12-19-508.pdf. [71]

Swedish Investment Fund Association (2013), *Facts and myths about the premium pension*, Swedish Investment Fund Association. [58]

Tapia, W. and J. Yermo (2007), "Implications of Behavioural Economics for Mandatory Individual Account Pension Systems", *OECD Working Papers on Insurance and Private Pensions*, No. 11, OECD Publishing, Paris, http://dx.doi.org/10.1787/103002825851. [53]

Thaler, R. and S. Benartzi (2004), "Save More Tomorrow: Using Behavioral Economics to Increase Employee Saving", *Journal of Political Economy*, Vol. 112/1. [45]

The Australian Government the Treasury (2016), *Development of the framework for Comprehensive Income Products for Retirement*, The Australian Government the Treasury. [70]

Thorp, S. et al. (2017), *Flicking the switch: Simplifying disclosures to improve retirement plan choices*, https://dx.doi.org/10.2139/ssrn.2783113. [52]

Vanguard (2017), *How America Saves.* [19]

Yildiz, Y., M. Karan and S. Bayrak Salantur (2017), "An Investigation on Early Voluntary Withdrawals from Individual Retirement Accounts: An Empirical Study on an Emerging Market", *Geneva Papers on Risk and Insurance: Issues and Practice*, http://dx.doi.org/10.1057/s41288-016-0037-9. [69]

Chapter 6. Mortality differences across socioeconomic groups and their implications for pension outcomes

This chapter assesses the potential differences in pension outcomes across socioeconomic groups due to differences in mortality and given the rules of the pension system that are in place. The analysis uses four indicators to conclude that low socioeconomic groups may indeed face a disadvantage for their pension and retirement, but this disadvantage may be partially offset when considering public pension benefits and progressive taxation.

Differences in mortality and the fact that lower socioeconomic groups tend to have lower life expectancies may lead to differences in pension outcomes across socioeconomic groups because of the rules in place. This is largely because in many jurisdictions the rules governing access to pension assets for retirement use age as a reference. These rules include minimum age limits to access pensions, minimum and maximum withdrawal limits, and the rate at which accumulated assets can be converted into a lifetime stream of guaranteed income payments.

First, minimum age limits at which people can have full access to their pension savings may have an impact on pension outcomes across socioeconomic groups. For a given retirement age, lower socioeconomic groups will have to work longer relative to the time they can expect to spend in retirement given their lower life expectancy. Furthermore, if this age is linked to average increases in life expectancy, this disadvantage may grow over time to the extent that differences in life expectancy across socioeconomic groups continue to diverge.

Rules imposing maximum or minimum withdrawal limits may also reference average life expectancy measures. In this case, maximum limits may impede lower socioeconomic groups from having a higher level of income than they otherwise could have given their expected time in retirement. On the other hand, minimum limits could potentially lead higher socioeconomic groups to have a higher chance of exhausting their pension savings in retirement.

Finally, the annuitisation rate at which accumulated pension assets can be converted into a lifetime income stream will depend on some underlying mortality assumptions. Where annuitisation is mandatory, this could result in a poor value for money for lower socioeconomic groups having lower than average life expectancies. Where it is voluntary, this could result in an exclusion of lower socioeconomic groups from the annuity market as they could find that the annuities are too expensive relative to the time they expect to spend in retirement, thereby limiting their options for managing their longevity risk in retirement.

This chapter presents a framework to assess the differences in pension outcomes across socioeconomic groups due to differences in mortality given the rules of the pension system in place. The analysis demonstrates that low socioeconomic groups may indeed face a disadvantage for their funded pension and retirement, but this disadvantage may be partially offset when considering the entire pension system. The analysis shows that low socioeconomic groups work and contribute more time per year spent in retirement for a given retirement age. Low socioeconomic groups also ultimately receive less from their pension savings when they take it as regular income because they will spend less time in retirement. However, progressive rules for public pensions and marginal tax rates can offset some of these relative differences in pension wealth and income, raising the question as to whether this is the appropriate and/or sufficient way to address longevity inequalities in retirement.

The analysis in this chapter introduces metrics that assess the differences in gross pension outcomes for funded pension arrangements as well as account for the impact that public pensions and tax rules will have on the ultimate pension income that individuals of different socioeconomic groups will receive.[1]

Section 6.1 of the chapter presents the four indicators used to assess the pension outcomes across socioeconomic groups. Section 6.2 applies this framework to calculate the pension outcomes for six countries: Canada, Chile, Great Britain, Korea, Mexico, and the United States.[2,3] Section 6.3 concludes with a discussion of policy implications.

6.1. Indicators used to measure the impact of mortality differences on pension outcomes

This chapter uses four indicators to assess pension outcomes for each socioeconomic group. These indicators aim to capture the value of time spent in retirement, the return on the savings made for retirement, the potentially offsetting impact of public pensions and tax systems for the pensions received by individuals of lower socioeconomic groups, and finally the change in relative income pre- and post-retirement.

The first indicator, the "retirement ratio", is the number of years spent working for each expected year in retirement given life expectancy at retirement. In other words, it is the number of years spent contributing to pensions divided by the life expectancy at the age of retirement. This is a measure of the time spent in retirement relative to years contributing.

The second indicator is the "asset pay-out ratio", which measures the expected present value of pension income relative to the amount of retirement assets accumulated. This is calculated by taking the present value of gross pension income at retirement over the expected time spent in retirement (i.e. the life expectancy at retirement) divided by the assets accumulated at retirement. This is a way to measure the value, or return, that pensioners receive from their investment for retirement.

The third indicator is the "pension wealth ratio", which measures the expected present value of pension income at retirement relative to annual earnings just before retirement. This measure has been introduced in order to be able to assess the impact that public pensions and tax policy can have in reducing the inequalities of pension outcomes. As such, it is calculated for gross pension income for funded pension arrangements, total gross pension income from both funded and public pension arrangements, and total net-of-tax pension income from both sources.[4]

The final indicator, referred to as the "income ratio", focuses on the change in relative income in retirement compared to before retirement. This indicator shows the average combined net public and private pension income in real terms over the expected time spent in retirement for each group relative to the average real pension income for the average earner. While this measure does not provide an indication of how well-off individuals are in their retirement, it can show whether existing inequalities are exacerbated in retirement given the rules of the pension system in place.

6.2. Impact of mortality differences on pension outcomes

This section assesses the impact of mortality differences on pension outcomes using the indicators introduced in the previous section. In each case, the analysis takes the perspective of the individual at the time of retirement, assuming that the pension system and rules in place for defined contribution plans at the age of retirement have been unchanged over the lifetime of the individual. The calculations assume a full career with no breaks from age 20 to the statutory age of retirement, and do not consider differences due to unemployment, disability or maternity leave. Low and high-income groups earn 50% and 300% of the average wage, respectively.[5]

Retirement ratios

High socioeconomic groups can expect to spend a longer time in retirement and therefore work fewer years per year spent in retirement compared to low socioeconomic groups.

The retirement ratio, calculated as the number of years spent contributing to pensions divided by the life expectancy at the age of retirement, captures this result that is common to all jurisdictions assessed. Table 6.1 shows the differences in life expectancies at retirement and the retirement ratios across socioeconomic groups for both males and females. It also shows the age at which each group could retire to spend a third of their adult life in retirement (i.e. a ratio equal to two years spent contributing per year spent in retirement).

Table 6.1. Life expectancy and retirement ratios

		Males				Females			
Country	Income level	Life expectancy at retirement	Ratio - Entry age 20	Ratio - Entry age varies	Retirement age to equalise ratio @ 2[1]	Life expectancy at retirement	Ratio - Entry age 20	Ratio - Entry age varies	Retirement age to equalise ratio @ 2[1]
Canada	Low	20.8	2.2	2.3	63	23.0	2.0	2.0	65
	Average	21.1	2.1	2.1	64	23.4	1.9	1.9	66
	High	23.0	2.0	1.8	67	24.5	1.8	1.7	68
Chile	Low	17.7	2.5	2.7	60	28.3	1.4	1.5	65
	Average	20.0	2.2	2.2	63	30.2	1.3	1.3	67
	High	21.8	2.1	1.9	66	31.4	1.3	1.1	69
Great Britain	Low	19.6	2.3	2.4	62	21.7	2.1	2.2	64
	Average	20.1	2.2	2.2	63	22.6	2.0	2.0	65
	High	22.7	2.0	1.8	67	25.1	1.8	1.6	68
Korea	Low	20.2	2.2	2.3	63	28.3	1.6	1.7	68
	Average	22.1	2.0	2.0	65	29.7	1.5	1.5	69
	High	24.3	1.9	1.7	68	30.0	1.5	1.4	71
Mexico	Low	17.4	2.6	2.7	60	19.5	2.3	2.4	62
	Average	17.5	2.6	2.6	61	19.6	2.3	2.3	63
	High	17.6	2.6	2.3	63	22.8	2.0	1.8	67
United States	Low	17.4	2.6	2.8	60	20.9	2.2	2.3	64
	Average	18.6	2.5	2.5	63	21.2	2.2	2.2	65
	High	20.0	2.3	2.1	65	21.5	2.1	2.0	66

Note: Retirement age is 65 except for Chilean females (60) and in the United States (66). Figures are in years. Life expectancy is cohort life expectancy that accounts for future expected mortality improvements. (1) The retirement age to equalise the retirement ratio at 2 is the age at which each group could retire to spend a third of their adult life in retirement

Large differences in life expectancy translate into large differences in the retirement ratios and the ages needed to equalise the ratio across socioeconomic groups. Looking at the retirement ratios for the countries having the largest differences in life expectancy at retirement shows the potential magnitude of these impacts. The largest differences observed for the jurisdictions assessed are in Chile and Korea for males and in Mexico and Great Britain for females, where high socioeconomic groups can live around 4.1 years and 3.3 years longer, respectively, than low socioeconomic groups. Assuming an entry age into the labour force at 20 and retirement age 65, low-income males in Chile work an additional 0.5 years per year spent in retirement than high-income males. For Mexican females, the gap in life expectancy at retirement results in low earners working 0.3 years longer per year in retirement.

Differences in the retirement ratios across socioeconomic groups increase when entry age varies. Assuming that low-income workers begin to contribute at age 18, average earners at age 20, and high earners at age 24, low-income workers need to work even more years per year spent in retirement. Low-income males in Chile would need to work an additional 0.8 years and low-income females in Mexico an additional 0.6 years per year spent in retirement compared to their high-income counterparts.

Low-income groups would need to retire much earlier than high-income groups to spend an equivalent proportion of their adult lives in retirement, especially when entry age is assumed to vary. Low-income males in Chile would need to retire six years earlier than high-income males to maintain a ratio of time spent working and contributing to time spent in retirement that implies that they will spend one third of their adult life in retirement. For most other countries, the difference in retirement age for males would be three to five years. For Mexican females, a five-year difference in retirement age would be needed to maintain a constant ratio of years spent working to years in retirement assuming that age of entry into the labour force varies across the income groups. For the other countries, the difference in retirement age for females would be two to four years.

Low-income females will have to work longer than the average male to have an equivalent number of years in retirement and sufficient assets to generate an equivalent pension. This is because females in low socioeconomic groups still have a life expectancy higher than the average male, even though differences in life expectancy across socioeconomic groups tend to be smaller for females.

Asset pay-out ratios

The relative value that pensioners receive from their retirement assets is typically higher for high-income than low-income pensioners because they receive their pension for a longer period. The asset pay-out ratio captures this notion. This ratio is calculated as the present value of gross pension income over the expected time spent in retirement divided by the assets accumulated at retirement.

Options involving some sort of annuitisation, either alone or combined with programmed withdrawals, result in the largest differences in asset pay-out ratios across socioeconomic groups. Table 6.2 shows that for the jurisdictions assessed here, programmed withdrawals never result in the largest differences in asset pay-out ratios between the low and high socioeconomic groups, despite the fact that the analysis assumes the same withdrawal limits across all groups.

Table 6.2. Pay-out option resulting in the largest difference in asset pay-out ratios across socioeconomic groups

	Males			Females		
Jurisdiction	PW	Annuity	Combination	PW	Annuity	Combination
Canada			X			X
Chile		X				X
Great Britain			X			X
Korea		X			X	
Mexico		X			X	
United States			X			X

Note: Combination pay-out options combine programmed withdrawals and annuity products, through either a deferred annuity or a delayed purchase. Shaded cells indicate that the given option is not available.

Annuity options can result in the highest asset pay-out ratios for all socioeconomic groups despite the implicit premium that low socioeconomic groups pay due to their lower life expectancies. Table 6.3 shows that this is true for males in Canada, Chile, and Mexico. However, this result will also depend on the level of anti-selection observed in the annuity market and the magnitude of the differences between the expected mortality of the low socioeconomic group and the difference in payments compared to those offered by programmed withdrawals. We could expect that low-income males in Great Britain, for example, would pay a higher premium due to both anti-selection and unisex pricing, so programmed withdrawals are more likely to be a better option. However, allowing for enhanced annuities eliminates the implicit premium and this option therefore results in the highest ratio for low earners.

In contrast to the result for males, programmed withdrawals tend to result in higher asset pay-out ratios for females than other options. The underlying reasons for this differ from one country to the next. In Canada, for example, limits on programmed withdrawals are the same for both genders whereas annuity pricing is gender distinct, which implies that programmed withdrawals will allow females to take a higher pension relative to their life expectancies. In Chile, the earlier retirement age of females drives this result.

Lump sums result in the highest ratios for Koreans and for males in low socioeconomic groups in the United States. In Korea, the mortality assumptions used for the pricing of the annuity drives this result, as they are based on a select group of insured individuals in Korea and therefore result in much higher life expectancies than those of the average population.

The remainder of this section looks at the actual asset pay-out ratios for each country specific pay-out options.[6]

Table 6.3. Pay-out option resulting in the highest asset pay-out ratio

Jurisdiction	Income level	Males				Females			
		PW	Annuity	Combination	Lump sum	PW	Annuity	Combination	Lump sum
Canada	Low		X			X			
	Average		X			X			
	High		X			X			
Chile	Low		X			X			
	Average		X			X			
	High		X			X			
Great Britain	Low	X						X	
	Average			X				X	
	High			X				X	
Korea	Low				X				X
	Average				X				X
	High				X				X
Mexico	Low		X			X			
	Average		X			X			
	High		X			X			
United States	Low				X	X			
	Average			X				X	
	High			X				X	

Note: The option of an enhanced annuity in Great Britain is not considered here. Shaded cells indicate that the option is not available. Combination pay-out options combine programmed withdrawals and annuity products either through a deferred annuity or the delayed purchase of an annuity.

Asset pay-out ratios for Canada

Depending on the type of plan, the pay-out of defined contribution plans in Canada can be subject to maximum or minimum withdrawal limits, and in most cases the option to use the accumulated assets to purchase a life annuity is also available. Some types of pension plans may also allow lump sums. Given the potential range of pay-out options, the analysis assesses the following options for Canada:

- Withdrawal at the minimum limit
- Withdrawal at the maximum limit
- The purchase of an immediate life annuity at retirement
- Withdrawal at the minimum limit until age 75 at which point an immediate life annuity is purchased with the remaining assets
- Withdrawal at the maximum limit until age 75 at which point an immediate life annuity is purchased with the remaining assets
- Withdrawing assets as a lump-sum at retirement[7]

The annuity option results in one of the smallest differences in outcomes across income groups. Table 6.4 shows that the pay-out option resulting in the largest difference in outcomes across income levels is the combination of taking minimum programmed withdrawals and deferring the purchase of an annuity to age 75.

Table 6.4. Asset pay-out ratios for Canada

Male

Income level	min PW	max PW	annuity	min PW + ann75	max PW + ann75	lump sum
Low	82.6%	99.8%	108.9%	104.9%	104.9%	101.0%
Average	83.7%	101.3%	110.1%	106.5%	106.3%	101.0%
High	89.3%	108.8%	115.8%	114.1%	112.9%	101.0%
spread	6.7%	8.9%	6.9%	9.2%	8.0%	0.0%

Female

Income level	min PW	max PW	annuity	min PW + ann75	max PW + ann75	lump sum
Low	89.2%	108.6%	106.1%	106.1%	105.9%	101.0%
Average	90.4%	110.2%	107.2%	107.5%	107.2%	101.0%
High	93.3%	112.5%	109.8%	111.0%	110.2%	101.0%
spread	4.1%	3.9%	3.8%	4.9%	4.3%	0.0%

For males, the purchase of an annuity results in the highest ratio for all income groups. For females, however, taking the maximum allowed programmed withdrawals results in the highest ratio. This result is reflective of the fact that the limits are the same for both genders, so would allow females to take a higher total level of income on average compared to males due to their longer lives.[8]

Pensioners taking programmed withdrawals at the minimum limit cannot expect to get back their assets in retirement with a return greater than the risk free rate, as indicated by ratios under 100. This is true even for the maximum withdrawal limit for low income males given that they have the shortest life expectancies.

Asset pay-out ratios for Chile

At retirement, individuals in Chile have the choice of using their assets accumulated within the mandatory defined contribution plan to take a programmed withdrawal, purchase an inflation indexed life annuity, purchase a deferred annuity combined with a programmed withdrawal, or take some combination of these options. The analysis therefore assesses the following pay-out options for Chile:

- Programmed withdrawal[9]
- Purchase of an inflation indexed annuity at retirement[10]
- Purchase of a 10-year deferred inflation indexed annuity at retirement, equal to 75% of the first temporary payment, combined with a programmed withdrawal for 10 years drawing the account to zero

For males, the purchase of an annuity at retirement results in a higher asset pay-out ratio than other options for all income groups (Table 6.5). Nevertheless, the difference in ratios across income groups is the largest for the annuity option. Programmed withdrawals result in the lowest ratio. For low-income males, ratios are below 100% for all pay-out options, indicating that they cannot expect to get back their accumulated assets with a return greater than the risk free rate.

Table 6.5. Asset pay-out ratios for Chile

Income level	Male			Female		
	PW	Annuity	Deferred annuity	PW	Annuity	Deferred annuity
Low	92.5%	98.6%	97.1%	103.0%	101.1%	97.7%
Average	98.9%	108.6%	106.1%	106.6%	105.6%	102.5%
High	102.8%	115.9%	112.6%	108.8%	108.6%	105.6%
spread	10.2%	17.3%	15.5%	5.8%	7.5%	7.9%

For females, programmed withdrawals result in the highest ratios for all income groups. This is driven again by the earlier retirement age of 60 (compared to 65 for males).[11] Programmed withdrawals also result in the smallest dispersion of outcomes across income groups, while the deferred annuity option results in the largest difference in ratios across income groups.

Asset pay-out ratios for Great Britain

Since 2015, pensioners face no restrictions regarding how to withdraw their savings at retirement from their defined contribution pension plan. As such, the analysis assesses several options:

- Programmed withdrawals based on an annuity factor calculated using gender distinct population mortality and the risk-free discount rate
- The purchase of an immediate annuity at retirement with 75% of assets, and taking the rest as a tax-free lump sum[12]
- The purchase of an immediate annuity at retirement

- Programmed withdrawals based on an annuity factor calculated using gender distinct population mortality and the risk-free discount rate until the age of 75, at which point an immediate annuity is purchased with the remaining assets
- The purchase of a 20 year deferred annuity at retirement with 10% of the accumulated assets, drawing down the remaining assets to zero over the twenty year period
- The purchase of an inflation indexed annuity at retirement
- The purchase of an enhanced annuity[13]
- Withdrawing all assets as a lump-sum at retirement[14]

The purchase of an enhanced annuity results in the lowest difference in the asset pay-out ratios between the low and high income groups (Table 6.6). This option allows low-income groups to purchase an annuity that provides higher payment given their lower life expectancy, and as such, it results in the highest overall asset pay-out ratio for the low income groups compared to other options.

Apart from the enhanced annuity option, options involving the purchase of an annuity generally result in a larger difference in the asset pay-out ratios across income groups for both genders, with the purchase of a 20-year deferred annuity resulting in the largest differences. Low earners tend to benefit relatively more from taking programmed withdrawals. For low-income males, no option involving regularly priced annuities results in a ratio over 100% due to a double penalty from their lower life expectancy and the unisex pricing of annuities. High earners benefit most from the option of combing programmed withdrawals with a deferred annuity, as they benefit more on average from the longevity risk protection that this option provides.

Table 6.6. Asset pay-out ratios for Great Britain

Males

Income	PW	Annuity + 25% lump sum	annuity	PW + ann75	PW + defann+20	Escalating annuity	Enhanced annuity	Lump sum
Low	101.8%	98.0%	97.0%	99.6%	99.7%	93.7%	111.4%	101.0%
Average	102.6%	99.1%	98.4%	100.7%	106.3%	95.4%	98.4%	101.0%
High	106.3%	104.7%	105.9%	107.1%	111.8%	104.7%	105.9%	101.0%
spread	4.5%	6.6%	8.9%	7.5%	12.0%	11.0%	-5.5%	0.0%

Females

Income	PW	Annuity + 25% lump sum	annuity	PW + ann75	PW + defann+20	Escalating annuity	Enhanced annuity	Lump sum
Low	103.5%	102.5%	103.0%	104.6%	104.2%	101.1%	109.4%	101.0%
Average	104.9%	104.4%	105.5%	107.0%	111.5%	104.3%	105.5%	101.0%
High	107.9%	109.1%	111.9%	112.9%	116.2%	112.6%	111.9%	101.0%
spread	4.4%	6.6%	8.8%	8.2%	12.0%	11.5%	2.5%	0.0%

Asset pay-out ratios for Korea

Defined contribution plans in Korea allow only two options for withdrawing assets. Individuals must either purchase a life annuity with the accumulated assets or take them as a lump sum.[15] This section assesses both of these options.

For both genders, lump sums result in a higher asset pay-out ratio than the purchase of an annuity at retirement for all income groups, with the difference between the two options for high income groups being smaller than that for low income groups. The mortality assumptions used for the pricing of the annuity drive this result because they imply much higher life expectancies than those of the average population and therefore lower incomes from the annuity. The difference in outcomes across socioeconomic groups for the annuity pay-out is particularly significant for males, with high income groups having a higher ratio than low income groups by 9.8 percentage points (Table 6.7).

Table 6.7. Asset pay-out ratios for Korea

Income level	Male		Female	
	annuity	lump sum	annuity	lump sum
Low	85.3%	101.0%	92.3%	101.0%
Average	90.1%	101.0%	94.5%	101.0%
High	95.1%	101.0%	95.0%	101.0%
spread	9.8%	0.0%	2.7%	0.0%

Asset pay-out ratios for Mexico

Mexico has two mandatory defined contribution pension systems into which employees are required to contribute, one for private sector workers and one for public sector workers. At retirement, individuals have the option of either using the accumulated assets to purchase an inflation-indexed life annuity or taking programmed withdrawals at a rate that changes with life expectancy. The analysis here assesses these two pay-out options for private sector workers.

Differences in the asset pay-out ratios for males across socioeconomic groups are expectedly small given the low gap in life expectancies, as shown in

Table 6.8. There is also little difference between the options of taking a programmed withdrawal or taking an inflation-linked annuity, though the ratio for the annuity is slightly higher.

The differences are larger for females, and in particular for the annuity, where the highly educated women can expect to receive 11.5 percentage points more from the retirement savings than the lower educated groups. However, for females the ratio for programmed withdrawals is higher than that for the annuity. Given the assumptions made for this analysis, the low and average income individuals would be required to take the programmed withdrawal option, as the income that an annuity would provide would be lower than the minimum guaranteed pension.[16]

Table 6.8. Asset pay-out ratios for Mexico

	Males		Females	
Income level	Programmed withdrawal	Inflation annuity	Programmed withdrawal	Inflation annuity
Low	91.2%	91.8%	96.7%	89.7%
Average	91.3%	92.0%	96.9%	90.0%
High	91.7%	92.7%	104.1%	101.2%
spread	0.5%	0.9%	7.4%	11.5%

Only high-income females can expect to receive a return on their accumulated assets of at least the risk-free rate in retirement, with ratios over 100% for both options. This result is largely due to low coverage of these types of pension plans, which results in a larger difference in mortality between the general population and the pensioner population. The mortality assumptions referenced for the pay-out amounts reflect the higher life expectancy of those covered by this pension system in Mexico.

Asset pay-out ratios for United States

The only constraint for withdrawing assets from a defined contribution plan in retirement is a required minimum distribution level from the age of 70 and a half. The analysis therefore considers a wide range of pay-out:

- Programmed withdrawals based on an annuity factor calculated using gender distinct population mortality and the risk free discount rate
- Programmed withdrawals at the required minimum distribution (RMD) level[17]
- The purchase of an immediate annuity at retirement
- Programmed withdrawals based on an annuity factor calculated using gender distinct population mortality and the risk free discount rate until the age of 75, at which point an immediate annuity is purchased with the remaining assets
- The purchase of a 20 year deferred annuity at retirement with 10% of the accumulated assets, drawing down the remaining assets to zero over the twenty year period
- The purchase of an inflation indexed annuity at retirement
- Withdrawing all assets as a lump-sum at retirement[18]

The pay-out option resulting in the largest differences in the asset pay-out ratio across socioeconomic groups for both genders is the combination of a programmed withdrawal and a 20 year deferred annuity. This option is also the one that results in the highest ratio for both genders for the aerage and high socioeconomic groups (Table 6.9).

Table 6.9. Asset pay-out ratios for the United States

Males

Income level	avg PW	min PW	annuity	PW + ann75	PW + ann def20	inflation annuity	lump sum
Low	98.0%	60.3%	95.3%	95.6%	92.9%	91.0%	101.0%
Average	100.6%	64.5%	99.5%	99.1%	102.4%	95.9%	101.0%
High	103.0%	69.1%	104.0%	102.7%	106.3%	101.3%	101.0%
spread	4.9%	8.7%	8.7%	7.1%	13.4%	10.3%	0.0%

Females

Income level	avg PW	min PW	annuity	PW + ann75	PW + ann def20	inflation annuity	lump sum
Low	102.6%	72.2%	101.0%	101.8%	102.2%	98.0%	101.0%
Average	103.1%	73.2%	101.9%	102.6%	108.3%	99.1%	101.0%
High	103.6%	74.3%	102.8%	103.4%	108.9%	100.2%	101.0%
spread	1.0%	2.1%	1.8%	1.6%	6.7%	2.2%	0.0%

For low socioeconomic groups, programmed withdrawals result in higher ratios compared to options involving annuities, which result in much lower pension income in retirement compared to other options.[19] However, the only option offering a ratio of at least 100% for low-income males is taking a lump sum.

Pension wealth ratios[20]

The pension wealth ratio looks at the expected present value of pension income relative to gross salary at retirement rather than relative to accumulated assets. This measure allows the analysis to account for the impact that public pensions and taxes have on pension outcomes across socioeconomic groups. The difference in the wealth ratios between the high and low groups and how this difference changes for the indicators for private pensions, total pension and net pensions indicate the impact that public pensions and tax have on the differences in relative pension outcomes across socioeconomic groups.[21]

The pension wealth ratio for private pensions is greater for high-income groups than low-income groups for all jurisdictions assessed except for Mexico. Table 6.10 shows in the first numerical column for each gender the difference in pension wealth ratios across socioeconomic groups for annuities and programmed withdrawals. In Mexico, low-income groups can expect a higher pension wealth by around one times their annual salary. This is because the total contribution levels in Mexico vary depending on income, with the government providing higher matching contributions for low-income workers into their defined contribution plan. This results in a higher pension for low earners relative to their pre-retirement income.

Table 6.10. Difference in pension wealth ratios between the high and low socioeconomic groups

Annuity[1]

Jurisdiction	Males					Females				
	Private	Total	*public pensions impact*	Net	*tax impact*	Private	Total	*public pensions impact*	Net	*tax impact*
Canada	0.4	-6.4	6.8	-8.2	1.8	0.2	-7.2	7.4	-8.8	1.6
Chile[2]	1.0	0.1	0.9	-1.8	1.9	0.3	-1.0	1.3	-2.3	1.3
Great Britain	0.5	-5.9	6.3	-6.3	0.4	0.5	-6.4	6.9	-6.9	0.5
Korea	1.2	-6.0	7.2	-7.1	1.0	0.3	-9.3	9.6	-10.1	0.8
United States	0.5	-3.6	4.1	-5.1	1.5	0.1	-4.9	5.0	-6.4	1.5

Programmed withdrawal[3]

Jurisdiction	Males					Females				
	Private	Total	*public pensions impact*	Net	*tax impact*	Private	Total	*public pensions impact*	Net	*tax impact*
Canada[4]	0.5	-6.3	6.8	-7.9	1.6	0.2	-7.2	7.4	-8.9	1.6
Chile	0.5	-0.4	0.9	-1.9	1.6	0.2	-1.1	1.3	-2.4	1.3
Great Britain[5]	0.2	-6.1	6.3	-6.4	0.3	0.2	-6.6	6.9	-7.0	0.4
Mexico	-1.0	-5.1	4.1	-5.1	0.0	-0.8	-5.4	4.7	-5.4	0.0
United States[5]	0.3	-3.8	4.1	-5.3	1.5	0.1	-5.0	5.0	-6.5	1.5

1. Mexico is not included as low and average income individuals will not have accumulated sufficient assets to be allowed to take an annuity at retirement.
2. Annuities in Chile are indexed to inflation.
3. Korea is not included, as programmed withdrawals are not allowed.
4. Maximum limit for Canada
5. Average withdrawal for Great Britain and United States based on annuity factor calculated with average population mortality.

Public pensions offset the relative differences in total pension wealth from differences in life expectancy for all jurisdictions assessed here. Table 6.10 also shows how the inclusion of public pensions and taxes affects these differences. A negative figure in the second numerical column for each gender of Table 6.10 indicates a higher total wealth ratio for low earners than for high earners. Low-income males in Canada, for example, can expect to receive a lower total pension by 0.4 times their annual pre-retirement income from purchasing an annuity relative to what high-income males can expect to receive. However, when public pensions are taken into account, they can expect to receive 6.4 times more their annual income relative to high earners. The difference between the pension wealth ratio based on total pension and that of the private pension ratio only is shown in the column labelled 'public pensions impact'. For the jurisdictions assessed here, the public pension in Korea has the largest offsetting impact for pension outcomes across socioeconomic groups when an annuity pay-out is selected. For programmed withdrawals, the public pension has the largest impact in Canada.

Tax rules can further offset the differences in pension outcomes across socioeconomic groups. The tax rules in all jurisdictions apart from Mexico further reduce the relative difference in pension income (Table 6.10). In Mexico, the high tax credits or exemptions that are in place result in little to no tax owed on pension income. Taxes generally have less of an offsetting impact than public pensions apart from Chile, where the impact of progressive taxation is equivalent or higher.

Income ratios[22]

The income ratios show whether the relative differences in pre-retirement income change during retirement. The calculations compare the expected average real income in retirement relative to that of the average earner. For all jurisdictions, progressive tax rules mean that the relative inequalities of pre-retirement salary between low and high earners are lower on a net basis than a gross basis.

Accounting for the progressivity of both public pensions and tax rules, reduces further the relative income differences across socio-economic groups in retirement. Relative differences in total pension income in retirement are smaller than the relative difference pre-retirement in all jurisdictions examined. Table 6.11 shows the total net pension income ratios for someone receiving income from public pensions and an annuity purchased with retirement savings. Low earners can expect to receive at least 59% of the total net pension income of the average earner. The pension of high earners is also significantly reduced below 300%, primarily because they receive relatively lower public pension benefits.

Table 6.11. Total net income ratios for males from an annuity pay-out

Jurisdiction	Low Earner	High Earner
Canada	0.59	1.54
Chile	0.64	2.45
Great Britain	0.76	1.95
Korea	0.62	2.02
Mexico[1]	0.94	2.34
United States	0.60	1.99

Note: The ratios for females are very similar.

1. Figures for Mexico are shown for the programmed withdrawal option.

6.3. Main results and policy implications

The objective of this analysis has been to assess the differences in pension outcomes across socioeconomic groups given differences in life expectancy observed in the general population. The indicators used attempt to highlight the differences in pension outcomes, as well as the potential for public pensions and tax rules to offset inequalities in pension outcomes across socioeconomic groups. This section first summarises the main results of the analysis, it then provides some qualifiers based on the assumptions made and finally presents some of the policy implications.

Main results

- The four indicators used capture different aspects of the disadvantage of low socioeconomic groups with respect to pension outcomes, but none of these measures on their own fully captures this disadvantage. Together, however, they can provide an indication of the potential disadvantage that low socioeconomic groups can face with respect to the time spent in retirement and their relative financial position in retirement given the contributions that they have made and existing relative differences in income.
- Retirement age would need to differ across socioeconomic groups in order to equalise the time spent working and contributing to pensions compared to the time spent in retirement. The retirement ratio shows this result by capturing the disadvantage that individuals in low socioeconomic groups may have due to a shorter expected time spent in retirement relative to their working lives. This is perhaps the most obvious disadvantage that those with shorter life expectancies will have for their retirement, but it cannot capture any financial disadvantage that these groups may experience in retirement.
- For a given retirement age, lower socioeconomic groups have a financial disadvantage from funded pension sources. They will receive a pension for a shorter expected period, and therefore will receive a lower 'return' on the contributions they have made towards their pension over their working lives.
- Taking an annuity at retirement often results in one of the highest asset pay-out ratios for all socioeconomic groups, but also the largest disparities across socioeconomic groups. Low earners pay an implicit tax on the price of the annuity to subsidise the longer lives and annuity payments for high earners because annuities are priced using average life expectancies. Low earners tend to benefit relatively more from taking programmed withdrawals, particularly low-income women.
- Higher public pension benefits for low-income individuals can reduce or even reverse the financial disadvantage they have relative to high earners. Nevertheless, with these measures the more subjective question of whether these inequalities are reduced 'enough' cannot be answered. Even if the rules can reverse relative difference, absolute differences, of course, remain.

Caveats

The results presented in this report are best-case scenarios in terms of the retirement assets accumulated and level of pension earned. First, contribution gaps are not considered, yet low socioeconomic groups are likely to have higher rates of disability and unemployment that could negatively affect the amount of pension income they can ultimately receive in retirement. Alternatively, the unemployment or disability benefits that these individuals receive could help to offset any negative impact on pensions. Second, the analysis assumes the same earnings patterns for all income groups, whereas low-income groups are more likely to experience flatter income profiles. Considering this would also increase the inequalities in pension outcomes.

The analysis also relies on the differences in mortality observed for the general population, rather than using life expectancy estimations based only on individuals receiving pensions from funded sources.[23] One advantage of this approach is that it provides a fuller picture of the potential for the entire pension system to ameliorate or exacerbate the disadvantage of low-income groups in retirement since the analysis takes into account public pensions. Another advantage is that the analysis can more easily be expanded to more jurisdictions, as mortality by socioeconomic group for the general population is more widely available than mortality for the population receiving pensions from funded sources. However, this approach is less reflective of the reality that in many countries the population receiving pensions from funded sources tends to be skewed towards higher socioeconomic groups. Within this population, the differences in life expectancy across socioeconomic groups would therefore be smaller compared to the differences across the entire population, and the resulting impact on pension outcomes reduced. Furthermore, the approach assumes that the low earners are receiving the full potential pension from both public and funded sources, whereas low earners are likely not making full contributions to private pension systems throughout their working life, particularly where contributions are voluntary. The analysis here may therefore present on the one hand an overstatement of the differences in pension outcomes from funded sources, and on the other hand an overly optimistic view of the reduction of relative income differences when considering all pension sources.

In addition, the current analysis assumes deterministic market and mortality variables. The stochastic nature of these variables could significantly affect pension outcomes and determine the optimal strategy for drawing down pension income. Programmed withdrawals, for example, would be more attractive in high-return environments, and traditional annuity products would be more beneficial in high volatility environments. Furthermore, as the analysis relies on average life expectancies, it does not capture the main advantage of annuity products to protect individuals from outliving their savings in retirement in the event that they live longer than expected.

The analysis also ignores considerations such as liquidity needs or the desire to leave a bequest to heirs. Both of these aspects could lead to a preference for less annuitisation of assets.

Finally, the assessment considers total life expectancy rather than healthy life expectancy. However, to the extent that differences in healthy life expectancy could be even larger across socioeconomic groups than total life expectancy, low socioeconomic groups could be at a particular disadvantage as they may not even be capable of working as long.

Nevertheless, the analysis does lead to several potential policy implications for reducing the inequalities in pension outcomes across socioeconomic groups.

Policy implications

First, annuities are a valuable option for pension pay-out for all socioeconomic groups, despite the implicit tax that lower socioeconomic groups pay. Allowing for segmentation of the annuity market and pricing based on variables that can be correlated with socioeconomic status (e.g. health, smoking) could reduce the implicit tax paid by low socioeconomic groups and improve further the benefit they can receive from an annuity.

However, some flexibility in the design of the pay-out phase and pension products is desirable. Annuities do not necessarily result in the best outcomes in all scenarios. Programmed withdrawals can be a valuable option particularly for low-income individuals and those retiring early.

In considering the entire pension system, the progressivity of the public pension system and tax rules can do a lot for reducing financial disadvantages in retirement. Old age safety nets and lower marginal tax rates for low incomes can significantly reduce or eliminate relative inequalities in pension outcomes across socioeconomic groups. The Mexican case demonstrated that additional contributions provided for low-income groups can also reduce differences in the relative total pension received.

Nevertheless reducing inequalities with respect to time spent working versus time spent in retirement will require some allowance for differences in retirement ages for different people. Having explicit rules that differ across socioeconomic groups, however, is not likely to be feasible or realistic in practice, but indirect ways to allow for differences could be considered. For example, linking the number of years spent contributing to the age at which full pension benefits can be received would allow lower educated individuals - who likely started working earlier than the highly educated - to also retire earlier. Such policies have been put in place, for example, in France, Germany and Portugal. Measures to encourage those who are able to continue working to do so could also be considered. For example, Sweden offers tax credits to individuals who decide to work beyond the statutory retirement age.

Differences in life expectancies between genders raise additional questions relating to fairness. The longer life expectancies of females imply that even those in low socioeconomic groups may need to work longer than males to maintain an equivalent proportion of time in retirement. Females are also more likely to have career interruptions relating to care-taking roles, which would reduce the level of assets they would have otherwise been able to accumulate at retirement. This implies that females are not only at a financial disadvantage when reaching retirement, but they are also more likely to outlive their male spouse. Joint and survivor pensions, discussed in more detail in Chapter 7, could help to mitigate this disadvantage by ensuring that the surviving female will continue to receive a portion of the pension of the deceased spouse. Pension legislation in Canada, for example, requires pension members with a spouse or common-law partner at the time of retirement to take a joint and survivor pension that pays at least 60% of the member's pension to the surviving spouse at the expense of a lower initial income when the member retires.

In addition, the ability of females to work longer may be an issue, as females can also expect to spend a longer time disabled in old age. Pension policy will therefore need to consider ways to account for the length of time individuals can expect to spend in retirement in good health as opposed to total life expectancy alone.

Policies intending to improve the sustainability of pension systems in light of the increases in life expectancy will need to consider how those in different socioeconomic groups and different genders may be impacted. Working longer on average will be required, but not all groups will necessarily be able to work longer. Increased flexibility around the age at which individuals can retire will be key to improving pension outcomes for all groups and ensuring that lower socioeconomic groups are not penalised in retirement due to having shorter life expectancies.

Notes

[1] The technical annex provides details regarding methodologies and mortality assumptions used for the analysis as well as more detailed results.

[2] Data availability and the fact that DC plans are common guided the choice of countries.

[3] The mortality assumptions used are those of Great Britain, not the United Kingdom.

[4] This measure has the advantage of being able to reflect differences in absolute financial outcomes across socioeconomic groups independent of income inequalities existing before retirement. However, it falls short in capturing the differences in terms of individual effort towards their retirement income. For example, if we assume that low earners enter the labour force earlier yet retire at the same age (so work longer), this measure can result in a higher relative pension wealth for low earners than high earners. This is because the additional pension income that low earners receive from the earlier pension contributions accumulated over 45 years is greater than the present value of pension income lost at the end of retirement due to shorter life expectancies.

[5] The general assumption is that low income and high income correspond with low and high socioeconomic groups regardless of the socioeconomic indicator used to derive life expectancy.

[6] The specific results for each country are not comparable across countries as the assumptions used and scenarios assessed are country-specific. For example, programmed withdrawals are not always calculated in the same manner, and the mortality assumptions on which annuity pricing is based may differ to varying degrees from the mortality of the general population in that jurisdiction. Country-specific results and assumptions can be found in the Technical Annex.

[7] This option will always result in a ratio of 101% rather than 100% as the analysis assumes that assets are withdrawn at the end of the year after retirement.

[8] Note, however, that the maximum limits also quickly exhaust the account, with all assets withdrawn at age 89.

[9] This is based on an annuity factor discounted at the expected real investment return of 3%.

[10] The ability to take this option is conditional on being able to finance an annuity at the level of the Basic Solidarity Pension. For this analysis, this option is not available for low-income females.

[11] However, for females, low-income workers will not have accumulated sufficient assets to opt for an annuity at retirement due to the earlier retirement age and higher life expectancies.

[12] Since 2012 insurance companies in the EU are required to price on a unisex basis, so unisex rates are assumed here for annuities, except for the enhanced annuity, which is assumed to be specifically underwritten for the low-income group based on gender distinct mortality.

[13] This is equivalent to the purchase of an immediate annuity for average and high-income groups, with only low-income groups receiving a higher annuity income from this option.

[14] This option will always result in a ratio of 101% rather than 100% as the analysis assumes that assets are withdrawn at the end of the year after retirement.

[15] The lump sum option will always result in a ratio of 101% rather than 100% as the analysis assumes that assets are withdrawn at the end of the year after retirement.

[16] The minimum guaranteed pension (PMG) was equivalent to MXN 33 180.36 for private sector workers as of December 2016 (OECD, 2017[5]).

[17] The RMD is defined in terms of a uniform lifetime table, and the RMD in amount is the account balance divided by the distribution period given in the table. This level is not defined before age 70, and is therefore assumed to be equivalent to 1.75 times the life expectancy of the male population, which is in the same order of magnitude as the limit at age 70.

[18] This option will always result in a ratio of 101% rather than 100% as the analysis assumes that assets are withdrawn at the end of the year after retirement.

[19] Excluding the option of taking the minimum required distributions, which results in a very low ratio indicating that it is not the optimal design for pay-out.

[20] Detailed results of the actual pension wealth calculations by country and pay-out option can be found in the Technical Annex.

[21] The assessment of the impact of public pensions relies on the replacement rate calculations presented in *Pensions at a Glance 2017*.

[22] More detailed results of the income ratio calculations by country can be found in the Technical Annex.

[23] Except for Chile, where the mortality assumptions are derived from those affiliated with the pension system, including pensioners with a pension amount lower than the PBS (Pensión Básica Solidaria).

References

Baulch, B. and A. Quisumbing((n.d.)), *Testing and adjusting for attrition in household panel data*. [8]

Cairns, A. et al. (2016), *Modelling Socio-Economic Differences in the Mortality of Danish Males Using a New Affluence Index*, Pensions Institute. [7]

Dercon, S. and I. Outes-Leon (2008), *Survey Attrition and Attrition Bias in Young Lives*. [9]

Luy, M. et al. (2015), "Life Expectancy by Education, Income and Occupation in Germany: Estimations Using the Longitudinal Survival Method", *Comparative Population Studies*, Vol. 40/4, pp. 399-436. [2]

Murtin, F. et al. (2017), "Inequalities in longevity by education in OECD countries: Insights from new OECD estimates", *OECD Statistics Working Papers*, No. 2017/2, OECD Publishing, Paris, http://dx.doi.org/10.1787/6b64d9cf-en. [1]

OECD (2017), *Pensions at a Glance 2017: OECD and G20 Indicators*, OECD Publishing, https://doi.org/10.1787/pension_glance-2017-en.. [5]

OECD (2016), *OECD Reviews of Pension Systems: Mexico*, OECD Publishing, Paris, http://dx.doi.org/10.1787/9789264245938-en. [10]

OECD (2015), *The tax treatment of funded private pension plans*, OECD Publishing, https://www.oecd.org/daf/fin/private-pensions/tax-treatment-pension-plans-country-profiles.pdf. [6]

OECD (2014), *Mortality Assumptions and Longevity Risk: Implications for pension funds and annuity providers*, OECD Publishing, Paris, http://dx.doi.org/10.1787/9789264222748-en. [3]

Superintendencia de Pensiones de Chile; Superintendencia Valores y Seguros de Chile; (2015), *Norma de Carácter General SP/SVS No. 398*. [4]

Annex 6.A. Technical annex

This Annex details the methodologies and assumptions used for the analysis in this chapter. The first section describes the Longitudinal Survival Method (LSM), which was used to derive the mortality rates across socioeconomic groups for Korea and Mexico. The following section explains how OECD data was used to derive life expectancies by educational group for Canada, Great Britain and the United States and how these estimates differ from those detailed in (Murtin et al., 2017[1]). The final sections describe the general and country-specific assumptions and results, including the specific details of the pay-out scenarios assessed, detailed results for the pension wealth ratios and income ratios, and the mortality assumptions used. The methodology used to derive mortality rates and life expectancy estimates for Chile, which relied directly from pensioners' data, is explained in the section pertaining to Chile.

Longitudinal Survival Method (LSM)

The main challenge in deriving estimates of mortality for different socioeconomic groups is the lack of mortality data linked to socioeconomic variables. One potential source of data is longitudinal surveys, as they can track whether individuals are still alive and typically ask a number of questions that can indicate an individual's socioeconomic level. The number of respondents for such surveys, however, is usually not sufficiently large to derive robust mortality assumptions on their own.

The Longitudinal Survival Method developed by (Luy et al., 2015[2]) is a method inspired by indirect methods of mortality estimation which have been developed to estimate the mortality of populations with incorrect, incomplete or no data. However, methodological similarity enables LSM to estimate the mortality of the population of interest and its various subgroups based on the direct observation of mortality provided by longitudinal studies. It derives its estimations by adjusting the observed mortality of population subgroups from the known mortality of the entire population, as measured by life tables developed based on historical mortality data of the general population. As such, it overcomes the need for large amounts of data and has the potential to produce reasonable estimates for mortality and life expectancy based on a rather limited number of observations and a small number of inputs. The only inputs needed are the period of observation, the observed mortality of the general population over the period of observation (typically given by the life tables developed by national statistical bodies), the observed mortality of the respondents to the longitudinal survey, and basic demographic information for the respondents including birthday, gender and any socioeconomic variable that will be used for the analysis.

The accuracy of the methodology relies on the representativeness of the population sample of the longitudinal survey to that of the general population. That is, the total mortality of the sample is expected to be the same as that of the general population, and the improvements in life expectancy of the sample and all of its subpopulations over the period of observation mirror that of the general population.

Three main quantities are calculated to derive the estimated survival rates per age:

1. S_R - the observed probability of survival of respondents to the longitudinal survey between the first and last survey waves (the period of observation, z)
2. S_L - the expected probability of survival for a given cohort of the population over the period of observation, z (i.e. accounting for mortality improvements experienced over the period)
3. S_P - the expected probability of survival in the year corresponding to the central year of the period of observation, t (i.e. no mortality improvements accounted for)

For the calculation of S_R, respondents are grouped corresponding to their exact age, resulting in an average age of respondents of $\bar{x}$ over an average time between the first and last survey of $\bar{z}$. In practice, there are often not a sufficient number of observations to observe a death at every age in the longitudinal survey. S_R is therefore calculated based on a rolling weighted average of a larger age group, e.g. S_R for individuals aged 65 at their last birthday is estimated by summing the deaths and observations for the ages 60 to 70.

With these inputs, the estimated survival rate from age $\bar{x}$ to $\bar{x} + \bar{z}$ in year t becomes:

$$_zp_x = S_{R_x} \cdot {}^{S_{P_x}}\!/_{S_{L_x}}$$

The ratio S_{P_x}/S_{L_x} is thus used as an adjustment factor to convert the observed cohort survival (which would have experienced mortality improvements over time) to the period survival rate which would have been experienced in the central year of observation.

The z-year estimated survival rates for each age $\bar{x}$ are then converted into single year survival rates at each age x with these steps:

1. For each age x, the l_x given by the period life table (i.e. the number of expected survivors at age x) is interpolated between x and x+1 to calculate the l_x for the average exact age of the observations $\bar{x}$ and $\bar{x} + \bar{z}$.
2. An adjustment factor is calculated by dividing the z year survival for age x by the observed survival for $\bar{x}$ (based on the l_x calculated in Step 1) to adjust the survival rate from $\bar{x}$ to the exact age x at last birthday.
3. An adjustment factor is calculated by taking the difference of the logit of S_R and the logit S_P, taking into account the adjustment calculated in Step 2, to adjust the general population mortality to the mortality of the subgroup of interest.
4. The adjustment factor calculated in Step 3 is applied to the logit of the single year survival probabilities given by the period life table to obtain the estimated single year mortality rates for the subgroup of interest.

These steps are repeated for each $\bar{x}$, each resulting in an estimated set of mortality rates for year t. The final estimated mortality rates for the subgroup for each age x is obtained by taking a weighted average of these sets of rates. Additional smoothing can then be applied using the Brass methodology to change the shape of the survival curve, given a sufficient number of observations, to improve the fit of the estimated rates to the observed data, but is not necessary in all cases.

OECD mortality estimates by education

The data used to derive life expectancy estimates by educational attainment are described in (Murtin et al., 2017[1]). Low education refers to individuals having an educational attainment up to lower secondary level, average education refers to those having completed secondary education, and high education refers to those having completed tertiary education. This data was used as a basis for the estimations provided in this report for Canada, Great Britain and the United States, however there are some methodological differences to derive the mortality rates and life expectancies.

Life expectancy estimates in (Murtin et al., 2017[1]) use Chiang's method for abridged life tables based on smoothed mortality pooled into five year age groups and extrapolated to ages over 94 using the Gompartz methodology.

Estimates for this report use cubic splines with a smoothing parameter of 0.5 to interpolate the pooled mortality rates for individual ages through age 90, and use the Kannisto methodology fitted to ages 76-90 to extrapolate beyond age 90 to age 120, unless otherwise stated in the country specific assumptions. In addition, cohort life expectancies for 2016 were used for this analysis assuming the mortality improvement scale indicated for the given country rather than the period life expectancies given in (Murtin et al., 2017[1]).

General assumptions used for the analysis

The baseline scenario presented assumes an entry age of 20 and the statutory retirement age specific to the jurisdiction assessed. The salary of the average worker is based on average worker earnings in 2016, with low-income individuals earning 50% of the average income, and high-income individuals 300% of the average income.[1] The calculation of total pension payments received (private pension + public pension) is based on the replacement rates for public pensions using these same income assumptions, and is assumed to be indexed to inflation unless otherwise noted.[2] Net indicators are calculated based on the tax rules specific to each jurisdiction and assume that thresholds given for future years change in line with inflation.[3] For all jurisdictions assessed, assumptions are that salary increases each year in line with inflation (2%) and productivity (1.25%), real investment returns are 3% and the real risk-free rate is 2%.[4] All contributions and pension payments and withdrawals are assumed to occur at the end of the year.

Country specific results and assumptions

Canada

This analysis considers defined contribution pension plans in Canada. The two main types are Registered Pension Plans (RPPs) and Registered Retirement Savings Plans (RRSPs).

RPPs are established by employers. These plans are portable, and upon leaving their employer, employees may either transfer their accumulated assets into their new employer's plan or into a locked-in retirement account. At retirement accumulated assets must be used to purchase either a Life Income Fund (LIF) or a life annuity from an insurer. If a LIF is chosen, annual withdrawals are allowed from age 55 and are subject to minimum and maximum withdrawal limits which increase with age. Some provinces require that funds remaining in the LIF at a certain age be used to purchase a life annuity.

RRSPs are tax-deferred voluntary personal retirement savings plans into which contributions may be made up until the age of 71. There is not an effective minimum age at which withdrawals can begin, however by age 71 the funds must be transferred into a Registered Retirement Income Fund (RRIF), used to purchase a life annuity from an insurer, or withdrawn as a lump-sum. If an RRIF is chosen, withdrawals are subject to an annual minimum percentage of assets which increase with age. No maximum withdrawal limit is imposed.

The analysis assumes that individuals contribute 8.5% of their annual salary to their pension plan.

Pension wealth ratios

The pension wealth ratios for Canada, shown in Annex Table 6.A.1 demonstrate that public pensions can significantly offset the financial disadvantage that lower income groups have with respect to the pension income they can receive in retirement. While low income groups can expect 20-50% of their annual income less from private pensions compared to the high income groups, when public pensions are accounted for they can expect to receive six to seven times more their annual salary in total. Taxes further offset these differences at the income levels assumed. While low and average earners benefit from tax credits which offset most if not all of the tax owed on their pension, high earners still pay additional tax.

Annex Table 6.A.1. Pension wealth ratios for Canada

		Males				Females			
		Low	Average	High	spread	Low	Average	High	spread
min PW	Private	4.6	4.6	4.9	0.4	4.9	5.0	5.2	0.2
	Total	14.0	11.9	7.6	(6.4)	15.2	12.9	8.0	(7.2)
	Net	14.0	11.9	6.5	(7.5)	15.2	12.9	6.8	(8.3)
max PW	Private	5.5	5.6	6.0	0.5	6.0	6.1	6.2	0.2
	Total	15.0	12.9	8.7	(6.3)	16.2	14.0	9.0	(7.2)
	Net	15.0	12.9	7.1	(7.9)	16.2	14.0	7.4	(8.9)
annuity	Private	6.0	6.1	6.4	0.4	5.9	5.9	6.1	0.2
	Total	15.5	13.4	9.1	(6.4)	16.1	13.8	8.9	(7.2)
	Net	15.5	13.4	7.3	(8.2)	16.1	13.8	7.3	(8.8)
min PW + annuity at 75	Private	5.8	5.9	6.3	0.5	5.9	5.9	6.1	0.3
	Total	15.3	13.2	9.0	(6.3)	16.1	13.8	9.0	(7.1)
	Net	15.3	13.1	7.3	(8.0)	16.1	13.8	7.4	(8.7)
max PW + annuity at 75	Private	5.8	5.9	6.2	0.4	5.9	5.9	6.1	0.2
	Total	15.3	13.2	8.9	(6.3)	16.1	13.8	8.9	(7.2)
	Net	15.3	13.2	7.2	(8.0)	16.1	13.8	7.3	(8.8)
lump sum	Private	5.6	5.6	5.6	-	5.6	5.6	5.6	-
	Total	14.8	12.8	8.2	(6.6)	15.5	13.3	8.3	(7.2)
	Net	12.9	10.4	5.6	(7.3)	13.5	10.9	5.7	(7.9)

Income ratios

The rules around public pensions and taxation also mean that the relative differences in pension income across income groups is reduced in retirement compared to the relative differences over working lives. Annex Table 6.A.2 shows that low income individuals earning 53% of the net average salary can receive nearly 60% of the average pension in retirement.

Annex Table 6.A.2. Post-tax total pension income ratios for Canada

	Males			Females		
	Low	Average	High	Low	Average	High
pre-retirement	0.53	1.00	2.52	0.53	1.00	2.52
min PW	0.60	1.00	1.54	0.60	1.00	1.54
max PW	0.59	1.00	1.56	0.59	1.00	1.51
annuity	0.59	1.00	1.54	0.59	1.00	1.54
min PW + ann75	0.59	1.00	1.56	0.59	1.00	1.55
max PW + ann75	0.59	1.00	1.55	0.59	1.00	1.55
lump sum	0.64	1.00	1.43	0.64	1.00	1.43

Mortality assumptions

Canadian population mortality is based on the 2009-2011 life tables from Statistics Canada for males and females. The life expectancy of the average earner is based on this data.

Life expectancies for those with low and high education/income were based on the data used in (Murtin et al., 2017[1]) by educational attainment for a central year of 2009.

Mortality improvements for all socioeconomic levels are based on the mortality improvements developed in the Canadian Pensioners Mortality study (as described in (OECD, 2014[3])).

Factors used to price the annuity options were based on the GAM-94 mortality table with the mortality improvement assumptions developed by the Canadian Institute of Actuaries (as described in (OECD, 2014[3])).

Chile

All formally employed individuals in Chile must contribute 10% of their salary to an individual defined contribution pension up to a limit of 73.2 UF.[5] For low-income individuals, the state makes additional contributions in the form of a subsidy for young workers with low incomes.[6]

The analysis assumes the statutory retirement ages of 65 for males and 60 for females. At retirement, individuals have the choice of using their accumulated assets to take a programmed withdrawal, purchase an inflation indexed life annuity, purchase a deferred annuity combined with a programmed withdrawal, or take some combination of these options.[7] Programmed withdrawals are subject to maximum limits based on an actuarially neutral annuity factor calculated with the expected return on investment. For the deferred annuity option, the income received must be at least 50% but less than 100% of the first temporary payment withdrawn.

If accumulated assets are not sufficient to purchase an annuity providing the legal minimum pension,[8] individuals must draw down their assets by taking a programmed withdrawal.

Pension wealth ratios

Annex Table 6.A.3 shows that low-income individuals can expect to receive an overall lower pension relative to their level of income from private pensions compared to high income individuals.

Annex Table 6.A.3. Pension wealth ratios for Chile

Males

Pension income	Programmed withdrawal			Annuity			Deferred annuity		
	Private	Total	Net	Private	Total	Net	Private	Total	Net
Low	6.3	7.2	6.6	6.7	7.6	7.0	6.6	7.5	6.9
Average	6.6	6.6	5.5	7.2	7.2	6.0	7.0	7.0	5.9
High	6.8	6.8	4.7	7.7	7.7	5.2	7.5	7.5	5.1
spread	0.5	(0.4)	(1.9)	1.0	0.1	(1.8)	0.9	(0.0)	(1.8)

Females

Pension income	Programmed withdrawal			Annuity			Deferred annuity		
	Private	Total	Net	Private	Total	Net	Private	Total	Net
Low	5.9	7.2	6.9	5.8	7.1	6.8	5.6	6.9	6.6
Average	6.0	6.0	5.5	5.9	5.9	5.4	5.8	5.8	5.3
High	6.1	6.1	4.5	6.1	6.1	4.5	5.9	5.9	4.4
Spread	0.2	(1.1)	(2.4)	0.3	(1.0)	(2.3)	0.3	(1.0)	(2.2)

The relative levels of the ratio for low and high earners equalise or reverse when accounting for public pension benefits to which low-income individuals are entitled. Low-income males receive nearly an additional year of their annual income when public benefits are accounted for, and females around 1.3 additional years of salary.

Taxes further offset the difference in pension outcomes between high and low income groups. The dispersion of net pension wealth between low and high earners is similar across all types of pay-outs, with low earning males receiving around 1.8 times their income more than high earners, and females around 2.3 times their income more.

Income ratios

Relative differences in pension income decrease in retirement when total pensions and taxes are accounted for Annex Table 6.A.4 shows that income taxation reduces income inequality for pre-retirement income compared to the 0.5 for low-income earners and 3.0 for high-income earners gross of tax. The inclusion of public pensions and the specific tax treatment of retirement income results in more significantly reduced income inequalities in retirement for all types of pay-out.

Annex Table 6.A.4. Post-tax total pension income ratios for Chile

Income level	Pre-retirement	Males			Females		
		PW	Annuity	Deferred annuity	PW	Annuity	Deferred annuity
Low	0.57	0.67	0.64	0.65	0.67	0.65	0.66
Average	1.00	1.00	1.00	1.00	1.00	1.00	1.00
High	2.73	2.41	2.45	2.44	2.40	2.40	2.42

Mortality assumptions

Programmed withdrawals are based on an actuarially neutral annuity factor derived using the 2016 Chilean pensioner mortality table and the expected real investment rate of return. Annuity conversion factors are based on this same mortality table and the risk free discount rate.

Mortality rates by socioeconomic group were derived from an analysis of the data of affiliates to the Chilean pension system. Low, average and high socioeconomic groups are defined as being in the first, third and fifth quintile of the first pension income received by pensioners. The analysis assumed mortality improvements from the 2014 Chilean mortality tables for the calculation of the indicators.

Derivation of mortality rates

Mortality rates were derived from 1.3 million observations of pension affiliates between 2008 and 2016. Death and exposure calculations relied on the methodology used to develop the 2014 Chilean mortality tables, as detailed in (Superintendencia de Pensiones de Chile; Superintendencia Valores y Seguros de Chile;, 2015[4]). The resulting mortality rates for a central year of 2012 were smoothed using the Whittaker-Henderson method of graduation between the ages of 55 and 95. For older ages, mortality rates were extrapolated to 110 using the Kannisto method fitted to the graduated mortality rates for those aged 80 to 95.

Annex Table 6.A.5 shows the estimates of period life expectancy at age 60 for females and 65 for males by quintiles of first pension income calculated using the rates smoothed and extrapolated as described above. The difference in life expectancy between the 1st and 5th quintile is 3.3 years for females and 4.3 years for males.

Annex Table 6.A.5. Period life expectancy at age 60 (females) and 65 (males) by quintile of first pension income

	First pension income quintile				
Gender	1	2	3	4	5
Female	25.6	26.7	27.3	27.9	28.9
Male	15.9	17.9	18.3	19.0	20.2

Note: These figures do not incorporate mortality improvements. However, the calculation of the indicators assumes the mortality improvements from the 2014 Chilean mortality tables.

Great Britain[9]

Since 2012, employers have been required to auto-enrol employees into workplace pension schemes, with full rollout completed in 2018. These schemes are usually defined contribution schemes, and minimum contributions are building to 8% of earnings in 2019. The analysis therefore assumes that contributions are 8%.

Statutory retirement age is currently 65 for men and 62.5 for females, though the age will be 65 for both genders in 2018 and increase further to age 67 for both genders by 2028 (OECD, 2017[5]). The analysis assumes a retirement age of 65 for both genders.

Following the removal of an effective requirement to purchase a life annuity at retirement in 2015, pensioners face no restrictions regarding how to withdraw their savings at retirement.

Pension wealth ratios

In order to account for the impact that public pensions and tax rules can have on pension outcomes, Annex Table 6.A.6 shows the pension wealth ratios for DC pensions, total pensions, and total pensions net of tax.

Annex Table 6.A.6. Pension wealth ratios for Great Britain

		Males				Females			
		Low	Average	High	spread	Low	Average	High	spread
	Private	5.3	5.3	5.5	0.2	5.4	5.5	5.6	0.2
PW	Total	13.1	9.3	7.0	(6.1)	13.8	9.8	7.2	(6.6)
	Net	12.7	8.7	6.3	(6.4)	13.5	9.3	6.5	(7.0)
	Private	5.1	5.2	5.5	0.3	5.3	5.4	5.7	0.3
Annuity + 25% lump sum	Total	12.5	8.9	6.8	(5.7)	13.4	9.6	7.2	(6.2)
	Net	12.2	8.4	6.1	(6.1)	13.1	9.0	6.4	(6.7)
	Private	5.1	5.1	5.5	0.5	5.4	5.5	5.8	0.5
Annuity	Total	12.8	9.1	7.0	(5.9)	13.8	9.8	7.4	(6.4)
	Net	12.2	8.3	5.9	(6.3)	13.1	9.0	6.3	(6.9)
	Private	5.2	5.2	5.6	0.4	5.5	5.6	5.9	0.4
PW + ann75	Total	13.0	9.2	7.0	(5.9)	13.9	9.9	7.5	(6.4)
	Net	12.5	8.5	6.2	(6.3)	13.4	9.2	6.5	(6.8)
	Private	5.2	5.5	5.8	0.6	5.4	5.8	6.1	0.6
PW + defann+20	Total	13.0	9.5	7.3	(5.7)	13.9	10.2	7.6	(6.2)
	Net	12.6	8.9	6.5	(6.1)	13.5	9.5	6.8	(6.7)
	Private	4.9	5.0	5.5	0.6	5.3	5.4	5.9	0.6
Escalating annuity	Total	11.8	8.0	5.9	(6.0)	12.7	8.7	6.2	(6.5)
	Net	11.4	7.4	5.0	(6.3)	12.3	8.1	5.4	(6.9)
	Private	5.8	5.1	5.5	(0.3)	5.7	5.5	5.8	0.1
Enhanced annuity	Total	13.6	9.1	7.0	(6.6)	14.1	9.8	7.4	(6.7)
	Net	12.8	8.3	5.9	(6.9)	13.4	9.0	6.3	(7.1)
	Private	5.3	5.3	5.3	-	5.3	5.3	5.3	-
Lump sum	Total	13.0	9.2	6.7	(6.3)	13.7	9.6	6.8	(6.9)
	Net	12.2	7.6	4.2	(7.9)	12.8	8.0	4.3	(8.5)

The inclusion of public pensions largely offsets the relative differences in pension outcomes across socioeconomic groups.[10] While for funded DC pensions, low earners could expect to receive around one to two thirds of their annual salary less in total pensions relative to high earners, with public pensions they can expect to receive on average around 6 to 7 times more their annual salary in total. Tax rules can further reverse these differences, but to a lesser extent.[11]

Income ratios

Annex Table 6.A.7 shows that relative differences in income are significantly reduced in retirement. Whereas the low earner could expect to earn a net salary 53% that of the average earner, in retirement they can expect a pension that is 75-80% that of the average pension.

Annex Table 6.A.7. Post-tax total income ratios for Great Britain

	Males			Females		
	Low	Average	High	Low	Average	High
Pre-retirement	0.53	1.00	2.50	0.53	1.00	2.50
PW	0.75	1.00	1.94	0.76	1.00	1.89
Annuity + 25% lump sum	0.75	1.00	1.95	0.76	1.00	1.92
Annuity	0.76	1.00	1.95	0.76	1.00	1.93
PW + ann75	0.75	1.00	1.96	0.76	1.00	1.94
PW + defann+20	0.73	1.00	1.99	0.74	1.00	1.94
Escalating annuity	0.79	1.00	1.85	0.79	1.00	1.83
Enhanced annuity	0.79	1.00	1.95	0.77	1.00	1.93
Lump sum	0.85	1.00	1.46	0.85	1.00	1.41

Mortality Assumptions

Population mortality was based on the 2013-2015 life tables for Great Britain from the Office of National Statistics. The mortality rates in the life tables were extrapolated from age 100 to age 120 with the Kannisto methodology. The rates assumed for programmed withdrawals is based these assumptions.

For low and high education/income groups, life expectancies were based on the data used in Murtin et al (2017) by educational attainment for a central year of 2011. Enhanced annuity rates rely on the mortality rates for those with low educational attainment.

Normal annuity rates are based on the LML08 and LFL08 tables developed for life annuitants. Unisex rates were derived by taking the average of the male and female rates.

All mortality assumptions are projected forward with improvements using the CMI model calibrated to data from England and Wales, and a long term improvement assumption of 1.25%.

Korea

This assessment assumes contributions go towards a defined contribution plan, and that pension payments can be taken either as a lump sum or an annuity at retirement. Private pensions in Korea are occupational, which are quasi-mandatory and take the form either of a defined benefit or defined contribution plan, or voluntary personal pension savings accounts. Pay-outs from either plan can be received as a lump sum or annuity. Other types of pay-outs are not allowed.

Total contributions are assumed to be 18.3%, with 8.3% assumed to be paid by the employer (the minimum allowed employer contribution) and the remaining 10% assumed to be paid by the employee (OECD, 2015[6]). Retirement age for both males and females is assumed to be 65.[12]

Pension wealth ratios

Public pensions and progressive taxation offset the relative differences in total pension wealth from differences in life expectancy. Annex Table 6.A.8 shows that while low income individuals can expect to receive an overall lower pension relative to their level of income from private pensions compared to high income individuals, the relative levels of the ratio reverse when accounting for public pensions. Low income individuals receive at least eight times their annual income in additional pension wealth when public pensions are accounted for, compared to around three times more for high-income people.

Annex Table 6.A.8. Pension wealth ratios for Korea

Males

Pension income	Annuity			Lump sum		
	Private	Total	Net	Private	Total	Net
Low	10.2	20.2	18.9	12.1	22.1	18.5
Average	10.8	18.0	16.3	12.1	19.3	15.0
High	11.3	14.2	11.8	12.1	14.9	10.2
spread	1.2	(6.0)	(7.1)	-	(7.2)	(8.3)

Females

Pension income	Annuity			Lump sum		
	Private	Total	Net	Private	Total	Net
Low	11.0	23.9	22.5	12.1	24.9	21.3
Average	11.3	20.2	18.4	12.1	21.0	16.7
High	11.3	14.6	12.4	12.1	15.3	10.7
spread	0.3	(9.3)	(10.1)	-	(9.6)	(10.6)

Taxes further offset the difference in pension outcomes between high and low income groups, shown in the 'Net' columns. When an annuity is taken, pension wealth decreases by a factor of nearly 1.5 annual income when accounting for taxes paid for low income compared to just under 2.5 for high income earners, so in other words low income earners pay relatively lower taxes. The result is that low income males can expect to receive 7.1 times their annual income more in pension net of tax from an annuity than high income males, and low income females expect to receive 10.1 times more.

Annuities remain an attractive option for all income groups compared to lump sums. Lump sums are taxed relatively more than the annuity option, so while pension wealth is higher for lump sums compared to annuities on a gross basis, the annuity option provides a higher pension wealth ratio on an after tax basis.

Income ratios

Annex Table 6.A.9 shows that while income taxation only slightly reduces relative income differences for pre-retirement income, the inclusion of public pensions and the specific tax treatment of retirement income results in more significantly reduced differences in retirement. This is true for both annuity and lump sum pay-outs.

Annex Table 6.A.9. Post-tax total pension income ratios for Korea

Income level	Pre-retirement	Males		Females	
		annuity	lump sum	annuity	lump sum
Low	0.51	0.62	0.68	0.63	0.67
Average	1.00	1.00	1.00	1.00	1.00
High	2.70	2.02	1.80	1.98	1.76

Mortality assumptions

Annuity conversion factors are based on the 6th EMT mortality table along with improvements projected using the Lee-Carter model using Korean life tables from 1997-2011.[13]

Mortality rates for the different socioeconomic groups have been derived using the Longitudinal Survival Method (LSM) applied to the data obtained from the KLoSA longitudinal study carried out between 2006 and 2014 and based on self-evaluated economic status. This analysis produced mortality estimates for a central observation year of 2010. The same mortality improvements from the Lee-Carter model were applied to these estimates. The following section details the results and caveats of the LSM applied to Korean data.

LSM applied to Korean data

The initial KLoSA is a total sample of 4 463 men and 5 791 women. 1 968 observations (811 men and 1 157 women) are dropped due to nonresponse to the final survey, resulting in total input data of 3 652 men and 4 634 women aged between 45 and 98.[14] For the LSM, respondents over the age of 80 were also dropped.

Annex Table 6.A.10. Grouping of self-reported economic status for KLoSA

Economic category	Self-evaluated economic status	Freqency	Percent
Low	0	519	6.64%
	1	326	4.17%
	2	563	7.21%
Medium	3	981	12.56%
	4	751	9.61%
	5	1,645	21.06%
	6	884	11.32%
High	7	1,087	13.92%
	8	731	9.36%
	9	226	2.89%
	10	98	1.25%
Total		7,811	100.00%

The reported self-evaluation of economic status was used as the socioeconomic indicator to derive mortality rates by socioeconomic group.[15] Respondents answered a question asking how satisfied they were on a scale of 0 to 10 with their economic situation relative to their peers. While this measure is subjective, it has the advantage of being able to capture more broadly the economic situation of the individual than is possible from using a single quantitative measure based on income or wealth, for example, which have not by themselves to be robust indicators of socioeconomic status (Cairns et al., 2016[7]). The responses were grouped as shown in the Annex Table 6.A.10 into low, medium and high socioeconomic groups.

The resulting life expectancies at age 65 calculated for the low, medium and high economic groups for males and females are shown in Annex Table 6.A.11.

Annex Table 6.A.11. Life expectancies at age 65 by economic status for Korea using the LSM

Socioeconomic group	Males	Females
Low	15.0	20.1
Medium	17.6	21.4
High	19.4	22.0

Mexico

Mexico has two mandatory defined contribution pension system into which employees are required to contribute: one for private sector workers and one for public sector workers. For private sector workers, the system which is assessed for this analysis, total contributions of 6.5% of earnings are made up of 1.125% from workers, 5.15% from employers and 0.225% from the government. On top of these contributions, the government provides a supplementary contribution called the social quota which varies based on income level. This results in total contributions of 8.2%, 7.4% and 6.5% of annual salary for the low, average and high income workers that are assessed here, respectively.

At retirement, which is assumed to be the statutory retirement age of 65, individuals have the option of either using the accumulated assets to purchase an inflation-indexed life annuity or taking programmed withdrawals at a rate which changes with life expectancy. If the accumulated assets are not sufficient to purchase an annuity providing an income at least as high as the minimum guaranteed pension, the individual must instead take the programmed withdrawal at this level until the account is depleted, after which the government will provide the minimum guaranteed pension.

These two pay-out options are therefore assessed here: the purchase of an immediate inflation-indexed annuity at retirement and programmed withdrawals.

Pension wealth ratios

The pension wealth ratios, shown in Annex Table 6.A.12 are highest for low-income individuals even before public pensions and taxes are accounted for due to the additional social quota contributions that vary by wage level. Low and average earners cannot take an annuity because the income provided would be lower than the minimum guaranteed pension. Public pension benefits significantly increase these ratios for low-income groups in particular. These ratios do not change when taxes are taken into account, however, as pension benefits are tax-exempt up to 15 times the annual minimum wage, which is higher than the benefits calculated for all income groups for this analysis.[16]

Annex Table 6.A.12. Pension wealth ratios for Mexico

Males

Income level	Programmed withdrawal			Inflation annuity		
	Private	Total	Net	Private	Total	Net
Low	4.9	9.0	9.0	4.9		
Average	4.4	4.8	4.8	4.5		
High	3.9	3.9	3.9	3.9	3.9	3.9
spread	(1.0)	(5.1)	(5.1)	(1.0)	-	-

Females

Income level	Programmed withdrawal			Inflation annuity		
	Private	Total	Net	Private	Total	Net
Low	5.2	9.8	9.8	4.8		
Average	4.7	5.1	5.1	4.4		
High	4.4	4.4	4.4	4.3	4.3	4.3
spread	(0.8)	(5.4)	(5.4)	(0.5)	-	-

Income ratios

Annex Table 6.A.13 shows that relative differences in income are reduced in retirement for total pension income from programmed withdrawals, the only option available to all income groups. As both low and average income individuals receive the minimum guaranteed pension in most years, their income in retirement is very close.

Annex Table 6.A.13. Post-tax total pension income ratios for Mexico

Income level	Pre-retirement	Programmed withdrawal	
		Males	Females
Low	0.64	0.94	0.97
Average	1.00	1.00	1.00
High	2.61	2.34	2.25

Mortality assumptions

Average population mortality is based on 2009 figures from CONAPO, extrapolated to age 110 using the Kannisto methodology. Population mortality is assumed to follow the improvements used in the EMSSA 09 mortality table.

The maximum limits for programmed withdrawals are based on an actuarially neutral annuity factor derived using the EMSSA 09 mortality table and the risk-free rate of return. Annuity conversion factors are based on this same table and discount assumptions.

Mortality rates for the different socioeconomic have been derived using the Longitudinal Survival Method (LSM) applied to the data obtained from the Mexican Health and Aging Study (MHAS) longitudinal study carried out between 2001 and 2015.[17] Socio-economic groups are based on quartiles of the number of years of completed education for a central observation year of 2008, and subsequent mortality improvements are assumed to follow those used for the EMSSA 09 table.

The LSM is based on data collected by the MHAS in 2001, 2003, 2012, 2015 and panels for individuals born between 1895 and 1982. This resulted in a total sample of 6,504 men and 8,682 women, with 2,253 observations (937 men and 1,316 women) dropped from nonresponse to the final survey.[18] The input data is therefore composed of 5,567 men and 7,366 women aged between 20 and 105. People aged below 33 and over 69 (1,263 men and 1,440 women) are excluded from the analysis. Final estimates used for the analysis were based on quartiles of the years of education. The resulting estimates for period life expectancy for both genders is found in Annex Table 6.A.14.

Annex Table 6.A.14. Estimates of the life expectancy at age 65 in Mexico using the LSM

Educational Level	Males	Females
1st Quantile	16.2	18.0
2nd Quantile	16.5	18.5
3rd Quantile	16.3	19.3
4th Quantile	16.4	21.4

United States

Voluntary defined contribution pension plans in the United States can be either occupational or personal plans. Withdrawals from these types of plans are usually taxed at the marginal rate. Contributions are assumed to be 9%, and retirement at age 66, which is the statutory retirement age for a public pension for those reaching age 66 in years 2009 through 2020.[19]

Pension wealth ratios

Annex Table 6.A.15. Pension wealth ratios for the United States

		Males				Females			
		Low	Average	High	spread	Low	Average	High	spread
avg PW	Private	5.9	6.1	6.2	0.3	6.2	6.2	6.3	0.1
	Total	13.3	12.2	9.5	(3.8)	14.7	13.0	9.7	(5.0)
	Net	13.3	11.4	8.0	(5.3)	14.7	12.2	8.2	(6.5)
min PW	Private	3.6	3.9	4.2	0.5	4.4	4.4	4.5	0.1
	Total	11.0	10.1	7.4	(3.6)	12.9	11.2	7.9	(4.9)
	Net	11.0	9.8	6.5	(4.5)	12.9	10.9	6.9	(6.0)
annuity	Private	5.8	6.0	6.3	0.5	6.1	6.2	6.2	0.1
	Total	13.1	12.2	9.5	(3.6)	14.6	13.0	9.7	(4.9)
	Net	13.1	11.5	8.1	(5.1)	14.6	12.3	8.2	(6.4)
PW + ann75	Private	5.8	6.0	6.2	0.4	6.2	6.2	6.3	0.1
	Total	13.1	12.1	9.5	(3.7)	14.6	13.0	9.7	(4.9)
	Net	13.1	11.3	8.0	(5.1)	14.6	12.2	8.2	(6.4)
PW + defann+20	Private	5.6	6.2	6.4	0.8	6.2	6.6	6.6	0.4
	Total	13.0	12.4	9.7	(3.3)	14.7	13.4	10.0	(4.6)
	Net	13.0	11.3	8.2	(4.8)	14.7	12.3	8.5	(6.2)
Escalating annuity	Private	5.5	5.8	6.1	0.6	5.9	6.0	6.1	0.1
	Total	12.9	12.0	9.4	(3.5)	14.4	12.8	9.5	(4.9)
	Net	12.9	11.3	7.9	(4.9)	14.4	12.1	8.1	(6.3)
Lump sum	Private	6.1	6.1	6.1	-	6.1	6.1	6.1	-
	Total	13.5	12.3	9.4	(4.1)	14.6	12.9	9.6	(5.0)
	Net	12.0	10.5	7.2	(4.8)	13.2	11.2	7.4	(5.8)

Both public pensions and tax rules contribute to offsetting the relative differences in pension wealth for low-income groups. Annex Table 6.A.15 shows that on average, public pension benefits result in low income males generally receiving at least 3.5 times their annual salary in total more than high income males, and around 5 times more for females. Tax rules result in around an additional 1-1.5 years more in total annual salary for low-income groups compared to high-income groups.

Income ratios

Annex Table 6.A.16. Post-tax total pension income ratios for the United States

	Males			Females		
	Low	Average	High	Low	Average	High
pre-retirement	0.53	1.00	2.69	0.53	1.00	2.69
avg PW	0.61	1.00	1.99	0.61	1.00	1.99
min PW	0.59	1.00	1.88	0.60	1.00	1.89
annuity	0.60	1.00	1.99	0.60	1.00	1.97
PW + ann75	0.61	1.00	2.00	0.61	1.00	1.99
PW + defann+20	0.60	1.00	2.04	0.61	1.00	2.04
Escalating annuity	0.60	1.00	1.99	0.60	1.00	1.97
Lump sum	0.61	1.00	1.90	0.61	1.00	1.90

Existing differences in income before retirement do not become relatively worse in retirement. Annex Table 6.A.16 shows that whereas low-income individuals earn 53% less than average income individuals after tax, in retirement for most scenarios they can expect to receive around 60% of the average pension income.

Mortality assumptions

Population mortality was based on the 2014 life tables from the Human Mortality Database (HMD). Programmed withdrawals that are not based on the Required Minimum Distribution levels are based on this mortality.

For low and high education/income groups, life expectancies were based on the data used in Murtin et al (2017) by educational attainment for a central year of 2011. For females, these old age mortality rates were extrapolated from age 85 to centre the resulting estimated life expectancies around the observed population average. Nevertheless, the resulting mortality curves still demonstrate significant crossing of mortality rates at older ages due to the accelerating slope of mortality derived for the high income group beyond the age of 65. The average life expectancies at age 65, however, still follow the expected pattern that low educated groups also have lower life expectancies.

The base assumptions for the price of annuities are based on the IAM-Basic rates for 2012.

Mortality improvement assumptions were based on the MP-2017 improvement scale for all populations and annuity pricing.

Notes

[1] Average wages as shown in *Pension at a Glance 2017*, Table 6.5.

[2] Replacement rates assumed for public pensions are those calculated in Pensions at a Glance 2017. The case of Mexico is an exception, with the total replacement rate calculated directly.

[3] Rules and thresholds provided typically correspond with the rules in place for 2015 (OECD, 2015[6]) but are applied for 2016.

[4] These assumptions are those in *Pensions at a Glance 2017*.

[5] All analysis assumes currency in Unidad de Fomento (UF), a unit of account indexed to prices.

[6] Starting in July 2011, the worker directly receives a state subsidy in his/her individual pension savings account equivalent to 50% of the pension contribution, calculated on a minimum wage, for the first 24 contributions that he/she makes between the ages of 18 and 35, where his/her wage is equal to or lower than 1.5 times the minimum monthly wage.

[7] An amount of 15 UF is taken from the account at retirement to cover funeral expenses.

[8] This threshold is equal to the PBS, 3.5 UF in December 2016 (OECD, 2017[5]).

[9] Great Britain is assessed rather than the United Kingdom because the mortality assumptions used are based on Great Britain only.

[10] Public pensions are assumed to grow annually at the minimum rate of 2.5% rather than the assumed rate of inflation of 2%.

[11] Tax calculations assume that 25% of withdrawals are tax-free (whenever they are withdrawn), and that income from annuities do not benefit from this tax exemption.

[12] While currently the statutory retirement age for public pensions in Korea is 61, it is planned to be increased to 65 by 2033 (OECD, 2017[5]).

[13] Korean life tables are issued by KOSIS and found here. Note that the 6th EMT tables produce a life expectancy significantly higher than that of the Korean population, and the projections of mortality improvements based on the limited amount of historical data are relatively high. The price of an annuity used for this analysis is therefore quite conservative.

[14] Sensitivity analysis to attrition based on health status and a probit regression on the KLoSA data indicate that the remaining sample is not health biased, though a Wald test indicates that there may be a bias in relation to other demographic characteristics.

[15] The LSM was also tested based on educational attainment, but this resulted in less robust results for females.

[16] The minimum wage for 2014 is MXN 21 609.

[17] Estimates using the LSM were chosen over the data used by Murtin et al (2017) mainly because the former estimates were more in line with the observed life expectancy of the entire Mexican population. Estimates based on Murtin et al. (2017) for both genders result in figures for those with low education which are higher than estimates of life expectancy at age 65 for the general Mexican population.

[18] Sensitivity analysis indicates that attrition was not health biased.

[19] Contribution rate is consistent with that used in (OECD, 2017[5]).

Chapter 7. Are survivor pensions still needed?

This chapter describes survivor pension schemes in OECD countries. It first documents expenditures on survivor pensions the number of recipients and the average level of benefits. It then provides details about eligibility rules and benefit determination across countries. The chapter includes a discussion of how survivor pensions have developed in the recent decades and whether these trends are related to the more general evolution of pension systems and the deep changes in socio-economic environments. Simulations based on the OECD pension model estimate the impact of the survivor pensions on the financial situation of survivors, including how pension splitting can affect survivor pensions in OECD countries. Main results and key policy insights follow.

As with old-age pensions, survivor schemes first started by covering selected groups of the population. A few countries, among which Ireland, Sweden, the United Kingdom and the United States, introduced survivor pensions in the 19th or first half of the 20th century, in particular for civil servants (Flora, 1986[1]). The expansion of the Welfare State in many OECD countries after 1945 included the coverage of survivor risks by placing greater emphasis on social assistance (Hannikainen and Vauhkonen, 2012[2]). Yet, potential beneficiaries were less numerous than today because more people worked in jobs, in agriculture in particular, that did not provide pension coverage (Gillion et al., 2000[3]).

The introduction of survivor pensions improved the economic situation of widows at a time when the family representation was dominated by the male-breadwinner model.[1] In such a family, the husband worked and earned pension entitlements while his wife provided care and unpaid work that gave her limited pension rights. Moreover, the marriage was both widespread and a life-long contract that ended by death, most often of men, rather than by divorce.

Following the death of a partner, survivor pensions have pursued two main objectives. First, they have protected widows or widowers from poverty risks to offset sharp drops in disposable income to low *absolute* levels. Second, they have contributed to insuring against the decrease in disposable income *relative* to the situation prevailing before the death of the partner, in the same way as old-age pensions help avoid a sharp drop in income when moving out of paid work upon retirement: this is the so-called consumption-smoothing objective aiming at preserving standards of living.

Nowadays, all OECD countries provide instruments directly targeted at poverty alleviation, i.e. basic and minimum pensions as well as social assistance benefits including housing allowances.[2] In many countries, the level of these benefits is low, but there is no obvious justification why widowed persons should be granted higher safety-net benefits than other individuals in a similarly poor income situation. Some countries where poverty relief was the main objective have indeed eliminated survivor pensions. Moreover, scaling down survivor benefits has also been connected to a gender-equality motive, as in Sweden for example (Section 7.4). Yet, survivor pensions still effectively reduce the gender pension gap in most countries. The consumption-smoothing rationale is today the main justification for the existence of survivor pensions.

While both parents work in more than half of couples with children on average in the OECD, the single-breadwinner family model is still frequent in many countries, at least in households with dependent children (Section 7.2). Moreover, the need of a policy instrument to avoid the drop in disposable income following the death of a spouse applies beyond the male-breadwinner model, even if both partners achieve similar pension entitlements. This is because living in a couple benefits from economies of scale in the cost of running the household. It is generally estimated that the cost of living for a single household exceeds 50% of the cost of living for a couple (Section 7.1). According to the equivalence scale used by the OECD, a drop of total household income larger than roughly 30% after the death of a partner leads to a fall in the living standards of the survivor. Hence, the absence of survivor pensions typically implies that the death of one partner causes a drop in living standards of the survivor, even in couples where both partners earned the same own (50% of the couple's) pension income.

One way to cover the survivor's income risk is to purchase targeted financial products like joint-and-survivor annuity contracts which pay an agreed pension until the second partner dies. However, standard problems in insurance markets commonly referred to as market failure, such as adverse selection due to asymmetric information about health problems (Akerlof, 1970[4]), may lead to the lack of supply of adequate products. On top of that, the demand for a voluntary contract might also be limited by myopic behaviour – driven for example by the underestimation of the probability of a premature death of the partner or its financial consequences. Consequently, couples may not be well prepared financially to cope with the death of the partner through voluntary private insurance markets, and mandatory survivor pension schemes overcome market failures by enlarging the pool of insured people sharing the related risks.[3]

Most existing survivor pensions in pay-as-you-go (PAYGO) schemes are financed through contributions and taxes. As individuals within couples typically do not pay higher contributions or receive lower old-age pension benefits before death, these schemes imply redistribution from singles to individuals eligible for survivor pensions. Means-testing of survivor pensions limits the level of benefits, and therefore also limits this type of redistribution, but it favours single-breadwinner over dual-breadwinners couples (Section 7.5).

Moreover, survivor pensions might hamper the employment of women as the benefits could reduce incentives to work, potentially leading to labour market exit or reduced working hours. For this reason, survivor pensions typically set an age threshold or are, at younger ages, granted for a limited period to facilitate the adaptation to the new situation. When means-tested, survivor pensions reduce incentives to work even more as the benefit amount declines with own earnings. Disincentives to work at younger ages could even be at play before the age of eligibility to survivor pensions due to anticipation effects, especially when large differences in age or health status between partners make acquiring own old-age pension rights less important.

The socio-economic basis for the design of survivor and old-age pension systems has evolved substantially in various dimensions over the last decades. Ultimately they might question the *raison d'être* of survivor pensions. Survivor pension reforms over the past decades have indeed mainly focused on tightening or eliminating these schemes. This Chapter provides a description of survivor schemes in OECD countries and analyses whether they are well-designed and adapted to the ongoing profound socio-economic changes. It seeks to contribute to answering three main interrelated questions:

- What is the role pension systems should play to protect survivors given existing old-age safety nets?
- Are current survivor schemes well-designed given the deep developments societies are going through?
- Beyond country-specific historical contexts, are survivor pensions still needed and if so how would they look like if they were now built from scratch?

The rest of the chapter is organised as follows. The first section gives an overview of the current survivor benefits (total expenditures, recipients and benefit levels) and the second one examines how the socio-economic environment that has been central in the design of survivor pensions, including female employment, gender gap in pensions and family structure, has changed over time. Section 3 focuses on the current rules while Section 4 discusses the reforms to survivor pensions and how systemic reforms of old-age pensions have affected survivor schemes over the last decades. Based on the OECD pension model, the chapter then explores the impact of survivor pensions on the financial situation of survivors and how pension splitting can affect survivor pensions. Section 6 presents a general discussion of what survivor pensions should look like in the current socio-economic context while the final section summarises the main results and concludes.

7.1. Survivor benefits today: Expenditures, recipients and benefit levels

There is a great variety in the type and scope of survivor pension schemes across OECD countries. This materialises in substantial differences in the number and characteristics of total expenditures for survivor benefits, nowadays recipients and average benefit levels. Survivor benefits is indeed a broad category that includes permanent and temporary payments targeted at widows and widowers and other surviving dependent family members.

Expenditures

OECD countries spend on average about 1% of GDP on survivor benefits in mandatory schemes (Figure 7.1.). Greece, Italy and Spain are the OECD countries which report the highest spending on survivor benefits, more than 2.3% of GDP. By contrast, twelve OECD countries (Australia, Canada, Estonia, Ireland, Korea, Latvia, Lithuania, Mexico, New Zealand, Norway, Sweden and the United Kingdom) spend less than 0.5% of GDP.

Figure 7.1. Expenditures on survivor benefits, % of GDP, 2017 or latest

Total expenditures from mandatory schemes

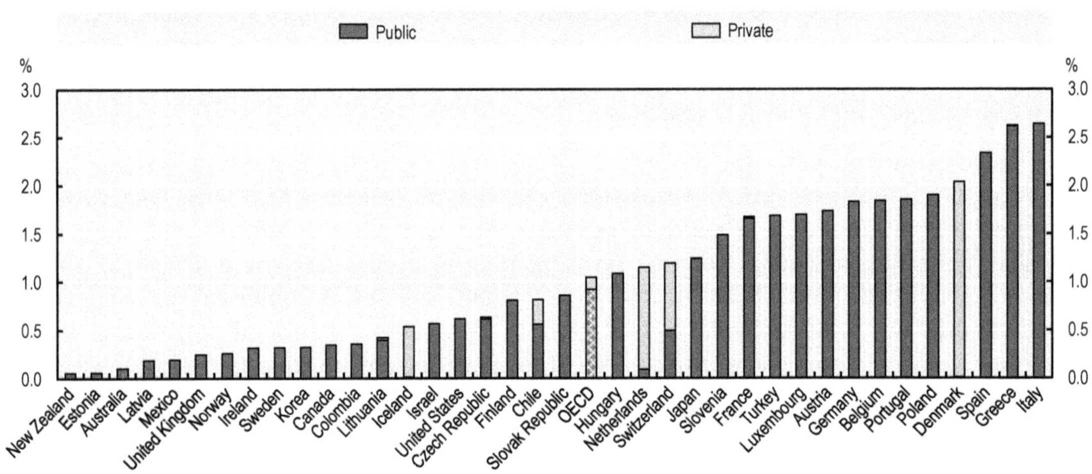

Note: The data on the United Kingdom are based on data provided by Department for Work and Pensions.[4] Data on (mandatory and voluntary) survivor pensions in mandatory private schemes in Denmark (ATP), Estonia, Israel, Mexico, Norway, the Slovak Republic and Sweden are not available. Data for Chile, Israel, Korea, New Zealand and the United States are 2017. Australia and Mexico are 2016. Poland is 2014. The other countries are 2015.
Source: OECD preliminary social expenditure database and information provided by countries.

StatLink http://dx.doi.org/10.1787/888933850260

In most countries, spending on survivor benefits is mostly public while mandatory private schemes dominate in Denmark, Iceland, the Netherlands and Switzerland only. In Chile, the mandatory private pension scheme, introduced in 1981, is still maturing and makes up for less than one-third of all expenditures on survivor benefits. Beyond survivor benefits, safety-net benefits and basic pensions, especially those which are residency-based as e.g. in Australia, the Netherlands and New Zealand, provide income unrelated to work experience and cover poverty risks for everyone including surviving spouses.

Relative to mandatory old-age benefit spending, expenditures on survivor benefits differ substantially across countries. On average, about one dollar is spent on survivor benefits for each eight dollars spent on old-age benefits, or a ratio of 13% (Figure 7.2.). Belgium, Chile, Denmark, Germany, Luxembourg, Poland, Spain and Turkey spend more than 20% while Australia, Estonia, Latvia, New Zealand and Norway spend less than 5%. However, in some countries including Australia, the spending data do not account for the fact that the remaining account balance in the private-sector schemes is typically transferred to the surviving spouse.

Figure 7.2. Expenditures on survivor benefits relative to old-age benefits, 2017 or latest

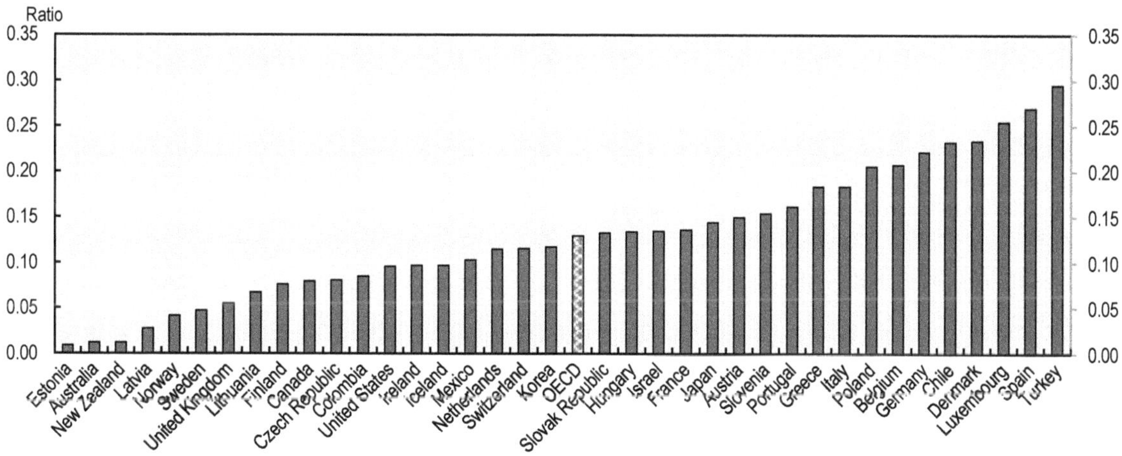

Note: See preceding figure.
Source: OECD preliminary social expenditure database and information provided by countries.

StatLink http://dx.doi.org/10.1787/888933850279

Survivor expenditures consist mainly of survivor pensions, but they may also include funeral expenses and other benefits in cash or kind. In all countries except Latvia and Lithuania the share of pensions in survivor expenditures exceeds 85%. In Latvia, survivor pensions are granted only to orphans. In Lithuania, assistance for families of deceased persons in the public scheme and special benefits for survivors in the private scheme provide comparatively large benefits in addition to the pension.

Recipients

There are 22 survivor benefit recipients for each 100 beneficiaries of old-age pensions within public schemes on average in the OECD (Figure 7.3). Comparatively many survivor benefits are paid in Germany, Lithuania, Luxembourg, Spain and Turkey; close to or more than 40 per each 100 old-age pension payments. By contrast, only few recipients of survivor benefits within public scheme – less than 5 for every 100 recipients of old-age pensions - are recorded in Australia, Estonia, Latvia, the Netherlands and Norway.[5] In Australia, the Netherlands and Norway, survivors' income risks after retirement age are basically not covered by survivor schemes but indirectly by residency-based basic pensions.

Figure 7.3.Number of recipients of survivor pensions in 2014

Recipients of survivor pensions per each 100 recipients of old-age pensions

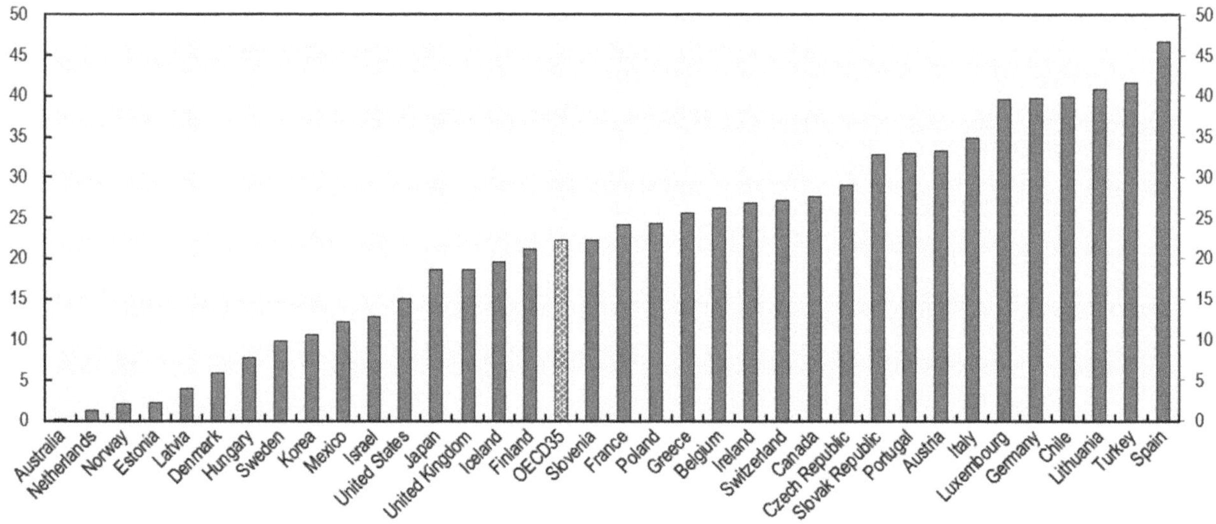

Note: Data refer to public schemes, except for Chile where it includes the mandatory private scheme. See the StatLink for more details.

Source: OECD social benefits recipients' database and information provided by countries. See the StatLink for more details.

StatLink http://dx.doi.org/10.1787/888933850298

Detailed information on recipients of survivor pensions reveal the following features.[6] First, in Canada, Ireland and Korea survivor pensions cover only widows and widowers; social benefits for orphans in these countries are not related to the accumulated old-age pension entitlements of their parents. Also, over 90% of survivor pension recipients in the Czech Republic, Finland, Germany and Sweden are widows or widowers. Conversely, orphans make up for a large share of survivor pension recipients in Hungary and the United States, amounting to 43% and 28%, respectively, and in Latvia where only orphans can be granted survivor pensions since 1996. Second, most of recipients of survivor pensions also receive own old-age pensions if such accumulation is allowed. In 2016, in the Czech Republic and the United Kingdom, for example, it was the case for 95% and 72% of recipients of survivor pensions, respectively.

Third, women represent more than 85% of survivor-pension recipients for widowed persons on average across 25 OECD countries (Figure 7.4). This is because they tend to live longer, be the younger partner within a couple and accumulate lower individual pension entitlements. The share of women is lower than 80% only in Denmark at 67% where gender differences in both old-age pensions and life expectancy are comparatively small.

On average across OECD countries, less than two-thirds of widowed people older than 65 receive some survivor benefits. That share varies greatly across countries. For example, countries with a very high share of widowed persons such as Hungary, Korea and Mexico have very few recipients.

Average benefit levels

Based on data reported by 26 OECD countries, the mean survivor pension to widows and widowers is equal to 56% of the mean old-age pension on average (Figure 7.5). It is 8%

in Lithuania, which grants a low flat benefit, and lower than 20% in Norway where survivor pensions are subject to strict means-testing (and will be phased out for survivors reaching the retirement age and born in 1963 or later).[7]

Figure 7.4. Share of women among recipients of survivor pensions for widowed persons in OECD countries

2016 or latest available

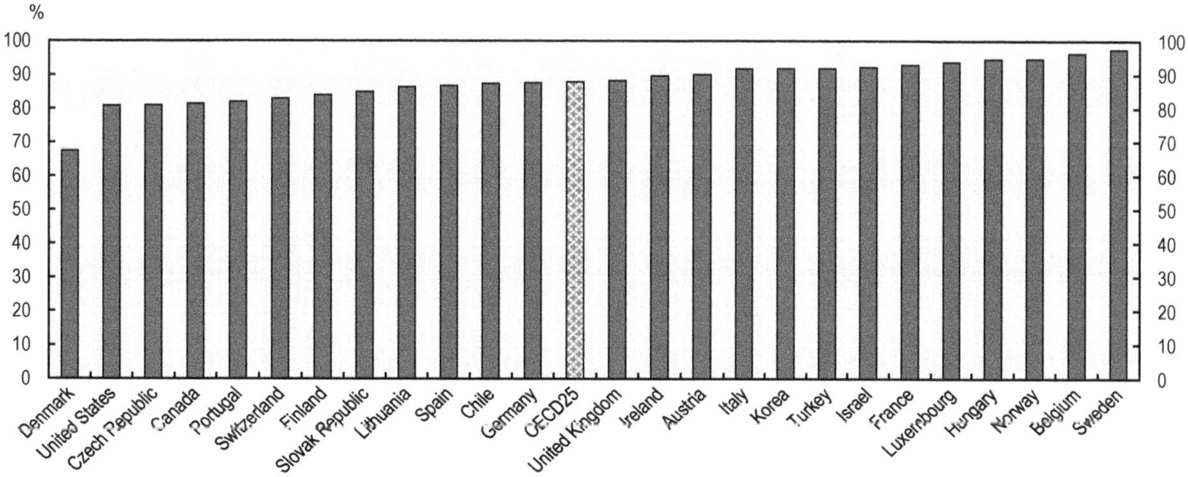

Note: Data refer to the main mandatory schemes.

Source: Data provided by countries for 2016 or 2017 and, for Ireland, OECD social benefit recipients database 2014.

StatLink http://dx.doi.org/10.1787/888933850317

Figure 7.5. Average level of survivor pensions relative to old-age pensions

2016 or latest available

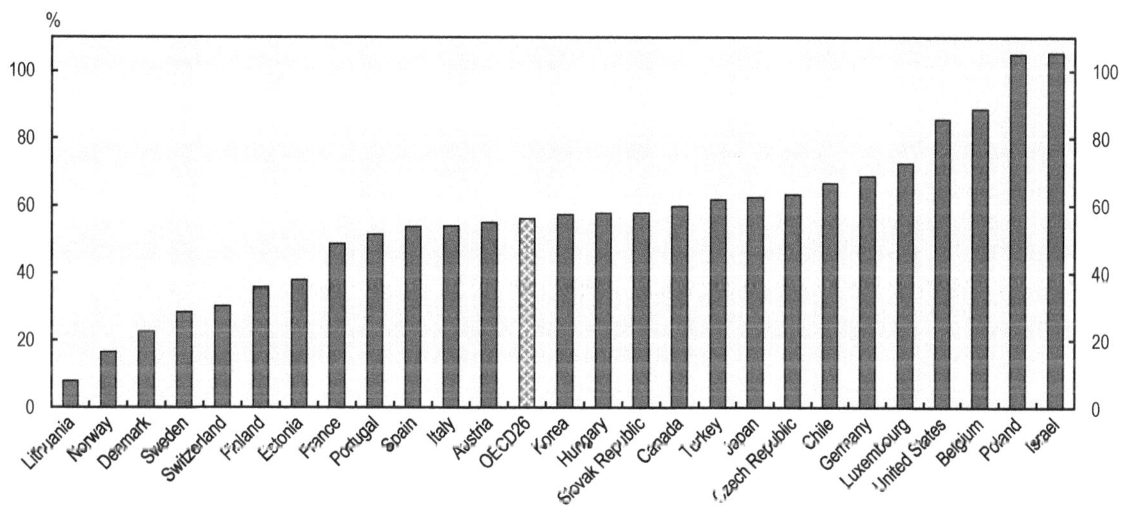

Note: Data for both, old-age and survivor pensions, refer to the main mandatory scheme paying survivor pensions in year 2016 or 2017.

Source: Information provided by countries. For Germany data stem from Deutsche Rentenversicherung ($2017_{[5]}$) and for Poland from ZUS ($2018_{[6]}$).

StatLink http://dx.doi.org/10.1787/888933850336

Conversely, it is higher than 80% in Belgium, Israel, Poland and the United States. In Israel, 50% of the basic pension is paid to survivors on top of their own entitlement to a full basic pension and even 100% if the survivor has no own entitlements.[8] High levels of the average survivor pension relative to the average old-age pension in Belgium and the United States are consistent with the high survivor replacement rate from the public scheme (Section 7.3). This also applies to Poland, where in addition old-age benefit levels of current pensioners from the old pension scheme are comparatively high. Comparable data across countries about the share of individual income provided by survivor pensions are missing. In France, as an example, among people receiving their own pension benefits, survivor pensions represented 23% of pension income for women and only 1% for men in 2015 (Lavigne, 2018[7]).

7.2. A changing socio-economic environment

The socio-economic environment matters to assess whether survivor pensions are necessary and well-designed. Female employment levels, the structure of family formation and survival rates have changed substantially from the time when survivor pensions were introduced in most OECD countries. Hence, the number of survivor-pension recipients as well as total expenditure are affected, in particular due to means-testing, which often applies to survivor pensions (Section 7.3).

Women work more often and gender employment gaps are narrowing

Although large gender gaps remain in some countries, more often than in the past women of young generations participate in the labour market, earn money and acquire pension rights. Female labour force participation rates increased substantially from 61% in 2000 to 69% in 2017 on average in the OECD (Figure 7.6). The increase exceeded 10 percentage points (p.p.) in Austria, Chile, Germany, Hungary, Latvia, Luxembourg, the Netherlands and Spain. This added to a longer trend in many countries, with the strongest increases of over 15 p.p. between 1983 and 2000 in Ireland, Luxembourg and Spain.[9] Higher education levels and lower fertility rates have contributed to these developments.

Still, the average male labour force participation rate is at a much higher level, equalling 80% in 2017. The gender gap exceeds 20 p.p. in Chile, Colombia, Korea, Mexico and Turkey while it is below 5 p.p. in Finland, Lithuania, Norway and Sweden. Moreover, the share of part-time and temporary workers among women is still higher than for men.

Female employment is strongly influenced by the persisting imbalances in sharing various tasks within partnerships. The pure single-breadwinner family model, where one partner works full time while the other does not work at all, represents 31% of households with children (OECD Family Database, Chart LMF1.1C). The single-breadwinner family model is frequent in Turkey (65%) and in Greece and the Slovak Republic (more than 40%). However, among couples with children younger than 15 years-old, both parents work in 59% of households on average across 24 OECD countries in 2014, with (both working full time in 41% of them. The share of couples with two full-time earners exceeds 60% of couples with children in Denmark, Portugal, Slovenia, Sweden and the United States.

Gender gap in pensions and old-age poverty

Weaker labour market attachment for women than for men and lower wages result in lower pensions and lower coverage by contributory pension schemes. On average across the 25 OECD countries for which data are available since 2007, women had pensions 24% lower than men in 2015, slightly less than the 2007 average of 27% (Figure 7.7).

In 2015, that gap was below 10% in Denmark, Estonia and the Slovak Republic only and larger than 40% in Germany, Luxembourg and the Netherlands. In this context, survivor pensions, which are predominantly paid to women lower the gender pension gap. In France, for example, survivor pensions diminish the gender pension gap by about one-third (DREES, 2018[8]).

Figure 7.6. Labour force participation in the age group 15-64 by gender since 1983

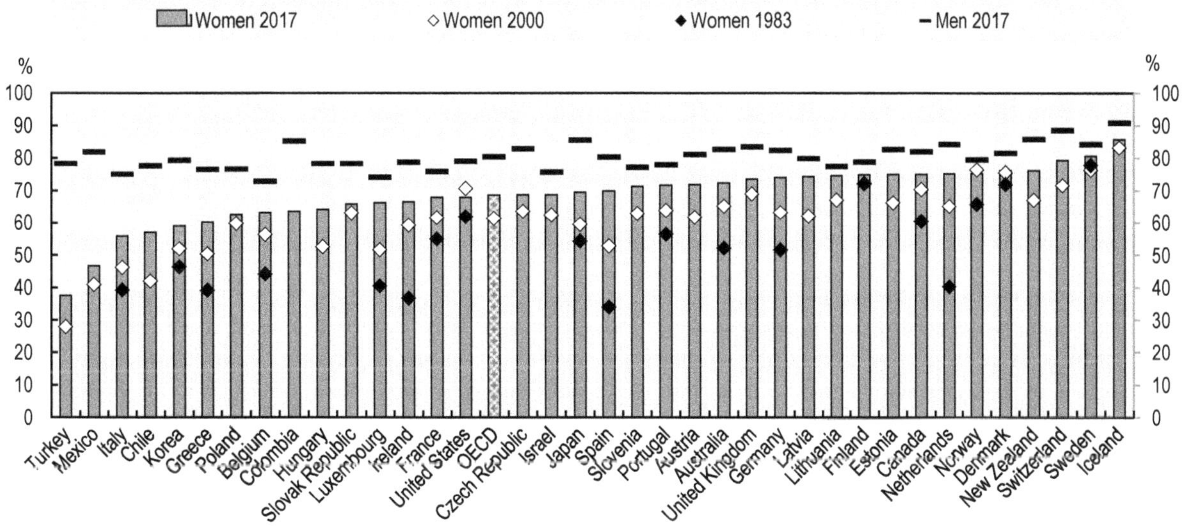

Note: OECD average calculated for all countries for which data were available.
Source: OECD Labour Force Survey indicators.

StatLink http://dx.doi.org/10.1787/888933850355

Lower pension entitlements and higher longevity result in higher poverty rates among older women. On average in the OECD, 17% of women older than 75 years fall below the relative poverty line defined at 50% of median equivalised income, against 10% for men at the same age and 12% for women aged 66-75. Many pensions are indexed to prices which tend to grow less than wages, implying that the relative value of pension in payments tends to fall, especially for people who survive long enough during retirement. Beyond potentially lower pensions due to indexation rules, very old people face higher poverty risk as they live more often in single-person households, hence not benefiting from the economies of scale that larger households provide (Box 7.1).

Box 7.1. Economies of scale in living costs and household income equivalence scales

Living expenses usually rise less than proportionally with the size of a household. Collective goods such as fixed living costs (like base rates of utilities or rental costs for common spaces such as kitchens and bathrooms) can be shared. These economies of scale in living costs reduce the per-person cost, especially accommodation cost, and mean that one dollar of a couple's income leads to higher individual living standards than for a single person with 50 cents of income.

Income equivalence scales are commonly used to compare the income of individuals living in households of different size and composition. These scales are based on defining the number of consumption units which are equivalent full-cost family members for each household.

Exactly how this adjustment for household size and composition should be made is debated in the literature, and several alternative scales exist (James, 2009[9]). One common equivalence scale, the standard scale, weights the first adult in the household as 1, each additional adult as 0.5 and each child as 0.3. Recent OECD publications divide the total income of a couple by the square root of the size of the household, i.e. the square root of 2 ($\approx$1.4) when comparing with single-person households - cf., e.g. OECD (2017[10]). The ratio of total household income divided by the equivalence scale is the "equivalised income" at the individual level. This publication follows the recent OECD approach. It implies that if each individual has an income of 100, then the equivalised income of a couple at the individual level is equal to $2*100 / \sqrt{2} \approx 141$ and a single person would have a standard of living which is only 100 / 141 = 71% of the individuals living in a couple. With the standard scale, it is slightly lower at 67%.

These orders of magnitude might not capture well the situation of widowhood. In particular they assume that widowed persons downsize their house after the death of the partner, which is typically not the case. Bonnet and Hourriez (2008[11]) estimate that when widows or widowers do not change accommodation, their living cost is 8% larger than what the above scales assume. That is, 71% becomes 77%, and in that case if the total income falls by more than 23% after the partner's death then the standards of living of the survivor decline.

Figure 7.7. Gender gap in total pension income

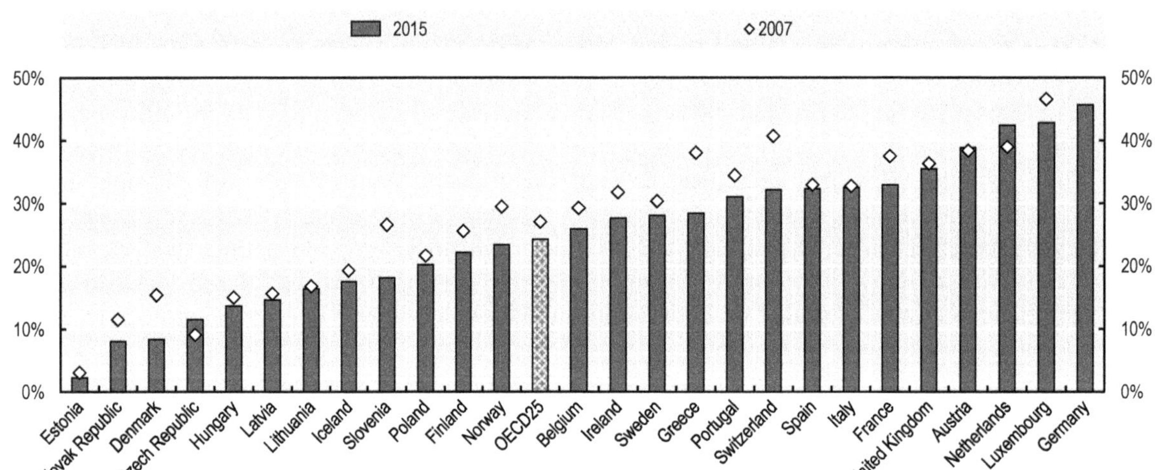

Note: The gender gap in pensions is calculated as the difference of average pensions between men and women divided by the average pension of men. The average for OECD25 does not include Germany as the value for 2007 was not available. The "2015" values for Germany and Iceland are from 2014. The "2007" value for France is an average of 2006 and 2008.
Source: EU-SILC, 2016.

StatLink http://dx.doi.org/10.1787888933850374

Figure 7.8. Trends in family formation reduce the number of widows

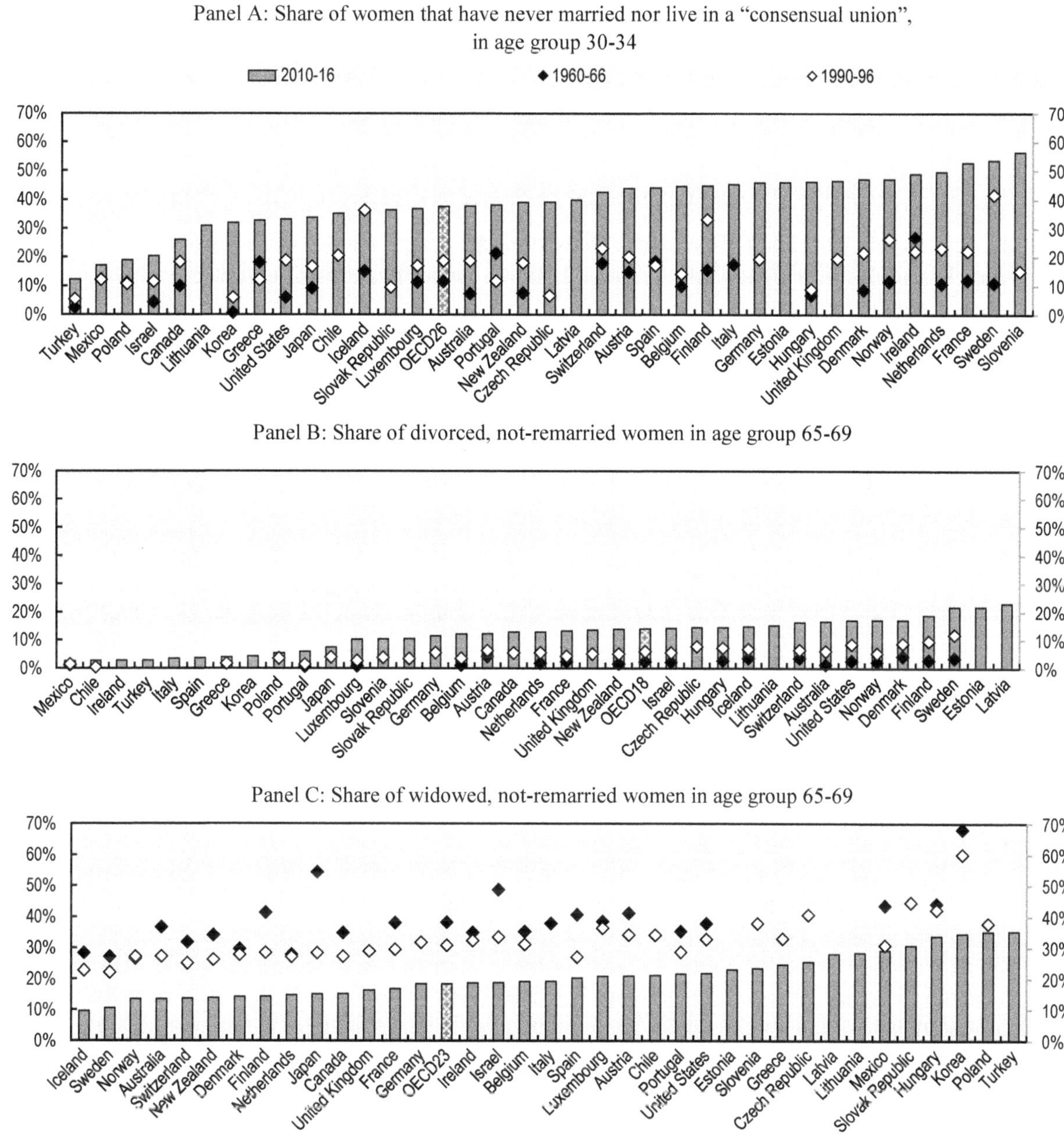

Note: OECD average calculated for all countries for which data are available for all three time periods. Observations from different sources (censuses, surveys) averaged for each 7-years span.

Source: OECD calculation based on the UNSD Demographic Statistic database (http://data.un.org). For Chile, data are from CASEN and period is 2009-2015 instead of 2010-16. For the United States in Panel B and C, the age group is 65-74 instead of 65-69.

StatLink http://dx.doi.org/10.1787/888933850393

Changes in families

Couples and marriages are being formed later and are less stable than in the past. In the 2010-2016 period, 38% of women aged 30-34 have never been married nor were living in a "consensual union"[10] compared to 19% in 1990-1996 and 12% in 1960-1966 on average across 26 OECD countries (Figure 7.8, Panel A). In France, the Netherlands, Slovenia and Sweden, more than half of women aged 30-34 in 2010-2016 have never been married nor were living in a "consensual union". The increase between 1990-1996 and 2010-2016 was spectacular, larger than 10 percentage points in all countries but Canada, Iceland, Israel, Mexico, Poland and Turkey. The increasing role of less formal partnerships only offsets part of this trend, such that the share of singles has risen.[11]

Moreover, between 1960-1966 and 2010-2016 the share of divorced, not remarried women aged 65-69 increased from 2% to 14% on average in the 18 countries for which data are available (Panel B). The highest levels in 2010-2016 of more than 20% were recorded in Estonia, Latvia and Sweden.

Along with improvements in men's life expectancy, fewer marriages and more frequent divorces contributed to more than halving the share of widows in the age group 65-69, from 38% in 1960-66 to 18% in 2010-16 for the OECD23 average (Panel C). In 2010-16, the highest shares of widows of more than 30% are found in Hungary, Korea, Poland, the Slovak Republic and Turkey, in part related to large gender gaps in life expectancy.

Life expectancy gaps between women and men

Life expectancy gains have been impressive. On average, female life expectancy at birth increased from 69 to 82 years between 1960 and 2015. It is expected to increase further, although at a slower pace, reaching 88 years in half a century. For men, life expectancy has been increasing faster since the 1990s across OECD countries, narrowing the gender gap from a peak of 7.1 years in 1985 to 5.6 years in 2015 on average (Figure 7.9).

Central and Eastern European Countries made a large contribution to this reduction, which is likely to be linked to the decline in heavy industry jobs, the increase in female alcohol and tobacco consumption and perhaps the reduction in gender paid-work gaps. Some health-care improvements such as better treatment of heart-related diseases may have also benefitted men more than women (Barthold et al., 2014[9]). Lower gender differences in life expectancy imply that the duration of widowhood should also diminish. The narrowing of the gender gap is less clear when focusing on remaining life expectancy at age 65, for which the peak was reached in 2000, with only a small decline since. Yet, the downward trend is expected to continue with the average gender gap in life expectancy at birth reaching 4.0 years and 2.8 years at age 65 in the middle of the century based on UN projections.

Figure 7.9. Gender gap in life expectancy at birth and at age 65, 1960 - 2060

Difference between female and male life expectancy, averaged across OECD countries, historical data until 2015 and the UN projections onwards

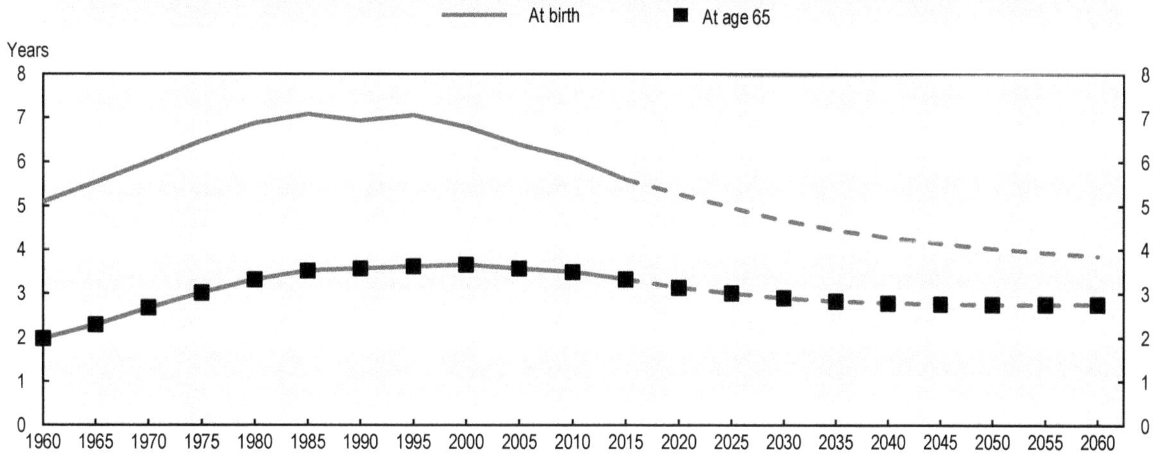

Note: Life expectancy is calculated for 5-year intervals; the upper bound of which is displayed at the horizontal axis.
Source: United Nations, Department of Economic and Social Affairs, Population Division (2017). World Population Prospects: The 2017 Revision, DVD Edition.

StatLink http://dx.doi.org/10.1787/888933850412

7.3. Eligibility criteria and benefit determination

Almost all OECD countries cover survivor risk through survivor pensions for at least some parts of the population. The following discussion focuses on future derived pension entitlements of widowed persons – who neither are disabled nor have dependent children - from the main mandatory scheme covering private-sector workers.[12] It is thus a narrower category than the survivor benefits discussed in Section 7.1. Neither survivor pension programmes in Australia, Latvia, New Zealand, Norway[13], Sweden and the United Kingdom, which were abolished over the past decades but still exist during the phase-out period, nor survivor schemes providing only temporary benefits or lump-sum payments are covered here. Detailed rules are shown in the Annex 7.A. Only policy changes enacted by the end of August 2018 are accounted for.

Eligibility criteria

Eligibility criteria to survivor pensions for widows and widowers vary significantly across countries as they depend on gender and age of both the survivor and the deceased as well as on the forms of partnerships. As for the eligibility of the deceased, most countries require having contributed for a minimum period to the disability or old-age pension scheme (see Annex 7.A).

Gender differences in eligibility have been eliminated over the last decades in many countries (Section 7.4) but a few exceptions remain. In Switzerland, for example, unlike women, men are only eligible for survivor pensions as long as they have a dependent child. Also in Israel and Japan the access for men is more restricted than for women.

Age-related criteria for widowed people are commonly applied for survivor pension eligibility to limit their negative impact on labour market participation. No minimum age requirements apply in Austria, Canada (from 2019), Chile, Ireland, Italy, Korea, Luxembourg, Mexico, Norway, Spain and Turkey while only widowed persons above a certain age can receive permanent survivor pensions in 17 OECD countries (Table 7.1). Widowed persons who are not able to work - with disabilities or caring for children - are usually exempted from these age tests.

Among the countries which set a minimum age for permanent benefits within survivor pension programmes, the lowest minimum age is 35 years in Portugal. Many countries set a minimum eligibility age below the statutory retirement age to reflect that, after a short work experience, the earnings capacity from e.g. age 50 is reduced. Estonia, Hungary, Lithuania and the Slovak Republic do not grant access to permanent survivor pensions before the recipient reaches the retirement age. The strictness of the eligibility age condition varies across countries. Indeed, a survivor who is younger than the age threshold when the spouse deceases never acquires the right to a permanent survivor pension in some countries including Finland, Israel and Japan; by contrast, in Belgium, France, Germany and Greece it is only delayed until the survivor reaches the required age.

Before the eligibility age to a permanent survivor pension is reached, many countries grant survivor benefits for a limited time period to help the survivor adjust to the new situation without limiting work incentives in the longer term. For example, in Greece, survivor pensions are paid for only 3 years if the survivor has not reached 55 years of age. In Portugal, the pension is paid to the spouse under 35 years-old for only 5 years, and in Hungary for only one year before age 63. In France, widowhood allowance is payable for 2 years if the widowed is younger than 50 years-old or until age 55 otherwise, which serves as a bridge to the survivor pension starting from age 55.

In Norway, permanent survivor pensions cease at the statutory retirement age when residents start to receive a basic pension. Survivor pensions are therefore a bridge benefit that provides income between partner's death and access to their own pension. The same applies to the basic component of survivor pensions in Finland while access to the earnings-related component continues after the retirement age.

While marriage used to be required to access survivor pensions, an increasing number of countries have expanded survivor benefits to civil unions and even registered cohabitations (Table 7.1). Sixteen countries provide survivor benefits to civil unions, while Canada, Hungary, Japan, Korea, Mexico, Norway, Portugal, Slovenia and Spain grant survivor pensions to cohabitants, upon meeting additional conditions. In Spain for example, five years of cohabitation are needed. Fourteen countries require a minimum length of marriage to grant survivor benefits varying from 6 months to 5 years.[14]

In many countries survivor pensions are indirectly linked to family policies. Having or caring for a dependent child can increase the survivor benefits or waive some eligibility conditions such as age or length of marriage requirements. For example, in the Czech Republic, Germany, Hungary, Israel, Portugal, the Slovak Republic, Switzerland and the United States, the age requirement is waived if the survivor is caring for a dependent child. Also, the length of marriage condition is waived in Finland, Greece, Israel, Lithuania, Luxembourg, Norway, Portugal and Switzerland if there is a child from this marriage.[15]

After divorce or separation, the death of the former partner does not cause any drop in income to the survivor (unless alimony was granted) because there were no shared income any longer. Still, nineteen countries grant survivor pensions after divorce treating this entitlement as a right acquired during marriage (Table 7.1) as long as the spouse meets additional conditions. For example, a minimum marriage period of 5-10 years is required in Greece, Switzerland and the United States. In Estonia, the divorced spouse can receive the benefit when reaching the statutory retirement age within 3 years after divorce and if the marriage has lasted for at least 25 years.

Table 7.1. Eligibility criteria for survivor pensions: Minimum age and family situation of the surviving spouses within the main mandatory survivor pension scheme

Permanent payments to non-disabled surviving spouses without dependent children

	Minimum eligibility age	Civil union	Cohabitation	After divorce	After remarriage		Minimum eligibility age	Civil union	Cohabitation	After divorce	After remarriage
Austria	-	√		√		Japan	55/-		√		
Belgium	46.5					Korea	-		√		
Canada	-	√	√	√	√	Lithuania	63.3/61.6*				
Chile	-	√				Luxembourg	-	√		√	
Czech Republic	55/58					Mexico	-	√	√	√	
Estonia	63*			√		Norway	-	√	√	√	
Finland	50	√		√	√A	Poland	50			√	√
France	55/60			√	√	Portugal	35	√	√	√	
Germany	45.5	√		√		Slovak Republic	62*				
Greece	55			√		Slovenia	55	√	√	√	
Hungary	63*	√	√	√		Spain	-	√	√	√	√A
Ireland	-			√		Switzerland	45	√		√	
Israel	40	√				Turkey	-	√			
Italy	-	√		√		United States	60			√	√A

Note: Rules apply to surviving spouses with no dependent child nor disability[16]. * = same as retirement age. – = no requirement age. √ = pension is payable. √ A = Eligibility or period of payment differs depending on the age of remarriage.
Source: Information provided by countries.

Also remarriage affects the entitlements to survivor pensions in some countries. If the widowed spouse is remarried, the survivor pension ceases in most OECD countries, while in some they are still paid for a certain time period or as a lump sum. In Estonia, for example, the survivor pension is paid for 12 months after remarriage. In the Czech Republic and Mexico, the survivor receives a lump sum equal to one or three years of the survivor benefits, respectively (see Annex 7.A for further details).

Benefit determination

The level of the survivor pension depends mostly on the pension entitlements of the deceased spouse and the replacement rate that the survivor pension guarantees. If the deceased did not reach the retirement age, some countries (for example Belgium, Finland, Luxembourg and Norway) assume for the calculation of the survivor pension that the deceased would have continued her career until the retirement age. In addition, means-tests against the survivor's own income (or of other household members) apply in many countries (details of benefit rules are shown in the Annex 7.A).

Survivor pensions are not limited to earnings-related schemes. In the Czech Republic, Ireland, Israel and Luxembourg contribution-based basic pensions are paid to survivors who never contributed.[17] Moreover, in Canada, Denmark, Finland, New Zealand and the Netherlands, residence-based basic pensions – which are not part of contributory pensions - help smooth consumption after the death of a partner as the benefit level for individuals exceeds 50% of the couple's rate.

One half of OECD countries will have a survivor replacement rate at least equal to 60% based on legislated measures. However, on average in the OECD, future survivor pensions will automatically replace 50% of the deceased's mandatory contributory pension at the retirement age, when no other income is taken into account for any household member including the survivor (Figure 7.10). When in addition the voluntary survivor option is taken into account where available, survivor pensions will replace 58% in total on average. In Denmark, Latvia, Lithuania, the Netherlands, Norway and Sweden, the replacement of the deceased's contributory pension comes only from the voluntary option. Even if the option is chosen, the survivor pension replacement rate remains very low in Latvia, Lithuania, Norway and Sweden. At the upper end of the range, survivor pensions will grant at least 80% of the deceased's mandatory contributory pension in Belgium, Ireland, Mexico, Poland and the United States.[18]

Figure 7.10. Survivor pension as a share of the deceased's pension

Mandatory contributory pension schemes only, paying permanent survivor pensions after the retirement age and not accounting for means-testing against other income

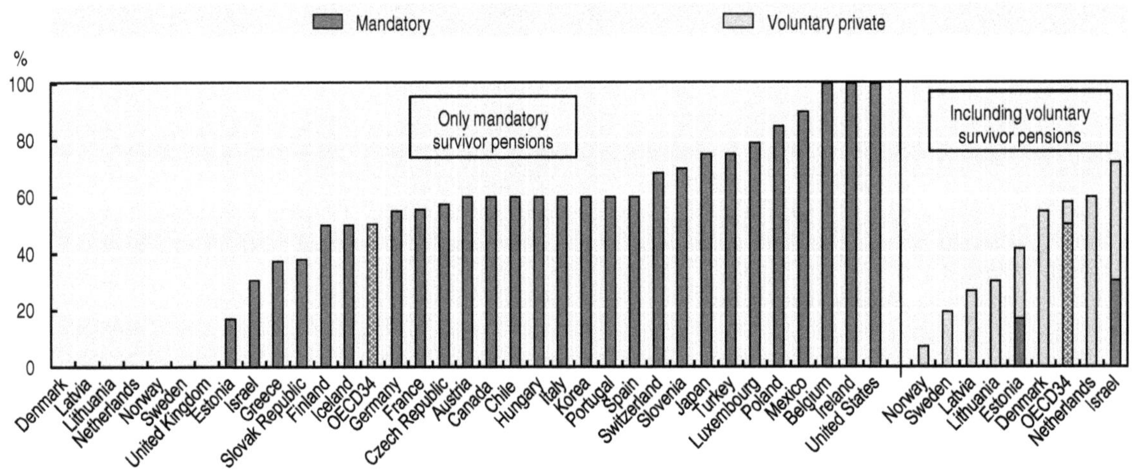

Note: Private-sector rules apply to surviving spouses of the cohort aged 20 in 2016 with no dependent child, no disability and no work history. If voluntary survivor options in mandatory private pension schemes are not specified by law, it is assumed that the joint-and-survivor annuity reduces the payments to 60% upon the death of the primary holder (Box 7.2). Calculations are made at male's normal retirement ages assuming same-age couples. Australia is not included in the chart because joint annuities are not modelled given that most mandatory earnings-related pensions (superannuation) are paid out as lump sums. New Zealand is excluded as there is no mandatory contributory pension schemes. When countries have several components in the mandatory pension, the average value is shown using the shares of each component in the total contributory pension of a full-career average earner as weights.
Source: SSA (2018[10]), MISSOC (2018[11]) and information provided by countries.

StatLink http://dx.doi.org/10.1787/888933850431

Box 7.2. How much does a joint-and-survivor annuity cost?

Joint-and-survivor annuities are financial instruments that transform assets into a stream of payments which continue as long as one annuitant is alive: they thus protect against longevity and survivor risks. Joint life expectancy is not a very intuitive concept, although it is based on a simple fact: even when both partners have the same individual life expectancy, the expected remaining time until the first partner dies (it is initially unknown who this is) is shorter than this same individual remaining live expectancy while the expected remaining time until the second partner diesis longer.

Joint-and-survivor annuities which pay the same amount to the survivor (100-percent joint-and-survivor annuity) provide lower initial payments compared to the sum of two single-life (unisex) annuities because the full benefits are paid for a longer period. The following calculations assume: independent mortality rates between partners; same-age couple retiring together at 65; and indexation of annuities to price inflation.

Based on future mortality tables (using average unisex rates across OECD countries), an annuity that provides a constant payment until the survivor dies should pay a benefit that is approximately 14% lower than the sum of two single annuities.[19] As alternative to the 100-percent joint-and-survivor annuity, the annuity can pay more upfront if the survivor receives a reduced benefit. As discussed above (Box 7.1), an about 70-percent joint-and-survivor annuity is sufficient to maintain standards of living upon the death of a partner. This 70-percent annuity implies an initial adjustment of about 6%. In the case of 50-percent joint-and-survivor annuity, no adjustment is needed, because the *expected* pay-outs are the same as for two single-life annuities: 100% until the first person dies and 50% thereafter.

Existing joint-and-survivor annuities are often designed in a similar way as survivor pensions within PAYGO schemes, but a distinction should be made between joint annuities *with* or *without* a primary annuity holder. Similar to PAYGO schemes, the annuity *with* a primary holder will pay a fixed amount until the death of the primary holder no matter whether his/her partner is alive. The payment is reduced only when the primary holder dies first. Conversely, the annuity *without* a primary holder reduces the payment upon the death of either partner. The annuity *without* a primary holder corresponds to the cases discussed in the previous paragraph.

The annuity *with* a primary holder provides higher payments than the annuity *without* a primary holder when the primary holder's partner dies first. Thus, the latter annuity requires a lower adjustment to initial payments. For example, if a partner without own pension is entitled to receive a survivor pension (or a joint-and-survivor annuity with a primary holder who is the partner) equal to 50% of the deceased's pension, the initial pension will be 8% lower instead of 0% in the case *without* primary holder discussed above. The 70% survivor replacement rates option requires adjustment of 11% instead of 6%.

The simulations in the chapter assume that voluntary survivor options in mandatory pension schemes takes the form of the joint-and-survivor annuity *with* a primary holder that provides the survivor with 60% of the deceased's pension, if not regulated differently. This gives an adjustment of 9%. This common to all countries assumption makes the voluntary survivor options comparable to the mandatory survivor options. Indeed, on average across 26 OECD countries that provide mandatory survivor pensions, the survivor receives 62% of the deceased's pension before means testing (Figure 7.10).

Individual earnings, individual pensions or even total household income reduce survivor pensions in 24 OECD countries (Table 7.2). Means-testing is absent in Chile, Israel (women), Lithuania, Mexico, Portugal and Spain only (and France for the mandatory occupational scheme).[20] In Finland, for example, an own old-age pension beyond about 20% of average earnings reduces the survivor pension proportionally. In the Czech Republic, Ireland and Poland the higher of the two benefits, own old-age and survivor pensions, is paid. In addition in the Czech Republic, 50% of (the earnings-related component of) the lower of the two benefits is also added. Section 7.5 provides some further analysis of the impact of basic pensions and means-testing on the level of survivor pensions.

Own labour income reduces or suspends survivor pensions in 14 countries. This is aimed to better target the survivor benefits at people in need, but it coincidently encourages partial or full withdrawal from the labour market. In Belgium, labour earnings above about half of average earnings cannot be combined with receiving survivor pensions. Poland reduces or suspends survivor pensions when labour income exceeds 70% or 130% of average earnings, respectively. France (main public scheme), Israel (only men) and Turkey apply regular means-testing against all household income.[21]

Table 7.2. Means-testing of survivor pensions against old-age pensions and other income

Mandatory permanent survivor pension payments to non-disabled spouses without dependent children

Affected by income of any household member	Affected by own old-age pensions and individual earnings	Affected by own old-age pensions but not by earnings	Neither affected by individual nor by household income
France (main public scheme)	Austria	Canada	Chile
Israel (men)	Belgium	Czech Republic	France (occupational)
Turkey	Estonia	Finland	Israel (women)
	Germany	Hungary	Lithuania
	Greece	Ireland	Mexico
	Italy	Korea	Portugal
	Japan	Slovak Republic	Spain
	Luxembourg	Switzerland	
	Norway	United States	
	Poland		
	Slovenia		

Note: Some countries are not included (see note to Table 7.1).[22]
Source: SSA, MISSOC and information provided by countries.

Survivor risks in private schemes

As with public pension schemes, not all private schemes – either mandatory or voluntary - pay survivor pensions. Old-age pension pay-outs can take different forms in funded private schemes (OECD, 2016[12]). For survivor pensions, private defined benefit (DB) schemes mostly pay, as in Iceland, the Netherlands or Switzerland, a fraction of the deceased's pension, similar to many public schemes.

In mandatory funded DC plans, survivor schemes are often voluntary and relate to the remaining capital in the individual account at the time of death, but some plans exclude payments to survivors explicitly. Chile and Mexico stand out, granting a fraction of the deceased's annuity to the survivor on a permanent basis.[23] Moreover, in Chile as well as in Norway, the pay-out of the old-age pension in the form of programmed withdrawals includes survivor benefits until the balance of the account is drawn down. In Australia lump-sum payments at the age of retirement are widespread and, outside survivor pensions, the capital from accumulated pension assets that is not consumed at death is inherited by the spouse. In other countries, at least some schemes pay survivor pensions only temporarily or make them optional. Funded DC schemes in Iceland pay survivor benefits on a temporary basis, at an about 50% rate of the deceased's pension for 3-5 years. Similarly, temporary payments are granted for 2 years in the Slovak Republic. In occupational plans in Denmark, survivor pensions are the default option.[24]

Voluntary pensions are typically even less regulated in the pay-out phase than mandatory schemes and cover the survivor risks mainly through the inheritance of unspent pension capital. In the Czech Republic, only the remaining pension capital minus state subsidies can be inherited. In the United States, the market share of DC plans in voluntary pension schemes has been increasing. Traditionally, DB plans have required annuitisation and included survivor options; moreover, opting out from the default survivor pension requires spousal consent in some schemes. By contrast, DC plans have more freedom, allowing for lump sums at the age of retirement and programmed withdrawals. These options are becoming more and more popular (Orlova, Rutledge and Wu, 2015[13]). Even if annuities are chosen, annuities without survivor option prevail. As a result, the increasing prevalence of DC plans has been associated with less coverage of longevity risks for surviving spouses.

Even in the case of a lifelong marriage, it is critical to distinguish whether survivor schemes are primarily about transferring pension assets to the surviving spouse or about ensuring a predictable flow of benefits to the survivor until he or she dies. Lump-sum payments and inheritance of remaining capital in programmed withdrawals ensure the transmission of accumulated pension assets to the survivor.

Lump-sum payments and programmed withdrawals do not insure against longevity risks. But this is the case for all households within those schemes, singles and couples. If policy makers assess that longevity risks should not be covered – which might be questionable normatively - and for example opt for lump sums, then survivor pensions within those schemes cannot be expected to address longevity risks. Yet, survivors are more vulnerable to longevity risk than other pensioners as they by definition live longer. In short, lump sums deal with the transmission of pension assets, but raise risks of survivors being exposed to insufficient income in old age.

7.4. Reforms to survivor pensions

Over the last thirty years, various reforms of the survivor pension were enacted in OECD countries. The most common trend was the extension of pension eligibility to men based on the same conditions as for women. This took place in Belgium, Canada, Chile, the Czech Republic, Finland, Germany, Hungary, Ireland, Israel, Japan, Korea, the Netherlands, Sweden, the Slovak Republic, Spain and the United Kingdom. In EU countries, this change occurred mainly in the 1990s in line with the 1984 EC Directive requiring the progressive implementation of equal treatment between men and women in social security matters. Some countries extended the coverage of the beneficiaries to same-sex partners or civil partners (Table 7.1).

Survivor pension reforms within evolving pension systems

In some countries systemic reforms of old-age pensions led to the elimination of survivor protection while in others it had no impact. First, in the 1990s, Italy, Latvia, Poland and

Sweden reformed their public pay-as-you-go (PAYGO) pension schemes from DB into notional (non-financial) defined contribution schemes (NDC). Norway did so in 2011. The core of the NDC design mimics funded DC schemes with strong links between individual lifetime contributions and benefits. Redistribution features such as survivor pensions can be added within NDC schemes on top of this core principle.

Sweden eliminated survivor pensions in the public scheme in 1990, almost a decade before the introduction of NDC pensions. Disincentives for women to build their own entitlements, induced to some extent by survivor pensions, and the view that derived pension rights do not fully recognise the autonomy of women and change the balance of power against women within families was the main factor that drove this change. In line with this argument, recent simulations for the United States indicate that abandoning both survivor pensions and spousal pension supplements would increase women's employment (Nishiyama, 2018[14]; Sánchez-Marcos and Bethencourt, 2018[15]).

In Latvia, as part of the move towards more individualised pension entitlements, survivor pensions for spouses were eliminated when the NDC scheme was introduced in 1996. In Norway, benefit levels were tightened in 2002 for survivors younger than 55 who do not work. With the introduction of the NDC scheme in 2011, survivor pensions received after the retirement age from the public scheme were gradually eliminated, with full effects for the generations born in 1963 and later. There is an ongoing debate in the country about whether survivor pensions after retirement age should be part of the NDC system and about transforming the survivor pensions paid until the retirement age into a temporary benefit, for a few years only, so as to improve incentives to participate in the labour market at working age.

In Poland, survivor pensions were almost unaffected by the introduction of NDC: survivor pensions were not incorporated into the NDC scheme and still pay a fraction of the deceased's old-age pension without adjustment for the remaining life expectancy of the survivor. By contrast, Italy incorporated survivor pensions into the NDC design. To ensure financial balances of the NDC scheme including survivor pensions, the NDC cohort-specific annuity factor used to compute NDC old-age pensions is adjusted to account for the expected expenditure on survivor benefits. Second, the introduction of point systems - in the 1990s in Germany and Estonia, in the 2000s in the Slovak Republic and in 2018 in Lithuania - which also have tight links between earnings and benefits, did not affect benefit rules for survivor pensions in these countries.

Third, in the United Kingdom, after many substantial reforms since the 1960s, the 2016 reform linked old-age benefits only with the length of the contribution period and not with past earnings. At the same time survivor pensions for spouses were generally eliminated.[25] Similarly, survivor pensions had been eliminated from the public schemes in Australia in 1997 and in New Zealand in 2013. The Netherlands which has a residence-based basic pension decided to eliminate the flat-rate survivor pension from their public schemes after the retirement age as indeed it was providing a higher flat-rate old-age safety net to widows and widowers than to singles.

Fourth, the role of private provisions within pension systems has increased in a number of OECD countries including Australia, Chile, Estonia, Lithuania, Latvia, Mexico, Norway, the Slovak Republic, Slovenia and Sweden. However, there have been some reversals in Lithuania, Hungary, Poland and the Slovak Republic more recently, with no major reforms in the direction of privatisation since 2007 (Bielawska, Chłoń-Domińczak and Stańko, 2015[16]; Kay, 2014[17]). All these changes have been accompanied by shifts from DB to DC schemes within occupational plans. For example, Mexico moved in 1997 from a PAYGO

DB to a mandatory funded DC scheme. In the new system, survivor pensions are financed by additional contributions (Social Security Administration, 2018[10]). Already in 1981, Chile substituted its PAYGO DB scheme with the mandatory funded DC scheme, with survivor benefits remaining a strong component. Beyond these two countries, the move from DB to DC was often accompanied by a drop in the coverage of survivor risks.

In short, pension reforms in OECD countries have tended towards more individualisation through closer links between old-age benefits and lifetime contributions, and less redistribution within schemes. This might create some tension for the continuity of mandatory survivor pensions.

Trends in expenditures

Survivor benefit expenditures have been influenced by both pension reforms and population ageing. Expenditures on survivor benefits have been stable compared to 1990 at around 1% of GDP on average across 24 OECD countries for which data are available. Austria, Belgium and Germany exhibit the strongest decline of more than 0.7 percentage points of GDP while the rise was most pronounced in Luxembourg, Portugal, Spain and Turkey (about 1 p.p. or more).

On average in the 24 OECD countries, survivor benefit expenditures have not kept pace with old-age pension spending which substantially increased from 5.5% of GDP in 1990 to 8.0% in 2017 (or latest). Indeed, survivor benefit expenditures from mandatory pensions represented 13% of old-age spending in 2017 (or latest), down from 20% about twenty-five years earlier on average (Figure 7.11). Higher women's own contributory pensions driven by their increasing employment, a lower gender gap in life expectancy and changes in couple formation may have contributed to this fall (Section 7.2). Additionally, stricter means-testing and a tightening of benefits and eligibility conditions partly explain this trend.

Figure 7.11. Trends in survivor benefit expenditures in mandatory schemes as a share of old-age spending, %

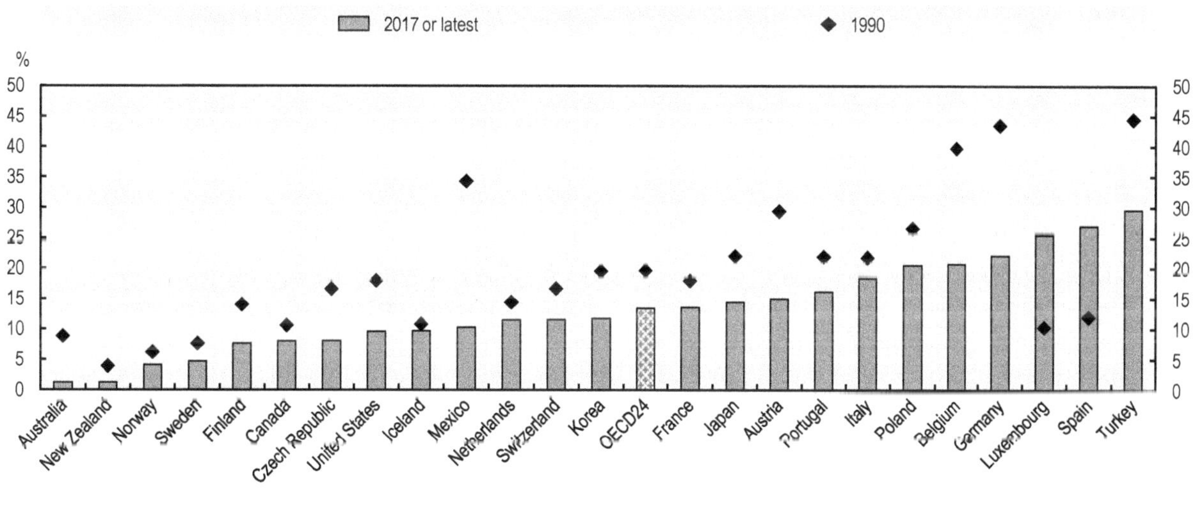

Note: See Figure 7.1. Data for Chile, Denmark, Greece and Ireland were not included due to break in series. Data for the other missing OECD countries are not available for 1990.
Source: OECD preliminary social expenditure database.

StatLink http://dx.doi.org/10.1787/888933850450

The strongest declines in survivor benefit spending relative to old-age pension expenditures between 1990 and 2017 are recorded in Belgium, Germany and Mexico. Germany broadened the means-tests to nearly all kinds of income in 2001, limited the duration of some survivor benefits to two years, introduced a one-year requirement on the minimum length of marriage and cut benefit levels from 60% to 55% of old-age pensions. For Mexico, the fall is less meaningful as old-age pension spending was very low in 1990. Other countries have also tightened access to survivor pensions, such as France and Norway.[26] New Zealand went further by abolishing the survivor benefit altogether in 2013.

Only in Luxembourg and Spain have expenditures on survivor benefits risen more strongly than on old-age pensions. Both countries increased the survivor benefits and expanded the coverage: Luxembourg for the same-sex couples and Spain for the registered cohabitations.

7.5. Future survivor pensions

Despite the recent trend towards more individualisation of old-age pensions and the abolishment or tightening of survivor pensions in several countries, the great majority of OECD countries still has mandatory survivor schemes for future pensioners. For people entering the labour market now, the current legislation does not include any automatic transfer of pension entitlements to the surviving spouse after the retirement age in only seven countries: Australia, Latvia, the Netherlands, New Zealand, Norway, Sweden and the United Kingdom. There, pension adequacy risks for survivors are covered through safety nets or are left to individuals who can either opt for survivor pensions within private schemes or buy an annuity with a survivor option from private insurers (Box 7.2).

This section is structured as follows. First, it discusses how own pensions affect the level of survivor pensions. Second, it shows how survivor pensions contribute on top of existing safety nets to protecting retirement income and preserving standards of living after the death of a spouse. Finally, this section presents the impact of introducing pension-rights splitting on top of or in place of existing mandatory survivor pensions.

This section is based on modelling the old-age and survivor pension entitlements from mandatory pension schemes for individuals entering the labour market in 2016. For simplicity, it focuses on same-age couples and assumes that the wife outlives her husband who dies shortly after retiring at the normal retirement age.[27] For most countries, the results also apply to husbands outliving their wife and to same-sex couples.[28]

How much is the pension of the deceased replaced by survivor schemes alone

Taking into account all sources of contributory pensions - and ignoring residency-based basic pensions - a never-working survivor would, on average across OECD countries, receive a survivor pension equal to 46% of the pension of the deceased spouse who had a full career at the average wage. Figure 7.12 shows zero or minimal numbers for countries without mandatory survivor pensions, plus Denmark and Lithuania.[29] Apart from these, the replacement from survivor pensions is 25% or lower in only Estonia and Israel. It is 75% or larger in Belgium, Luxembourg, Mexico, Poland and Turkey.

The average survivor pension of 46% of the deceased's pension remains below the replacement level of 50% shown in Figure 7.10. The main reason is that several countries grant spousal pension supplements to pensioners if their spouses have no or low own pensions, but not to survivors thereby lowering the effective survivor replacement rate compared to Figure 7.10. Such supplements play a large role in Ireland where the basic pension increases by 90% in case of having a spouse without own contributions as well as in Israel and the United States, where it can equal 50% of own public pensions, and in Belgium (25%). Except for low earners, supplements are less important, in Japan and Korea which pay flat-rate benefits. Also, Switzerland has mandatory pension splitting during marriage, which increases the old-age pension of a spouse without work history but reduces the survivor pension.

Figure 7.12. Survivor pension relative to the contributory old-age pension of the deceased spouse

Same age couple, the deceased has worked a full career from age 20 in 2016 at the average wage and died just after having retired at the normal retirement age, mandatory pension schemes

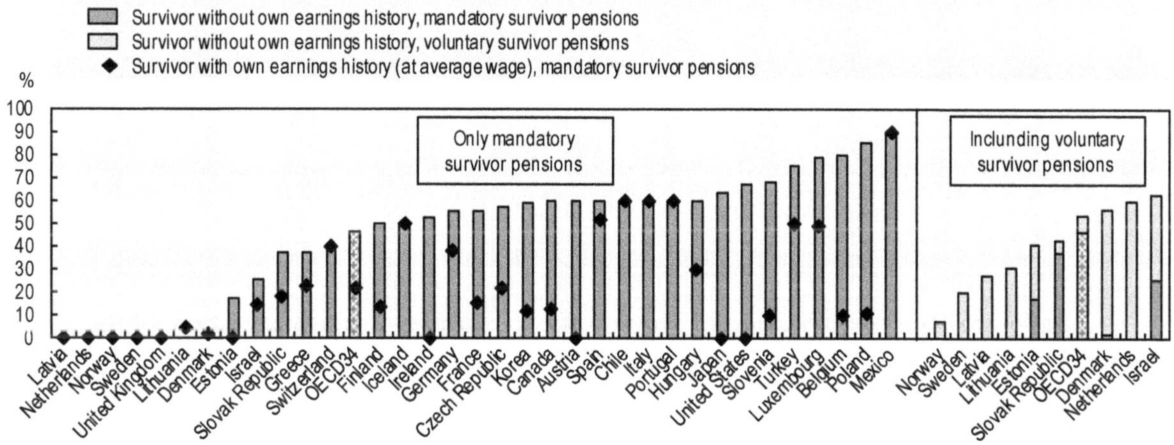

Note: For voluntary survivor options in private mandatory schemes the simulation assumes that a couple buys a joint-and-survivor annuity that lowers the payment to 60% upon the death of the primary holder (Box 7.2). The only exception is the Slovak Republic where the survivor receives the same pension as the deceased but only for two years. Australia and New Zealand are not included (see note of Figure 7.10).
Source: OECD pension model.

StatLink http://dx.doi.org/10.1787/888933850469

An own pension reduces survivor benefits in many countries. On average in the OECD, the survivor replacement rate in mandatory schemes decreases from 46% for a single-earner couple to only 22% when both individuals had the same baseline career (Figure 7.12). The impact of having an own pension varies a lot across countries. In Austria, Estonia, Ireland, Japan, and the United States, own pensions fully eliminate entitlements to survivor benefits in the case of spouses having the same earnings history at the average wage. By contrast, in Chile, Iceland, Italy, Mexico, Portugal and Switzerland mandatory survivor benefits remain unaffected.

In many private mandatory pension schemes, survivor pensions are voluntary and survivor benefits are financed by an upfront reduction of earnings related pensions. When voluntary survivor pensions (in mandatory pension schemes) are accounted for, the survivor replacement rate for a non-working partner increases from 46% to 54% on average. It is less than 25% only in the United Kingdom, which have no mandatory earnings-related schemes and no survivor scheme for basic pensions (unlike Ireland), as well as in Norway and Sweden, where the contributions to the private DC scheme are relatively low compared to the public scheme. By contrast, when accounting also for the voluntary option, the survivor replacement rate in Denmark, Israel and the Netherlands exceeds the OECD34 average from mandatory survivor pensions.

Contribution of survivor pensions to survivors' total pension income

Survivor pensions can provide substantial additional income to widowed persons. On average across 35 OECD countries, basic pensions and safety nets currently provide an income of 20% of the gross average wage for those who have never worked. Based on economic assumptions used in the OECD pension model, current indexation rules imply that when those who entered the labour market in 2016 will reach the retirement age this average will fall from 20% to 16%. A spouse who has never worked and survived a full-career average-earning partner would additionally receive 15% of the average wage from mandatory survivor options, thereby 31% in total, almost doubling retirement income (Figure 7.13). Voluntary survivor pensions add a further 3 percentage points, or 34% in total.

Figure 7.13. Gross total pension income of a survivor without own earnings history

Same age couple, the deceased worked a full career from age 20 in 2016 at the average wage and died just after having retired at the normal retirement age, mandatory pension schemes

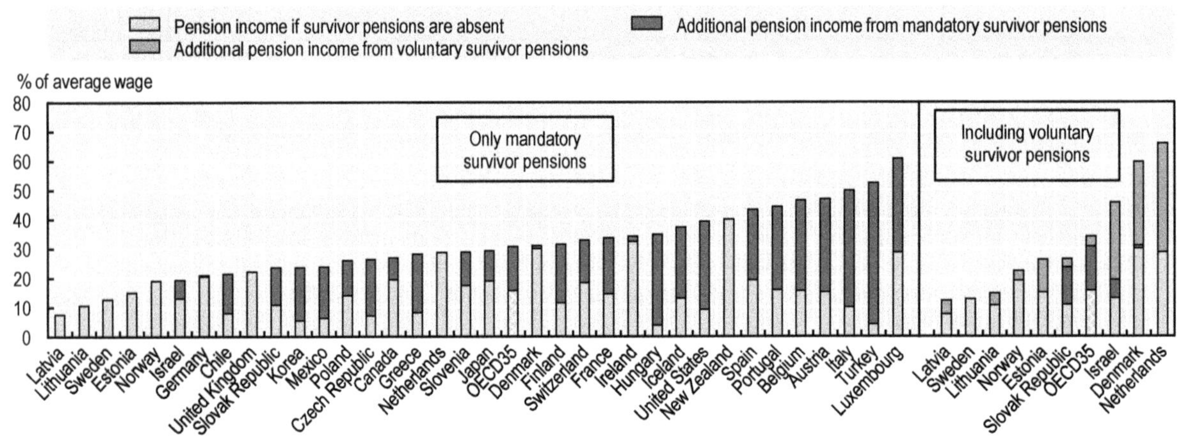

Note: The "pension income if survivor pensions are absent" series calculates total pension income that would be paid if survivor pensions were ignored, taking into account additional benefits from first-tier pensions that would become available. Additional pension income from survivor pensions then displays the effective additional income stemming from survivor pensions. Australia is excluded due to comparability reasons.
Source: OECD pension model.

StatLink http://dx.doi.org/10.1787/888933850488

Based on mandatory survivor pensions alone, the total pension income of a widowed spouse who never worked and was partnered to a full-career average-wage worker exceeds 40% of the gross average wage in Austria, Belgium, Italy, Luxembourg, Portugal, Spain and Turkey. On the other side of the spectrum, no additional total income stems from mandatory survivor pensions in Estonia, Latvia, Lithuania, Norway, Sweden and the United Kingdom where the surviving spouse would receive less than 25% of the gross average wage. Also in Germany, where the old-age safety net is withdrawn, additional income from survivor pensions is close to zero in that case.

The own pensions of a survivor diminish survivor pension levels to some extent: on average in the OECD, a surviving spouse of a two-average-earners couple can expect the own gross pension of 53% of average wage to be topped up by a mandatory survivor pension of 11 percentage points – instead of 15 p.p. when the surviving spouse never worked - to 64% (Figure 7.14). Still, in that case survivor pensions substantially improve the situation of the survivor compared to a single person with a similar work experience in Austria, Belgium, Chile, Iceland, Luxembourg, Mexico and Southern European countries.

Figure 7.14. Gross total pension income of a survivor with own earnings history

Same age couple with an identical full career from age 20 in 2016 at the average wage, deceased died just after having retired at the normal retirement age, mandatory pension schemes

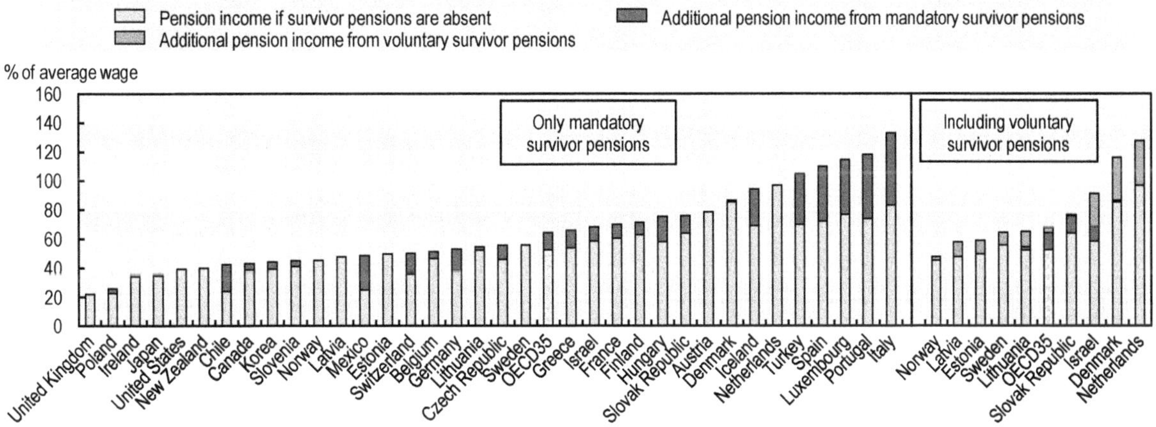

Note: The "pension income if survivor pensions are absent" series calculates total pension income that would be paid if survivor pensions were ignored, taking into account additional benefits from first-tier pensions that would become available. Additional pension income from survivor pensions then displays the effective additional income stemming from survivor pensions. Australia is excluded due to comparability reasons.
Source: OECD pension model.

StatLink http://dx.doi.org/10.1787/888933850507

Preserving living standards after partner's death

Economies of scale that benefit couples can be significant, but stop playing for survivors (Box 7.1). In particular, living costs do not drop by half upon the partner's death, even when downsizing the accommodation. Based on the OECD equivalence scale, a drop of more than 30% in the *total* income of the couple household reduces the standards of living of the survivor upon the partner's death.

After the death of their spouse, survivors without work history would have, on average across 35 OECD countries, an equivalised disposable income equal to 76% of its pre-death level (Figure 7.15). This means that they would lose on average 24% in standards of living (18% if voluntary survivor options are taken). Mandatory survivor pensions offset three-fifths of the financial impact induced by the loss of the breadwinner's entitlements, as without survivor pensions the loss would reach 61%.

Countries which record the largest losses in standards of living following the death of a partner, more than 25%, are those that combine low first-tier benefits with low replacement from survivor pensions: Estonia, Finland, Greece, Iceland, Ireland, Latvia, Lithuania, Norway, the Slovak Republic and Sweden. By contrast, the equivalised disposable income increases for survivors in Belgium, Luxembourg, Mexico, Poland, Slovenia and Turkey. Single-breadwinners outliving their spouses who never contributed to pensions also experience rising living standards in most countries. On average in the OECD, their equivalised disposable income increases by about 25%.

Figure 7.15. Total pension income of survivor of single-earner couple relative to equivalised pension income before the death

Same age couple, the deceased worked a full career from age 20 in 2016 at the average wage and died just after having retired at the normal retirement age, mandatory pension schemes

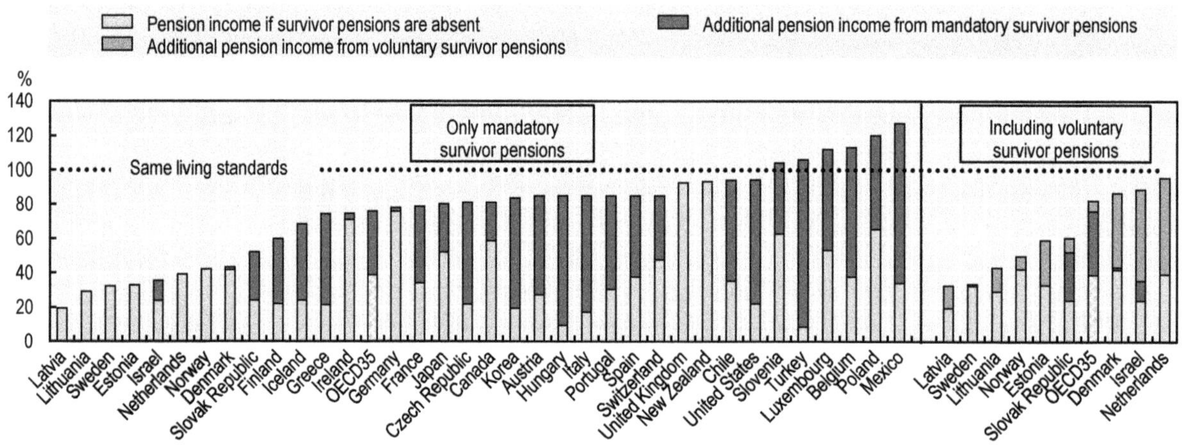

Note: The "pension income if survivor pensions are absent" series calculates total pension income that would be paid if survivor pensions were ignored, taking into account additional benefits from first-tier pensions that would become available. Additional pension income from survivor pensions then displays the effective additional income stemming from survivor pensions. Australia is excluded due to comparability reasons.
Source: OECD pension model.

StatLink http://dx.doi.org/10.1787/888933850526

Pension splitting and survivor pensions – policy scenarios

The splitting of pension rights is often discussed as an alternative to survivor pensions, even though both can be combined. Splitting of pension rights means that old-age pension entitlements of partners are first totalled and then divided between partners, half-half or in any other proportion. The splitting can take place when contributing, separating or retiring. Hence, splitting increases the old-age pension of the surviving partner who has accumulated fewer own entitlements than the deceased partner. At the same time, it reduces the old-age pension of the surviving partner who has higher own entitlements. Moreover, pension splitting may reduce the survivor pensions that are subject to a means-test against other pension income.

Switzerland is the only country that has made pension splitting mandatory, in its public scheme since 1997. Germany introduced in 2002 the choice, at least for some restricted cases, to trade the entitlement to a survivor pension against a fifty-fifty splitting of pension claims between partners upon the retirement of the younger spouse. Take-up rates in Germany are very low though as only couples who were either married after 2001 or born after 1961 are eligible; but this may be also due to the financial disadvantage of pension splitting compared to survivor pensions. The next section provides a discussion about what splitting brings while highlighting that it is not a substitute to survivor pensions.

The following simulations assume that fifty-fifty splitting of total pensions is introduced in all countries, first to replace mandatory survivor pensions. Such a shift from the current mandatory survivor schemes to splitting would generate significant changes in many countries, but on average across 35 OECD countries the total pension of the survivor who never worked and was married to an average earner will be similar (Figure 7.16).

Figure 7.16. The impact of introducing pension splitting on the survivor's pension income

Change in total gross pension income of a survivor without own earnings history compared to current legislation

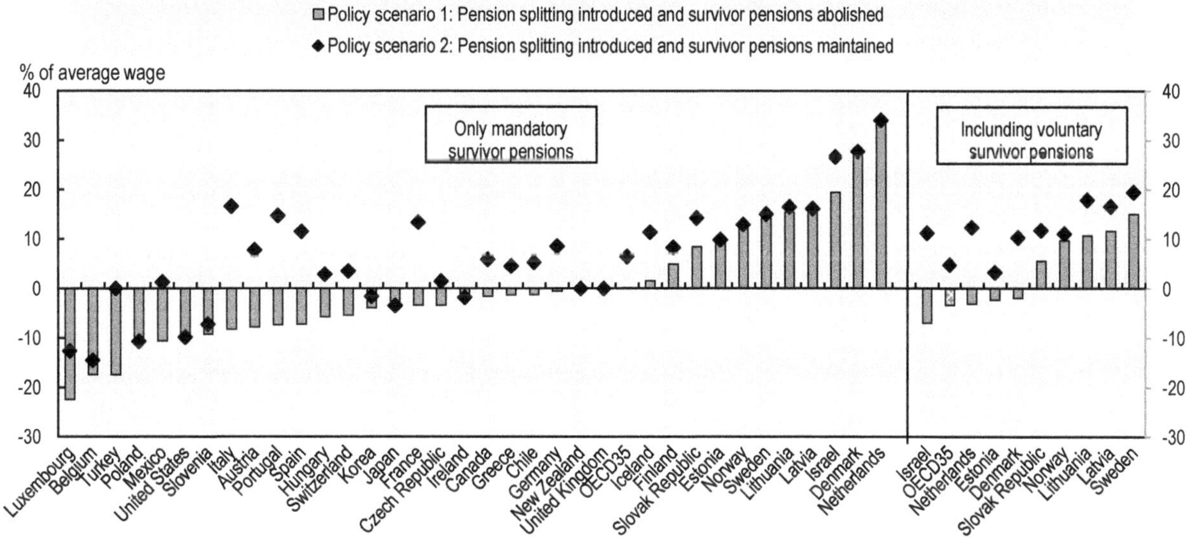

Note: The simulation assumes the deceased of the same age couple had a full career from age 20 in 2016 at the average wage and died just after having retired. Latvia, the Netherlands, New Zealand, Norway, Sweden and the United Kingdom do not provide mandatory survivor pensions in that case. The introduction of pension splitting splits total pension income with the exception of Switzerland where it only applies to the mandatory occupational scheme as splitting already exists in the public scheme. Australia is excluded due to comparability reasons.

Source: OECD pension model.

StatLink http://dx.doi.org/10.1787/888933850545

Pension splitting would increase the pension income of survivors by more than 15% of the average wage in Denmark, Israel, Latvia, Lithuania, the Netherlands and Sweden due to the lack of a mandatory survivor pension in the earnings-related schemes. By contrast, in the majority of OECD countries (22 exactly) the existing survivor pensions are more beneficial than splitting for survivors who were married to average earners and without own earnings-related pension. In Belgium, Luxembourg and Turkey the total pensions of survivors would decrease by more than 15% of average wage if survivor pensions were replaced by pension splitting due to high survivor replacement rates, markedly above 50%.

Moreover, a worker outliving his never-earning spouse would never benefit from the introduction of pension splitting as he/she would give up own old-age pension entitlements without receiving survivor pensions in the first place.

Including voluntary survivor pensions turns the average impact of splitting negative, equalling -3% of average wage across OECD countries (right part of Figure 7.16). Survivors covered by the voluntary survivor options would be worse off if splitting replaced survivor pensions in Denmark, Estonia, Israel and the Netherlands while they would be still better off in Latvia, Lithuania, Norway, the Slovak Republic and Sweden.

The second policy scenario looks at the introduction of pension splitting while preserving the existing mandatory survivor pension rules. In this simulation survivor pension rules apply to the old-age pension of the deceased after splitting. Such a change would raise the pension income level of survivors who have never worked by 7% of average wage on average in the OECD. In France, Italy, Portugal and Spain total pension income of a survivor would increase by more than 10% of average wage upon introducing pension splitting while maintaining current survivor pension rules, compared to a decline in the scenario that survivor pensions are simply replaced by splitting. By contrast, in Belgium, Luxembourg and Poland pension splitting would lead to a reduction of survivor's total pension income by more than 10% of average wage whether survivor rules are maintained or abolished. There, strict means testing against other pension income reduces survivor pension payments drastically upon the introduction of pension splitting in mandatory schemes.

7.6. General discussion

Survivor pensions is a complex topic and is often integrated within social policies. It mixes various elements of old-age pensions, family policies and inheritance rights. Historically, survivor pensions were designed to smooth standards of livings after the death of a spouse and help widows fight poverty. Nowadays, poverty relief is a policy objective that is targeted by specific instruments which do not differentiate between singles and widows or widowers. Hence, consumption smoothing is currently the key objective pursued by survivor pensions, which in many cases de facto helps reduce the pension gap between men and women.

Inheritance of pension entitlements

Are pension entitlements part of inheritable assets? Whether pension entitlements are viewed as a more or less explicit part of own accumulated assets influences whether they should be treated as part of inheritance rights. In practice, the principles governing survivor pensions still mix the wealth and redistribution rationale.

In general, PAYGO entitlements until being withdrawn are promises and cannot be transmitted unless survivor schemes come into play. Then in the absence of survivor schemes, the contributions made for example by people who die before the retirement age are lost to the heirs, which tends to increase the pensions of people who survive until that age. Most funded defined benefit schemes also fall in this category. In all these schemes, the pension entitlements of a single person are not part of her estate.

Individual funded defined contribution accounts are closer to the idea of personal assets that can be inherited, even though recent measures have questioned the strength of pension property rights in some countries.[30] This is typically the case during the accumulation phase if the contributor dies before retiring. If the contributor survives and starts to withdraw, the choice might need to be made between lump sums (which then fall within private assets), programmed withdrawals or individual annuities which might obey some specific rules for survivor pensions, or joint-life annuities which directly address survivor risks.

Survivor pensions and redistribution

The original design of survivor pensions refers to a timeworn family model. The man was working, the woman was taking care of children and house, and everyone was assumed to be part of a unique, lifelong heterosexual marriage. The foundations of this model have been questioned, female formal employment has progressively expanded, and family formations have been less stable and more diverse (Section 7.2). In the meantime, pension entitlements have become more individualised, potentially creating some tension with redistribution mechanisms such as those inherent in survivor pensions. Over the last decades, most of survivor pension reforms, especially in Nordic and Anglo-Saxon countries, have tended to limit access to derived rights (Section 7.4).

These societal changes have been occurring in a challenging period for pension systems. Demographic changes driven by increased longevity and low fertility put pressure on old-age support ratios, weakening the finances of defined benefit schemes and the rates of return of defined contribution pensions. One policy implication has been to emphasise that pension policies should promote labour force participation for everyone.

Making a surviving partner eligible to a permanent survivor pension at an age lower than the normal retirement age is therefore inconsistent with these general principles.[31] Instead, being eligible to a permanent survivor pension should be consistent with retirement age rules. For survivors of younger ages, in order to offset the financial burden created by the death of a partner, a temporary allocation – e.g. during a couple of years or until dependent children reach adulthood – should be granted to help adapt to the new situation. When the survivor reaches the retirement age, the full survivor pensions could kick in. An alternative is to set a given age threshold (lower than the retirement age) at the time of a partner's death, from which the surviving partner is entitled to part of the survivor pension when reaching the retirement age, with that part increasing steadily with the age at partner's death and reaching 100% for death occurring if the survivor reached the retirement age.

Survivor pensions could take the form of a redistribution within a given household through time, i.e. from before to after the death of a partner. Their current designs, however, typically involve redistribution across households which might have unintended consequences.[32] If survivor pensions are combined with the same contribution rates and benefit levels for individuals being single or living in a couple, they imply some redistribution, which is difficult to justify, from singles to couples and from dual-career couples to single-earner couples, especially to those with large age differences (James, $2009_{[18]}$). For example in that case, singles get no benefit from survivor schemes and yet they contribute to financing the extension of entitlements to survivors. This arises because the individual pension amount does not account for the cost of joint-life insurance.[33] The financing of survivor pensions by singles is also questionable because survivor pensions help compensate for lost economies of scale that singles never benefited from.

Internalising the cost of survivor pensions

There are two ways to avoid these undesirable forms of redistribution. First, as in Chile and Sweden for the funded schemes for example, partners while benefiting from economies of scale in their cost of living receive (or can choose to in Sweden) lower individual pension benefits when both partners are alive to finance the survivor benefit upon death. Financing a survivor benefit equal to 60% of the deceased's pension reduces initial pensions - when both partners are alive - by about 9% compared to singles with the same contribution history (Box 7.2). Because this reduction is meant to finance survivor pensions which are currently financed by lowering the own pensions of everyone, a budget-neutral reform which implements such a mechanism would lead to an increase of pensions for singles, and therefore a much lower total reduction than 9% for couples. This internalises the expected cost of survivor pensions within a given household or at least, more generally, among couples.[34] The second way of internalising is by splitting pension entitlements within couples, as discussed further below.

Less common lifelong marriage and increased female employment surely diminish the role survivor pensions have to play. Yet, beyond remaining gender gaps, consumption smoothing upon the death of a partner is still a worthwhile objective to be pursued by social policies, and in particular through survivor pensions. While fewer and fewer pensioners will rely on survivor pensions, those who have to will still be particularly vulnerable after the death of their partner. Even in the case where both partners had the same career, the standards of living of the survivor would decline by about 30% due to economies of scale of living in a couple.

Both myopic behaviour and incomplete information lead to insufficient insurance of survivor risks at a fair price through private insurance and efficient annuity markets (Barr and Diamond, 2008[19]; Blake, 2012[20]; Findley and Caliendo, 2008[21]), which justifies the need for mandatory survivor pensions.[35] In particular, short-slightness, compulsory behaviour, low financial knowledge and information procession costs mean that people do not insure themselves well against especially distant, future events. These limitations may be stronger for survivor pensions than for old-age pensions because they require planning beyond the horizon of own life.

Taking stock of the recent trends in couple formation, survivor pensions should in principle be extended beyond marriages to civil unions and formal partnerships. One open question though might be whether survivor pensions should be limited to partnerships which have some legal or financial obligations in terms of solidarity within couples. If there is no formal obligation, a partner might not be protected to start with by his or her partner when both partners are alive; it might therefore be questionable whether consumption-smoothing when the partner dies is a valid objective for public policy. There is also some concern that such an extension of eligible partnerships could reinforce unions of convenience as partners approach retirement ages. However, as for marriages, if the cost of survivor pensions is internalised within couples as suggested above, these concerns will be limited. If it is not internalised then at least, in order to justify the cost to the public purse more fairly, survivor pensions should be based on the prorated length of the current union as a share of the total contributed period.

Splitting pension rights

The situation is very different for divorced and separated partners, to whom survivor pensions should not be eligible. Indeed, the consumption-smoothing motive does not apply to old partnerships because there is no current consumption to smooth. The main question, however, refers to past pension entitlements. During the partnership, resources were typically shared and some decisions such as those related to the allocated time for formal employment - that generates pension rights - and informal activities such as home-based work – that does not – have typically been taken jointly. Some OECD countries, including Estonia, France, Germany and Luxembourg, endorse this resource sharing by taxing spouses or partners jointly or allowing them to fill a joint tax statement. Therefore, pension entitlements accumulated during the partnerships can be considered at least partly to be common to the partners.

In that sense, there is a strong case to split, at least partially, the pension entitlements of both partners (Box 7.3). For example, in the case of a full split, each partner gets half of the total entitlements accumulated by both partners during the union.[36] Splitting also facilitates separation arrangements; court judgements upon divorce typically split some (private) pension rights acquired during marriage similarly to splitting assets and granting alimony. With splitting, pension entitlements are automatically prorated for the duration of partnerships.

One advantage of splitting is that this mechanism focuses on entitlements earned during the partnership and minimises the impact of the ex-partners' career after a separation. However, while splitting is fairly easy to implement in defined contribution and point systems or in defined benefit systems that are based on straightforward accrual rates, it is more complicated to introduce splitting in complex and fragmented pension systems as well as in schemes with loose links between contributions and pension entitlements.[37]

Box 7.3. Survivor pensions combined with splitting pension

The own pension of the survivor and of the deceased in the absence of splitting are denoted PS and PD, respectively, following Bonnet and Hourriez ($2012_{[22]}$). Assume that the share *s* of accumulated pensions is split between partners. Equal or fifty-fifty splitting corresponds to *s* = ½.

This implies that when both partners are alive the survivor gets (1-s) PS + s PD and the deceased gets s PS + (1-s) PD. After the partner's death, the survivor thus gets a total pension including the survivor pension at rate λ of (1-s) PS + s PD + λ [s PS + (1-s) PD].

Based on the equivalence scale used by the OECD, the couple's equivalised household income when both partners are alive is (PS + PD) / √2.

So upon death, the survivor maintains standards of living, i.e. can successfully smooth consumption, when:

$$(1-\mathrm{s})\,\mathrm{PS} + \mathrm{s}\,\mathrm{PD} + \lambda\,[s\,\mathrm{PS} + (1-\mathrm{s})\mathrm{PD}] = (\mathrm{PS} + \mathrm{PD})/\sqrt{2}$$

Solving this for λ leads to:

$$\lambda = (\sqrt{2}-1) + \left(1-\frac{\sqrt{2}}{2}\right)\left(1-\frac{PS}{PD}\right)\frac{1-2\,s}{1-s\,(1-\frac{PS}{PD})}$$

The case of surviving a single breadwinner corresponds to PS = 0 while the case of a similar career between both partners is PS = PD.

When there is equal splitting (s=1/2), a survivor replacement rate $\lambda = (\sqrt{2}-1) = 41\%$ ensures consumption smoothing after the death of the partner whatever the career patterns. Likewise, if partners had the same career (PS=PD), $\lambda = 41\%$ ensures that standards of living are maintained upon the death of a spouse.

The general condition in the single-breadwinner case is $\lambda = (\sqrt{2}-1) + \left(1-\frac{\sqrt{2}}{2}\right)(1-2s)$. If the split is one-third / two-thirds (s=1/3) then consumption smoothing is achieved for the spouse who never worked with $\lambda = 51\%$.

Splitting pension rights should replace survivor pensions for separated couples, but is not a substitute to survivor pensions for ongoing partnerships. With split entitlements during the accumulation phase, current partnerships are still exposed to risks of lower standards of living after the death of the partner due to lost economies of scale. For example, based on OECD equivalence scale, transmitting 41% of the deceased partner's entitlements to the survivor would fulfil the consumption-smoothing objective in the case of full splitting (Box 7.3). It follows that a benchmark framework would combine splitting pension rights, at least partly, between partners when these entitlements are accumulated and granting eligibility to survivor pensions for current partnerships, prorated based on the length of the partnership.

However, some countries including Sweden abandoned survivor pensions because they are associated with a family model which has contributed to reproducing gender inequality. In turn, maintaining survivor pensions would endogenously limit women's autonomy. This view insists on the financial independence of partners and might not support the idea of splitting pension rights. A key stone of that argumentation refers to the balance of power within couples. However, if decisions are truly taken jointly, splitting pension rights might not be inconsistent with and even could actually support financial independence.

Splitting pension rights may incur additional spending on earnings-related pensions – i.e. abstracting from survivor pensions - because on average it transfers pension rights from men to women, who tend to live longer and to have lower own entitlements. However, when accounting for survivor pensions, the fifty-fifty pension splitting would reduce the total pension spending (Bonnet and Hourriez, 2012[22]). However, as discussed before, the fifty-fifty splitting alone fails to preserve standards of living upon the death of a partner.

7.7. Conclusion: main results and key policy implications

Main results

- Almost all OECD countries cover survivor risk through survivor pensions for at least some parts of the population, with eligibility criteria and coverage differing substantially across countries.
- Nowadays, all OECD countries provide instruments directly targeted at poverty alleviation. There is no obvious justification why widowed persons should be granted higher old-age benefits than other individuals in a similarly poor income situation.
- The consumption-smoothing motive has thus become the main objective of survivor pensions for widowed persons. Survivor pensions are helpful to insure against the decrease in disposable income relative to the situation prevailing before the death of the partner, in the same way as old-age pensions help avoid a sharp drop in income upon retirement. Moreover, survivor pensions effectively lower gender gaps in pensions in most countries.
- While marriage used to be required to access survivor pensions, an increasing number of countries have expanded survivor benefits to civil unions and even cohabitations, including same-sex partners.
- Only nine OECD countries do not grant survivor pensions after divorce, even though the consumption-smoothing objective is not relevant when a partner from a former union dies.

- Survivor schemes have been tightened over the last decades, especially in Nordic and Anglo-Saxon countries. Yet, overall survivor spending has been stable at about 1% of GDP. This means, however, that expenditures on survivor benefits have not kept pace with the increase in old-age benefit spending, with the relative spending ratio (survivor vs old-age) being reduced from 20% to 13% in about 25 years on average across countries.
- Spending on survivor benefits is currently very low in Australia, Estonia, Latvia and New Zealand while it is larger than 2.3% of GDP in Greece, Italy and Spain. As a share of expenditures on old-age benefits, it is the highest – more than 25% - in Luxembourg, Spain and Turkey. In Germany, Lithuania, Luxembourg, Spain and Turkey, there are about two survivor pension recipients or more for each five old-age pension recipients, the highest ratios within the OECD. On average, 88% of survivor pension recipients are women.
- No minimum age requirements apply for receiving a permanent survivor pension in Austria, Canada, Chile, Ireland, Italy, Korea, Luxembourg, Mexico, Norway, Spain and Turkey while only widowed persons (who are neither disabled nor have dependent children) above a certain age are eligible in 17 OECD countries. The lowest minimum age is 35 years in Portugal and 40 years in Israel. Estonia, Hungary, Lithuania and the Slovak Republic do not grant access to permanent survivor pensions before the recipient reaches the retirement age. In Norway, mandatory survivor pensions cease at the statutory retirement age when residents start to receive a basic pension.
- Before the eligibility age to a permanent survivor pension is reached, many countries grant survivor benefits for a limited time period to help survivors adjust to the new situation without limiting work incentives in the longer term.
- Before any means-test applies, survivor pensions will replace 50% of the deceased's mandatory contributory pensions on average across OECD countries, with the highest rates in Belgium, Ireland, Mexico, Poland and the United States. In some countries, the survivor pension is optional leading to lower own entitlements for those who choose to be insured.
- Individual earnings, individual pensions or even total household income reduce survivor pensions in all countries except Chile, Israel (for women), Lithuania, Mexico, Portugal and Spain.
- Based on current legislated rules and taking into account non-contributory pensions and means-testing, the surviving spouse who never worked and was married to a full-career average-wage worker will receive at retirement age a total pension equal to 31% of the average wage on average across countries.
- Across countries, the range lies from less than 25% in Chile, Estonia, Germany, Israel, Korea, Latvia, Lithuania, Mexico, Norway, the Slovak Republic, Sweden and the United Kingdom to more than 45% in Austria, Belgium, Italy, Luxembourg and Turkey.
- Given the living-cost equivalence scale used by the OECD, the standards of living of the surviving spouse with no work experience will fall by more than 30% at the partner's death in Estonia, Finland, Iceland, Latvia, Lithuania, Norway, the Slovak Republic and Sweden. The standards of living of the surviving spouse with no work experience does not fall in Belgium, Luxembourg, Mexico, Poland, Slovenia and Turkey.

- Introducing fifty-fifty pension splitting while abolishing mandatory survivor pensions does not affect the total income of a survivor with no work experience and who was married to a full-career average-wage worker, on average in the OECD. The impact strongly differs across countries though, ranging from a 22% drop in Luxembourg to a 34% increase in the Netherlands when ignoring voluntary survivor pensions. If splitting is introduced while survivor rules are maintained and applied to the split pensions then the income of survivors would increase in most countries.
- Pension reforms in OECD countries have tended towards more individualisation and less redistribution within schemes. The socio-economic environment in terms of female labour force participation, family composition and gender gaps in life expectancy has been changing drastically. All these create some tension for the continuity of mandatory survivor pensions.
- Yet, systemic reforms to PAYGO pensions have affected survivor pensions in very different ways. For example among countries which implemented an NDC scheme, Norway has been eliminating survivor pensions after the retirement age (though no final decision on this matter has been made) while Italy integrated them in the NDC scheme. In general, survivor pensions can be included in the main PAYGO scheme or be added to it and be financed separately.

Key policy implications

- Survivor pensions for widowed persons should more clearly focus on smoothing survivors' standards of living – a still needed policy objective - while limiting disincentives to participate in the labour market and removing some redistribution across households which are difficult justify.
- Myopic behaviour strengthens the need for mandatory survivor pensions, while voluntary survivor options in private schemes may limit the efficient functioning of annuity markets.
- Recipients should not be eligible to a permanent survivor pension before the retirement age. Instead, at these younger ages a temporary benefit should be accessible following the partner's death to help adapt to the new situation.
- The cost of survivor pensions for widowed persons should be internalised within a given couple or at least among all couples. This means that for the same accumulated entitlements the old-age pension of someone living in a couple should be lower than that of a single, in order to finance survivor pensions. In a budget-neutral reform, this implies that the pension level of singles will be higher while that of individuals living in a couple will be lower.
- Survivor pensions might be extended beyond marriages to civil unions and formal partnerships. One open question though might be whether survivor pensions should be limited to partnerships which have some legal or financial obligations within couples.
- Survivor pensions should not be eligible to partners from former unions as in that case there is no current consumption to smooth. For former partnerships, the issue is rather about sharing past pension entitlements related to the common partnership.
- Splitting pension rights within couples – at the time of accumulation of pension rights, i.e. even for current partnerships – (but not necessarily half-half) offers

some advantages although some countries favour the individual treatment of partners, including as part of a broader way to promote gender equality.

- Splitting is fairly easy to implement in defined contribution and point systems or in defined benefit systems that are based on straightforward accrual rates. It is more complicated to introduce splitting in complex and fragmented pension systems as well as in schemes with loose links between contributions and pension entitlements.
- Splitting pension rights should replace survivor pensions for separated couples, but is not a substitute to survivor pensions for ongoing partnerships. For the latter, survivor pensions should still play a role even though the survivor replacement rates on the split pensions should be lower than those currently applied without splitting.

Notes

[1] Survivor schemes may cover all dependent family members of the deceased and often integrate pensions for widows and orphans in one scheme. Unless otherwise stated, this chapter focuses on pensions for widows and widowers.

[2] Chapter 2 in (OECD, 2015$_{[26]}$) provides an in-depth analysis of these schemes.

[3] Occupational funded defined benefit (DB) schemes, for example in Denmark or the United States, make the coverage of survivors the default option and opting out sometimes requires spousal consent; hence they also, at least partially, overcome the market failure.

[4] Widowhood B pensions are included while widowhood supplements in category (AB pensions) are excluded as expenditures for supplements cannot be distinguished from those for old-age pensions. Total survivor expenditures in the United Kingdom are therefore underestimated in the chart.

[5] Survivors who receive survivor pensions on top of their public earnings-related pension are not included in Norway.

[6] Detailed data on recipients are not available for 17 OECD countries.

[7] This is based on current legislation. However, the Norwegian government has not yet fully decided whether there should be survivor pensions for old-age pensioners born in 1963 and later.

[8] In the latter case, 100% of the basic pension correspond to a two-thirds replacement of the full basic pension income of the deceased spouse who received the 50% spouse supplement which stops upon widowhood.

[9] In Denmark, Finland and Sweden women's participation rates had increased earlier, and were already above 70% in 1983.

[10] Eurostat refers to a consensual union as the situation when two persons belong to the same household, and have a 'marriage-like' relationship with each other, and are not married to or in a registered partnership with each other.

[11] See e.g. http://www.pewsocialtrends.org/2014/09/24/record-share-of-americans-have-never-married/.

[12] More precisely, rules described here apply, consistent with the standard typical case in OECD (2017$_{[23]}$), to someone who entered the labour market in 2016 at age 20, i.e. to the cohort born in 1996.

[13] See endnote 7.

[14] The fourteen countries are Belgium, Chile, Estonia, Finland, Germany, Greece, Israel, Lithuania, Luxembourg, Mexico, Norway, Portugal, Switzerland and the United States.

[15] In France, the amount of benefit is increased if having a dependent child (main public scheme). In Japan, survivor pension from national pension system is paid only to the survivor with a dependent child.

[16] Data for Iceland are not available. Australia, New Zealand, Sweden and the United Kingdom are not included as no mandatory survivor pension programmes for widowed person exist except for transitory rules. Denmark is not included as it provides temporary payment only. The Netherlands is not included as survivor pension is not provided to surviving spouses with no dependent child nor disability. In Belgium the threshold age is gradually rising to age 55 by 2030. Data for Chile refers to the mandatory private scheme. In the Czech Republic the minimum age is 55 for widows and 58 for widowers, and lump sum pension is payable after remarriage. For Estonia, temporary pension is payable after remarriage. In Finland, divorced widow or widower can receive a survivor pension only if there has been a maintenance agreement. In France, age 55 will also apply to AGIRC from 2019. Pensions are payable after remarriage in the main public scheme, but not in the occupational scheme. In Germany, the age threshold is gradually rising to 47 by 2029. Israel refers to public scheme. In Italy, the benefit is payable to a divorced spouse only if the judge assigned to her a maintenance allowance after the divorce. In Japan, the minimum age is set at 55 only for men in earning related scheme. For Lithuania, the minimum age is 63.3 for men and 61.6 for women. In Luxembourg, a temporary pension is payable after remarriage. In Norway, cohabiting partner is eligible for survivor's pension only if they had children together or if they had been married previously. The pension ceases upon the remarriage, but the right is recovered if the new marriage ends in divorce within 2 years. For Slovenia the age threshold is gradually increasing by six month a year to reach 58 by 2022. In the United States, the availability of survivor pensions for civil union differs by state. Benefit is not available for cohabitation except for certain limited circumstances. Survivor pensions are payable to the divorced spouse if the marriage lasted at least 10 years and not remarry before age 60.

[17] Basic pensions in Luxembourg refer to the basic component in the public earnings-related pension.

[18] For the United States, the benefit level varies from 71.5% to 100% depending on the age of the survivor.

[19] The actual average costs of joint-and-survivor annuities relative to single-life annuities might differ from these calculations due to many reasons. First, men tend to have higher pensions and are more prone to be the first-to-die in the couple, which increases the cost of survivor payments. For example, if the gender-specific pricing of annuities was allowed, the 100-percent joint-and-survivor annuity would require an adjustment of 19% compared to a male single-life annuity. Second, couples with one partner having a low life expectancy are more likely to opt for the joint-and-survivor pensions (adverse selection). Third, people living in couples might live longer than singles (Johnson et al., 2000[27]) while the timing of death among partners is correlated. Indeed, couples are exposed to similar risk factors in long- (e.g. similar diet) and short- (e.g. car accident) run; and the stress caused by the partners' death can speed up own death (OECD, 2016[12]).

[20] The implementation of a reform in Spain in the summer of 2018 lifts the replacement rate of survivor pensions from 52% of the deceased's pension to 60% for survivors without any other income. This can be seen as the introduction of a partial means-test of survivor pensions.

[21] In Israel the means-test does not apply if the widowed person is a women or lives with a dependent child.

[22] In Belgium earnings affect pension only below the statutory retirement age. In France, the survivor pension in main public scheme is means-tested while in the occupational scheme (*ARRCO-AGIRC)* it is not. In Germany, means-testing applies only above an income threshold (15,750 EUR for labour earnings or 10,989 EUR for public pension income in 2016). In Greece, the survivor pension drops by 50% after 3 years in case of labour or other pension income. In addition, survivor pension are not paid to divorced spouses whose monthly taxable income exceeds twice the amount of the Social Solidarity Benefit. In Israel, the survivor gets own basic pension and the seniority increment from the decedent, which cannot be higher than 50% of basic pension. For Japan, the rules refer to earning related survivor pension. In Korea, labour income affects the value of survivor pension only for those younger than 55 years. In Norway, in order to receive survivor pension below 67 one must work while when older one must choose between own or 55% of joint pension entitlements. In the Slovak Republic the lower of own and survivor pensions is reduced by 50%. In Spain, combined own and survivor pensions cannot exceed the maximum pension level. In Switzerland, the survivor's occupational pensions are reduced if the sum of the own and occupational schemes exceed 90% of couples income before death; in case of public scheme only higher of the two can be claimed. In the United States earnings affect pension only below the statutory retirement age.

[23] In Chile, if a contributor deceases during the accumulation phase of the pension contract, the Disability and Survivor insurance steps in where necessary and fills up the DC account to pay a minimum survivor pension.

[24] In the Netherlands, with funded DB, survivor pensions are the default option and offer a large flexibility that, however, creates some complexity in mandatory private DB schemes, during the accrual phase either someone builds up pension entitlements with survivor benefits (*opbouwbasis*) or only in case of death during active membership (*risicobasis*). In the latter case, not being an active member anymore, for example by switching pension funds, leads to ineligibility to survivor benefits later on, but part of the entitlements can be converted into survivor benefits. At retirement those who built up survivor benefits (*opbouwbasis*) can choose to convert their pension into a higher pension without survivor benefits. Reciprocally, those with only a survivor option during active years (*risicobasis*) can choose to convert part of their pension in a survivor pension in exchange for lower benefits.

[25] There are some transitional arrangements to smooth the ending of inheritance in the reformed system subject to satisfying certain rules.

[26] In France, means-testing was introduced in 2003. Belgium has been increasing the eligible age of the survivor pension since 2015. In Norway, after the 2002 reform, in order to enhance work incentives recipients below age 55 who do not work have their pension reduced.

[27] The normal retirement age refers to the age at which the receipt of an old-age pension without deductions is possible for a full-career worker with labour market entry at age 20 (OECD, 2017[23]).

[28] However, deviations may be significant in Israel and Mexico, where DC schemes apply gender-specific annuity factors based on gender-specific life expectancy, or in countries with different future retirement ages for men and women (Chile, Israel, Poland, Switzerland and Turkey). Temporary monthly benefits to survivors right after the death of the spouse such as continued payments of the deceased's old-age pension for a three-month period in Denmark and Germany are not included in the simulations. After annuitising them, as a permanent survivor pension, they would have a negligible impact on simulated values.

[29] Mandatory survivor pensions in Lithuania and Denmark are limited, respectively, to low flat benefits in the public scheme and a lump-sum payment in the ATP scheme. The simulations in this section annuitise the lump-sum payment in the ATP scheme.

[30] The example of reversals in Hungary and Poland, where DC assets were mostly transferred back into the PAYGO accounts, shows that, even in the simplest case of individual DC accounts during the accumulation phase, there always remain some caveats in treating these accounts as inheritable, especially when the funds are not sufficiently protected legally.

[31] For those who need it, the emphasis should be placed on active policies to return to work rather than on the long-term, passive receipt of benefits.

[32] See Section 7.4. Moreover, means-testing survivor pensions - when the benefit falls if the survivor earned some own income - might discourage second-income earners from working longer and creates the usual trade-off between work incentives and cost.

[33] If the measures benefiting couples are, for example, actually meant to reward having children – which typically raises the pension rate of return - survivor pensions are not the best policy instruments to achieve this.

[34] In theory, internalisation could also be done through higher contribution rates for individuals living in couples, but this adjustment throughout the accumulation phase would be much more complicated to manage.

[35] This might reflect a chicken and egg problem. The market does not have sufficient size and is prone to anti-selection because taking a joint-and-survivor annuity is often not mandatory in DC schemes.

[36] If the splitting applies to only half of the total entitlements, then each partner becomes individually entitled to three-quarters of the own entitlements and one-quarter of the partner's entitlements.

[37] Two important questions arise with the splitting of pension rights. The first pertains to when the splitting should take place, during the accumulation phase, upon separation or at retirement. The main problem with splitting pension entitlements conditional on terminating the partnership can induce undesirable financial incentives about whether or not to continue the partnership depending on the implication for each partner's entitlements. There is therefore a clear case for splitting – fully or partially depending on the political choice – when entitlements are accumulated. The second question refers to whether splitting should be optional, a default option or mandatory. Optionality is the first-best solution because it leaves more freedom to adapt to individual preferences. However, it is based on assuming perfect foresight by individuals and equal decision-making power within couples. Imperfect foresight or myopic behaviour which justifies the existence of pension systems in the first place can also lead to suboptimal choices in terms of survivor pensions. Moreover, in practice, this "common" choice can be decided by the person who has more effective power within the couple, who is likely to be the person with the larger entitlements and who might then opt not to split, leaving the weaker partner with more vulnerability risks. This is why mandatory splitting at the time when pension rights are built is probably the best solution, at least up to a threshold amount, beyond which it could become optional. Switzerland is the only country that has made pension splitting mandatory in the public scheme and take up of voluntary options like in Germany is low.

References

Akerlof, G. (1970), "The Market for "Lemons": Quality Uncertainty and the Market Mechanism", *The Quarterly Journal of Economics*, Vol. 84/3, p. 488, http://dx.doi.org/10.2307/1879431. [4]

Barr, N. and P. Diamond (2008), *Reforming Pensions*, Oxford University Press, New York, http://dx.doi.org/10.1093/acprof:oso/9780195311303.001.0001. [19]

Barthold, D. et al. (2014), "Analyzing Whether Countries Are Equally Efficient at Improving Longevity for Men and Women", *American Journal of Public Health*, Vol. 104/11, pp. 2163-2169, http://dx.doi.org/10.2105/ajph.2013.301494. [9]

Bielawska, K., A. Chłoń-Domińczak and D. Stańko (2015), *Retreat from mandatory pension funds in countries of the Eastern and Central Europe in result of financial and fiscal crisis: Causes, effects and recommendations for fiscal rules.*, https://www.researchgate.net/publication/292643291_Retreat_from_mandatory_pension_funds_in_countries_of_the_Eastern_and_Central_Europe_in_result_of_financial_and_fiscal_crisis_Causes_effects_and_recommendations_for_fiscal_rules. [16]

Blake, D. (ed.) (2012), *Pension Economics*, John Wiley & Sons, Inc., Hoboken, NJ, USA, http://dx.doi.org/10.1002/9781119205968. [20]

Bonnet, C. and J. Hourriez (2012), "La prise en compte du couple par le système de retraite : réversion et partage des droits", *Population*, Vol. 67/1, p. 159, http://dx.doi.org/10.3917/popu.1201.0159. [22]

Bonnet, C. and J. Hourriez (2008), "Veuvage, pension de réversion et maintien du niveau de vie suite au décès du conjoint: une analyse sur cas types", *Retraite et société*, Vol. 4/56, pp. 71-103. [24]

Deutsche Rentenversicherung (2017), *Rentenversicherung in Zahlen*, https://www.deutsche-rentenversicherung.de/cae/servlet/contentblob/238692/publicationFile/61815/01_rv_in_zahlen_2013.pdf. [5]

DREES (2018), *Les retraités et les retraites*, https://drees.solidarites-sante.gouv.fr/IMG/pdf/retraites_2018.pdf. [8]

European Commission (2006), *Joint Report on Social Protection and Social Inclusion*, European Commission, Luxembourg, http://ec.europa.eu/social/BlobServlet?docId=1996&langId=en. [28]

Findley, T. and F. Caliendo (2008), "The behavioral justification for public pensions: a survey", *Journal of Economics and Finance*, Vol. 32/4, pp. 409-425, http://dx.doi.org/10.1007/s12197-008-9036-4. [21]

Flora, P. (1986), *Growth to limits: the Western European welfare states since World War II*, Walter de Gruyter, Berlin. [1]

Gillion, C. et al. (eds.) (2000), *Social security pensions: Development and reform.*, International Labour Office, Geneva. [3]

Hannikainen, M. and J. Vauhkonen (2012), *The history of Finnish earnings-related pension in the private sector*, https://www.etk.fi/wp-content/uploads/2015/10/Ansioiden%20mukaan_eng.pdf. [2]

James, E. (2009), *Rethinking Survivor Benefits*, Washington DC: World Bank., http://documents.worldbank.org/curated/en/500701468331226085/Rethinking-survivor-benefits. [18]

Johnson, N. et al. (2000), "Marital Status and Mortality", *Annals of Epidemiology*, Vol. 10/4, pp. 224-238, http://dx.doi.org/10.1016/s1047-2797(99)00052-6. [27]

Kay, S. (2014), *Political Risk and Pension Reform in Latin America and Central and Eastern Europe*, http://web.isanet.org/Web/Conferences/FLACSO-ISA%20BuenosAires%202014/Archive/2677a879-ef44-43b9-8359-81d529482d7b.pdf. [17]

Lavigne, A. (2018), *Quelle réforme pour la réversion en France?*, https://halshs.archives-ouvertes.fr/halshs-01715935. [7]

MISSOC (2018), *Mutual Information System on Social Protection*, https://www.missoc.org/. [11]

Nishiyama, S. (2018), "The joint labor supply decision of married couples and the U.S. Social Security pension system", *Review of Economic Dynamics*, http://dx.doi.org/10.1016/j.red.2018.08.001. [14]

OECD (2017), *Pensions at a Glance 2017: OECD and G20 Indicators*, OECD Publishing, Paris, http://dx.doi.org/10.1787/pension_glance-2017-en. [23]

OECD (2017), *The Pursuit of Gender Equality: An Uphill Battle*, OECD Publishing, Paris, http://dx.doi.org/10.1787/9789264281318-en. [25]

OECD (2016), *Life Annuity Products and Their Guarantees*, OECD Publishing, Paris, http://dx.doi.org/10.1787/9789264265318-en. [12]

OECD (2015), *Pensions at a Glance 2015: OECD and G20 indicators*, OECD Publishing, Paris, http://dx.doi.org/10.1787/pension_glance-2015-en. [26]

Orlova, N., M. Rutledge and A. Wu (2015), "The Transition from Defined Benefit to Defined Contribution Pensions: Does It Influence Elderly Poverty?", *SSRN Electronic Journal*, http://dx.doi.org/10.2139/ssrn.2634699. [13]

Sánchez-Marcos, V. and C. Bethencourt (2018), "The effect of public pensions on women's labor market participation over a full life cycle", *Quantitative Economics*, Vol. 9/2, pp. 707-733, http://dx.doi.org/10.3982/qe667. [15]

Social Security Administration (2018), *Social Security Programs Throughout the World*, https://www.ssa.gov/policy/docs/progdesc/ssptw/. [10]

ZUS (2018), *Informacja o świadczeniach pieniężnych z funduszu ubezpieczeń społecznych oraz o niektórych świadczeniach z zabezpieczenia społecznego*, http://www.zus.pl/documents/10182/167627/Biul0217.pdf/533d444f-2047-49a9-acf7-cbb19c738f7b. [6]

Annex 7.A. Survivor pension rules of main mandatory programmes for widows and widowers

Annex 7.A. is available ONLINE ONLY at the following DOI:
http://dx.doi.org/10.1787/pens_outlook-2018-11-en

ORGANISATION FOR ECONOMIC CO-OPERATION AND DEVELOPMENT

The OECD is a unique forum where governments work together to address the economic, social and environmental challenges of globalisation. The OECD is also at the forefront of efforts to understand and to help governments respond to new developments and concerns, such as corporate governance, the information economy and the challenges of an ageing population. The Organisation provides a setting where governments can compare policy experiences, seek answers to common problems, identify good practice and work to co-ordinate domestic and international policies.

The OECD member countries are: Australia, Austria, Belgium, Canada, Chile, the Czech Republic, Denmark, Estonia, Finland, France, Germany, Greece, Hungary, Iceland, Ireland, Israel, Italy, Japan, Korea, Latvia, Lithuania, Luxembourg, Mexico, the Netherlands, New Zealand, Norway, Poland, Portugal, the Slovak Republic, Slovenia, Spain, Sweden, Switzerland, Turkey, the United Kingdom and the United States. The European Union takes part in the work of the OECD.

OECD Publishing disseminates widely the results of the Organisation's statistics gathering and research on economic, social and environmental issues, as well as the conventions, guidelines and standards agreed by its members.

OECD PUBLISHING, 2, rue André-Pascal, 75775 PARIS CEDEX 16
(21 2018 04 1 P) ISBN 978-92-64-30540-3 – 2018

www.ingramcontent.com/pod-product-compliance
Ingram Content Group UK Ltd.
Pitfield, Milton Keynes, MK11 3LW, UK
UKHW051459290926
15471UKWH00008B/1304

9 789264 305403